Evolutionary Tax Reform in Emerging Economies

Evolutionary Tax Reform in Emerging Economies

An Income-Based Approach

Robert F. Conrad
and
Michael Alexeev

OXFORD
UNIVERSITY PRESS

OXFORD
UNIVERSITY PRESS

Great Clarendon Street, Oxford, OX2 6DP,
United Kingdom

Oxford University Press is a department of the University of Oxford.
It furthers the University's objective of excellence in research, scholarship,
and education by publishing worldwide. Oxford is a registered trade mark of
Oxford University Press in the UK and in certain other countries

Published in the United States of America by Oxford University Press
198 Madison Avenue, New York, NY 10016, United States of America

British Library Cataloguing in Publication Data

Data available

Library of Congress Control Number: 2023946229

ISBN 9780192847089

DOI: 10.1093/oso/9780192847089.001.0001

Printed and bound by
CPI Group (UK) Ltd, Croydon, CR0 4YY

MIX
Paper | Supporting
responsible forestry
FSC
www.fsc.org   FSC® C013604

Preface

This volume is based on my experiences working on tax issues in more than fifty countries over forty years. My tax work in emerging economies began in 1973 with Glenn Jenkins and Malcolm Gillis who were Fellows at the Harvard Institute for International Development (HIID). I worked for Glenn as a research assistant prior to enrolling in graduate school at Wisconsin in 1974. He encouraged me to study public finance and went out of his way to have me involved in his projects. Malcolm directed the Indonesian Tax Reform project, the first major reform in which I participated. The success of the Indonesian reform in 1983 is a testament to his skills. Glenn and Malcolm were wonderful mentors.

I continued to work on projects for HIID in Ecuador among other places and in 1985 had the opportunity to direct my first reform programme in Malawi with funding from the World Bank. The fall of the Iron Curtain in 1989 created a demand for assistance from the emerging economies of Central and Eastern Europe. Eric Zolt, who founded the US Treasury Tax Advisory Program for Central and Eastern Europe, asked me to direct the programme at the end of his term. So, my family and I moved to Paris, and I spent two years (1992–1994) commuting to 14 countries to work on policy, developing the programme, and recruiting resident and short-term advisors.

Andrei Shleifer contacted me when I returned to the United States in 1994. He asked me to return to Russia and work with Maxim Boycko, among others, at the Russian Privatization Center. The initial work led to a collaboration of more than 15 years—first with the Russian Privatization Center, then the Ministry of Finance, and ultimately with Mr Yegor Gaidar and his colleagues at the Institute for the Economy in Transition (now the Gaidar Institute for Economic Policy). One result of this work was the passage of the Russian Tax Code in 2001 and the subsequent changes through 2010.

In 1996, I was contacted by Mr George Soros, who asked me to discuss with him the tax situation in Ukraine. This meeting developed into a professional relationship of more than 25 years. Mr Soros asked me to support reforms in a wide variety of countries, including Nigeria, Guinea, Greece, Armenia, Pakistan, Ukraine (where I have worked periodically for more than 30 years), Mongolia, and Myanmar (from 2011 until the coup in 2020), among other countries. His support provided me with a unique opportunity to work on my own, representing no institution. My only instruction was to give my best effort to support productive reforms. I will always be grateful to Mr Soros for his support as well as the support of his son, Alex Soros, and the opportunities afforded me.

My thinking about tax reform evolved with each experience and each interaction with numerous individuals working in government, the IMF, the World Bank, and other institutions. I never had the opportunity, however, to systematically express my view on the overall structure and approach to tax reform until Mr Soros agreed to sponsor the work in this volume. I have always been an advocate of income taxation and believe that there are ways to simplify the approach so that the income tax can evolve as an economy reforms.[1] Consumption taxation, while inferior to income taxation in my view, is needed in the form of a VAT in emerging economies for administrative and revenue reasons. The VAT is a transaction-based charge where the taxpayer's (the domestic resident's) liability is discharged in a series of prepayments (advanced payments in the text) through the chain of value added. It was a natural extension to adopt the VAT prepayment approach to the income tax. This can be done by expanding withholding to a series of transaction-based advanced taxes to develop what is called a collection-driven tax system. The separation of the taxpayer from the person charged with collecting the advanced payment on behalf of the government is the third element of the framework upon which this volume is based.

As a graduate student, I learned that my best approach to success was to find the smartest people in the class and learn from them. That lesson has been key to my career. I have been extremely fortunate to have learned from some of the best experts in the tax field, and the most important person for this volume is Mike Alexeev. Mike was a graduate student at Duke when I was an assistant professor. When I first started working in Russia in 1992, Mike was the first person I contacted. We worked together in Russia for more than 15 years and continued to work in other places. The success of the tax changes in Russia are a direct result of Mike's involvement.

I had intended to draft this volume as the sole author, and I completed the original drafts. Mike carefully read and commented on numerous drafts. The more I wrote and reread, the more it became clear to me that Mike's ideas and mine are so intertwined that this is really a jointly authored volume. I am most grateful that Mike agreed to join me in publishing this manuscript. I know the work, and my career, are all the better for his contributions and friendship.

My thinking has been influenced by many others, including, but certainly not limited to: Malcolm Gillis, Glenn Jenkins, Victoria Perry, Thomas Horst, Andrei Schleifer, Maxim Boycko, Richard Bird, Don Lubick, Ward Hussey, Joesph Bell, Arnold Harberger, Emil Sunley, Paul Collier, Yegor Gaidar, and, of course, the officials and others in the countries where I have worked. These individuals have been willing to cooperate with me, to share their concerns, and even to accept some of my

[1] A companion manuscript called: 'Income Taxation Reform: A Proposal that can be Administered' contains a proposal for income taxation in advanced countries. This volume is based on my view that advanced economies such as the United States have much to learn from the experience of emerging economies. The discussion in Chapter 3 of this volume is based on the companion manuscript.

advice. Their willingness to explore options and their good cheer will always be most appreciated.

None of my work would have been possible without the love and support of my family. Helen, Selby, and Dan tolerated my absences, sometimes on short notice, and moved a number of times both domestically and internationally, always with grace. I have been truly blessed.

Robert Conrad

Hillsborough, NC
June 2023

When I received my PhD in Economics from Duke University in 1984, I never thought that I would become involved in tax policy issues. In fact, I never thought this until Bob Conrad contacted me in 1992 and asked me to help him in his work on tax policy in the newly created Russian Federation. Bob taught me public economics at Duke, and he was on my dissertation committee, but my dissertation was not about tax policy. Nonetheless, the general background in economics and the expertise in the Russian economy and institutions made it relatively easy for me to contribute to Bob's team. Moreover, some of my connections to the Russian economists and my ability to communicate with them and with Russian officials in Russian proved very useful for the entire project. Several years of interacting with Bob and others who worked in the Russian tax project gave me sufficient knowledge and experience to be able to work on tax policy issues in several other emerging economies such as Egypt, Kazakhstan, and Zambia largely on my own while continuing to work with Bob on tax policy and other economic issues in Russia. Bob and I wrote a number of policy memos together, but he always was the primary author. Over the years, we have converged on similar views on main tax policy issues and so when Bob asked me to comment on the two major manuscripts he was writing, I was glad to do it. As with the memos I mentioned above, Bob is clearly the primary author of both of these manuscripts, but I hope that my contribution has also been sufficient to justify my role as the secondary author.

Michael Alexeev

Professor of Economics
Indiana University
Bloomington, IN

Acknowledgements

The Open Society Foundation, via a grant from Mr George Soros, funded the project of which this volume is one result. This support is gratefully acknowledged.

Six anonymous reviewers made a number of important suggestions. We hope that this text reflects those contributions.

Ms Gina Brosius has worked with Robert Conrad for almost 30 years. She has been a wonderful associate and friend. The thanks expressed to her here will not do justice to the significance of her contributions.

Contents

*Unpublished memoranda and related documents are available for review
and download from www.emergingtax.com*

List of Figures

List of Tables

List of Boxes

1

One Framework for Tax Reform

1.1 Introduction

The context in which tax reforms are undertaken is discussed here. This discussion
is followed by a description, and one critical evaluation, of what will be defined as
the standard approach to tax reform; an approach that combines direct and indirect
taxes with property taxation. The approach, in general, is useful for thinking about
how to structure policy. Some evaluative comments are made in order to provide
some context for the collection-driven approach to the evolution of tax systems that
is the basis for this volume. This approach, described in Chapter 2, is based on a collection driven, but relatively efficient, tax system that can evolve through time based
on modifications to the standard approach. Two annexes supplement the text. Annex
A1.1 contains a discussion of basic economic notions used in tax analysis for those
who wish to become familiar with the concepts. Optimal taxation is summarized in
Annex A1.2.

Making tax changes is a messy undertaking. All sectors of the economy have an
interest in taxation and all individuals are affected either directly or indirectly by
a country's tax regime. Investors monitor the tax systems of a number of countries
to determine the potential effects on investment and to use comparative information as input for negotiating either special incentives or general policy changes in
countries in which investments are made or contemplated. The business and legal
communities, taxpayer organizations, and the population more generally use the
political process to advocate for particular policies, so political factors are important
and should be understood to be an integral part of the process.

Tax changes in any country are monitored by other countries in the region and
around the world for at least two reasons: first to learn, and perhaps to duplicate[1] or
to reject, the experience of other countries, and second to determine potential competitive effects on trade and investment, foreign investment in particular.[2] Changes

---

[1] In addition, policy makers may not want to be perceived as being either outside the mainstream or
as allowing their countries to be subject to experiments for novel recommendations and to being overly
influenced by nonresident advisers. On more than one occasion during our careers, the response to our
recommendations by policy makers has been: 'What other countries do this?'

[2] Major accounting firms publish international comparisons as well as country summaries that are
available to clients and to the general public. Online versions such as https://www.pwc.com/gx/en/
services/tax/worldwide-tax-summaries.html are available. Deloitte publishes summaries, annual highlights by country, and some in-depth analysis. For example, see https://dits.deloitte.com/#TaxGuides.
International organizations such as the OECD and the International Bureau of Fiscal Documentation,
among others, gather similar information, publish comparative analyses, and support research. For
example, OECD has a comparative tax database: https://www.oecd.org/tax/tax-policy/tax-database/.

Evolutionary Tax Reform in Emerging Economies. Robert F. Conrad and Michael Alexeev, Oxford University Press.
© Open Society Institute (2024). DOI: 10.1093/oso/9780192847089.003.0001

in technology and research in academic institutions and in think tanks are also part of the milieu. Finally, tax policies are a subject of intellectual interest and academic research, in particular for economists, political scientists, lawyers, and accountants. In short, there is an active market in both ideas and application of taxation reflecting the competitive forces in the domestic and international markets more generally. Thus, like any competitive market in the real world, the market for tax policy and the change process is messy.

For emerging economies, tax policy is perceived, correctly we believe, as an important element in any programme for economic and political stabilization and development. Taxation is one structural element used by international financial institutions (IFIs, such as the IMF and World Bank[3]) as a basis for performance requirements. IFIs, bilateral donors, and some NGOs[4] provide financial support for tax changes as well as technical assistance. Such assistance is motivated, at least in part, by the objective of reducing international aid flows over the longer term by promoting increased efficiency and growth.[5] Each of these factors may interact to affect tax changes and implementation efforts.

Tax reform may be understood as a continuous process, sometimes with significant incremental changes or major reform episodes such as Japan (1949),[6] the United States (1954),[7] Colombia (1971),[8] Bolivia (1981),[9] Indonesia (1983),[10] Jamaica (1990),[11] Malawi (mid-1980s-1990s),[12] the Dominican Republic (1990),[13] and Russia

---

[3] The IMF maintains an extensive library of technical assistance reports. See: https://www.imf.org/en/Publications/SPROLLs/Publications-on-Technical-Assistance#sort=%40imfdate%20descending. The World Bank provides assistance for policy as well as significant support for tax administration (in conjunction with the IMF). For example, the administrative effort for the Russian tax reform was supported by the World Bank (World Bank, 2003).

[4] For example, The Open Society Foundation's Fiscal Governance Program has an active portfolio of support for tax efforts with some emphasis on natural resource policy.

[5] Assistance, particularly financial support, may be a type of double-edged sword. First, the intent of some types of assistance, structural adjustment for instance, is to promote economic reform and to lay the foundation for economic growth. On the other hand, technical assistance amounts to a type of wealth transfer. In effect, the value to the local economy of concessionary financing is a gift of capital from the rest of the world equal to the present value of the aid or concessionary financing that is retained by the domestic economy. While conditional aid may be tied to specific projects, it is impossible to isolate the economic effects of such wealth transfers on the overall economy. There are increased local expenditures, domestic labour is employed, and domestic resources are attracted to aid-financed activities; all of these factors can change some domestic relative prices as well as the exchange rate because of their size. For example, the foreign currency support from the IMF amounted to a minimum of 6% of total imports in Ukraine in 2015 ($5 billion in disbursements and $83 billion in total imports). Some have claimed that these actions amount to assistance-induced 'Dutch disease' (Nkusu, 2004). Of course, the purpose of aid is to assist in making domestic citizens better off, and there is no reason to believe that such transfers are harmful on a net basis even if the consequences are unintended. Also, aid flows may affect tax effort, at least measured as a share of taxes to GDP (Besley & Persson, 2014).

[6] Modern tax reforms might be traced to the mission headed by Carl Shoup to Japan at the end of World War II (*Report on Japanese Taxation by the Shoup Mission*, 1949). Shoup's strong academic approach combined with pragmatism set a standard for those who followed (Mehrotra, 2012).

[7] The 1954 US Internal Revenue Code is still the basic document for US taxation.

[8] Musgrave and Gillis (1971).

[9] Musgrave (1981).

[10] Conrad & Gillis (1984), Conrad (1986).

[11] Bahl (1991).

[12] For the basic document that was the foundation for the reform that continued until the early 1990s, see Chamley, Conrad, Shalizi, Skinner, & Squire (1985).

[13] Conrad (1990).

(2002).[14] In this context, a relatively short time period means between five and ten years. For example, tax reform was a significant policy issue in every country in Central and Eastern Europe during the period after the initial liberalization. The countries introduced an invoice-credit system VAT, significantly modified their excise tax regimes, restructured both the enterprise profits tax and individual income taxes, introduced, or at least significantly modified, the property tax, and changed their tariff structures. Other examples of significant tax reform include New Zealand (beginning in 1984)[15] and Indonesia (1983) when the country implemented a VAT, changed the basic structure of the income tax, and began a property tax reform process.

Of course, there is no clear-cut distinction between marginal,[16] incremental, or significant tax changes, particularly over time, but some examples may illustrate the distinctions. Incremental reforms for our purposes are tax changes within the existing structure. All countries make frequent changes in marginal rates. For example, Myanmar in 2017,[17] Ukraine's tax changes in 2015,[18] and Greece's statutory changes between 2013 and 2014.[19] Such changes may be part of a planned reform (as in Russia in 2002), in response to political pressure, or in response to economic events, such as the COVID pandemic. The United States increased the use of tariffs in 2017, lowered some tax rates, and changed the derivation of the base (capping state and local tax deductions for individuals, allowing expensing for certain assets for a limited time, and moving to a modified territorial system for corporations). There are also frequent changes in methodology such as the technical changes to transfer pricing in Ukraine in 2019,[20] or there may be changes in the computation of the base such as the exemptions in Kenya in 2019.[21] Incremental or significant reforms include the changes made in Eastern Europe during the post 1989 period, the introduction of Value Added Taxes by most countries, and the wholesale reform of the New Zealand system in the 1980s.

Marginal and incremental changes through time can have significant effects as the changes accumulate and experience is gained. For example, there has been a trend,

---

[14] Alexeev & Conrad (2013, 2015).

[15] The New Zealand Tax reform is well known and many of the changes introduced have been used in other countries. In particular, the VAT in New Zealand has been used to modernize VAT systems that had been based on the Sixth Directive of the European Union. The tax reform was part of an overall economic reform programme (Atkinson, 1997) and has been a topic of some discussion (Stephens, 1993). One aspect of the tax reform was the extensive use of foreign experts such as Eric Toder (who became Deputy Assistant Secretary for Tax Policy in the United States) and Susan Himes (a tax counsel for the Senate Finance Committee and later a resident adviser in Romania as well as a short-term adviser to a number of countries).

[16] Marginal changes can have significant effects. For example, a change in personal exemption levels holding all other things fixed can have a significant effect on the total number of taxpayers, progressivity, the levels of compliance, and the growth of tax revenue.

[17] The Taxation of the Union Law 2017. Available at: https://www.ird.gov.mm/sites/default/files/The%20Union%20Taxation%20Law%202017.pdf.

[18] A tax reform working group was organized in Ukraine in 2015 (Ukraine Ministry of Finance, 2015).

[19] Conrad (2013).

[20] There is still an effort to impose what is called the tax on distributed profits, which is a type of cash flow tax.

[21] See https://taxnews.ey.com/news/2019-2045-kenya-enacts-finance-act-2019.

Top marginal income tax rate, 1980 to 2017

Top marginal tax rate of the income tax (i.e. the maximum rate of taxation applied to the highest part of income)

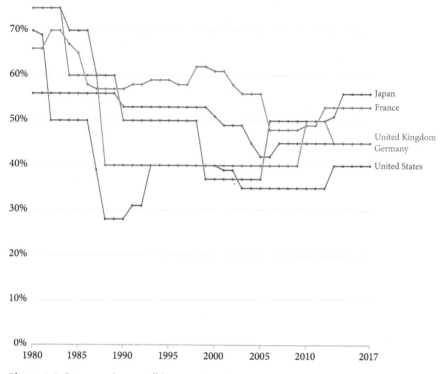

Figure 1.1 Decrease in overall income tax rates

Source: Alvaredo, F., Chancel, L., Piketty, T., Saez, E., & Zucman, G. (eds) (2018). *World Inequality Report 2018.* Belknap Press. Published online at OurWorldInData.org. Retrieved from: https://ourworldindata.org/grapher/top-income-tax-rates-piketty (online resource).

at least in more developed economies, for a decrease in overall income tax rates (see Figure 1.1) as well as a significant decrease in corporate taxation in many countries (see Figure 1.2).

1.2 Objectives of Tax Reform

Approaches to tax reform[22] may vary depending on the economy's current conditions, the commitment of the government and other stakeholders, the resources available for reform (including the source of funding), and whether tax reform is part of a more general reform programme.[23] Tax reform can be a short-term initiative

---

[22] This material is based on 'One Strategy for Tax Reform Assistance', prepared by R. F. Conrad on behalf of Japan International Cooperation Agency (JICA) (June 2004).

[23] It is often the case that tax reform is part of a more general economic reform programme, including privatization, liberalization of the trade system, deregulation of the economy, legal reform, expenditure

Statutory Weighted and Unweighted Corporate Income Tax Rates, 1980–2022

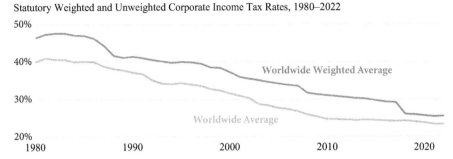

Figure 1.2 Corporate tax rates have continuously declined over the past decades but have levelled off in recent years

Note: The number of countries included in calculated averages varies by year due to missing corporate tax rates for years prior to 2022; that is, the 1980 average includes statutory corporate income tax rates of 73 jurisdictions representing roughly 60% of 1980 world GDP, compared to 180 jurisdictions representing above 95% of world GDP in 2022.
Sources: Statutory corporate income tax rates were compiled from various sources. GDP calculations are from the US Department of Agriculture,
'International Macroeconomics Data Set'.

- Reprinted from The Tax Foundation Blog: Enache, Cristina. 'Corporate Tax Rates around the World, 2022', *Corporate Tax Rates around the World, Tax Foundation,* 13 December 2022.

implemented by simply changing some laws or procedures. More often, however, tax reform is a long-term process, and appropriately so. Tax systems must accommodate changes in the economic environment, institutional development (both within the tax system, the tax administration in particular, and throughout the economy), and other factors.

Despite the differences in initial conditions and circumstances, many tax reform[24] efforts, and tax changes more generally, have had a number of common elements and themes. These commonalities are the basis for the discussion that follows and the development of what we will call the 'standard model'.

1.2.1 Shift the Relative Emphasis from Direct to Domestic Indirect Taxation

Prior to the widespread adoption of VAT, tax systems often displayed a relatively greater emphasis on income-based taxes (either corporate, individual, or both), trade

reform, and restructuring of intergovernmental relations. Tax reform should be understood in such a context because the success of tax reform (measured in terms of revenue gains, buoyancy, distributional goals, and other objectives) may depend on how other economic reforms evolve.

[24] The term 'tax reform' is being used rather loosely in the sense that there may be no overt intention to change the structure of taxation but to change only some technical aspects of a particular tax. Nevertheless, such changes can become either an impetus for or an indicator of longer-term tax adjustments. Such a process took place in Nigeria where Conrad became involved at the behest of Paul Collier and Ngozi Okonjo-Iweala. There were discussions of a major tax reform but what happened initially was a series of technical changes to the income tax, including such things as thin capitalization rules. The initial changes helped lay the foundation for further positive changes that were supplemented by training and administrative reform.

taxes, and certain excise taxes in addition to cascading sales taxes.[25,26] The dynamic change in relative emphasis on indirect taxes like VAT is illustrated in Figure 1.3. In addition, the upward trend was accompanied by a fall in income taxes as a share of total tax revenue. There has been a lively debate both within academia and in the public more generally about consumption relative to income taxation (see Annex A1.1 and Chapter 3). There is also the possible demonstration effect of the supply-side tax policies enacted in the US (The Economic Recovery Act of 1981) and UK[27] during the early 1980s. Finally, a shift towards consumption taxation has been part of technical assistance advice of emerging economies. The relative trend for developing countries is confirmed in Figure 1.3.

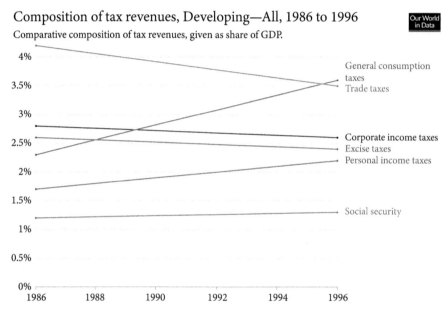

Composition of tax revenues, Developing—All, 1986 to 1996

Comparative composition of tax revenues, given as share of GDP.

Figure 1.3 Composition of tax revenue

Source: Todaro, M. and Smith, S. (2014) *Economic Development, 12th Edition.* Pearson. ISBN: 1292002972. Published online at OurWorldInData.org. Retrieved from: https://ourworldindata.org/grapher/composition-of-tax-revenues-regional (online resource).

---

[25] The classic reference has been Tait (1988). Tait, in our view, along with individuals like Sijbren Cnossen, is one of the more influential proponents of the VAT. From his position at the IMF Fiscal Affairs Department, he had much influence over technical advice supplied about tax reform. Tait (1988) was based on the use of the *Sixth Directive of the European Union* (1977). Recent innovations, particularly the New Zealand approach to VAT, are being incorporated into technical advice now. More recent IMF advice on VAT is reflected in Ebrill, Keen, & Perry (2001).

[26] Income-based taxes can be complicated to administer and to collect, particularly in an environment where compliance is relatively low. Reliance on tariffs distorts domestic markets and may retard export development, while also creating opportunities for corruption and rent seeking.

[27] Under various prime ministers, the basic individual tax rate was reduced from 33% to 23% between 1979 and 1997.

It has been argued that several purposes are served by shifting the relative emphasis towards domestic indirect taxes (or consumption taxes). An economic argument in support for indirect taxation is that the sales taxes (including VAT) may not distort intertemporal decisions, unlike income taxation, with the result that saving might be encouraged. Second, domestic consumption taxes such as VAT are claimed to be easier to administer relative to income-based taxes.[28] There may be fewer taxpayers to monitor because methods limit the taxpaying population to relatively large suppliers of goods and services as well as most importers. The requirements for suppliers subject to tax are perceived to be simpler relative to income-based taxes. As a result of the shift in emphasis, the tax system's administrative resources might be expected to be more revenue productive, other things equal. Third, most consumption taxes—VAT, in particular—are accounts-based taxes. Thus, tax administrators (and taxpayers) gain familiarity with income accounting, experience that can help to develop the income tax system. Fourth, a broad-based consumption tax can be used to tax, indirectly, the incomes of individuals who do not comply with other taxes.[29] In effect, a broad-based consumption tax can expand the effective taxpaying population while reducing the number of taxpayers who must officially comply with the law. That is, the statutory intent is to have the tax burden fall on all resident consumers, the true taxpayers (broadening the base), but the effective result is to limit tax reporting to high-turnover suppliers (reducing administration). In effect, VAT is a type of advanced payment system: a concept that is exploited in this volume.

Two other points about this approach might be noted. First, there is the perception that shifting towards an indirect tax system, VAT in particular, can be a source of relatively rapid revenue increases; an important characteristic of a reform path dictated in part by pressure to reduce relatively large domestic deficits. Indirect tax changes can be introduced in any month, and revenues generally accrue every month. Such revenue generally represents the full discharge of the tax liability for that time period (again, generally one month). This is unlike the income tax which is usually perceived to be an annual tax. That is, income tax payments, while periodic, are constructed based on some indicator, or estimation, with possible reconciliations at the end of the year (with the possible exception of simple wage withholding). This statement applies to entities and higher income individuals, while administration may be simplified for wage earners by Pay as You Earn (PAYE) systems where advanced payments via wage withholding are final payments. Thus, the government can change rates and procedures for indirect taxes with revenue consequences supposedly arising within one or two months instead of annually as in the case of income taxes.[30]

---

[28] This claim is questioned later in our discussion.

[29] This claim has been critically evaluated (Auerbach, 2013).

[30] It is true that increasing withholding rates for income taxes, such as wage withholding, can have an immediate effect on a cash flow basis. The issue is whether withholding is a final tax. This issue may be particularly relevant for high-income taxpayers and entities where withholding and estimated taxes are

Second, reliance on indirect taxes might enable a shift in orientation from taxes on trade to domestic consumption taxes while preserving the collection point at imports, at least for VAT. Decreasing reliance on trade taxes can have numerous positive effects. Tariffs can create a range of economic distortions, including mis-allocation of domestic resources, higher domestic prices, reduced exports (via the impact on exchange rates and other effects), and incentives for corruption and rent seeking. Shifting the tax base from trade taxes[31] to domestic consumption and income taxes reduces the domestic production bias and provides a more neutral treatment for exports. The use of VAT may be a natural instrument for such a shift because, like tariffs, significant revenue can be collected at a few points and at the time of importation.

1.2.2 Reduce the Use of the Tax System for Non-Revenue Objectives

In general, a tax system is a poor instrument for objectives such as targeting investment or encouraging the consumption of particular goods or services (food for low-income people or activities sponsored by nongovernmental organizations, for instance).[32] Using the tax system to pursue these types of targets may be ill advised for at least three reasons.

First, mixing non-revenue with revenue objectives unnecessarily complicates the tax system. Administrative costs are increased, and compliance is likely to suffer.

Second, tax instruments may be too crude, in general, for targeting to be cost effective. For instance, consider the use of a consumption tax exemption for food. The standard argument in favour of this incentive is to reduce the tax burden on the poor (and perhaps reduce the regressivity of a flat-rate indirect tax).[33] Such an exemption is available to people in all income groups, however. In general, high-income

prepayments for the annual tax. In effect, this is an issue of 'tax revenue' relative to 'tax collections'; an issue of accrual relative to cash-based accounting.

[31] One of Conrad's first applied lessons was the claim that many emerging economies would use the ports as choke points to collect taxes regardless of the type of tax imposed. Thus, one justification for the VAT (as opposed to other types of indirect tax) is that the use of points of importation would be maintained. The story was that the countries were going to tax imports, so they might as well impose a more efficient tax relative to tariffs. Of course, the success of such a strategy depends on whether the VAT on imports gets credited further down the chain of value added and whether the export regime (zero rating in particular) works.

[32] Of course, whether a tax system is a poor instrument for targeting depends on the availability of alternatives. For example, programmes such as food subsidies, cash payments to low-income individuals, and other social programmes may be more complicated (and even nonexistent) in emerging economies. Such programmes may depend on means testing and other targeting methods that depend on knowledge about the population, knowledge that may not exist within the government.

[33] It is not clear, at least to us, whether a flat-rate comprehensive consumption tax is regressive, particularly in emerging markets. A flat-rate consumption tax is a proportional tax over an individual's life cycle because saving is generally consumed at some point during an individual's life. In addition, a flat-rate consumption tax may be progressive in application. Only official market goods are subject to consumption taxes. Thus, household production is not taxed. As well, goods and services supplied in informal, rural, or other small markets are not taxed. Low-income people tend to consume proportionally more of such goods and services.

individuals spend more on food, even though the proportion of income spent on food is lower, relative to lower-income individuals. This is particularly true of food purchases from suppliers in the modern sector such as supermarkets as opposed to small open-air markets which often are not taxed at all, e.g., due to the fact that many sellers in these markets fall under the VAT threshold. Thus, high-income people tend to benefit from an exemption for food more than the poor. The overall regressivity of the VAT could increase as a result.[34]

Third, tax incentives for investment tend to be anti-competitive. To take advantage of an incentive, taxpayers must first have a tax liability that is eligible to be reduced by the incentive. Thus, larger established enterprises are more likely to benefit relative to smaller, more marginal enterprises or start-ups. Such a result is the opposite to what might be efficient, because these marginal and smaller firms may account for the greatest growth in employment and potential through time.

1.2.3 Improve the Tax System's Elasticity, Flexibility, and Diversification

An elastic tax system may be a desirable property so that the revenue can be responsive to short-term macroeconomic changes and can provide greater flexibility for government expenditures as the economy grows. This flexibility results because revenues increase (decrease) more than proportionally when income increases (decreases): a type of automatic stabilization. For instance, publicly provided goods such as education might be income-elastic goods and thus a greater share of GDP accruing to government might match revenues with expenses in a relatively efficient manner. Alternatively, an elastic revenue system can allow the government to reduce rates, keeping the share of government expenditure constant (or even reducing that share), leaving a greater proportion of resources to the private sector. The overall tax structure might change over the longer term in response to changes in the economic environment. For instance, the balance between direct and indirect taxes might change through time, as experience with the reformed tax system is gained, growth continues, and the economy becomes more sophisticated. In addition, the tax system should be able to accommodate changes in the structure of economic investment, such as when new industries enter the domestic market or existing industries exit.[35]

The coordinated use of a variety of revenue instruments may help to diversify the government's revenue base. A type of portfolio effect may be possible, whereby

---

[34] Willingness to pay is not based on proportions but on total valuations placed on the consumption of goods and services. Thus, a reduction in the tax rate for food provides a greater increase in purchasing power for the rich than for the poor.

[35] Early in his career, Conrad was exposed to the conjecture that introducing the VAT was one step towards the longer-term development of the income tax. Administrative experience combined with the relatively higher elasticity of the income tax would eventually cause the share of VAT in total revenue to fall. This conjecture is one basis of the collection-driven system developed here where there is a clear intention for VAT revenue to fall, both relatively and absolutely, through time.

the variability of government revenues is decreased. For instance, income and consumption are not perfectly correlated. Under some changing conditions, reductions in consumption tax yield might be buffered by increasing reliance on income taxes.[36] Note should be made of the fact that income and consumption are positively correlated, so diversification is not complete. In fact, all taxes, no matter how narrow, depend on income (as a measure of the change in wealth on a flow basis). This basic point will receive some emphasis in the evaluation below.

1.2.4 Simplify

There is no such thing as a tax system that is simple to administer. Taxpayers do not want to pay taxes, just like they would prefer to obtain gasoline, or any commodity, for free. The problem with taxes, however, is that, unlike the gasoline market, there is no necessary relationship between the payment (the tax) and the benefits received (a legal structure, roads, education, etc.); thus, it makes sense for any individual to reduce tax payments to a minimum via legal avoidance and perhaps through evasion. Therefore, it is necessary to keep compliance costs as low as possible in order to reduce the incentive for noncompliance. A simplified tax system can reduce the potential for tax arbitrage via incentives, complicated definitions, rules, exemptions, and other means. In addition, administration can be simplified so that administrative resources can be allocated to difficult-to-tax sectors and groups where revenue and compliance potential are relatively high. As a result, vertical and horizontal equity may be promoted by the effort to pursue simplification as a component of reform initiatives.

1.2.5 Ensure Compatibility with the International System

Governments are aware of the need to respond to the increased importance of international trade and world economic integration. Emphasis on export-oriented economic growth and increased globalization have been one part of this trend. Governments have begun to adjust their domestic tax policies to accommodate, and to take advantage of, globalization and membership in organizations such as the World Trade Organization (WTO), efforts such as the Base Erosion and Profit Shifting (BEPS) project of the OECD, and the recent agreement about minimum taxation of multinational enterprises.[37]

Constraints on domestic policies are one cost of such integration. These constraints include restrictions on the use of special zones and discriminatory

---

[36] There are other potential benefits to diversification. For example, a consumption tax may have an elasticity of about unity with respect to the base while an income tax might have a greater elasticity if the tax is progressive (i.e., the average tax rate increases). Excises tend to be inelastic relative to other taxes given the targeted nature of the charge (fuel, alcoholic beverages, and tobacco products are the primary taxed commodities). Thus, the relative importance of each tax might change over the business cycle, providing some stabilization properties while preserving some revenue.

[37] In addition, countries in Central and Eastern Europe have been concerned with satisfying standards for EU membership.

tax incentives. On the other hand, reducing tariffs and developing compatible customs procedures are one benefit of this trend. This compatibility may also force lower-income countries to further reduce their dependence on tariffs for revenue, at least overtly.

Finally, domestic income tax policies might be constrained by both international organizations such as the WTO and by bilateral agreements such as tax treaties. Governments may find it necessary to adopt developed country standards for source rules, residence rules, valuation methods (such as the OECD transfer pricing rules), and the derivation of income for tax purposes, in order to ensure that domestic income taxes qualify for credit in the investor's home country, depending on the home country's basis for taxation (source or residence).

1.2.6 Enhance Sustainability

Sustainability should imply more than collecting adequate revenue, although being able to pay the bills may be a necessary condition for a successful evolution of the tax system. Such an objective may mean that taxpayers and tax administrators should be able to undertake medium-term (three to five years) planning without concern about radical changes, reversals in particular, through time. Phased introduction of reforms can then be incremental and planned, to the extent possible, to build on the implementation of earlier changes. In addition, the level of public acceptance may need to be sufficient to ensure reasonable compliance. Acceptance may be increased with familiarity, and, if practice is reasonable, acceptance may grow over time. Sustainability does not mean a fixed tax regime because change is inevitable. Rather, sustainability may imply that the framework in which tax changes are made is predictable once any basic reform is implemented. Such a property may include adequate public awareness, such as a formal transparent public comment process for proposed tax changes.

1.2.7 Shift to a Relatively Progressive System

A tax reform may increase the effective progressivity of the system, at least relative to the prior system and within administrative constraints. Of course, such changes should be based on progressivity in fact as opposed to law. For example, reducing the number of personal income tax brackets may increase the overall progressivity of the system. In addition, the elimination of the personal exemption might be considered progressive if other elements of the tax system, such as the taxation of nonwage income, expands.

1.2.8 Increase Economic Efficiency

One objective of economic policy, in general, is to increase the real wealth of the economy. Increases in real wealth expand individual choices, which may increase both investment and consumption through time. Economic efficiency, in the standard sense,[38] is always reduced by either an introduction, or an increase, in a particular tax relative to a situation where revenue for public goods production is collected via lump-sum taxes.[39] This does not mean that there is always a tradeoff between other objectives of economic policy and taxation because taxation is but one of the instruments, including the overall legal and regulatory framework and expenditure policy, available for government to affect decisions. That said, there is every reason to install a tax system that is efficient enough to force tradeoffs between increased efficiency and other objectives of economic policy such as distribution and provision of publicly supplied goods and services. For us, this implies that governments should choose the mix of instruments and relative levels of each tax to reduce administrative costs, uncertainty in application, opportunities for rent seeking, and the adverse incentives created by any tax system.

1.3 Tax Policy: A Standard Model

Given the variety of objectives, a standard model of taxation has evolved into a tax regime with multiple instruments; a modernized tax administration; special regimes for particular groups such as small business, agriculture, and mineral enterprises; and a system of fiscal decentralization.[40] The structure of the standard model is described below.

1.3.1 The Tax Instruments

The tax instruments advocated in the standard model include:

- A Value Added Tax (VAT) as the clear choice for general sales taxation;
- An excise tax system restricted to petroleum products, alcoholic beverages, and tobacco products in addition to a few other commodities such as automobiles, communications such as cell phone service, and luxury goods;
- An income tax consisting of both a personal income tax and a separate tax on enterprises (generally corporations) that may have some level of corporate integration;

---

[38] By 'standard sense', we mean the ceteris paribus change in the economy's real, as opposed to financial, ex ante net worth resulting from the imposition of a tax. See Annex A1.1 for further discussion.

[39] There are second-best considerations when preexisting distortions exists. See Annex A1.1.

[40] Various government levels generally impose various taxes and fees. These charges are payments in exchange for specific benefits and thus are not taxes as such. Pricing for these services should be determined, economically speaking, by rules regarding public sector pricing. The same statement applies to pollution and other environmental charges. Such charges, often called taxes, are really payments in exchange for the use of environmental services (or to repair environmental damage). Thus, such charges are not taxes but adjustments to market prices that might not exist. Marginal environmental charges should be determined relative to the public sector pricing rules. The danger of doing otherwise, or treating environmental charges as taxes, is to lose sight of the function served by such prices. Revenue considerations may begin to dominate at the expense of corrective pricing (Atkinson & Stiglitz, 2015) (Lecture 15).

- Either selective tariffs or a uniform tariff for protection; and
- A property tax administered by and providing revenue for local government.

Instruments for particular groups include a small business tax paid in lieu of either income tax and/or VAT, special taxes on agriculture, estate (or inheritance) taxes, and special regimes for natural resources including royalties and environmental charges.

Much of this volume is devoted to a discussion of the technical and administrative aspects of each tax instrument, although with a somewhat different emphasis. Thus, the discussion in this chapter is in summary fashion and is supplied to provide some context for the discussions to follow.

1.3.1.1 A Modern Value Added Tax

A consumption-type destination-based VAT has certainly been the instrument of choice for taxing sales.[41,42] One-hundred and sixty-six countries have adopted a VAT as of 2018.[43] The reasons for adopting VAT and a critical evaluation of VAT as applied is contained in Chapter 4. Properties considered desirable for VAT include:[44]

- A base that is defined as broadly as possible. Exemptions might be restricted to a selective negative list of goods and services, such as gold sold to the central bank, certain financial transactions not considered current consumption, and supplies made by certain types of entities, particularly services supplied by government and nonprofit institutions; and
- A single rate (with the exception of zero-rating exports).

VAT is an accrual-based tax. VAT administration is based on invoices, perhaps computer generated and maintained,[45] and generally includes monthly reporting, perhaps a rapid refund process for qualified exporters, a minimum turnover level, and voluntary and/or mandatory registration. VAT is not an easy tax to administer (although on balance it might be easier to administer relative to other alternatives (see Chapter 4)). Successful application may depend on the public's and the tax administration's understanding of the statutory and economic purpose of the VAT:

---

[41] Ebrill et al. (2001).

[42] We do not want to imply that a VAT is the best indirect tax system in all situations or even that the VAT is the best choice in any situation for reasons discussed in Chapter 4. The retail sales tax still functions reasonably well in the United States. There are local option sales taxes on selected goods in a number of countries, and there is a question about whether the VAT is reasonable for countries with large amounts of trade. It is not our purpose to discuss the tradeoffs between a VAT and sales tax now, but there is some discussion in Chapter 4. Properly designed and administered, the VAT can be the most significant revenue source for many countries (accruing more than 40% of total revenue in some cases).

[43] OECD (2018).

[44] The VAT has many desirable elements (Tait, 1988). The IMF Fiscal Affairs Department has been active in assisting with VAT implementation and monitoring (Ebrill et al., 2001).

[45] The invoice might be entirely electronic and never printed.

in particular, imposing a tax on domestic consumers. Export refunds are an integral element of the VAT's purpose.

1.3.1.2 An Excise Tax System Limited to a Few Selected Items

An excise tax can be an important revenue source for emerging/developing economies. It is generally a tax imposed at the point of production or importation.[46] Thus, unlike VAT, administrative emphasis is placed on physical control. One recommended structure[47] is to limit the list of excisable goods to petroleum products, tobacco products, and alcoholic beverages, plus telecommunication. The list might be expanded to include automobiles and a few luxury goods. The reasons to restrict excises to only a few goods include balancing administrative expense relative to revenue and choosing goods with relatively inelastic demands. Thus, revenues can be significant for those commodities even when high rates are imposed.

Tax rates can be either per unit or ad valorem. Per unit taxes have been the tradition when the tax has been collected at the factory gate. There are now methods to maintain the advantage of per unit taxes at a few collection points, combined with physical control, while approximating an ad valorem retail tax (see Chapter 4).

1.3.1.3 Income Tax

Direct taxation of income has been a significant element in the basic tax regimes of Western Europe and the United States for more than one hundred years.[48] Some elements of income taxation are also part of the tax systems of most countries. While known as an 'income tax', the base employed to compute the tax may, or may not, be income in an economic sense. For example, if there is only an individual tax on wage withholding combined with a cash flow tax at the entity level, then the economic effect of the tax over time can be similar to a consumption tax such as a VAT.

The income tax is often discussed as two separate taxes: a personal income tax and an enterprise (or corporate) tax. The separation between the personal tax and entity tax is maintained here for discussion purposes only and is abandoned in Chapter 2. Figure 1.4 illustrates the relative importance of income taxes in developed relative to emerging economies. It is clear that income taxes are relatively less important in terms of revenue for emerging economies. Policy proposals and the recommended approach are based on treating the entity tax, the personal tax, and the capital gains

---

[46] Excises for commodities like gasoline are sometimes collected at the retail level in more developed economies. Such practices are discussed in developing and emerging economies for administrative and compliance reasons.

[47] For a discussion and comparative data, see OECD (2018). For the set of recommendations noted here, see Conrad (2016). Much of the discussion in this section is based on that Memorandum.

[48] The income tax was introduced in the United States in 1910 and in Europe at earlier dates. For example, a tax on wages was introduced in the UK in 1799.

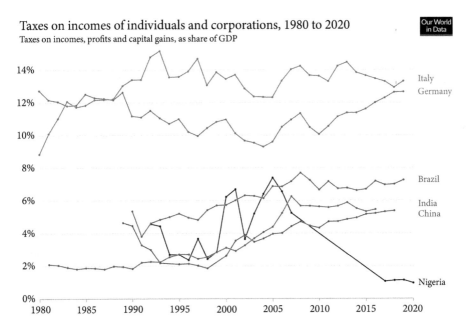

Taxes on incomes of individuals and corporations, 1980 to 2020
Taxes on incomes, profits and capital gains, as share of GDP

Figure 1.4 Relative share of income tax

Source: OECD Revenue Statistics; OECD Latin American Tax Statistics; IMF Government Finance Statistics (GFS); IMF Article IV Staff Reports; CEPALSTAT Revenue Statistics in Latin America. Published online at OurWorldInData.org. Retrieved from: https://ourworldindata.org/grapher/taxes-on-incomes-of-individuals-and-corporations-gdp (online resource).

tax as part of an integrated regime to impose tax on income accruing to individuals, either resident or nonresident (see Chapter 3).

a. A Personal Income Tax (PIT)

Personal income tax (PIT)[49] has not been a significant revenue source in either the near or the intermediate term in emerging economies. For example, the OECD reports that the average share of PIT in total taxes is 18%.[50] Per capita income may be too low, and participation in the modern sector by a significant proportion of the population may be too small (much income is generated in agriculture or informal markets for instance), to justify more extensive reliance on the PIT, at least as currently configured.[51] Administrative difficulties of required filing by individuals, especially higher-income individuals who do not have wage income (doctors,

---

[49] Social taxes may also be an important element of the revenue system. Reform of the social tax system should be coordinated with reform of the benefits provided by the system (pensions, health, unemployment, and other benefits). Until that time, it is generally recommended that the tax be uniform and applied to a base essentially the same as the PIT tax base to ease administration.

[50] OECD Revenue Statistics in Africa 2022. Available at https://www.oecd.org/countries/ghana/revenue-statistics-africa-ghana.pdf.

[51] One issue is how to define the personal income tax base, at least from an economic perspective. See Chapters 2 and 6.

lawyers, other professionals, and business owners supplying services), may also contribute to the relatively low dependence on PIT. It could also be the case that the share of PIT in total tax revenue in emerging economies will begin to mirror those in higher-income economies as income increases and administration improves. That is, the PIT may be designed to enable the economy to 'grow into' the PIT as per capita income grows, more individuals participate in the modern sector, and the aggregate tax base expands. Recommended strategies might vary depending on the emphasis placed on consumption relative to income tax elements in the PIT, but some common elements include extensive use of withholding on wages and other types of income at a flat rate. Administration may be enhanced with a flat rate tax in countries with computerization and enhanced compliance activities, including taxpayer education. The extent of withholding might vary from withholding tax only on wages (where the tax might be a final tax), to withholding on types of capital income including interest and other payments such as royalties and honoraria.[52]

b. An Enterprise Income Tax

The enterprise income tax is usually a significant revenue source for emerging economies but has been a declining share of total revenue in more advanced economies. The relative significance in emerging economies may arise because of the importance of foreign investors, and the fact that the tax administration has less difficulty monitoring activity in the modern sector. On the other hand, the falling share of enterprise taxation in advanced economies may be due to competitive pressure resulting from globalization,[53] the possible inability of individual countries to control the tax base as currently defined because of the presence of transfer pricing and other methods to legally avoid taxation without losing investment, the change in industrial structures from manufacturing to services which might be more difficult to tax, and policy shifts that may have changed the relative emphasis of the overall tax system towards consumption and individual taxation. If growth and enhanced competition for emerging economies mimics more developed economies today, then the share of enterprise profits taxes may be expected to fall.

Notwithstanding the importance of enterprise taxes in overall tax revenue, recommended reforms have included expanding the base and lowering the rate. Base expansion proposals have included reduction or elimination of tax incentives as well as tightening administrative procedures such as transfer pricing rules. Such base expansions may be perceived as partial financing of rate reductions. In effect, a

---

[52] It is important to distinguish between withholding on all persons as opposed to withholding on cross-border transactions.

[53] Of course, the tax structures, particularly the tax rates, have not been constant in all countries and may respond to factors such as globalization. The 2017 Tax Act in the United States may be a case in point.

broad base and lower rates[54] may be perceived as a more effective, economically efficient, and administratively easier method of attracting investment relative to using incentives (sometimes targeted) within a narrower overall tax base with, perhaps, higher rates.

A debate continues about the structure of enterprise taxes even if there is agreement among analysts and policy experts about the need for a broader base. The income tax base is one standard where there is an attempt to empirically measure the change in net worth, or the net return to equity capital, using full accrual accounting, depreciation, and interest deductions. This approach may be coupled with methods to integrate the corporate and individual tax such as dividend exemptions (Slovakia and Greece, for example) and split-rate systems (such as Germany). The consumption tax base at the entity level is an alternative. This approach includes cash flow taxation[55] of which the Border Adjustment Tax (Devereux et al., 2021) is one example.[56] At the entity level, the consumption base becomes a tax on economic rent. These issues are discussed in Chapter 3.

1.3.1.4 Decreased Reliance on Tariffs
It is now common to see reductions in discriminatory tariffs as part of a reform.[57] Reliance on tariffs might be reduced when increased emphasis is placed on VAT, which is capable of preserving the tax on imports while, perhaps, changing the nature of the economic results. Tariffs, to the extent that they are retained, should be relatively small, used for revenue purposes only, and levied at a uniform rate as in Chile.

1.3.1.5 A Property Tax (Attributed to Local Governments)
It is common to recommend that a property tax be one basis for local government finance. The tax base is either the quantity of the stock (as initially in Georgia) or the value of a stock (common in most developed countries such as the United States). Accordingly, the property tax should be perceived as one element of a more general tax on either the stock (when units are taxed) or on some measure of total gross or net worth (when the value is taxed). The tax, however, can be complicated and administratively cumbersome in any economy given different valuation methods and the presence of numerous exemptions. The administrative issues have been sidetracked

[54] For a popular description of the trend towards a broad base and lower rates in taxation ('BBLC', as he labels the term), see Reid (2018).
[55] There are many expositions of the incentive effects of cash flow relative to income taxation. For an excellent reference for readers with some knowledge of basic economics, see Boadway (1979). The approach has been advocated by some advisers, particularly in the context of the liberalization of Central and Eastern Europe (McLure, 1991).
[56] The Border Adjustment Tax was recommended in one proposal for US tax reform (GOP, 2016).
[57] For one example of a proposal for a radial reduction in tariffs in Russia, see Conrad (2000).

a bit in emerging economies by the development of simple valuation procedures and administration designed to enhance compliance.[58]

1.3.2 Special Circumstances

Tax structures may include particular regimes for what are considered special situations.

1.3.2.1 Small Business Taxation

Small businesses, according to some empirical definition, may be subject to a special income tax regime and may be exempt from VAT, because the sector's compliance with the generally applicable tax is deemed either inappropriate or unworkable. Taxing small businesses is an issue in all economies for a number of reasons. First, there is concern that the compliance cost of imposing the normal tax regime on such businesses is not worth the relatively small revenue gain. Second, and related to the first, small businesses may operate in sectors in which trade is dominated by either cash transactions or barter; a situation that makes auditing difficult. Finally, there is a question about whether maintaining accrual-based accounts is cost effective for at least some small businesses, even if owners are knowledgeable about the methods (see Chapter 5).

1.3.2.2 Natural Resource Revenue

Natural resource revenue may be important in particular economies; a topic discussed in depth in Chapter 6. Natural resources can interact with the general tax system in at least two ways. First, the state as the resource owner either enters into contracts with private entities or produces itself, generally via a state-owned enterprise. The generally applicable tax system may be reflected in the contracts or may be modified by the contracts. Second, the importance of natural resources for total government revenue may extend beyond the specific sector, particularly if the natural resource sector is a significant economic sector. Total government revenue can be influenced by changes in natural resource prices. The direct effect of changes in profitability can affect total revenue if natural resources are a major revenue source. There is also the indirect effect via linkages with other economic sectors. Both effects could combine to be significant, particularly if the economy is not diversified. For these and other reasons, natural resource policy emerged as an important topic for countries with significant resource endowments, regardless of income levels or overall stage of development.

---

[58] Kelly (2014).

1.3.2.3 Agricultural Taxation

Agriculture is a difficult sector to tax in all economies, in part because of the nature of the industry and in part because much agriculture is conducted by effectively small business. Some countries address such difficulties by introducing a large exemption for the PIT and having a relatively large threshold for VAT. Small farmers will generally be exempt from both taxes in this case. In addition, farmers can be treated as a special case of a small business if small business taxes are used.

1.3.2.4 Estate and Inheritance

Estate and inheritance taxes are relatively minor taxes in terms of revenue generated, again regardless of a country's level of development. Such taxes may be perceived as important elements for progressivity on an intergenerational basis.

1.3.3 Administration

Tax administration reform is generally an essential element of, and perhaps the driving force for, general tax reform. For example, one justification for increasing the reliance on indirect taxation is the perception that such taxes are not as administratively cumbersome as income taxes. Tax administration reform is a long-term process, like tax reform in general. Today it is generally recognized that tax policy reform needs to be linked to administrative reform, or at least to the evolution of the tax administration, in order for the objectives of tax reform to be realized. Approaches to administrative reform depend on local circumstances, but all reforms are considered to be relatively long term in their initial implementation (three to five years at a minimum but a reasonable expectation is a generation). One longer-term trend in tax administration has been the emphasis on voluntary compliance.[59] Emerging trends in tax administration have been the extensive use of computers and the use of large data sets. Computerization has facilitated electronic filing and reductions in filing requirements when coupled with withholding and adjustments to the definition of the tax base.[60] Powerful computers and large datasets have enabled cross-matching of withholding records and taxpayer records and expanded audit capabilities, among other important functions.[61]

---

[59] In general, the term is used to connote self-reporting by the taxpayer to the tax authorities of both the data necessary to compute the tax liability as well as the amount of tax. Such an approach may be contrasted to an assessment system where the amount of tax is computed by the tax authorities. This approach will be critically evaluated in Chapter 2. Voluntary compliance has been one basis for the US tax system as well as other advanced economies and is one basis of administrative reform in emerging economies. For one historical perspective, see Manhire (2015). For an applied example, see Okello (2014).

[60] See Joseph & Avdic (2016), e-Estonia https://e-estonia.com/solutions/e-governance/, and https://www.techrepublic.com/article/how-estonia-became-an-e-government-powerhouse/.

[61] See Chapter 3, OECD (2016), as well as Cotton & Dark (2017) and Keen & Slemrod (2017) more generally.

1.3.4 Fiscal Decentralization

One trend among tax reform efforts is the movement to decentralize expenditure responsibilities while providing regional and local governments with the fiscal resources necessary to meet their expanded obligations. This trend is based on an increasing body of evidence that economic growth is enhanced if the subnational governments control particular types of public expenditures (Kelly, 2014). It is argued that, through time, public expenditures tend to be more transparent and more targeted to the population's needs because local decision makers can be better held accountable by the voters for their actions (if information is available and the population is mobile).

This trend has developed because central governments may be slow to respond to reform initiatives while much of the impetus for real growth can be developed at the subnational level. For example, local small business interests can initiate much employment and investment growth. These small businesses respond to changes in the local investment climate, and thus it is important that a coincidence of interest be developed between local government and the small business sector. That is, an increase in local public services and a decrease in the regulations imposed on small business can yield growth in local investment and employment and, in turn, the local tax base.

Unfunded mandates can be created, however, if expenditure responsibilities are decentralized but tax and other fiscal resources are maintained by the centre. Revenue sharing, grants, equalization formulae, and other national-to-subnational transfers compose one set of tools to provide resources to subnational governments although they could result in dysfunctional incentives, such as a soft budget constraint, for subnational government. Also, these methods are mechanical and do not consider all local concerns even if distributions are transparent and well-funded. Thus, it is generally agreed that subnational governments need some types of own-source revenues at the margin in order to accrue resources sufficient for locally identified, publicly supplied goods and services.

Box 1.1 contains an illustration of how the standard approach has evolved over time. Some significant tax reforms are described spanning more than 20 years, including Indonesia in the 1980s, Malawi in the late 1980s, and Russia over the period 1992–2002. Of course, the approach has been used over a much longer period given the relative structural stability of European tax regimes since the VAT was first introduced in France in 1954.[62]

---

[62] Many analysts, including us, may trace their intellectual approach to tax reform to the Shoup mission to Japan at the end of World War II, so it may be appropriate, somewhat arbitrarily, to date the beginning of the modern era of tax reform to that mission as well as his work on VAT (*Report on Japanese Taxation by the Shoup Mission*, 1949). We believe that the report had some effect on the redrafting of the US Internal Revenue Code in 1954. In addition, Shoup and his students, including Richard Bird among others, have made continuing contributions to tax reform efforts throughout the world. Another early tax reform was in Korea, which began reforming its tax system in earnest about 1960 (Kwack & Lee, 1992).

Box 1.1 Selected cases of reform

Item	Indonesia	Malawi	Russia
Dates of Initial Reform	1982–1985	1986–1990	1992–2002
Initial Economic and Political Conditions	• Stable government for some years after the fall of the Suharto regime • Economic growth had averaged 7.3% during the period 1968–1980 • Economy depended on natural resource revenues to a significant degree (petroleum and minerals) • The impetus for reform was an awareness that Government could not depend on natural resource revenue over the longer run • Tax base was narrow, not diversified, and there was evidence of significant corruption	• Stable autocratic government under Hasting Banda • Among the poorest countries in the world • Basic agricultural economy with limited manufacturing • Landlocked and war in Mozambique increased cost of trade	• Initially post-Soviet adjustment with dissolution of Soviet Union • Inflation at high rates • Rapid privatization in an environment where some industries and firms were no longer profitable • Political environment reflected the uncertain nature of the structural adjustment

Continued

Box 1.1 *Continued*

Item	Indonesia	Malawi	Russia
Financing	Financed by Government	World Bank	USAID, Tacis, IMF, World Bank and George Soros via a number of technical assistance providers (including Georgia State University, US Treasury, IMF resident advisers and Harvard Institute for International Development)
Objectives	• Reduce reliance on natural resource revenue • Increase the integrity of the tax system • Broaden the base and reduce rates • Increase the progressivity of the system • Design a system that could be administered with existing staff while the administration underwent longer term modernization and reform	• Expand and broaden base • Tax reform part of structural adjustment lending and part of a package of overall reforms	• Adopt a market-oriented tax system • Stabilize revenue • Broaden base • Adopt non-Soviet accounting concepts • Simplify administration • Reduce corruption
Reforms	**VAT** • Set 10% base rate (zero-rated exports) • Repealed a set of three uncoordinated indirect taxes	**VAT** • Replaced the existing sales tax system with a VAT through the manufacturer's level • Initial rate about 30%	**General Notes** • Tax reforms were reflected in a two-volume tax code • The tax administration part of the code was enacted first with the policies enacted initially in 2001

Item	Indonesia	Malawi	Russia
	Profits Tax • Most incentives were eliminated • Introduced simplified depreciation • Lowered rate to 25% • Taxpayers began using generally accepted international accounting standards • Corporate integration was proposed, but not enacted **Personal Income Tax** • Replaced schedular tax regime with a unified personal income tax, including fringe benefits • Introduced two rates **Tariff System** • Not part of original reform	**Profits Tax** • Most incentives were eliminated • Introduced simplified depreciation • Lowered corporate rate • Implemented franking system to reduce double taxation of corporate profits **Personal Income Tax** • Introduced 3 rate system. • Expanded withholding **Tax Administration** • Introduced unique taxpayer identification numbers. • Began unification of audits into a comprehensive audit system • Redesigned forms	• The code reduced the number of taxes and provided for allocations between the centre and subnational governments, in addition to including the tax statutes and provision for tax administration **VAT** • VAT was introduced when the Soviet Union was dissolved, but the law was ambiguous, there was little understanding and there was much evasion • The introduction of standard accrual-based VAT took almost ten years. Rates were reduced from 30% to less than 19%. A differential rate for a specific list of goods (e.g., foodstuffs) was introduced. **Profits Tax** • Simplification of depreciation • Adoption of internationally accepted accounting standards on an accrual basis

Continued

Box 1.1 *Continued*

Item	Indonesia	Malawi	Russia
	Property Tax • Not part of initial reform • Reform began with some demonstration projects initiated at the end of the initial reform project **Tax Administration** • Introduced taxpayer identification numbers • Began computerization • Expanded withholding • Began reorganization of departments to a functional reorganization		• Partial integration of the profits and individual income tax • Provided rules for derivation of the base consistent with modern accounting **Personal Income** • Introduced a comprehensive flat rate tax (13%) • Simplified exemptions and broadened base **Excise Tax** • Introduced a reformed excise system with a restricted number of covered commodities • Adjusted rates for inflation **Tariffs** • Began a radical reduction of the tariffs **Small Business Tax** • Introduced a small business tax that included a choice between a turnover tax and cash flow tax **Tax Administration** • Introduced a revised taxpayer numbering system • Began computerization • Expanded withholding (including withholding tax on disposals of capital assets) • Introduced net worth comparisons and audit selection criteria • Attempted to address petty corruption

1.4 Rethinking the Standard Approach

The standard framework might be considered international best practice. While there may be unique features for the tax system in each country, and the relative importance of each charge may differ, it is true that most countries have adopted a framework that includes a mix of income taxation, sales taxation (usually the VAT, with the major exception being the United States), a selective excise tax regime, reduced reliance on trade taxes, and a property tax. Almost universal adoption does not, however, imply the existence of best practice or that this mix of tax instruments is appropriate for all countries if such best practice exists. In short, it is possible for all countries to get it wrong.

A working definition of taxation is needed in order to provide one perspective on the issue of tax structures. Taxes are defined in this volume as a compulsory payment made to the government for which no specific benefit is received. Accordingly, taxes should be taken in the context of ways (other than confiscation) that governments accrue resources from individuals. Other methods include, but are not limited to:

- constitutional ownership of assets (such as natural resource endowments and the right to issue currency[63]);
- charging for the supply of goods and services produced by the government, either via public sector enterprises, such as electricity in some countries, or by the general government (such as court costs, fees for the use of parks, or charges for the supply of medical care);[64]
- issuing debt, at least over some time period;[65]
- gifts and voluntary contributions;
- foreign aid; and
- seigniorage (the power of a state to issue a medium of exchange and to profit on the difference between the real value and cost).[66]

Social security might be included as a tax. Our view is that the issue of social insurance may be related to a payment in exchange for a good or service. For example, retirement benefits may be financed out of social security payments. In that case, we believe that social security, while a compulsory payment, is a tax only to the extent that the present value of the benefits to the individual is smaller than the costs. That is, the individual may value the present value of the benefits at 10 while having to pay 13 in present value terms. The compulsory payment for which no benefit is received is then equal to 3. The same approach applies to other forms of social insurance such as survivor's insurance, unemployment, and health insurance. In some cases, the benefit might not be related to the cost at all. In Ukraine for example, one could argue that the standard social security funding-distribution relationship does not apply, and thus it is a tax, particularly because benefits change over time.

---

[63] State ownership may be understood as type of confiscation of stocks or at least a prohibition on private sector ownership.

[64] Again, state enterprises, if they are monopolies (a state oil company for instance), may be understood to include taxation elements if prices are not equal to marginal cost. Distributional concerns can be taken into account by discriminatory pricing (Atkinson & Stiglitz, 2015) (Lecture 15).

[65] Debt issuance may be a type of deferred taxation depending on how debt service is financed.

[66] Again, monopoly power over the domestic medium of exchange might be a type of confiscation. Inflation is the most common method of profiting from the difference between the cost of printing money and the real value.

Given this definition, there are a limited number of ways the government can impose tax, including:

- Fixed fees or payments unrelated to either assets or flows of goods and services;[67]
- Periodic charges on assets (ad rem[68], i.e., ad valorem), such as a property tax, a net worth tax, or on other assets such as inventories;
- Charges on flows (ad rem or ad valorem), including production, title transfer (supply and demand), or triggered by a certain event such as death or arriving in or leaving the taxing jurisdiction; and
- Periodic ad valorem charges on flows of income (measured as the change in either net worth or net cash flow).

The standard approach fits well into this grouping because the only charge not employed in a majority of instances is a charge independent of any economic activity. That is, governments might use all the elements in their fiscal arsenal. A second potential explanation is diversification of government revenue sources.

Diversification, at least in an economic sense, is limited because there are only two economic classifications that can be taxed (as opposed to confiscation of assets) as a means to transfer resource flows from assets owned by private sector individuals to the public sector: flows and stocks. In addition, there are only two methods to determine the tax base: the number of stocks or flows, or the value of stocks or flows.[69] Thus, it could be the case that the standard model has evolved through time in an attempt to use as many tax handles as possible. In addition, using numerous tax handles may enable a government to obtain revenue without concentrating on one or two sources as means of keeping effective rates on each measured base relatively low (in order to be politically acceptable perhaps) and to diversify the revenue system. Basic elements of the standard model reflect the use of all elements that might be taxed and include:

---

[67] We assume fixed fees are different from lump-sum taxation as defined in economics, which we understand to be equivalent to a one-time asset transfer, an action that results in only income effects.

[68] Ad rem asset charges are used in emerging economies for property taxation. For instance, some jurisdictions (e.g., Georgia) impose a tax per unit of geographical area of agricultural land.

[69] From an economic perspective, it is easy enough to convert a per unit tax into an ad valorem tax by multiplication (or division, depending on if the tax is being held constant). If the ad valorem tax rate is 't' and the value of the tax base is 'V', then $tV = K$ where K is the per unit value of the tax. For example, if the tax rate is 12% and the value is 20 Kwacha, then the per unit equivalent is 2.4 Kwacha. There may be certain advantages to one taxation method relative to another. If a general sales tax is imposed, then either the effective tax rate across taxed goods and services would be different if a constant per unit value were used, or there would have to be different per unit taxes on each taxed good or service in order to keep the effective tax rate constant (where effective tax is used here to mean the proportion of the value of the tax base). A per unit tax may be preferred in situations where either the value is uncertain (such as sales of a specific good and service between related parties) or the tax is collected at a point where the market price of the good or service is not known. For example, alcoholic beverages taxed at the manufacturer's gates as opposed to the retail level.

1. Per unit taxes on flows of goods and services (some excises and tariffs).
2. Ad valorem taxes on the flow of goods and services (some excise taxes and sales taxes, including VAT, other general sales taxes, and turnover taxes).
3. Ad valorem taxes on income (the change in net worth).
4. Per unit taxes on stocks (some countries impose property taxes as a fixed value per hectare).
5. Ad valorem taxes on stocks (property taxes, asset taxes, net worth taxes,[70] and estate taxes or inheritance taxes); and
6. Fixed fees (such as the tax imposed by the Thatcher administration in the UK, or the fixed charge imposed on each Malawi citizen prior to 1990).

The list of potential combinations of stock and flows matched with per unit or ad valorem rates is not exhaustive. For example, there is no practical per unit tax on income (such as 10 Yen per 10,000 Yen of net income). In addition, the elements that compose the standard model may have evolved from administrative experience,[71] criteria other than revenue,[72] as well as economic conditions.

That said, there might still be questions about why to use all of the tax instruments in the standard approach given the fact that there is ultimately only one economic base: real income. One explanation is to match each instrument with a reform target.[73] For example, the VAT might be used as a significant revenue source. The income tax can be used to add progressivity to the overall system or perhaps to offset the perceived regressivity of sales taxation.[74] Excises can be used to discourage a specific activity such as smoking[75] or to add progressivity depending on the commodities taxed.[76] Property taxes might be a progressive revenue source that can be administered by local governments. Finally, fixed fees, independent of economic activity, may or may not be used for political reasons.[77] This explanation may justify the standard approach and may be sufficient. That said, even this justification does not explain why all the instruments in the standard approach should be used for all countries almost

---

[70] Taxes on gross or net worth are sometimes use as a either an estimated tax (a tax prepayment) or a minimum income tax. Such charges are not imposed on the intended base, however, which we take to be income. Rather, the charges are administrative means to attempt to tax some measure of income. True taxes on stocks include net worth charges or taxes on the gross value of assets (of which real property is one element).

[71] A general tax on the stock value of net worth is an example. Administrative difficulties include measuring the value of net worth at a point in time and incentives to leverage on the evaluation date.

[72] Multiple rate taxation of income is one example.

[73] Targets and instruments are a common approach in macroeconomics (Fleming, 1968).

[74] There is an extensive economics literature on the use of multiple instruments (Huang & Rios, 2016; Boadway, Garon, & Perrault, 2019).

[75] For one example to estimate the effect of excises on smoking, see Wasserman, Manning, Newhouse, & Winkler (1991).

[76] Excises on automobiles are sometimes based on models as in Russia. See cost_of_car_ownership_2016.pdf (pwc.ru).

[77] There are exceptions. Malawi had a minimum personal income tax that was a fixed fee. Conrad understood that the basis for the charge was the proposition that everyone has a stake in the success of the country and should contribute something in monetary terms to the state.

regardless of income levels, economic structure, income distribution, or whether a country is federal or unitary.[78]

A second justification for the approach could be portfolio diversification because different instruments become relatively more important at different points in the economic cycle. It is true that income taxes, sales taxes, and excise taxes are all positively correlated, but the correlations are not perfect, so there is some potential to reduce the overall variation of government revenue. In addition, excises are relatively inelastic and sales taxes such as the VAT may have an elasticity a bit greater than one,[79] while the income tax can be relatively elastic, holding the base and rate structure constant. Thus, even if correlated, the government may have access to some revenue during downturns and may benefit dis-proportionally from economic growth.

A third justification for the standard approach could be administrative efficiency—the government may want to use every instrument at its disposal to collect revenue in a way that diffuses taxpayer resistance and administrative costs. In this situation, the objective would be to choose the mix of tax instruments, and the relative levels of taxation, to satisfy government revenue needs while minimizing the administrative, compliance, and efficiency costs of the system while still recognizing the mutual dependence of each tax instrument on the underlying economic system. The use of multiple instruments means forgoing the benefits of going down the intensive margins of using one or two taxes, given administrative constraints. In addition, there could be administrative complementarities between the taxes that might increase total revenue holding administrative costs fixed. For example, comprehensive audits are advocated for the VAT and income tax because both taxes are accounts-based taxes.

With respect to emerging economies, it has been claimed that adopting a VAT, which is supposedly easier to administer than an income tax, provides an opportunity for the tax administration to learn by doing. Income tax administration is then enhanced, and through time, the share of income taxes to total tax revenue will increase both with increased growth and enhanced administrative efficiency.

While each of these is a potential explanation, a number of questions remain. First, it might appear as if there is some type of evolution to applied taxation.[80] That is, that taxation might begin with easy-to-identify and administer taxes such as production shares (of farm products), tariffs, excises, and a type of ad rem property tax; then move gradually to broader indirect taxes such as the turnover taxes and ultimately the VAT, wage withholding, and a crude profits tax applied to larger firms, including multinational firms; and finally, the introduction of more sophisticated

---

[78] We believe it is no coincidence that the last major economies to adopt a VAT were Australia and Canada, both federal countries, with the US being a significant outlier. In the US, sales taxes have been under the control of the states, and issues about adopting a national sales tax would mean developing a method to compensate the subnational governments. It is apparent that Australia and Canada found such a solution. The problem is somewhat the reverse in the European Union, where the loss of hard borders meant freer trade.

[79] The elasticity will not be unity in practice because the coverage of the VAT is not complete, and there are exempt taxpayers who may come into the system at different parts of the business cycle.

[80] Seelkopf et al. (2021).

income taxes. This type of evolution might be reflected in the relative importance of each tax in total revenue at various points in the development process and may be reasonable if tax policy evolves with per capita income as well as innovation. Issues remain, however. It might be reasonable to conjecture that the tax mix depends on the population and the diversification of the economy, even if the economy is relatively rich. For example, the Baltic States have relatively small populations, so it might be reasonable to ask whether Estonia's tax system would be more efficient, on some margins, if it had no profits tax or no VAT. Estonia's population is less than most major world cities, and cities are not expected to implement the entire mix of taxes used in the standard approach. In addition, the mix of tax instruments applicable for relatively high-income, low-population countries might not apply with equal force to low-income, low-population countries such as Timor-Leste. There is at least the question about whether it makes sense for such countries to employ administrative resources in a manner that mimics the tax mix of higher-income, large population countries.

Another issue is that there can be, and often is, significant variation with respect to each tax instrument, income taxes in particular. Income tax bases can vary as a matter of method from attempts to tax economic income to attempts to tax consumption. VATs vary in application and can include sales tax and even turnover tax elements. What might be efficient for a large, diversified economy might not be reasonable for a small economy that has little expectation of developing the degree of domestic diversification of larger economies, much less have a tax administration large and diversified enough to have a variety of tax specialists.

A third issue is whether changes in economic structure and technology affect either the choice of the tax mix or the administration. It may be the case that some tax instruments become obsolete and others more prominent through time, so what is a combination of tax instruments that compose the standard approach today may not be applicable in the future, even given the significant adjustment costs of changes in taxation. This might be true today for the profits tax as currently constructed given globalization and the cost of monitoring what are only portions of the overall activities of a globalized firm. The same might be said of the VAT, at least for high income economies,[81] the property tax, and the structure of excises.

Fourth, it might appear that the standard model has simply been exported from high-income countries. Countries with less experience might benefit, significantly, from the applied experience of higher-income countries. In effect, emerging economies might skip some steps that history imposed on other economies. The cost of such exportation is that emerging economies get systems that are less efficient relative to the the facts and circumstances in their countries. We believe it is important to note that such an experience might be a two-way street. It also might be the case, given the experience of emerging economies, that the potential exists for significant feedback to higher-income countries. That is, the experience and adaptations of emerging

---

[81] See Chapter 3.

economies might be helpful to higher-income countries, and such experience might assist in laying the foundation for the evolution of tax systems in the future.

Fifth, one element not explicitly incorporated in developing the standard model is risk sharing. All taxes, perhaps with the exception of one-time poll taxes, have some risk sharing characteristics. For example, in the ancient method of taxation via share-cropping where a fixed proportion of the harvest was taxed, revenue varied with the amount and price of output. Accordingly, risk averse producers might respond to the tax-induced change in net-of-tax variability of returns. For example, a tax of 20% on the harvest will decrease the net-of-tax gross expected value of the harvest by 20% while at the same time reducing the variability (measured by standard deviation) in the value of the net-of-tax harvest by the same proportion. Thus, there is a cost (the tax) and a benefit (risk sharing). The individual bears 80% of the revenue risk with the remaining 20% being shifted to the other citizens via changes in government revenue. In addition, it is well known that an income tax structured in a particular manner can be a relatively efficient risk-sharing device (Domar & Musgrave, 1944).[82] Furthermore, recent economic researchers have found that, in cases where uncertainty is present, individuals may prefer an income tax over consumption taxes even if consumption taxes have lower efficiency costs when there is perfect certainty.[83]

Finally, from an economic perspective, the efficiency cost of taxation is determined by the effects on the real income of individuals. Real income will fall, absent compensating for changes in the delivery of public goods and services financed by the taxes. Thus, the issue is how to choose a tax system that is most efficient in terms of the effect on real income, given the expenditure mix and levels[84] as well as distributional objectives. This does not mean that an income tax is an important, or even an essential, part of the tax mix. Rather, the choice of the tax mix should be made in the context of the combined effect on individual income and, perhaps, the idiosyncratic nature of any individual economy. As noted, this might imply a different tax mix, and even the abandonment of particular tax instruments as an economy evolves. For example, if revenue needs are low, then a per unit tax on one commodity might be the most efficient tax system. If revenue and distributional concerns are significant, then the level of taxation will be greater, given the distribution of wealth. If an economy has relatively low income, then the proportion of trade taxes, excises, and consumption taxes may be higher relative to an economy with greater wealth.

While we have used and endorsed the standard approach, these and other issues have become more prominent with more experience. Furthermore, we have a bias for using income taxes for reasons that will become clear. This bias has led us to

---

[82] The conditions include a proportional tax and perfect loss offsets.
[83] The result has been noted by Nishiyama & Smetters (2005) and Athreya & Waddle (2007). This issue is also noted by Auerbach (2006). Conrad and Alexeev (2021) use some simple simulations to confirm the result.
[84] Or more accurately, the present value of the level of expenditure mix.

be concerned about the almost universal adoption of taxes on consumption expenditures, such as VAT,[85] regardless of population size, per capita income, degree of economic diversification and all factors unique to any country. The efficiency benefits of such taxes, in the context of a tax mix, may not be present. VAT, however, has one significant administrative benefit. The tax is transactions based and is effectively an advanced payment on the ultimate tax paid by the taxpayer, the domestic resident. In effect, the government gets some, or all, of the tax revenue before, or at the time, the ultimate taxpayer obtains the rights to the good or service. Given the importance of revenue to emerging economies, it might be possible to expand the transaction based-advanced payment system to elements of income in order to develop a collection-driven tax system that is able to evolve through time. An attempt is made to develop such a system in this volume.

Given these concerns, this text is organized in a manner to reexamine some of the elements of the standard approach, both individually and collectively. The discussion begins in Chapter 2 with the development of a collection-driven tax system based on the individual as the taxpayer. The more technical discussion is included in the Annexes to Chapter 2 along with a discussion of the economic contributions to tax analysis.

The move from method to application becomes an important part of this discussion because a tax system that cannot be administered has little other than methodological value. Each separate tax is then discussed in chapters on direct (Chapter 3) and indirect taxation (Chapter 4), but in the context of what we call Advanced Payment Agents (APA) as the basis for collecting either the final tax or an estimate of the tax on the individual. Experience is used to discuss practical issues of application. Chapter 5 contains a discussion of small business taxation which, by practice, appears to be an appealing approach to the taxation of a particular economic group. There is also a chapter (Chapter 6) on natural resource policy because of the importance of government ownership of reserves throughout the world and the need to discuss, and to distinguish, tax policy from capturing the return from government ownership of a particular asset. There is not a separate discussion of tax administration. Rather, administrative issues pervade both the approach and the applications to each tax.

A summary is found in the final chapter, along with a discussion about how technological and market changes might affect the choice of tax instruments for countries considering reform.

---

[85] The concern is compounded when income taxes contain elements that exempt savings, such as deferred pensions, incentives for capital investment, and other exemptions for the income from nonhuman capital, such as exemptions on interest income. There are conditions under which a VAT combined with such an income tax is simply a double tax on the same consumption tax base. The only benefit of such an approach, as a matter of method, is that progressivity is added to the combined system.

References

Alexeev, M., & Conrad, R. (2013). The Russian Tax System. *The Oxford Handbook of the Russian Economy*. doi:10.1093/oxfordhb/9780199759927.013.0031.

Alexeev, M., & Conrad, R. (2015). *The Effect of Russia's Tax Reform*. Russia: IET.

Athreya, K. B., & Waddle, A. L. (2007). Implications of Some Alternatives to Capital Income Taxation. *Economic Quarterly*, *93*(1), 31–55. Retrieved from https://www.researchgate.net/publication/5053084_Implications_of_some_alternatives_to_capital_income_taxation.

Atkinson, A. B., & Stiglitz, J. E. (2015). *Lectures on Public Economics: Updated Edition*. Princeton, NJ: Princeton University Press.

Atkinson, P. E. (1997, 1997 April–May). New Zealand's radical reforms. *OECD Observer* *(205)*, 43+.

Auerbach, A. J. (2006). *The Choice between Income and Consumption Taxes: A Primer*. Paper presented at the Conference on Key Issues in Public Finance, New York University.

Auerbach, A. J. (2013). *Capital Income Taxation, Corporate Taxation, Wealth Transfer Taxes and Consumption Tax Reforms*. Paper presented at The Empirical Foundations of Supply-Side Economics, Becker Friedman Institute, University of Chicago.

Alvaredo, F., Chancel, L., Piketty, T., Saez, E., & Zucman, G. (eds) (2018). *World Inequality Report 2018*. Belknap Press. Published online at OurWorldInData.org. Retrieved from: https://ourworldindata.org/grapher/top-income-tax-rates-piketty (online resource).

Bahl, R. (Ed.) (1991). *The Jamaican Tax Reform*. Cambridge, MA: Lincoln Institute of Land Policy.

Besley, T., & Persson, T. (2014). Why Do Developing Countries Tax So Little? *Journal of Economic Perspectives*, *28*(4), 99–120. doi: 10.1257/jep.28.4.99.

Boadway, R. (1979). *Public Sector Economics*. Cambridge, MA: Winthrop Publishers, Inc.

Boadway, R., Garon, J.-D., & Perrault, L. (2019). Optimal mixed taxation, credit constraints, and the timing of income tax reporting. *Journal of Public Economic Theory*, *21*(4), 708–737. doi: https://doi.org/10.1111/jpet.12382.

Chamley, C., Conrad, R., Shalizi, Z., Skinner, J., & Squire, L. (1985). *Tax Policy for Malawi*. World Bank. Washington, DC.

Conrad, R. (1986). Essays on the Indonesian Tax Reform. *CPD Discussion Paper*, 86-8.

Conrad, R. (1990). *Tax Reform for the Dominican Republic*. International Tax Program and United Nations Development Program.

Conrad, R. (2000, 24 June). [Tariff and Customs Reform (Russia)].

Conrad, R. (2013, 13 July). [Memorandum: Various Matters (Greece)]. Mimeo.

Conrad, R. (2016). *One Approach to Tax Reform in Myanmar*. Mimeo.

Conrad, R., & Gillis, M. (1984). The Indonesian Tax Reform of 1983. *HIID Development Discussion Paper*, 162.

Conrad, R., & Alexeev, M. (2021). *Income Tax Reform: A Proposal that Can Be Administered*. Unpublished.

Conrad, R. F., Hool, B., & Nekipelov, D. (2018). The Role of Royalties in Resource Extraction Contracts. *Land Economics, 94*(3), 340–353. Retrieved from https://EconPapers.repec.org/RePEc:uwp:landec:v:94:y:2018:i:3:p:340-353.

Cotton, M., & Dark, G. (2017). Use of Technology in Tax Administrations 1: Developing an Information Technology Strategic Plan (ITSP). *IMF Technical Notes and Manuals No. 17/01.*

Devereux, M. P., Auerbach, A. J., Keen, M., Oosterhuis, P., Schön, W., & Vella, J. (2021). *Taxing Profit in a Global Economy*. Oxford: Oxford University Press.

Domar, E. D., & Musgrave, R. A. (1944). Proportional Income Taxation and Risk-Taking. *The Quarterly Journal of Economics, 58*(3), 388–422. Retrieved from https://EconPapers.repec.org/RePEc:oup:qjecon:v:58:y:1944:i:3:p:388-422

Ebrill, L. P., Keen, M., & Perry, V. J. (2001). *The Modern VAT*: International Monetary Fund.

Fleming, J. M. (1968). Targets and Instruments (Objectifs et instruments de politique économique) (Metas e instrumentos). *Staff Papers (International Monetary Fund), 15*(3), 387–404. doi: 10.2307/3866296.

GOP. (2016). *A Better Way: Our Vision for a Confident America, Poverty, Opportunity, and Upward Mobility*, Bethesda Md.: ProQuest.

Huang, J., & Rios, J. (2016). Optimal tax mix with income tax non-compliance. *Journal of Public Economics, 144*, 52–63. doi: https://doi.org/10.1016/j.jpubeco.2016.10.001.

Joseph, S., & Avdic, A. (2016). Where do the Nordic Nations' Strategies Take e-Government? *The Electronic Journal of e-Government, 14*(1), 3–17. Retrieved from www.ejeg.com.

Keen, M., & Slemrod, J. (2017). Optimal Tax Administration. *IMF Working Paper, WP/17/8.* doi: https://doi.org/10.5089/9781475570267.001.

Kelly, R. (2014). Implementing Sustainable Property Tax Reform in Developing Countries. In R. M. Bird & J. Martinez-Vazquez (eds), *Taxation and Development: The Weakest Link?* (pp. 326–363). United Kingdom: Edward Elgar Publishing Inc.

Kwack, T., & Lee, K.-S. (1992). Tax Reform in Korea. In T. Ito & A. O. Krueger (eds), *The Political Economy of Tax Reform* (pp. 117–136). Chicago: University of Chicago Press.

Manhire, J. T. (2015). What Does Voluntary Tax Compliance Mean?: A Government Perspective. *University of Pennsylvania Law Review Online, 164*(11). Retrieved from https://ssrn.com/abstract=2601613.

McLure, C. E. (1991). A Consumption-Based Direct Tax for Countries in Transition from Socialism. *World Bank Country Economics Department, Working Paper No. 751.*

Mehrotra, A. K. (2012). From Seligman to Shoup: The Early Columbia School of Taxation and Development. In W. E. Brownlee, Y. Fukagai, & E. Ide (eds), *The Political Economy of Transnational Tax Reform: The Shoup Mission to Japan in Historical Context* (pp. 30–60). New York: Cambridge University Press.

Musgrave, R. (1981). *Fiscal Reform in Bolivia: Final Report of the Bolivian Mission on Tax Reform.* Cambridge, Mass: Law School of Harvard University.

Musgrave, R. and Gillis, M. (eds) (1971) *Fiscal Reform for Columbia: Final Report and Staff Papers of the Colombian Commission on Tax Reform.* Cambridge, Mass: Law School of Harvard University.

Nishiyama, S., & Smetters, K. (2005). Consumption Taxes and Economic Efficiency with Idiosyncratic Wage Shocks. *Journal of Political Economy, 113*(5), 1088–1115. doi: 10.1086/432137.

Nkusu, M. (2004). Aid and the Dutch Disease in Low-Income Countries: Informed Diagnoses for Prudent Prognoses. *IMF Working Paper, WP/04/49.*

OECD. (2016). *Technologies for Better Tax Administration.*

OECD. (2018). *Consumption Tax Trends 2018.*

OECD Revenue Statistics; OECD Latin American Tax Statistics; IMF Government Finance Statistics (GFS); IMF Article IV Staff Reports; CEPALSTAT Revenue Statistics in Latin America. Published online at OurWorldInData.org. Retrieved from: https://ourworldindata.org/grapher/taxes-on-incomes-of-individuals-and-corporations-gdp (online resource).

Okello, A. (2014). Managing Income Tax Compliance through Self-Assessment. *IMF Working Paper, No. 14/41.* Retrieved from https://www.imf.org/en/Publications/WP/Issues/2016/12/31/Managing-Income-Tax-Compliance-through-Self-Assessment-41415.

Reid, T. R. (2018). *A Fine Mess: A Global Quest for a Simpler, Fairer, and More Efficient Tax System.* New York: Penguin Books.

Report on Japanese Taxation by the Shoup Mission. (1949). Tokyo, Japan: General Headquarters, Supreme Commander for the Allied Powers Retrieved from http://www.rsl.waikei.jp/shoup/shoup00.html.

Seelkopf, L., Bubek, M., Eihmanis, E., Ganderson, J., Limberg, J., Mnaili, Y., ... Genschel, P. (2021). The Rise of Modern Taxation: A New Comprehensive Dataset of Tax Introductions Worldwide. *The Review of International Organizations, 16*(1), 239–263. doi:10.1007/s11558-019-09359-9.

Stephens, R. (1993). Radical Tax Reform in New Zealand. *Fiscal Studies, 14*(3), 45–63. Retrieved from http://www.jstor.org/stable/24437312.

Tait, A. A. (1988). *Value Added Tax: International Practice and Problems*: International Monetary Fund.

The Tax Foundation Blog: Enache, Cristina. 'Corporate Tax Rates around the World, 2022', *Corporate Tax Rates around the World, Tax Foundation*, 13 December 2022.

Todaro, M. and Smith, S. (2014) *Economic Development, 12th Edition.* Pearson. ISBN: 1292002972. Published online at OurWorldInData.org. Retrieved from: https://ourworldindata.org/grapher/composition-of-tax-revenues-regional (online resource).

Ukraine Ministry of Finance. (2015). *Memorandum of Understanding.* Kyiv, Ukraine.

Wasserman, J., Manning, W. G., Newhouse, J. P., & Winkler, J. D. (1991). The Effects of Excise Taxes and Regulations on Cigarette Smoking. *J Health Econ*, *10*(1), 43–64. doi:10.1016/0167-6296(91)90016-g.

World Bank. (2003). Russia: Tax Administration Modernization Project (Loan 2853). *Project Performance Assessment Report No. 25915*. Retrieved from https://documents1. worldbank.org/curated/en/685011468757814711/pdf/multi0page.pdf.

Annex A1.1
Basic Notions Used in the Economic Analysis of Taxation

A1.1.1 Introduction

The economics of taxation has a rich and complex history dating back to Adam Smith.[1] Below, some of that literature is summarized from the perspective of what can be applied to tax policies in emerging economies.[2] Some basic notions that are important for the tradeoffs developed in the tax literature are discussed before proceeding to a summary discussion.

A1.1.2 Basic Issue: Efficiency

Economists emphasize the notion of economic efficiency. It is intuitive that efficiency implies getting the most out of limited resources. As a matter of method, however, economic efficiency has two components. Consumption efficiency is a situation where an individual can be made no better off by changing the combination of goods and services demanded given the economic value of the assets over which the individual has control.[3] Production efficiency is a situation where a producer constrained by technological factors cannot increase output (revenue) without increasing costs or reduce the use of any input necessary to produce a particular mix of outputs without having to increase the use of some other input.[4] Given efficiency at the level of the individual agent, aggregate consumption efficiency implies that it is not possible to make one individual better-off, in an economic sense, without reducing the economic welfare of at least one other individual, keeping the aggregate value of consumption fixed. Aggregate production efficiency is a situation where it is not

---

[1] See Dome for one perspective on Smith's theory of tax incidence (Dome, 1998). Smith had four maxims for tax policy: equality of burden (purportedly taxation related to benefits received), certainty in application, administrative convenience, and results in the lowest deadweight loss (Drenkard, 2015).

[2] Economists who address taxation deal with complex issues, and the proposed approaches are most impressive. In addition, the results and discussions provide the reader with a sense of humility not only about themselves relative to the ability of the authors, but regarding the lack of knowledge about the issues in general.

[3] There are two conditions for individual efficiency. First, the budget constraint is exhausted; second, the marginal rate of substitution is equal to the relevant relative price ratios.

[4] Technology is the constraint for producers given market structure. The producer will choose the inputs used to produce desired outputs in combination so that costs are at a minimum. Alternatively stated, given a cost constraint, derived from the technical constraint, the producer will choose input combinations and levels to maximize output.

Evolutionary Tax Reform in Emerging Economies. Robert F. Conrad and Michael Alexeev, Oxford University Press.
© Open Society Institute (2024). DOI: 10.1093/oso/9780192847089.003.0002

possible to increase the supply of one commodity[5] without decreasing the supply of at least one other commodity, keeping total amount of inputs fixed. Finally, overall economic efficiency is a situation where the marginal benefit of increasing the output of one good or service is equal to the marginal cost of production measured in terms of the decreased value of forgone production of other goods and services. Overall economic efficiency and each of its components are based on the Pareto criteria, a necessary feature of any type of economic efficiency concept. Facts and circumstances, the initial distribution of wealth for example, may limit the feasible set of potentially efficient outcomes.

Efficiency implies that tradeoffs are necessary, and the converse is true for inefficient situations. That is, if the situation is inefficient, it is possible, in principle, to increase either the production of all goods and services or the welfare of everyone. Thus, it is natural for economists to emphasize efficiency because there are no costs, at least in theory, to increasing output of any commodity or the welfare of one individual in inefficient situations.

It should be clear that efficient outcomes are not unique in any absolute sense and depend on technology, stocks of capital and labour, individual preferences, the distribution of wealth, and numerous other factors. For example, more food and fewer personal computers may be consumed when the income distribution is relatively equal compared to an unequal situation where less than 5% of the population accrues 50% of the income.

In addition, emphasis is placed on the fact that efficiency is defined relative to the preferences of the individuals who compose the economy. For example, an individual might prefer to grow tomatoes in her garden as opposed to buying tomatoes in the market, even when the financial cost of growing tomatoes at home is five times the financial cost of buying identical tomatoes in the market.[6] Economists believe such actions are economically efficient as long as the price signals upon which the individual's decision is based are not distorted. Accordingly, a tax, or other distortion, which would decrease this person's production of tomatoes, would be inefficient. This perspective is particularly important when examining public policy because much interest is placed, justifiably, on changes in observable GDP. All elements of how economists measure GDP, however, are not observable. The tomato-growing example is a case in point. It could be the case that the tax imposed to induce the individual to reduce the production of tomatoes resulted in that individual working more in the market (as opposed to her own garden), so measured GDP would rise.

This point deserves some emphasis because of the importance of economic growth in emerging economies. Material economic growth, poverty reduction, and measured GDP may provide an expansion of opportunities and choices for the population. How those choices are exercised is not an issue of the economic analysis itself. For example, a 10% expansion of agricultural production potential may result in a 6% expansion of production with agricultural producers forgoing the additional 4%

---

[5] A commodity includes both goods and services.
[6] The point is that the tomatoes are not identical in an economic sense.

of the potential to spend time with families. The point can be summarized by stating that 'self-interest' is a much different concept from material greed, production maximization, or selfishness.

All economies are not economically efficient, so it is possible, in theory, to make all individuals better off. That said, it is difficult, if not impossible, to develop public policies that make everyone better off. Most public policies, tax policies in particular, will generally make some individuals worse off. In practical situations where Pareto efficient tradeoffs are not feasible, economists appeal to the Kaldor-Hicks criteria where emphasis is placed on the potential rather than actual Pareto improvements. For example, suppose taxpayers are classified into three groups: high income, middle income, and low income. Suppose there is a policy proposal to increase the taxes paid by high-income taxpayers, to reduce taxes (or equivalently redistribute income) to low-income taxpayers, and to make no change to taxes paid by middle-income taxpayers. The changes are made so that total tax revenue stays the same. We would expect that high-income taxpayers would be made worse off even if they are concerned for the welfare of low-income taxpayers, and low-income taxpayers would be made better off. Middle-income taxpayers could be better off if middle-income taxpayers prefer a more equal income distribution, particularly when they do not have to pay for it. The policy would not be Pareto improving because middle and low-income taxpayers are made better off while high-income taxpayers are made worse off.[7] The policy could pass the Kaldor-Hicks (sometimes called the Cost-Benefit) Test if it is possible for the winners (middle and lower-income taxpayers) to potentially compensate the losers (the high-income taxpayers), with an amount sufficient to make the losers no worse off. In effect, the winners can pay the losers an amount sufficient to make the policy a potential Pareto improvement while ensuring the losers will not block the policy. Emphasis is placed on the term 'potential' because the compensation will not be made in practice. If the compensation were paid, then the policy initiative would be completely different in the sense that the policy could change the taxes paid by all taxpayers and adequate compensation might not be possible.

The Kaldor-Hicks notion of relative economic efficiency is important for tax analysis because price distortions are created by all taxes used for revenue purposes, as opposed to correcting market distortions (externalities), relative to the economic definition of efficiency. In theory, lump-sum charges would be neutral (create no efficiency costs), but lump-sum charges are methodological tools only and cannot be applied in practice.[8] In order to produce no distortions, a lump-sum tax must be

---

[7] The new allocation could be Pareto efficient, however. Thus, there is a difference between Pareto improving and Pareto efficient allocations. That is, it is possible for two points to be Pareto optimal but a movement from one allocation to another would not be Pareto improving simply because outcomes allocated by the Pareto criterion are only partial. Therefore, the Pareto criterion cannot be used to determine which Pareto efficient outcome is best. The same can be said of the Kaldor-Hicks rule: it cannot be used to determine the best outcome. Rather, the rule can be used to determine whether welfare is improved relative to some initial situation. In addition, policy changes that satisfy the Kaldor-Hicks rule do not have to be Pareto efficient.

[8] It might be possible to impose a surprise tax of a fixed amount once, but that charge would not be sufficient to fund the government for all time.

certain, independent of any characteristic over which the individual has control, and never be subject to change.[9] The absence of lump-sum charges implies that the economics of tax analysis will always be second best in the sense that there is no practical means to avoid efficiency costs.

If relative efficiency is the only criterion, then an efficient outcome will be defined relative to the particular economic environment in which the tax is imposed. Given those conditions, a tax regime will be deemed superior to another if the tax regime under investigation can satisfy some objective or set of objectives, given some initial conditions if real net national income is greater. Of course, there may be trade-offs with respect to the objectives themselves. Income distribution and the desire to change the production technologies, among other factors, may result in tradeoffs between some measure of efficiency and the other objectives.

All economies are operating in an inefficient manner because the empirical situation will never match the situation depicted in any methodological model. That said, relative economic efficiency will always be an economic criterion to evaluate policy because the basic objective of economic analysis is to increase the economic wellbeing of the individuals in an economy. In short, there is no need to impose a tax that can make a bad situation worse, when it may be possible to use tax policy to make relative improvements. Thus, any tax that fails to achieve this objective given levels of the other criteria will be judged inferior.

A1.1.3 Numerical Examples of Efficiency

A numerical example is used to illustrate how efficiency cost is measured and how a change in exogenous factors affects the preference of one type of taxation relative to another based on measured efficiency.[10] In particular, a tax on consumption expenditures (a VAT) is compared to an income tax in the case where perfect certainty is assumed as opposed to when there is a specific type of uncertainty.

Suppose an individual can consume a single consumption good in two periods ($t = 0$ and $t = 1$). Suppose further that the individual will work in $t = 0$ and retire in $t = 1$, and the individual has no savings at the beginning of $t = 0$. This means that the wages earned in $t = 0$ must be spent on consumption goods in both periods, so the budget constraint measured in present value terms is:

$$\hat{w}_0 L = \hat{P}_0 Q_0 + \frac{\hat{P}_1 Q_1}{(1 + \hat{r})},$$

where: w_0 = return to human capital (the market wage) in $t = 0$,

[9] For example, the UK imposed a type of lump-sum charge per annum during the Thatcher administration, and resources were diverted to repealing the charge. In effect, some UK residents were willing to pay more than the current value of the tax in order to increase the probability that the tax would be repealed. Such behaviour is one example of how substitution operates.
[10] The analysis is based on Conrad and Alexeev (2021).

$\bar{L}$ = labour supply (assumed to be exogenous),
r = return to non-human capital,
P_0 = price of consumption in $t = 0$[11],
P_1 = price of consumption in $t = 1$,
$\bar{Q}_0$ = quantity to be consumed in $t = 0$,
$\bar{Q}_1$ = quantity to be consumed in $t = 1$.
$\hat{}$ denotes expected values in the case where prices are uncertain.
and the individual's preferences are represented by:[12]

$$U^A(Q_0, Q_1) = K_A + \left(Ln(Q_0) + \frac{Ln(Q_1)}{1+z}\right),$$

where z = the individual's discount rate and
K_A = arbitrary positive constant.

What is not spent on consumption in t = 0 will be spent on consumption in t = 1, so saving is defined as:

$$S_0 = w_0\bar{L} - P_0 Q_0$$

Tax-exclusive prices are assumed to be:

$$\hat{w}_0 = 10,$$
$$\hat{r} = 0.10, \text{ and}$$
$$\hat{P}_0 = \hat{P}_1 = 1.0,$$

Two types of taxes are used to illustrate the welfare cost. An income tax will affect the returns to human capital (wages) and the return to saving. This means that the budget constraint with the income tax is:

$$w_0(1-t)L = \hat{P}_0 Q_0 + \frac{\hat{P}_1 Q_1}{(1+\hat{r}(1-t))},$$

where t = income tax rate assumed to be constant.

A VAT will increase the price of consumption goods in both periods, so the budget constraint in the case of a VAT is:

$$\hat{w}_0 L = \hat{P}_0(1+k)Q_0 + \frac{\hat{P}_1(1+k)Q_1}{(1+\hat{r})},$$

where: k = VAT rate.

[11] Some textbook applications of the basic savings model define $\hat{w}_0(1-t)L = \hat{P}_0 Q$ as the aggregate value of consumption (or C_t) in any time period. While reasonable for the issue at hand, we prefer to separate the p's and the q's in order to illustrate the effects of uncertainty. In addition, it is useful to define $\frac{W_t}{P_t}$ as the real wage, measured in units of labour supply.
[12] These preferences imply that individual is risk averse, which becomes important in the case where prices are uncertain.

The welfare function is well defined, so it is possible to solve for the individual's optimal choices given the constraint that revenue from the two taxes must be equal in present value terms. An income tax rate of 50% is chosen for the illustration. Then the VAT rate that generates the same present value of revenue is 104.44%. In the perfect certainty case, quantities consumed and welfare measures are found in Table A1.1.1.[13]

The VAT would be preferred because the same present value of revenue can be collected but the individual's welfare is higher. One measure of the relative efficiency cost of the tax would be the amount of the additional tax-free income needed to make the individual indifferent between having to pay an income tax relative to the VAT. The answer is supplied in the line labelled 'Amount of Compensation' in Table A1.1.1.

The well-known result that an individual would prefer a consumption tax to an income tax arises because an intertemporal distortion is created by the taxation of the income from saving. This distortion is evident by the fact that consumption is higher in $t = 0$ relative to $t = 1$ for the income tax while consumption is equal in both periods for the VAT.[14]

Consider now a situation where uncertainty is present. All prices (wages, interest rates, and the consumption prices in the two periods) are assumed uncertain for this illustration. Each price is assumed to be lognormally distributed with a standard deviation equal to the respective mean. The strategy used to examine the uncertain situation is to generate random prices (for all prices) and compute welfare and the present value of taxes and after-tax income. The results presented in Tables A1.1.2a and A1.1.2b are the expected value and standard deviations for 10,000 iterations of random shocks.[15] Table A1.1.2a and A1.1.2b contain the expected values and standard deviations for the income tax and the VAT, respectively.

Table A1.1.1 Perfect certainty

Variable	Income tax	VAT
Q_0	26.19	25.62
Q_1	25.00	25.62
Welfare	999.917	1000.000
Amount of Compensation	.0128723	

---

[13] Welfare values should not be considered absolute values. Values were normalized so that net-of-tax welfare with the VAT was equal to 1,000.00.

[14] No welfare cost is created by the VAT in this particular case because labour supply is exogenous. Accordingly, the VAT is equivalent to a lump-sum (perfect) tax given the assumptions. Such a result is not a demonstration that the VAT is a first best tax, because in reality labour supply is endogenous. Still, the VAT is generally superior to the income tax when there is perfect certainty and labour supply is variable. The VAT and a wage tax are equivalent in this example in the perfect certainty case, so the effective consumption tax can be measured relative to a tax on wages. In this case, a wage tax of 51.08% is necessary to raise the same present value of revenue relative to the income tax.

[15] More information about the computations can be found in Conrad and Alexeev (2021).

Note that now the income tax is preferred to VAT. Welfare is higher with the income tax, in an expected value sense, relative to VAT. The standard deviation of the income tax is higher relative to VAT, but this results because the average is higher. When the values are normalized, by using the coefficient of variation (the last row of Panels A and B) for example, the adjusted variability of the income tax is lower. So, even with the approximately identical expected value of income, in present value terms, an individual would prefer the income tax because it has better risk-sharing properties, at least relative to VAT. Variability of welfare is lower, at least in part, because of the tax on savings. VAT does not tax savings, so variability of the interest is not mitigated by VAT. On the other hand, the variability of after-tax interest to the individual is lowered by the income tax. The risk-sharing properties of income tax are well known if income is measured in a particular way.[16] Given the facts that uncertainty pervades all decisions and individuals are perceived to be risk averse, as a general matter, the demonstrations of the potential superiority of the income tax in risky situations should be part of any evaluation of tax reform strategies. This might be particularly true in emerging economies where a significant percentage of the population is poor and poorly diversified, making taxation perhaps one important mutual insurance device.

Table A1.1.2a Uncertainty: income tax

Statistics	Welfare	Present value of after-tax income	Present value of tax	Present value of tax-inclusive income
Mean	997.325	49.08	51.24	100.32
Standard deviation	319.144	50.37	52.6	102.97
Coefficient of variation	0.317628	1.02629	1.0265	1.0264

Table A1.1.2b Uncertainty: VAT

Statistics	Welfare	Present value of after-tax income	Present value of tax	Present value of tax-inclusive income
Mean	996.872	49.08	51.25	100.32
Standard deviation	318.999	50.53	52.77	102.97
Coefficient of variation	0.31811	1.02949	1.0295	1.0264

[16] This literature can be traced to 1944 (Domar & Musgrave, 1944). This issue about the superiority of the income tax has been studied in the case of wage shocks (Nishiyama & Smetters, 2005); with uninsurable, idiosyncratic risk (Athreya & Waddle, 2007); and in incomplete markets (Easley, Kiefer, & Possen, 1993). All the authors found that income taxation, including taxation of nonhuman capital, could dominate consumption taxes in terms of welfare.

A1.1.4 Tax Equity

Economists employ two measures of equity in tax analysis: horizontal and vertical equity.

A1.1.4.1 Horizontal Equity

Horizontal equity implies equal treatment of equals. While intuitive, application of the concept needs to be clearly specified. It is common to employ this concept in the context of equal pre-tax incomes. Accordingly, if two individuals have the same economic incomes, then the tax should be the same and incomes after tax will be the same. For example, if individuals A and B have observed market incomes perfectly measured of 10,000, then horizontal equity might imply that both individuals pay the same tax. But income is a flow measured[17] between two points in time. Thus, suppose that further investigation reveals that Individual A worked 10 hours per week to earn 10,000 while Individual B worked 50 hours per week. Both freely choose their market time, but Individual A enjoys much more time in nonmarket activities, given the same market purchasing power, relative to Individual B. It can be argued that Individual A's economic wellbeing is higher.[18] It could be the case that Individual A is more productive than Individual B or any number of other factors could be responsible for the difference in hours worked. The point is that it is not possible to specify what is meant by equal treatment of equals in an absolute sense, at least empirically.[19]

[17] Horizontal equity could potentially be defined relative to wealth, or the present value of the flow of tax-inclusive income. In this case, individuals with identical wealth, at a point in time, should pay equal taxes in present value terms. This means that the amount of equal tax, in present value terms, may result in a different time pattern of taxes. For example, Individual A could pay taxes of 10 and 12 in t = 0 and t = 1, respectively, while Individual B pays 0 and 24 in t = 0 and t = 1, respectively. The present value of the taxes is the same, however, if the discount rate is 20%. Thus, equal taxes at the same points in time may violate horizontal equity on a flow basis but satisfy horizontal equity on a present value basis. There are also issues with respect to the basis for comparison. For example, suppose a 20-year-old woman has a present value of income equal to 100 while a 40-year-old man has a present value of income equal to 100. Both have the same wealth, but the younger woman can consume the same wealth over a longer expected lifetime relative to the older man. An adjustment for age could be made, but this raises the issue of what is meant by equal incomes and wealth in the first instance.
[18] No statement can be made about whether Individual A is better off than Individual B. Individual B may prefer market work relative to household activities.
[19] It might be efficient to violate horizontal equity and not tax individuals with the same observed income the same (Mankiw & Weinzierl, 2010). These authors develop optimal income tax policies based on individual height because it is observed that, on average, taller individuals have higher incomes, at least in developed economies. Thus, a tall person and a short person with equal income would be taxed differently. Of course, the horizontal equity criterion being applied is equal income, but the two individuals in question are not equal on all margins, a point to which we return below. In addition, the optimal tax literature is based to some extent on interpersonal welfare comparisons, at least in the sense that the social welfare functions are employed to facilitate the analysis. See below. If economic welfare were measurable, then it might be possible to define horizontal and vertical equity with respect to comparisons of total welfare (either at a point in time or through time). Given differences in preferences, counterintuitive results might occur. For example, a person with low income (a monk, for instance) might have a higher level of economic welfare than a rich tycoon. Or two people with identical incomes could have significantly different levels of economic welfare (Feldstein & Taylor, 1976). Also, note that any tax system would satisfy horizontal equity if individuals have identical preferences and are identical on relevant margins because

While there are difficulties with the notion of horizontal equity, the concept has some uses. In particular, the notion can be used to justify equal taxation of different types of income. For example, an individual providing legal services as a sole proprietor and making 1,000 for her efforts should pay the same tax as an individual providing the same legal services for the same value via a corporate entity.[20] In addition, an individual investing in a project with a certain risk-adjusted present value should be taxed the same as another individual investing in a different project with the same risk-adjusted present value. Such comparisons can be one justification for the absence of discriminatory tax incentives and exemptions for particular types of income (honoraria, pensions, royalties, and interest, for example).

Finally, horizontal equity may imply the lack of discrimination. In terms of political economy, the unequal treatment of equals via discriminatory taxation is a source of both frustration and anger. Individuals and their agents who manage firms can begin to exert pressure on the government when discrimination is perceived. The basic example is when an individual making 1,000 in wages pays more (or less) tax than an individual making 1,000 in honoraria. This is an example where there is no difference in economic substance, but there could be a different after-tax income outcome based on the definition of the payment. An additional example is the case of tax incentives for individuals who export (either as individuals or via entities in which they have an equity participation), among many cases. One basis for such treatment is that other things equal, an increase in exports increases the supply of foreign exchange. If such a tax incentive is provided, then producers of import substitutes will claim they too deserve to be treated equally because increasing production of import substitutes, other things equal, frees scarce foreign exchange. Such pressure may either increase the complexity of the tax system and/or be one impetus for reform that can garner broad public support.[21]

A1.1.4.2 Vertical Equity

Vertical equity implies the unequal treatment of unequals. Ability to pay (as opposed to benefits received, perhaps) may be one basis for vertical equity: individuals who can afford (financially) to pay more tax relative to others should be required to do so.[22] Suppose the incomes, perfectly measured, of Individuals A and B are 10,000

---

individuals in the same tax bracket would have equal welfare (Rosen & Gayer, 2010: 376). Given differences in preferences, it might be difficult, if not impossible, to have a complete measure of horizontal equity.

[20] It might be the case that efficiency and horizontal equity are complementary in these situations.

[21] See the discussion of tax incentives in Chapter 3 and the discussion of corruption in Chapter 4 for other examples. Horizontal inequities can exist because persons with the same taxable incomes pay less tax, including bribes, relative to honest taxpayers.

[22] There may be a presumption in ability to pay that the individuals receive the same level of public goods and services. See the discussion below about the combination of tax and expenditure.

and 10,000,000, respectively. Application of vertical equity will imply that Individual B should pay more tax than Individual A, but the concept provides no guidance about how much more tax Individual B should pay. Vertical equity, by itself, also does not indicate the type of tax structure. For example, a tax of 100 imposed on Individual A and a tax of 101 imposed on Individual B can satisfy the general notion of vertical equity, even though the tax regime is regressive in the sense that the average tax rate decreases with pre-tax income and the average tax rate is lower for Individual B than Individual A.[23]

Vertical equity might be modified to state that the tax system should be progressive.[24] This notion, however, provides little guidance for the marginal rate structure. For example, a flat rate tax combined with a significant exemption (as recommended in the text) has a progressive statutory incidence because the average tax rate increases with income. Variable rate structures such as 10%–22%–40% or 10%–22%–23% also qualify, even though the rate of progression falls in the latter structure (40 – 22 = 18 and 23 – 22 = 1). Vertical equity, while intuitive, may benefit from further specification in order to inform practical policy. Ultimately, the degree of progressivity is a political economy problem holding compliance and related administrative issues constant. This is because economic method may provide little in the way of policy guidance about the degree of progressivity.[25]

A1.1.4.3 Distribution

Part of the ambiguity about both vertical and horizontal equity is that there is little specification about policy objectives, and there is no specification of the relative cost of achieving the specified objectives. In effect, the equity measures may be inputs, or indicators, of policy that can be used by policy makers, not necessarily economists, to evaluate policy. One approach is to require that the government needs to raise a specific amount of revenue and then to impose specific conditions about what is meant by the equity concepts. For example, the objective could be to raise 100 in revenue while requiring that individuals with the same before-tax income pay the same amount of tax, and there is one tax rate plus a personal exemption of 10. Given assumptions about individual characteristics, it is possible to determine whether such

---

[23] Vertical equity could also be measured relative to the value of assets. For example, a person with net worth of 1,000 should pay more tax, in present value terms, relative to a person with a net worth of 100. Note, again, the issue about timing of the tax payments. The individual with net worth of 100 could pay tax of 1 per annum while the individual with net worth of 1,000 could pay zero tax for 20 years and then pay 100 in tax in year 21. The 100 paid in year 21 could have a higher present value relative to the present value of the tax of 1 per annum.

[24] Economists generally define progressivity with respect to an increasing average effective rate.

[25] Economists might note that real GDP may increase or decrease with changes in measured progressivity, an efficiency issue, and may measure the income distributional outcomes of changes in progressivity measures (a positive economic issue).

a tax system is feasible and, if it is feasible, the rate can be determined. Such a specification satisfies both vertical and horizontal equity, as specified in the problem.
As well, the tradeoffs in terms of efficiency costs of achieving the objective can be
analysed. In addition, the cost (or benefit) of having horizontal or vertical equity, as
defined, can be examined by relaxing one constraint at a time.

Vertical equity may take on more meaning when tax and expenditure are combined
to determine statutory fiscal incidence of government actions on individuals. One
purpose of the tax system may be to redistribute income, but such redistribution can
be offset by expenditure policies. For example, a country could impose a tax system
with increasing average rates and then develop a spending programme that favours
the rich (subsidies for private higher educations, subsidized electricity for high-cost
housing, etc.). The implication of combining tax and expenditure is that the issues of
vertical (and horizontal) equity are placed in the context of the relationship between
pre-tax incomes and post-government intervention results.

Wealth redistribution may be one objective of government policy, so the use of
revenue is important in determining the net effect of government actions (tax and
expenditure) on the after-tax and after-expenditure distribution of wealth. The economic value of government expenditures accrues to individuals either directly via
the provision of cash and in-kind transfers, including public goods provided to all,
or indirectly via the payments to suppliers of factors of production used to produce
and distribute public goods and services.

Including government expenditure into the problem can help determine the issues
to be examined. For example, the issue at hand could be to design a tax system to raise
a specified amount of revenue while that revenue is transferred from some taxpayers to the lowest 10% of the wealth distribution, exogenously determined, via equal
grants. Now horizontal equity could be invoked so that there is a constraint that those
with the same pre-tax incomes have the same post-tax post-expenditure incomes.
Vertical equity is clearly implied by the redistribution. Note, however, that vertical
equity in a tax-expenditure sense may not be equivalent to vertical equity in a tax
sense. That is, it can be possible for those at the high end of the distribution to be
taxed at a lower marginal rate (perhaps zero) relative to individuals with lower initial wealth. This could arise because of the tradeoff between raising revenue and the
efficiency cost of the tax system. (See Annex A1.2.)

A1.1.5 Summary

In summary, the concepts of economic efficiency and relative efficiency via the
Kaldor-Hicks criterion have relatively clear definitions while, at least for economists,
notions of equity and redistribution need more structure in order to be analysed in
terms of the tradeoffs between equity and efficiency. It is clear, however, that one
implication from this discussion is that taxation and expenditure might be analysed together in order to obtain a better understanding of the equity implication
of government actions. The specification of equity and the analysis of tradeoffs is

one of the important contributions of the optimal tax literature discussed in Annex A1.2. Finally, it is important to note that equity concepts apply only to individuals (human beings). That is, equity concepts should not be applied to artificially created legal entities. For example, equal effective marginal, or average, tax rates measured at the corporate level are not an indicator of horizontal equity. It is the equality of the marginal, or average, tax rates of the individuals who own the corporate entities that matters. This is because only individuals matter in the sense that all economic income ultimately flows to the residual claimants of the legal entities. In effect, legal entities have no economic welfare independent of their individual owners.

References

Athreya, K. B., & Waddle, A. L. (2007). Implications of Some Alternatives to Capital Income Taxation. *Economic Quarterly*, *93*(1), 31–55.

Conrad, R., & Alexeev, M. (2021). *Income Tax Reform: A Proposal that Can Be Administered*. Unpublished.

Domar, E. D., & Musgrave, R. A. (1944). Proportional Income Taxation and Risk-Taking. *The Quarterly Journal of Economics*, *58*(3), 388–422.

Dome, T. (1998). Adam Smith's Theory of Tax Incidence: An Interpretation of His Natural-Price System. *Cambridge Journal of Economics*, *22*(1), 79–89.

Drenkard, S. (2015, 28 May). What Can Adam Smith Teach Us about Tax Policy? Retrieved from https://www.libertarianism.org/publications/essays/what-can-adam-smith-teach-us-about-tax-policy.

Easley, D., Kiefer, N. M., & Possen, U. M. (1993). An Equilibrium Analysis of Fiscal Policy with Uncertainty and Incomplete Markets. *International Economic Review*, *34*(4), 935–952. doi:10.2307/2526973.

Feldstein, M., & Taylor, A. (1976). The Income Tax and Charitable Contributions. *Econometrica*, *44*(6), 1201–1222.

Mankiw, N. G., & Weinzierl, M. (2010). The Optimal Taxation of Height: A Case Study of Utilitarian Income Redistribution. *American Economic Journal: Economic Policy*, *2*(1), 155–176. doi:10.1257/pol.2.1.155.

McLure, C. E., Jr. (1974). A Diagrammatic Exposition of the Harberger Model with One Immobile Factor. *Journal of Political Economy*, *82*(1), 56–82.

McLure, C. E., Jr. (1975). General Equilibrium Incidence Analysis: The Harberger Model after Ten Years. *Journal of Public Economics*, *4*, 125–161.

Nishiyama, S., & Smetters, K. (2005). Consumption Taxes and Economic Efficiency with Idiosyncratic Wage Shocks. *Journal of Political Economy*, *113*(5), 1088–1115. doi:10.1086/432137.

Rosen, H. S., & Gayer, T. (2010). *Public Finance*: McGraw-Hill/Higher Education.

Annex A1.2
Optimal Taxation

A1.2.1 Introduction

There is an important and growing literature on optimal taxation. Our intention is to describe some aspects of this literature and how the implications derived from the various results might be used in the applied emerging economy context. That is, it is not our intent to cover the numerous contributions to the economics of optimal taxation. Surveys of this literature are provided by Bradford and Rosen (1976), Sandmo (1976), Slemrod (1990), Heady (1993), and Gentry (1999).

A1.2.2 Structure of the Problem

The approach to optimal taxation is based on a shared common approach to economic analysis consisting of three elements. First, there is a well-defined objective. There might be a single objective such as to minimize the welfare cost of a tax, given revenue needs, or to maximize revenue subject to welfare constraint. The objective could be multifaceted, such as to improve both relative efficiency and some measure of equity. Tradeoffs might exist when the objective is multifaceted, so there needs to be a clear specification of how society (via the government) values the tradeoff at different combinations of measured equity and efficiency. This is commonly modelled by an analytical device known as a social welfare function, which reflects society's preference about the welfare of each individual in the economy.[1] Social welfare functions are helpful in situations where individuals are heterogeneous given the use of interpersonal comparisons. Second, there could be multiple means to achieve the objective. Multiple means include different marginal income tax rate schedules, different indirect tax schedules, or the combination of income tax and indirect tax schedules. There could be an entire universe of potential tax regimes that satisfy

---

[1] A social welfare function is a mathematical representation of alternative relative values assigned to each individual based on notions of social ranking and measurability of both the Social Welfare Function and the underlying utility. In effect, it is assumed that it is possible to tradeoff, in a social sense, the welfare of one individual for another. These assumptions violate microeconomic notions that individual economic welfare is not empirically measurable in either an absolute or relative sense. In addition, a social welfare function satisfying reasonable properties does not necessarily exist in the first instance (Arrow, 1950). These violations, however, are analytical devices to obtain some understanding of how different social preferences affect tax schedules. It should be obvious that the more equal the desired post-tax post-expenditure distributions relative to other variables in the system, the greater the transfers. The policy implications of the tax schedules, for the income tax in particular, may be similar in the sense that equity and efficiency tradeoffs will have a consistent impact.

Evolutionary Tax Reform in Emerging Economies. Robert F. Conrad and Michael Alexeev, Oxford University Press.
© Open Society Institute (2024). Doi:10.1093/oso/9780192847089.003.0003

the problem's constraints, but the search is for the one, or one potential combination, which is relatively the best, with best being defined as the highest value of the objective. Finally, there are one or more constraints. Depending on the problem, the constraints may include satisfying an exogenously given revenue constraint, the inability of the government to observe nonmarket behaviour, or lack of knowledge about the particular characteristics of individuals composing the economy.

One important constraint is either an implicit or explicit asymmetry of information in the modern approach to tax analysis. In many cases, the only information available to government is observable, the most common of which is observed pre-tax market income, as defined by the tax law in the case of practice and as defined by the analyst in the case of the methodology discussed. Other observable characteristics (or 'tags' in the literature) such as age, gender, and educational level might be used if such tags are indicators of one or more underlying individual traits. For example, in the landmark work of Mirrlees, it is assumed that individual innate abilities, 'human capital' hereafter, are distributed across the population (Mirrlees, 1971). These abilities enable those with more human capital to be more productive (other things equal). The tax authority cannot observe human capital, so reliance must be made on observed market incomes.[2] One tax schedule is applied to everyone and is assumed by individuals to be exogeneous. Lack of observability implies that observed pre-tax incomes are affected by the tax regime because individuals respond to the tax schedule by changing their labour supply and not revealing their true productivity. It is important to note that, while abstract, this is a realistic assumption. The government, both as a tax collector and a redistributor, may gather all sorts of information about individuals, including types of income (again relative to some empirical definition), the value of assets, marriage status, number of children, presence of any disabilities, sex, race, height (Mankiw & Weinzierl, 2010), and other factors. All these factors, even combined and independently observable (potentially), are not sufficient (either individually or collectively) to determine either the underlying human capital of any particular individual or their nonmarket activity. Thus, individual welfare cannot be inferred from market observations. Accordingly, the problem is second best by definition, because part of the 'game' on the part of the individuals is to disguise their income potential, when observed income may not be perfectly determined by ability and their individual preferences.

We believe it is important to note that the asymmetry of information might be interpreted as one means to model the fact that, unlike markets for private goods and services, taxpayers do not have an incentive to reveal their preferences at the margin in response to signals provided by taxes. That is, the tax system is not incentive compatible with the taxpayer revealing necessary information, because a tax is by definition a payment that is not made in exchange for any specific benefit. For example, suppliers of privately provided goods and services in a competitive economy are not necessarily concerned about the underlying characteristics of the

---

[2] We assume away lump-sum taxation, which appears to be politically and administratively infeasible.

individuals because the individuals have an incentive to reveal their willingness to pay at the margin. Suppliers of public goods or publicly supplied goods and services cannot rely on such incentive compatibilities because the taxpayer gets the benefits regardless of the amount of tax they pay.[3] Thus, the problem, at least in a primitive form, for a government, is to try to establish a relatively efficient tax regime knowing that taxpayers will attempt to evade by hiding their true abilities or willingness to pay.

There are other aspects about how the methodologies are developed. For example, there need to be assumptions about how individuals respond to changes in the relative prices as well as the income effects generated by particular taxes. Often, individual preferences are assumed to be either identical or at least have the same functional form. Technology, and the evolution of technology in the case of dynamic analysis, must be specified. Some researchers use technologies that ensure a competitive solution, and when combined with technological assumptions, this ensures that there is no transfer of economic rent from consumers to producers.[4] In effect, constant cost technologies may be assumed.[5] Technical issues must be addressed in order to ensure that the models are tractable and to ensure that at least one set of solutions exist.[6] Given the mathematical complexity and lack of realism, there is an issue about the relevance of the results produced by this vast literature. Specific results, however, are not the issue for us as practitioners. Rather, the results provide important input into how policy analysts think about the incentives created by different taxes as well as how to rigorously apply and enhance the distributional aspects of the tax-expenditure system.

A1.2.3 Income Taxes

In the modern era, Mirrlees provided the landmark study of the first analysis of how optimal income taxation is used for redistributive purposes in the context of asymmetric information (Mirrlees, 1971). The initial result illustrating the equity-efficiency tradeoff is that the marginal tax rate on the individual with the highest earnings potential should be zero.

---

[3] In the aggregate, the supply of the public good or service might be affected if all individuals try to avoid paying the marginal valuation for a particular mix of goods and services.

[4] There are sometimes discussions about taxing economic rents on the supply side of the market because such taxes are economically neutral. In economics, however, any rents accruing to the supply side of the market are income transfers from consumers. In fact, economic models are usually based on the assumption that the objective of any planner or economy in general is to maximize individual welfare; a proposition that translates into maximizing the economic rents in the economy because the rents are the surplus created when total benefits exceed total costs, as defined in the economic models.

[5] If income transfers from consumers to producers are part of the system, then there would have to be a means to distribute the rents to individuals, after tax. For instance, either the rents could be capitalized into asset prices, holding the return to nonhuman capital fixed, or the return to capital on a flow basis could change.

[6] Relative to a set of stipulated assumptions, it could be the case that no solution exists, or that multiple solutions exist.

A1.2.3.1 Tax Schedules Can Change the Average but Lower the Marginal to Mitigate the Equity-Efficiency Tradeoff

The original Mirrlees result provides a framework for the stark tradeoff between equity and efficiency. For example, suppose the tax schedule changes from 10%, 20%, 30% to 10%, 25%, 30%. As noted by Mankiw and Weinzierl, the increase in the middle bracket changes the marginal incentive to work for the individual in the 25% bracket (who used to be in the 20% bracket) and will increase the average tax rate for the individual in the highest tax bracket (Mankiw & Weinzierl, 2010).[7] There is, however, no marginal incentive for the individual in the 30% bracket to change his or her behaviour. That is, both the individual who is now in the 25% bracket and the individual in the 30% bracket pay more taxes other things equal, so the average tax rate increases, but there is no marginal incentive for the individual in the 30% bracket to work less at the margin.

One potential practical implication is that high marginal rates at the top of the observed pre-tax distribution may be in the interest of neither those at the high end of the distribution nor those, with presumed lower human capital levels, at the lower end of the income distribution. Again, other things equal, lowering the highest marginal rates, while paying at a higher average rate, could increase efficiency or aggregate income, increase tax revenue, and increase redistribution. That is, it may be in the interest of the poor to have lower marginal tax rates on the rich while increasing the average tax rate if taxes increase so there is more to redistribute to the poor.[8] We note, as a practical matter, that there are more ways to increase the average rate without changing or increasing the marginal rates, such as more accurate reporting, expanding the definition of the base, reducing corruption, and expanding compliance activities. Such increases are discussed in the text.

A1.2.3.1.1 Marginal Tax Rates at the High End of the Distribution Depend on Distributional Assumptions

The original Mirrlees result is that the marginal tax rate on the person with the largest endowment of human capital should be zero. The trick, of course, is that the government does not know who has the highest human capital endowment when the tax regime is determined. Subsequent work provided additional support for the result that the marginal rates should fall consistently at high income levels. As noted, these results illustrate the important tradeoff between equity and efficiency. Those with higher human capital are given incentives to increase effort relative to those with lower skills. For example, suppose two Individuals A and B are in the same marginal tax bracket, but Individual A has 50% greater human capital. Suppose both work the

---

[7] Horizontal equity is not an issue in this analysis because every individual will be subject to a different tax: human capital is unique to the individual. More generally, individuals that have identical abilities and preferences will pay the same tax.

[8] This is not a Laffer curve effect where decreases in marginal rates are self-financing. Rather, a lower marginal rate at the high end of the distribution while increasing the average can increase tax revenue if the supply response at the high end, in terms of value added, is greater than the loss at the middle brackets.

same amount with Individual B producing 1 per hour and Individual A producing 1.5 per hour. Suppose now that the marginal tax rate on Individual A is decreased enough for her to work one hour more while the tax rate on Individual B is increased so that he will work one hour less. Total value added in the economy will increase because the increased hour of effort by Individual A will be 50% greater than the loss in value added from the reduction by Individual B. In addition, tax revenue may increase because Individual A may pay more tax than is lost by Individual B's reduction of effort. This is because Individual A will have to pay higher taxes on the inframarginal units of effort. That is, Individual A will have to pass through the now higher tax rate imposed on Individual B in order to benefit from the lower marginal tax rate. For example, suppose there is a flat rate tax of 20% imposed on both individuals in the initial situation and that both individuals work ten hours, producing value added of 15 for A and 10 for B. Tax revenue will be 5 (or 3 from Individual A and 2 from Individual B). Suppose, however, that this flat rate tax schedule is replaced with a two-rate system where the tax rate is 22% on incomes up to 10 and 15% on incomes above 10. Given the assumptions, Individual B will work nine hours and Individual A will work 11 hours. Tax revenue will now be equal to 5.155, with Individual B paying 1.98 (.22*9) and Individual A paying 3.175 (or .22*10 + .15*6.5).[9]

Researchers have subsequently determined that the shape of the marginal tax rate function depends, at least in part, on assumptions about the distribution of human capital, distributional preferences, and other factors, such as the distribution of wealth at the highest income levels. Some extensions of the model[10] support high and increasing marginal tax rates for high-income earners while being critical of flat tax systems. In some cases, the tax rates are also relatively high at the low and high ends of the human capital distribution, with lower rates in the middle: a 'u-shaped' marginal tax rate schedule. Such rates may be reasonable at the low end of the distribution because we understand that the rate schedule includes both tax and expenditure. For example, it is common for some means-tested programmes (food subsidies, housing, and cash transfers) to be phased out as income increases. Such a phase out combined with a single marginal tax rate can yield an effectively high marginal tax rate at the low end of the human capital distribution. To illustrate, suppose there is a flat income tax of 20% and that a low-income individual receives 1,000 Kwacha if they do not work, but the grant is phased out at 25% for every Kwacha of income earned. In this case, the marginal tax rate on an additional Kwacha is 45% if the cash grant is not included in taxable income. (On 1 Kwacha of income, 0.2 Kwacha will be taxed, and 0.25 Kwacha of the grant will be reduced for the increase in pre-tax-pre-expenditure income.) One technical reason for such results is that the government observes results of only behaviour, not human capital, and the system is

[9] Note that vertical equity still holds in the sense that Individual A pays more tax. Vertical equity could be violated between Individuals A and B if vertical equity is defined as increases in the average tax rate. The average tax rate for Individual B is higher than Individual A's in this case (0.22 for B and approximately 0.19 for A). But the general result is ambiguous because the general result depends on the amount of tax paid in each bracket. For example, in the traditional Mirrlees case, the average tax rate is falling for the individual with the highest human capital because the marginal rate is zero for that individual.
[10] Saez (2001); Diamond & Saez (2011).

designed to keep those with higher human capital from gaming the system too much, thereby reducing efficiency.

Such expenditure programmes are not used as extensively in emerging economies, and it is true that most empirical applications, and discussions, of optimal tax theory have been applied to OECD countries.[11] There are some linkages to emerging economies, however, if specific, or targeted, groups are the unit of analysis instead of individuals. There are numerous government programmes in emerging economies designed to assist low-income groups such as microfinancing, training and support for small holder agriculture, subsidized education for girls, and subsidized access to cell phones, computer services, and water. Each of these programmes is multifaceted. For example, agricultural extension services and microfinancing are designed to help small holders increase their skills and productivity as well as access to intangible and physical capital. There are criteria, perhaps group identifiers (or tags), that identify the eligibility and those outside the targeted group who are not eligible. If the tags are related to income in the sense that individuals and/or groups can transition out of the lower income group, then the benefits would be lost: an effective tax rate of 100%. More importantly from the perspective of the methodology, we understand, is that those outside the group are not eligible and so there is no incentive for those with higher incomes to reduce their effort. This is the type of behaviour illustrated by the methodological result discussed here.

A1.2.3.1.2 Tagging

Mirrlees's original analysis was limited to one non-observable indicator of human capital and that indicator totally determined individual market productivity. There may be other indicators of earning capacity, however. The examples of small holder agriculture are one example (land tenure for example). Gender, health status or disability, race, age,[12] region of residence, educational attainment, measured IQ, and other factors may be correlated with market productivity in the sense that such tags are related to income earning potential. Thus, it may make sense for the government to use such tags to determine the tax schedule with different schedules being determined for each tag or set of tags. That is, the government might use all the information available to design a tax system in which the inefficient incentives are a minimum. Discrimination may be an inevitable result of using such information. Note that tags are not perfectly correlated with earning ability, and that tags may not be immutable. For example, an individual could move from the city to a rural area, or to another country, to avoid high tax rates, other things equal, if residence is a tag. To be effective, a tag should then be as immutable as possible so the individual cannot affect the information content provided by the tag and, to the extent possible, be a reasonable indicator of market ability. Note that an entire marginal rate schedule is determined for each tagged group. For example, Mankiw and Weinzierl find the marginal tax

[11] There are a number of examples (Diamond & Saez, 2011; Piketty, Saez, & Zucman, 2018).
[12] Kapička develops age-dependent tax schedules that take into account labour supply responses within a time period and through time in the context of an individual's life cycle (Kapička, 2015).

rates for one income group are 44% for short people and 51% for tall people (Mankiw & Weinzierl, 2010).

The notion behind tagging and tax schedules is intuitive. The government cannot observe the true ability of any individual, so using indicators is one way to limit the ability of individuals to game the system, or at least make it more costly. A tag needs to be a good indicator of the unobservable variable in order to be effective. We conjecture that increasing the number of indicators will in the limit create the individualized tax-expenditure system that is consistent with the original Mirrlees model.[13] It is important to note that tags are used to develop a completely different rate structure for individuals in different groups. For example, a tag might separate the population into two groups: Group A and Group B. The tax schedule for Group A could be 10% on income up to 50,000 and 20% on income above 50,000. On the other hand, the tax schedule for Group B could be 15% on income up to 42,000, 17% on income between 42,000 and 80,000, and 29% on income above 80,000. As noted below, there may be political constraints on having what are effectively two different rate structures apply to a single population.

Gathering data about individuals is not costless for either the government or the individuals, however, in terms of individual rights, constitutional limitations, and the cost of monitoring. Thus, there may be a limit to the use of tags in terms of increasing the efficiency of the tax-expenditure system. To return to the differences in administration between tax and expenditure, the use of tagging does not rule out a flat-rate tax system applied to all taxpayers, at least approximately. Tags, as noted above, could be used to affect the post-tax post-expenditure distribution of income when application is restricted to the expenditure side of the budget; a point to which we return below.

A1.2.3.1.3 Income from Nonhuman Capital

Optimal taxation of nonhuman capital, or savings other than investments in human capital, has also been the subject of considerable effort. The modern evolution of optimal nonhuman capital taxation begins with Chamley (1986) and Judd (1985), who demonstrate that in a dynamic context, taxes on the income from nonhuman capital should be zero, at least at the margin (a result strikingly similar to the Mirrlees result for human capital). The intuition for this result is that through time the supply elasticity of capital becomes effectively infinite. Thus, a tax on nonhuman capital in the steady state will reduce the productivity of labour, which in turn reduces income. In effect, a dynamic economy becomes similar to a small open economy in the sense that the elastic supply of capital relative to labour determines the zero (or low) taxation of capital income.[14]

This line of work has since been merged with the Mirrlees original static approach, including wealth distribution, to yield an emerging rich literature that illustrates a

---

[13] If individualized taxes are possible and if as the number of tags increase there is greater accuracy in predicting the underlying human capital, then lump-sum taxes may be possible.
[14] The intuition in the text differs from Judd's in the sense that Judd argues that taxing capital income distorts intertemporal decisions because the marginal tax rate on future consumption increases with time.

variety of results depending on assumptions and structures. In particular, the income from nonhuman capital might be taxed at positive rates, rates higher than the rates on human capital, or a zero rate. See, for example, tax in the context of political reform (Scheuer & Wolitzky, 2016); different savings rates for high- and low-skilled individuals (Saez & Stantcheva, 2018); and how particular types of uncertainty affect the conditions under which tax rates on the income from capital are positive (Golosov, Troshkin, Tsyvinski, & Weinzierl, 2013), as well as more general examples (Diamond & Saez, 2011; Piketty et al., 2018).

One line of argument will help to illustrate the intuition of at least some of the approaches. Individuals save in order to increase future consumption. Depending on the assumptions and conditions made by the authors, it is possible for some groups to save too much in the sense that individual savings are greater than the model's definition of the social optimal. This might arise because of uncertainty or differences in perceptions of risk among different groups. The tax system might provide incentives to over save if the tax on wage income is progressive in each tax period (say a year). High human capital individuals can work in early periods and save more than they would otherwise in order to be taxed less on their wage income in later periods. The present value of taxes for such individuals could be lower while maintaining per annum consumption levels. Taxes on nonhuman capital income and based on accumulated earnings may become relatively efficient options in such settings. The use of earnings history may be interesting in the sense that the Haig-Simons definition of income is equal to the change in net worth and net worth is a measure of the present value of all future income flows (see below). Knowing earnings history is one method to compute the current value of accumulated income[15] and may serve as an indicator of how current income is a measure of the change in net worth.

A1.2.3.2 Indirect Taxation and the Mix of Taxes

The search for relatively efficient indirect taxation has a rich history, beginning with Ramsey who developed the initial inverse elasticity rule that tax rates on consumption flows should be higher the lower the elasticity of demand: a justification for high taxes on cigarettes and similar goods and services (Ramsey, 1927). Corlett and Hague introduced second-best considerations by showing that it is not possible to tax all consumption flows because household consumption produced by nonmarket activity ('leisure' in the literature) cannot be taxed (Corlett & Hague, 1953). Their rule was to tax consumption flows at higher rates that were more complementary with leisure. Such a result could, however, lead to what are considered to be regressive taxes on food and other essential consumption flows.

---

[15] In effect, the present value of accumulated earnings is measured from the current, as opposed to the initial, period.

Two studies with important practical policy implications modified the Corlett-Hague result. Diamond and Mirrlees (1971) demonstrated that intermediate inputs should not be taxed (no cascading turnover tax) and Atkinson and Stiglitz (1976) developed the conditions under which indirect taxes are equal for all consumption flows. These results have been modified by more recent studies, including a discussion of the relationship between consumption of some goods and services relative to the distribution of wealth (Kaplow, 2008); assumptions that purchases of consumption goods are inputs into household production (Olovsson, 2015) and (H. J. Kleven, 2004); and one type of bounded rationality model (Allcott, Lockwood, & Taubinsky, 2018). Such studies contain conditions under which the Atkinson-Stiglitz result does not hold. This literature is amply summarized by Ebrill et al. who state: 'The general conclusion is that nonuniform (indirect) taxation has a role to play whenever the pattern of consumption contains information about the consumer's underlying–and unobservable–ability to pay taxes that is not fully exploited by the other tax instruments (such as income taxes) assumed to be available' (Ebrill, Keen, & Perry, 2001).

While there are important caveats, the Diamond-Mirrlees and Atkinson-Stiglitz result has been one justification for the VAT and the use of indirect taxes for revenue purposes with supplemental revenues and income redistribution being restricted to income taxation. In addition, the Diamond-Mirrlees result is counter to any type of uniform tariff. There may be a link between indirect and direct taxation, however. For example, McLure was among the first to demonstrate the conditions under which a uniform tax on income from labour and capital is equivalent to a uniform tax on consumption (McLure, 1974, 1975). That is, uniform taxation of income to the owners of productive factors can be equivalent to a VAT or other indirect taxes such as the sales tax. Of course, the equivalence also works in reverse. The intuition is that the sources of income must equal the uses of income, at least per unit of time and in present value terms, so that a uniform tax on one side is equivalent to a uniform tax on the other side of the identity.

In terms of progressivity, it might, as a practical matter, be easier to impose progressive taxes on the sources of income rather than the uses of income unless there is a clear distinction between consumption flows favoured by high relative to low-income taxpayers. For example, a high tax on first class (or business class) plane tickets, such as the one imposed by the UK, combined with a lower tax on inferior cuts of meat, may be progressive and might mimic a progressive income tax.

A1.2.4 Implications for Emerging Economies

The literature on efficient taxation is vast, is expanding, and is becoming progressively nuanced. Of particular relevance to emerging economies are extensions that include evasion (Cremer & Gahvari, 1993; Huang & Rios, 2016); bargaining (Piketty,

Saez, & Stantcheva, 2014); imperfections such as adverse selection (Stantcheva, 2014); migration (Heady, 1988); errors in taxpayer perceptions (Roeder, 2014); the presence of unemployment (Kroft, Kucko, Lehmann, & Schmieder, 2020); tax competition between countries with various degrees of uncertainty (Bierbrauer, 2014; Boadway & Sato, 2014); inclusion of household production (Olovsson, 2015); debt (Gottardi, Kajii, & Nakajima, 2015; Kapička & Neira, 2019); with an objective to reduce poverty (Kanbur, Paukkeri, Pirttilä, & Tuomala, 2017); limited commitment by government (Reis, 2013; Park, 2014); political constraints (Scheuer & Wolitzky, 2016); and limited administrative capacity (Heller & Shell, 1974; Slemrod, 1990; Mayshar, 1991; Agenor & Neanidis, 2012; Kaplow, 1990, among others). The extensions reinforce the basic results described above about the importance of information, preferences, responsiveness of taxpayers, and the distribution of wealth. All these extensions may have implications for emerging economies. In addition, there may be some limitations to the analytical work to date that temper the application. Both aspects are discussed in this summary.

A1.2.4.1 Clarification of Objectives

One benefit of the approach taken in the optimal tax literature, and in economics more generally, is that the objectives are clearly, as well as rigorously, defined, and there is transparency in the statement of the problem. It is not possible in a policy environment to stipulate objectives with the mathematical precision of a formal economic model. Nevertheless, there is something to be learned from attempting to clearly elucidate the objective for the policy change. In addition, clearly communicating the objective and being transparent will increase the ability to refine, and perhaps expand, the objectives. Finally, stating the objectives and the assumptions upon which they are based provides a basis for informed discussion and critical evaluation.

Examples of such communication include pre-budget statements, such as those advocated by The International Budget project;[16] general explanations of tax proposals, including examples and explicit definitions; and budget projections, including assumptions upon which they are based. We do not expect the type of critical evaluation supplied in academic seminars and in the technical evolution of the optimal tax literature. It is important, however, that transparency with respect to objectives, assumptions, and the basis for recommendations provide a dynamic environment in which informed policy discussions (as well as clarification) might evolve through time. Paramount to the conditional nature of the objective is that tax reform is conditional on the empirical situation and, accordingly, will change through time.

[16] https://internationalbudget.org/.

A1.2.4.2 The Importance of Coordinating Tax and Expenditure

The issues of tax and redistribution immediately imply tax and expenditure. Much discussion of tax reform, such as the discussion in this volume, is focused on the redistributive aspects of the tax system alone. At the minimum, the discussion should be expanded to include the interaction of tax changes with expenditures. For example, Conrad has argued in some countries that he would support a regressive tax system on some margins if such a system is the most effective means to raise revenue to support a strongly progressive expenditure policy.

The taxation of food in the VAT is a case in point. As noted above, it is the net effect of VAT and targeted food subsidies that matters. Of course, the combined effect of the VAT and targeted food subsidies could be progressive, but that progressivity might not be the point. In particular, it could be the case, and it is certainly argued,[17] that VAT exemptions increase complexity which, in turn, increases administrative costs and compliance, and perhaps decreases revenues. If revenues, net of administrative costs, fall, then there may be a decline in food subsidies, or other targeted programmes, resulting in a net regressive outcome. In addition, an exemption for food from the VAT could be regressive in terms of welfare, depending on how the exemption is implemented. High income individuals may, and probably do, spend more on food from formal market sources subject to VAT relative to the poor (who often buy food from vendors who are, formally or informally, exempt from VAT) even if those with relatively high income spend a lower proportion of their incomes on food. This implies that the welfare gains, or the net distribution of real wealth, may accrue to those with higher incomes: a net regressive result. To illustrate, suppose the VAT-inclusive price of food is 1.10 and low-income individuals spend 11 on 10 units of food and high-income individuals spend 110 on 100 units of food. Suppose now that food is exempt from VAT and so the tax-inclusive price falls to 1.0. Suppose that expenditure on food falls to 10.5 and 100.6 for the poor and rich, respectively.[18] Such a result is possible if the demand for food is inelastic. This means that consumption of food has increased by 0.5 units and 0.6 units for the poor and rich, respectively. The immediate result is that the rich have 9.4 units to spend on other goods and services while the poor's expenditures on other goods and services increases by only 0.5 units. That is, the net distributional gain to the rich is regressive because almost 95% of the revenue loss accrues to the rich.

Another example is the absence of a personal exemption during Georgia's initial reform efforts in approximately 2005. The income tax had no personal exemption in order to simplify administration.[19] In effect, those required to withhold on wages

---

[17] Tait (1988); Ebrill et al. (2001).
[18] The elasticity of demand is −0.55 and −0.068 for the poor and rich, respectively.
[19] Conrad opposed the implementation of the flat-rate tax without an exemption in Georgia (Conrad, 2004) and has subsequently reconsidered his views.

only had to report aggregate wages and total tax withheld. There were no withholding tables and individualized computations were not required.[20] Expanded to all sources of income, unified withholding could impose individualized taxes, for most types of income (capital gains being the major exception), without the need for individual returns.[21] If Georgia had a progressive expenditure programme, then the net effective tax-expenditure rate could be progressive, particularly if administrative costs are lower, compliance is improved, and revenues are higher than a system that is personalized.

A1.2.4.3 Administration of Tax and Expenditure

Little advice is provided in the optimal tax literature about how to administer the tax-expenditure system except for the assumption that coordination is necessary in order to obtain the relatively efficient outcomes. Coordination of tax and expenditure policies is difficult, at a minimum, because of historically different bureaucracies. There is a certain logic to the separation of administration because it is one thing to become organized to take resources from the private sector, for which nothing is immediately exchanged, and quite another to spend the resources or to give them away, particularly to targeted groups. That said, part of the reform process should be to enhance the coordination process. Actions in the area include examining the net impact of tax proposals in the context of the use of revenues and how incremental revenues (either positive or negative) will be used. Also, tax expenditures need to be measured. There are two aspects to this approach. First, there needs to be an explicit empirical definition of the object of taxation. For example, if the government wants to move towards consumption taxation, then exemptions for the income from nonhuman capital are an essential part of the system. If, however, the objective is to impose tax on an empirical measure of income (perhaps comprehensive), then exemptions such as wages contributed to retirement accounts should be a tax expenditure. Finally, some effort is necessary to examine the distributional implications of both tax-expenditures as well as the statutory incidence of normal government expenditures.

These implications are not simply trying to transform academic investigations into the public sphere, although the approaches to the academic study of optimal tax and expenditure are based on a common approach to problem solving. Rather, it is using the approach to engage policy makers and the public at large in a common discussion about means and ends.

---

[20] It is still necessary to report tax-inclusive and tax-exclusive wages to employees to foster understanding.
[21] Such an approach could be reasonable in terms of starting the system and developing the administrative apparatus. Individualized reporting can be developed through time as per capita income increases, the economy becomes more complex, the tax administration becomes more experienced and has access to larger budgets, and taxpayer education is expanded.

A1.2.4.4 A Flat Tax May Be Relatively Efficient

Separation of the administration of tax and expenditure may imply that a flat tax, perhaps with recognition of personal circumstances, can be relatively efficient. Such an approach may provide for delegation of additional distributional considerations, based on tagging and other methods, to the expenditure side of the budget. Specialization of labour and capital can be one means to justify the approach. There are two functions of the tax and expenditure system: to transfer resources from the private to the public sector and to spend those resources. Taxing need not be overly individualized, particularly in emerging economies where resources are severely constrained. In that context, it may be relatively efficient to devote tax administration resources to revenue collection without regard for fine tuning the system by attempting to further individualize the system. For example, flat rate withholding via the use of third-party withholding agents may be an effective and efficient means to raise necessary revenues. This approach and other options are discussed in the text.

By definition, tags are necessary for expenditures, particular those designed for distributional purposes. Thus, there is a logic to developing the specialized skills necessary to identify recipients, recipient groups, and even those receiving supply contracts from the government. In an emerging economy context, the tags may not be individualized. Noted above was the use of subsidies for small holders, rural health clinics, and other in-kind programmes, as well as the use of such tags to determine the individuals who receive subsidies (such as micro finance) and cash transfers.

A1.2.4.5 Situations Are Unique

It should be apparent that optimal tax structures depend on the facts and circumstances. Accordingly, there may be no such thing as 'international best practice' in terms of policy design or even in terms of using all the elements of the standard approach described in Chapter 1. For example, Alvaredo et al. review some of the relevant empirical data that are used to develop tax schedules, note their variation across countries, and discuss the variation in preexisting income transfer programmes in OECD countries (Alvaredo, Chancel, Piketty, Saez, & Zucman, 2017).[22] The factors determining the tax schedules and the mix of taxes, however, depend on the distribution of skills, the information system available in the country, the degree of openness, the relevant elasticities, and other factors. Thus, there is no reason to believe that the policies of one country, advanced economies in particular, should

---

[22] It is almost axiomatic to assume that the economy described in economic theory, of which the optimal tax literature is one element, corresponds to a country. There is no necessary reason for this to be valid. Mexico City, Delhi, Shanghai, and Sao Paulo, among other cities, have greater populations than most countries and could be treated as small open economies. In general, the issue may be how the tax policies of a subnational government interact, or are overridden by, national tax policies.

be exported to other countries, even if the methodologies applied to the development of the policies is the same. An exception might apply to tax administration via the use of administrative procedures that can be rapidly replicated in any number of countries. Computer systems such as those used for tariffs, master tax files, and the like are cases in point. There is an issue, however, about other aspects of tax administration such as the overall organization of the tax departments. For example, the use of Large Taxpayer Units common in large high-income countries may be of limited or no relevance in countries with small tax administrations and severely limited budgets.

In terms of economic policy prescriptions, it would seem that there are three important additional implications. First, there is a consensus about the need to avoid taxing intermediate goods and services. That is, tax either the sources of income or the uses of income but do not tax transactions (or goods and services) that are derived from fundamental sources of income but are used as inputs further downstream in production. The methodological reason for this result is that it makes no sense to distort input choices that, in turn, result in distortions of either relative output prices or the price of the fundamental productive factors (human and nonhuman capital). A related practical point is that taxing intermediate goods and services results in an uncertain pattern of both relative effective taxes (both average and marginal) and income distributional outcomes. Ultimately, the rule to not tax intermediate goods and services is derived from the fact that incidence and income distribution results, or objectives, affect individuals. Accordingly, the government should impose a tax on individuals directly either via sales taxation (uses of income) or the return to primary production factors (sources of income). This way, there will be a better correspondence between policy prescription (differential or uniform rates) and results.

Second, the original Mirrlees result that marginal taxes are zero for the most skilled human capital and the Judd-Chamley result that marginal taxes are zero for nonhuman capital in the long run need to be modified, if not rejected. Progressive comprehensive income taxation, as opposed to consumption taxation, may be indicated as a practical matter. Appeal may not be made to the literature in computing specific rate structures, but a comprehensive approach to the evolution of the tax system with variable and progressive rates on all components of income appears to be a reasonable inference.

Third, the government should use information other than observed income to determine a reasonably efficient tax-expenditure programme. Use of indicators or tags of capacity, wealth, or other characteristics may increase the effectiveness of both efficiency and income distributional outcomes as demonstrated in the optimal tax literature. We believe that most tags will be more effective on the expenditure side of the budget. This is because identifying qualified individuals or groups is fundamental to any expenditure programme intended to provide benefits that affect distribution or efficiency.[23] It is important to note that observable tags are used in optimal tax models

---

[23] There are exceptions such as separate tax treatment of small business.

to determine the underlying innate characteristic (or characteristics) that influence earnings potential. Thus, the ideal tag would not be subject to manipulation by the individual while being a perfect indicator of the unobservable variable. Some tags may not be subject to manipulation such as gender, ethnicity, and age. Whether such tags are relevant, however, depends on whether the characteristics are correlated with the unobserved variable and on the political acceptability of using the tag. For example, it could be the case that Gender 1 has higher earnings potential than Gender 2, but it may not be politically acceptable to develop separate tax schedules based on gender.

Tags, as a practical matter, can be useful as indicators for tax-expenditure policy even in situations where the tag itself might be subject to change or to manipulation. For example, educational attainment or health status may be indicators of income potential.[24] In addition, temporary, but exogeneous, indicators might be used as some notion of economic potential or circumstances. Extreme examples are individuals harmed by weather events such as floods. Less extreme examples are unemployment or membership in a particular group such as agriculture. The important point is that policy makers can make use of information other than expenditure in the case of indirect tax and observed income in the case of direct tax to reduce the disincentive effects of taxation and to identify objective conditions that help target particular expenditures.

A1.2.5 Limitations on Policy Relevance

While there are some implications from the optimal tax literature, a number of factors may limit the direct transfer of results to actual situations. We emphasize that the limitations noted here apply to the economic analysis of taxation in general. This approach is adopted here because it is important for policy makers to place the economic analysis of tax policy into a broader policy context. As economists, we believe the limitations are both a strength and weakness of economic methodology. The strength of the approach facilitates a reasonable, and rigorous, analysis relative to clearly defined objectives, axioms, and assumptions. In effect, there is a well-defined agenda that enables policy makers to focus on particular tradeoffs. The weaknesses include the fact that, like all analytical methods, the price of rigor and internal consistency limits application because of the assumptions employed. Accordingly, policy makers need to be aware of the limitations in order to place the recommendations into a broader context.

---

[24] The converse is not true, however. That is, lack of educational attainment is not an indicator of ability because there may be constraints on access to educational attainment. It is one thing to state that educational attainment is an indicator of ability but quite another to state that lack of educational attainment is an indicator of lack of ability. Educational attainment is a noisy signal.

A1.2.5.1 Nature of Government Expenditure and Composition of Government Ownership

Government actors do more than redistribute wealth, although all government expenditure may have redistributive characteristics. That is, there is more to the economic analysis of government action than the rather straightforward equity-efficiency tradeoff. Provision of public goods (national defence), or goods and services with public goods characteristics, public services (sanitation, public health, public safety, education among others), and infrastructure are among the activities that may or may not be intended to be redistributive, although there are redistributive effects. In addition, taxes are not the only source of government revenue. Revenues include receipts from provision of some public services (e.g., the court system and the post office) and public sector enterprises (electricity provision in some countries), returns to publicly owned assets (e.g., natural resources), debt (or future taxes perhaps), user fees, and other revenues.

Public sector provision of goods and services that is only indirectly related to redistribution may imply that the more traditional approach to tax analysis may have some relevance. Government decision makers must decide how to finance an exogenously given net budget (government expenditure less revenues from other sources) where the distributional implications of the government expenditures are predetermined. This approach may result in a tax system that either complements or offsets the distributional implications on the expenditure side of the budget. For example, it might be the case that provision of certain public services (port services for imported inputs and consumer goods) may have a regressive impact. The optimal tax system in that case may be called upon to both raise revenue and to serve some offsetting (or other) redistributive purpose.

There are two arguments against the traditional approach in this context. First, there is the issue of targets and instruments. Unless the redistribution and revenue functions are strongly positively correlated, then it is not possible to achieve two objectives with one tool. It might be argued, however, that there are two or more instruments in the tax system: the traditional use of indirect taxes to raise revenue and the use of income taxes for wealth redistribution and supplemental income. There is a bit of a false premise with such an approach, however, because consumption (even on a selective basis such as tobacco products) and income flows are ultimately determined by wealth, given preferences. Thus, taxing consumption is taxing at least part of income and comprehensively taxing consumption is comprehensively taxing at least some measure of income through time. There may be intertemporal uses for consumption taxes relative to income taxes, but ultimately government revenues must accrue from the returns to the assets held in the economy, both human and nonhuman and both privately and publicly owned.[25]

---

[25] There may be some ability to impose taxes on nonresidents to the extent that taxes can be exported. Governments are generally assumed to be unconcerned about the distributional aspects of taxes imposed on nonresidents.

Second, government decisions, like all decisions, are made under considerable risk and uncertainty. In addition, the government, even as a flow-through entity with zero net worth, has a portfolio of sources and uses of funds. Thus, at least as a matter of method, the optimal tax system should be determined in concert with efficient public sector prices, expenditures, and other government activities, unless the tax system is somehow independent from the other activities.[26] Such an approach is not possible analytically, particularly when decisions must be made on a timely basis with factors that are exogenous at one point in time changing, sometimes in unpredictable ways.

This limitation of optimal tax theory is not a criticism per se, but only an admission of the inability of any economic model to determine the globally efficient outcome even in a second-best sense.

A1.2.5.2 Definitions of Relevant Terms

It is important to clearly define the terms used in the literature.

A1.2.5.2.1 Definition of Capital and Labour

Capital and labour are rigorously defined and differentiated in the optimal tax literature. In reality, the distinction may be opaque,[27] particularly when the analysis is expanded to include entities such as corporations that may be subject to tax, a second tax perhaps.[28] Related to this point is the ability to clearly identify the separate returns to nonhuman capital and labour. For example, a lawyer may provide legal services via a sole proprietorship and her income would be taxed as income from labour. Alternatively, the lawyer may provide identical services via a corporate entity. From the perspective of the optimal tax methodology, the presence of a corporate entity is immaterial because the services are a return to labour, and the tax-inclusive value should be independent of the organizational form, other things equal. The issue may become more complicated, however, when intangible assets are included into the analysis. An inventor may discover a new product, patent the product, and receive lease (royalty) payments as a sole proprietor. Alternatively, the inventor may contribute the intangible asset to a legal entity in exchange for equity participation in anticipation of accruing a return to capital. This return, however, is the present value of the rewards to the individual's effort, the return to one part of the individual's human capital. It is not clear, at least to us, how the conversion of human effort into intangible assets is treated in the optimal tax literature, particularly when intellectual

---

[26] Such an approach would include tax expenditures (Saez, 2004).

[27] Christiansen and Tuomala have a model where labour income can be converted into capital income, an assumption that yields a positive tax on capital income (Christiansen & Tuomala, 2008). See also Diamond & Saez (2011).

[28] Nonhuman entities such as corporations are ignored in some of the literature such as Chamley (1986) and models based on that approach. Others explicitly consider the optimal taxation of corporate capital (Dávila & Hébert, 2019).

and intangible property can be sold as an asset separately from the supply of human services or become part of the public domain (in the case when patents expire).[29]

One implication of this point is that differential taxation of human and nonhuman capital becomes more complicated if humans are able to transfer the flow of labour services into a stock (intangible or intellectual capital) and sell it. The opposite is also true. Individuals operating as sole proprietors (or partnerships) can use capital in the supply of goods and services. For example, farmers may produce food using land (real property), capital (hoes or tractors depending on wealth), and labour. As a practical matter, it may be impossible to separately account for the returns to capital independently of labour. Economists can identify the marginal contribution, but the value of the total return may not be equal to the summation of the value of the marginal distributions. For example, if the marginal value of labour is 10 and 11 units of labour are used, and the marginal value of capital is 12 and 5 units of capital are used, then the total value of inputs is $110 + 60 = 170$. Total value added (or the value of total sales) may be 185 (or even 150) with the result that 15 (−20) remains unaccounted for. This difference is economic rent, or perhaps the ex-post return to risk sharing, and is by definition a value that cannot be attributed to any primary production factor, other things equal. It is clear in this case that the farmer owns the rent because the farmer is the sole proprietor. How, as a practical matter, it would be possible to separate the returns to capital and labour when there are different tax rates on the returns to capital and labour is not clear in the economic literature. Even in the case where an individual creates an entity, the separation of the returns to capital and labour may be opaque. The individual may forgo a wage if the tax on the return to corporate capital is lower than the marginal wage rate. Alternatively, the individual can strip the income from capital via higher stated wages if the tax on wages is lower than the one on capital.

The muddle becomes more apparent when labour is defined as human capital (see Olovsson (2015) for a good example of the use of human capital in the sense defined by Becker). As a practical matter then, the ability to arbitrage an empirical definition will increase the likelihood for uniform marginal rates applied to all returns to assets—both human capital and nonhuman capital.

The argument for uniformity may be enhanced by noting that much is made of the substitutability of capital and labour in the optimal taxation of capital literature as well as the fact that, relative to the assumptions, increasing the amount of capital per worker increases wages via an increase in the labour productivity. As noted above in the original Chamley (1986) analysis, there is a similarity between the long-run supply elasticity of capital and the supply elasticity of capital in a small open economy. Both supply elasticities are infinite, which implies that a tax on capital will reduce the capital stock and in turn reduce the wages via the indirect productivity effect. One assumption leading to this result is that labour productivity, holding the nonhuman capital stock fixed, is exogenous. This is not true as a practical matter. The effect of a change in capital on the productivity of labour is symmetric with regard to

[29] There is no claim here that capital is dated labour in the Marxist sense.

the change in productivity on capital with respect to a change in the tax on labour, other things equal. Thus, increasing the effective labour stock via either increases in the population or increasing the productivity of the existing labour force by investments in education, health, and other means will increase the productivity of capital, when the productivity of capital is exogenous holding the quantity of labour fixed. Therefore, imposing a tax on labour may reduce the productivity of nonhuman capital and reduce investment with a consequent reduction in welfare. In reality, both the human and nonhuman capital stocks change through time and are influenced by government policy. In summary, the issue may be the government's use of tax policy to affect the portfolio of assets used in the economy, including the stock of human capital, relative to simply increasing the nonhuman capital stock.

A1.2.5.2.2 Definition of Skills, Even with Tags and the Equity–Efficiency Tradeoff

There is a determinative relationship between specific human capital and value added in the original Mirrlees formulation of the income tax problem. There is no nonhuman capital, so the functional relationship is clearly identified. Individuals are then distributed along the skill spectrum. Even in cases where there are multiple outputs and inputs, as in indirect tax analysis (such as Diamond & Mirrlees, 1971), market forces will result in a situation where the productivity of labour, at the margin, is the same, either on a tax-exclusive or tax-inclusive basis as the case may be, in all sectors. In effect, either labour is assumed to be homogeneous, or productivity is exogenously determined, with some exceptions. In reality, human capital is both unique to each individual and multidimensional. That is, each individual at any point in time owns a portfolio of skills that can be applied in different ways in different occupations on both intensive and extensive margins. The individual's skill portfolio and its evolution are determined by the constraints imposed on the individual, again both now and through time. In effect, each individual has comparative and perhaps absolute advantages, both realized and potential, which are determined, at least in part, by relative prices and preferences.

Preferences are important because the economies depicted in the optimal tax literature are rather stark in the sense that there is only measured GDP and household production. Thus, the individual is provided little or no choice of occupation. For example, an individual with analytical skills sufficient to become a rich financial analyst may prefer to become a relatively underpaid schoolteacher in a no-tax situation. Measured GDP might be lower given that choice, but welfare will be higher as measured by economists. On the other hand, disregard for the individual's occupational choice in determining the purportedly optimal tax may induce the individual to become a rich financial analyst. In this case, measured GDP might increase (tax inclusive), but welfare measurement may fall.

One key element in this example is that the individual making this choice had the opportunity to choose in the first instance. That is, the individual's choice set is broad enough to provide such options. The expansive choice set may be determined by the individual's wealth, or the wealth of their parents, the culture, their tags (race or ethnicity, sex, and other factors), and the availability of options provided by the government and society more generally. Thus, it might be the case that one objective of government is to expand the choice sets available to the population, or to particular tagged groups: an expansion that might change the structure of relatively efficient taxation.

In particular, the efficient tax structure may involve a situation where the tax system would have little or no effect on occupational choice or on how an individual invests in their unique portfolio of skills. More important, for emerging economies, indeed for all economies, are the distributional effects of changing the choice set available to individuals. The simple microeconomic model has only one income constraint, but that constraint is multifaceted in the sense that the constraints determine the opportunities available to the individual. Thus, in both a static and dynamic context, the distributional aspects of the tax-expenditure policies may affect different margins. For example, the redistributive effects of a progressive income tax on measured monetary income of a child born in a highly educated high-income household may be minor compared to the expansion of the opportunity set of a child born into a low-income rural household who benefits from vaccinations, elementary education, nutritional education provided to her parents, and access provided to markets for the products produced by the household. In effect, taxation may be used to create multidimensional redistribution, which might be one interpretation of tagging, in a dynamic sense perhaps. While the various dimensions may be valued in monetary terms, it might be important to examine the various margins, both extensive and intensive, that affect the choices available to recipients.

A1.2.5.2.3 Definition of Uncertainty

Risk bearing is defined in the efficient tax literature as the ability to base decisions on both an expected outcome and the variability of that outcome, perhaps using implied probabilities. The types of risky situations tend to be specific to the question under investigation. For example, Bierbrauer assumes uncertainty with respect to the distribution of skills in the economy, an assumption that creates an incentive towards formation of coalitions that needs to be incorporated into the tax system (Bierbrauer, 2014). Boadway and Sato assume wage uncertainty and risk aversion on the part of individuals where the tax system now incorporates a type of insurance in addition to equity and efficiency considerations (Boadway & Sato, 2014). Gottardi et al. assume uninsurable risk and show that debt as well as positive taxes on capital and labour result (Gottardi et al., 2015).

One consequence of imposing taxes is that there is some type of risk sharing between the individual taking the actions and the entire taxpaying population, as noted by Boadway and Sato (2014) and authors dating to Domar and Musgrave (1944). In reality, uncertainty pervades all decision making. All actions will have uncertain consequences because of the time lag between the action and the consequence. The variation between actions and expected outcomes may be small if consequences are of short duration but may increase with a longer time lag. In addition, actions and consequences may be affected by learning. The fact that taxes are based on observable ex post outcomes means observed taxes and the observed tax base in each new time period can be used to learn more about the relationship between cause, effect, and uncertainty.

The numerous types of uncertainty are difficult to address. To be specific, suppose an individual changes their effective labour effort from 10 to 9 hours in response to a higher marginal tax rate and, holding things constant, expects to be in a 20% bracket when the expected tax-inclusive wage is 10. The reality, however, is that income is significantly higher or lower than 10, placing the individual into a different marginal tax rate ex post. This type of uncertainty, taken singly, can be accommodated in existing optimal tax models. Suppose, however, that the individual, knowing their particular level of specific human capital, must decide their occupation, how much to work per annum, whether they will marry and have children, how many years to work, how much to save per annum when there is uncertainty about the wages in different occupations, about whether the occupation will continue (computer card punchers in the 1960s and coal miners in the United States today), how long they will live, the probability of accidents, how many children they will have, the future macroeconomic conditions, the tax system, and the level of government expenditure. The computation time and effort necessary to take all these types of uncertainty into account may be prohibitive, and so it may be natural for individuals to move through time making adjustments based on circumstances and new information.

Such adjustments may imply that the path chosen by an individual at a point in time may be affected by learning and experience. In addition, choices today may affect subsequent future risks. An individual can only accept a job today based on the number of job offers available and the existing distribution of occupations. They can search more or accept a position from the currently existing set of options. If an option is selected, then the individual will begin a path that may generate additional opportunities, most of which are not known.

The type of adaptation based on experience, learning, and realizations of uncertain events may provide feedback on how government should decide on policy. For instance, suppose an individual believes they have a comparative advantage in agriculture and discovers during a training programme that they enjoy woodworking more than farming. The government may observe the occupation change and may be able to track the individual's work history, but the determination of the marginal tax rate to charge this year, much less the tax rates for the future, including taxes on the income from savings, may be computationally impossible because of the difficulty in determining the interaction of decisions with ex post outcomes needed to determine the relative specific human capital of the individual.

Given the fact that there is learning from experience, errors in perception, rational responses to the prohibitive costs of computing expected values, and variation of expected values before taking an action, individuals and the government might have to muddle through. That is, the conditions that determined the optimal tax-expenditure system last year may be different from the initial conditions and the stock of capital, including social capital and intangible capital via learning, at the beginning of this year.[30] In effect, the tax systems may be conditional on changes through time. The population may perceive such responses in tax changes as random, however, generating more risk and uncertainty in the system. Thus, it may be important for policymakers to explicitly state that they are basing decisions on current information (including estimates about the future), but that policy may be different in the future based on changes in exogeneous factors and experience.[31]

A1.2.5.2.4 Definition of Taxpayer and Residence

It appears in the optimal tax literature that the population of taxpayers defines the economy rather than the other way round, except in cases where migration is possible. Presumably, the taxpayer is a resident of the economy, but residence is not defined unless, again, there is migration in the model (Kleven, Landais, Muñoz, & Stantcheva, 2020). Taxation is assumed to be on a residence basis because in models with migration, it is possible for individuals in one jurisdiction to migrate and escape taxation in the economy under investigation.[32] There appears to be no risk of overlapping taxation, so if there is source taxation (the wages of a resident are attributed to foreign source), then the effective tax is the tax rate in the home country. That is, it could be inferred that countries, to the extent they interact in the models, tax on a residence basis so, as far as relevant, the income (from labour or capital) earned in a jurisdiction other than the individual's residence is taxed only in the residence country.[33] Real net national income is defined as income attributable to all residents in such models, we believe. In addition, all income is claimed to be observable and attributable to the person to whom the income is officially attributed. For example, if there are farm families, then the productivity and wages of each individual in the household are observable because there is no organization, or cooperation, for which gains from cooperative effort are attributed.

Market income attributable to an individual is observable by government by assumption. This means that, to the extent that flow-through entities are relevant to combining the uses of capital and labour (such as in Diamond-Mirrlees), the nature

---

[30] The COVID pandemic may be a case in point. It might have been thought that such a pandemic was a small probability event and so a relatively efficient tax system was developed on that basis.

[31] It might be the case that some tax regimes are random. For instance, suppose there is an annual balanced budget policy and expenditure is determined one year in advance. If wages are random, then, in a flat-rate tax system, the tax rate needed to balance the budget will be inversely related to the random wage. Tax rates will be low when wages are high and vice versa. The tax rate would then appear to be random, even though the rate is uniquely determined by the wage.

[32] The United States imposes taxes on all citizens regardless of residence. Thus, it might be a bit more difficult (at least in theory) for a US citizen to escape US tax by moving.

[33] This, of course, is an inference. It may be the case that source and residence are simply not addressed. The comment has some merit, however. It is common in this literature to use social welfare functions as a convenient method for weighting the presumed measurable utility of the individuals in the economy. It is claimed that the standard approach to economics where marginal values of individuals without regard to wealth are equal in a competitive economy is consistent with a utilitarian social welfare function with equal social weights. While a reasonable inference, we believe social welfare functions do not exist and are largely inapplicable for policy analysis. While we have views about distributional outcomes, we must admit that these views, while influenced by economics, are our personal normative judgements.

of the flow-through entities is irrelevant.[34] Observability may imply that income to
the household might be equivalent to income to the individual in cases where attribution between family members is not observable. In addition, nonmarket activity
appears to be unrelated to market activity in the models developed to date. That is,
individuals are paid their market productivity, so there is no return to the individual
for spending time outside the market engaging in additional labour effort.

Such definitions are clear in the methods under discussion, but they are opaque
in reality. Residence must be empirically defined, as do source and other concepts.
There is no superior definition, in our view, because there are gains and losses to any
definition. For example, consider a 183-day residence rule. An individual may intend
to live in one jurisdiction but have the wherewithal to game the system by being
absent the time needed to avoid being a taxpayer in the particular jurisdiction. On the
other hand, a multifaceted definition may require demonstration of 'intent' such as
the US definition of a tax resident. This definition is more complex and more difficult
to administer, and it is not clear whether the revenues or the ability of a taxpayer to
game the system are affected significantly relative to the 183-day rule. One approach
to this issue is to attempt, as much as practical, to make the definitions irrelevant for
the purposes at hand by creating a potential financial incentive to become a resident
or to develop simple clear and clearly arbitrary rules. This issue is discussed in the
text.

A1.2.5.2.5 Definition of Income and Consumption

With some exceptions, there is a clear distinction between consumption goods and
services and saving or the purchase of capital goods and services. In addition, income
is clearly defined as the market return to capital, either human capital or nonhuman
capital. Some externalities are examined, but externalities such as caring for others or
for some notion of the common good are not examined. In addition, capital goods
and services such as language or culture (social capital) appear to be exogenously
given and are either irrelevant or have a zero price. The practical definitions of consumption expenditures for consumption tax purposes and market income will be
discussed in the relevant chapters, but it should be clear from the discussion above
that market-determined income is only a component of real net national product for
economists. In addition, the definition of a consumption good or service for methodological purposes only provides guidance on the practical development of market
consumption for practical tax purposes. In economic models, consumption may be
produced because at least two inputs are required to consume anything: the commodity purchased and time needed to consume. For example, a meal purchased at
a café requires time in order to produce consumption. Accordingly, such consumption may be a substitute for using food and time to produce a meal to be consumed
outside the market. It is the value of the meal consumed that matters for economic
welfare and consumption, not the inputs (café meal plus time or meal produced at

---

[34] There are exceptions in the case of the optimal corporate tax (as opposed to the optimal capital
taxation) literature.

home plus time) used to produce the output. In sum, meals consumed in cafés and meals produced and consumed at home are the objects of desire and may be substitutes, as opposed to the expenditure on the café meal and the expenditure on food at the market because time is required to produce economic welfare.

Finally, the many externalities (concern for others) and the assets with zero market prices (the atmosphere), while not relevant for much of the optimal tax literature, may affect both the practical economy's structure and the resulting tax system.

A1.2.6 Summary

As noted, the limitations discussed here extend to the general economics of taxation and to economic analysis more generally. Our view is that such limitations do not reduce the value of the information or implications of the models discussed in this Annex. Rather, limitations provide the frame of reference within which the implications may be understood. Thus, the overall power of the inferences may be increased by understanding the context. This is true because the context provides an opportunity to examine the inferences relative to the empirical situation, and the policymaker is able to make tradeoffs needed to apply, and to adjust, the results given their constraints.

References

Agebirm P.R. abd Beabudusm K. C. (2014). Optimal Taxation and Growth with Public Goods and Costly Enforcement. *Journal of International Trade and Development*, 23(4), 425–454.

Allcott, H., Lockwood, B., & Taubinsky, D. (2018). Ramsey Strikes Back: Optimal Commodity Tax and Redistribution in the Presence of Salience Effects. *AEA Papers and Proceedings*, 108, 88–92. doi:10.1257/pandp.20181040.

Alvaredo, F., Chancel, L., Piketty, T., Saez, E., & Zucman, G. (2017). Global Inequality Dynamics: New Findings from WID.World. *American Economic Review*, 107(5), 404–409.

Arrow, K. J. (1950). A Difficulty in the Concept of Social Welfare. *Journal of Political Economy*, 58(4), 328–346.

Bierbrauer, F. J. (2014). Optimal Tax and Expenditure Policy with Aggregate Uncertainty. *American Economic Journal: Microeconomics*, 6(1), 205–257. doi:10.2307/43189659.

Atkinson, A. B. and Stiglitz, J. (1976). The Design of the Tax Structure: Direct versus Indirect Taxation. *Jounral of Public Economics*, 6(1–2), 55–75.

Boadway, R., & Sato, M. (2014). Optimal Income Taxation and Risk: The Extensive-Margin Case. *Annals of Economics and statistics* (113/114), 159–183. doi:10.15609/ann aeconstat2009.113-114.159.

Bradford, D. and Rosen, R. (1976). Optimal Taxation of Commodities and Income. *The American Economic Reviews* (66/2), 94–101. Retrieved from https://www.jstor.org/stable/1817204.

Chamley, C. (1986). Optimal Taxation of Capital Income in General Equilibrium with Infinite Lives. *Econometrica, 54*(3), 607–622.

Christiansen, V., & Tuomala, M. (2008). On taxing capital income with income shifting. *International Tax and Public Finance, 15*(4), 527–545. doi:10.1007/s10797-008-9076-x.

Conrad, R. (2004, 16 September). [Memorandum: Tax Issues: Georgia].

Corlett, W. J., & Hague, D. C. (1953). Complementarity and the Excess Burden of Taxation. *Review of Economic Studies, 21*(1), 21–30. Retrieved from https://EconPapers.repec.org/RePEc:oup:restud:v:21:y:1953:i:1:p:21-30.

Cremer, H., & Gahvari, F. (1993). Tax evasion and optimal commodity taxation. *Journal of Public Economics, 50*(2), 261–275. Retrieved from https://EconPapers.repec.org/RePEc:eee:pubeco:v:50:y:1993:i:2:p:261-275.

Dávila, E., & Hébert, B. M. (2019). Optimal Corporate Taxation under Financial Frictions. *NBER Working Paper Series, 25520*. Retrieved from https://www.nber.org/papers/w25520.

Diamond, P., & Saez, E. (2011). The Case for a Progressive Tax: From Basic Research to Policy Recommendation. *Journal of Economic Perspectives, 25*(4), 165–190. doi:10.1257/jep.25.4.165.

Diamond, P. A., & Mirrlees, J. A. (1971). Optimal Taxation and Public Production I: Production Efficiency. *The American Economic Review, 61*(1), 8–27. Retrieved from http://www.jstor.org/stable/1910538.

Domar, D. and Musgrave, R. A. (1944). Proportional Income Taxation and Risk Taking. *Quarterly Journal of Economics, 58*(3), 388–422.

Ebrill, L. P., Keen, M., & Perry, V. J. (2001). *The Modern VAT*: International Monetary Fund.

Gentry, W.M. (1999). Optimal Taxation. In J. J. Cordes, R. D. Ebel and J. G. Gravelle (Eds). *The Encyclopedia of Taxation and Tax Policy*. Washington: Urban Institute Press.

Golosov, M., Troshkin, M., Tsyvinski, A., & Weinzierl, M. (2013). Preference Heterogeneity and Optimal Capital Income Taxation. *Journal of Public Economics, 97*, 160–175. doi:10.1016/j.jpubeco.2012.10.006.

Gottardi, P., Kajii, A., & Nakajima, T. (2015). Optimal Taxation and Debt with Uninsurable Risks to Human Capital Accumulation. *American Economic Review, 105*(11), 3443–3470. doi:10.1257/aer.20110576.

Heady, C. (1988). Optimal Taxation with Fixed Wages and Induced Migration. *Oxford Economic Papers, 40*(3), 560–574. Retrieved from http://www.jstor.org/stable/2663023.

Heady, C. (1993). Optimal Taxation as a Guide to Tax Policy: A Survey. *Fiscal Studies 14*(1), 15–41.

Huang, J., & Rios, J. (2016). Optimal Tax Mix with Income Tax Non-compliance. *Journal of Public Economics*, *144*, 52–63. doi:10.1016/j.jpubeco.2016.10.001.

Judd, K. (1985). Redistributive Taxation in a Simple Perfect Foresight Model. *Journal of Public Economics*, *28*(10), 59–83.

Kanbur, R., Paukkeri, T., Pirttilä, J., & Tuomala, M. (2017). Optimal taxation and public provision for poverty reduction. *International Tax and Public Finance*, *25*(1), 64–98. doi:10.1007/s10797-017-9443-6.

Kaplow, L. (1990). Optimal Taxation with Costly Enforcement. *Journal of Public Economics*, *43*(2), 221–236.

Kapička, M. (2015). Optimal Mirrleesean Taxation in a Ben-Porath Economy. *American Economic Journal: Macroeconomics*, *7*(2), 219–248. Retrieved from http://www.jstor.org/stable/24739277.

Kapička, M., & Neira, J. (2019). Optimal Taxation with Risky Human Capital. *American Economic Journal: Macroeconomics*, *11*(4), 271–309. doi:10.1257/mac.20160365.

Kaplow, L. (2008). *The Theory of Taxation and Public Economics*. Princeton, NJ: Princeton University Press.

Kleven, H., Landais, C., Muñoz, M., & Stantcheva, S. (2020). Taxation and Migration: Evidence and Policy Implications. *Journal of Economic Perspectives*, *34*(2), 119–142. doi:10.1257/jep.34.2.119.

Kleven, H. J. (2004). Optimum Taxation and the Allocation of Time. *Journal of Public Economics*, *88*(3–4), 545–557. doi:10.1016/s0047-2727(02)00192-5.

Kroft, K., Kucko, K., Lehmann, E., & Schmieder, J. (2020). Optimal Income Taxation with Unemployment and Wage Responses: A Sufficient Statistics Approach. *American Economic Journal: Economic Policy*, *12*(1), 254–292. doi:10.1257/pol.20180033.

Mankiw, N. G., & Weinzierl, M. (2010). The Optimal Taxation of Height: A Case Study of Utilitarian Income Redistribution. *American Economic Journal: Economic Policy*, *2*(1), 155–176. doi:10.1257/pol.2.1.155.

Mayshar, J. (1991). Taxation with Costly Administration. Scandavian. *Journal of Economics*, *93*(1), 75–88.

McLure, C. E., Jr. (1974). A Diagrammatic Exposition of the Harberger Model with One Immobile Factor. *Journal of Political Economy*, *82*(1), 56–82. Retrieved from http://www.jstor.org/stable/1830900.

McLure, C. E., Jr. (1975). General Equilibrium Incidence Analysis: The Harberger Model after Ten Years. *Journal of Public Economics*, *4*, 125–161.

Mirrlees, J. A. (1971). An Exploration in the Theory of Optimum Income Taxation. *The Review of Economic Studies*, *38*(2), 175–208. doi:10.2307/2296779.

Olovsson, C. (2015). Optimal Taxation with Home Production. *Journal of Monetary Economics*, *70*, 39–50. doi:10.1016/j.jmoneco.2014.08.004.

Park, Y. (2014). Optimal Taxation in a Limited Commitment Economy. *The Review of Economic Studies*, *81*(2), 884–918. doi:10.1093/restud/rdt038.

Piketty, T., Saez, E., & Stantcheva, S. (2014). Optimal Taxation of Top Labor Incomes: A Tale of Three Elasticities. *American Economic Journal: Economic Policy*, *6*(1), 230–271.

Piketty, T., Saez, E., & Zucman, G. (2018). Distributional National Accounts: Methods and Estimates for the United States*. *The Quarterly Journal of Economics, 133*(2), 553–609. doi:10.1093/qje/qjx043.

Ramsey, F. P. (1927). A Contribution to the Theory of Taxation. *The Economic Journal, 37*(145), 47–61. doi:10.2307/2222721.

Reis, C. (2013). Taxation without commitment. *Economic Theory, 52*(2), 565–588. Retrieved from http://www.jstor.org/stable/23470312.

Roeder, K. (2014). Optimal taxes and pensions with myopic agents. *Social Choice and Welfare, 42*(3), 597–618. Retrieved from http://www.jstor.org/stable/43662491.

Saez, E. (2001). Using Elasticities to Derive Optimal Income Tax Rates. *The Review of Economic Studies, 68*(1), 205–229. doi:10.1111/1467-937X.00166.

Saez, E. (2004). The optimal treatment of tax expenditures. *Journal of Public Economics, 88*(12), 2657–2684. doi:10.1016/j.jpubeco.2003.09.004.

Saez, E., & Stantcheva, S. (2018). A simpler theory of optimal capital taxation. *Journal of Public Economics, 162*, 120–142. doi:10.1016/j.jpubeco.2017.10.004.

Sandmo, A. (1976). Optimal Taxation: An Introduction to the Literature. *Journal of Public Economics, 6*(1–2), 37–54.

Scheuer, F., & Wolitzky, A. (2016). Capital Taxation under Political Constraints. *The American Economic Review, 106*(8), 2304–2328. Retrieved from http://www.jstor.org/stable/43956913.

Slemrod, J. (1990). Optimal Taxation and Optimal Tax Systems. *Journal of Economic Perspectives, 4*(1), 157–178. doi:10.1257/jep.4.1.157.

Stantcheva, S. (2014). Optimal Income Taxation with Adverse Selection in the Labour Market. *The Review of Economic Studies, 81*(3 (288)), 1296–1329. Retrieved from http://www.jstor.org/stable/43551627.

Tait, A. A. (1988). *Value Added Tax: International Practice and Problems*: International Monetary Fund.

2
Collection-Driven Taxation

An Introduction

2.1 Introduction

The foundation for one adaptation to the tax reform standard approach is presented
here. Collection methods are emphasized, hopefully consistent with economic efficiency considerations. The individual (or household) is the economic basis for the
policy approach. That is, the individual is the taxpayer regardless of how resources
are transferred, what the collection method is called (VAT, corporate tax, or excise
tax, for example), and what is stated in the statute. In a perfect world, this means
that the individual would report and pay tax directly without the need for an intermediary. That is, the collection method (voluntary compliance by the individual
for example) corresponds with the policy intent of the tax and the identification of
the taxpayer. Practical difficulties, however, may prevent cost-effective application of
such an approach.

Collection methods, including the mix of tax instruments employed, and base
computations at any point in the tax system's evolution are determined relative
to economic conditions and institutional factors. The proposed collection-driven
methods are based on transactions with tax payments serving either as advanced
payments or the final tax depending on institutional factors. As discussed below, suppliers of market goods and services are not the taxpayers. The collection method
will be broad-based for most economies and will include both consumption and
income-based methods. This means that the tax on individuals is collected in bits
on a transaction-by-transaction basis, except for capital transactions (imperfectly
defined). In short, the collection method is based on taxing everything that moves
and most things that do not.

We believe successful application of this approach has three benefits. First, rates
would be as low as possible. Second, total administrative costs–including costs to taxpayers, those acting as collection agents, and the tax administration–are reasonable
so that private sector actors can concentrate on individual decision making.

Third, the proposed collection approach is built on market transactions between
suppliers and demanders and thus depends on the institutional environment and
state of the market at any point in time. This means that collection methods,

Evolutionary Tax Reform in Emerging Economies. Robert F. Conrad and Michael Alexeev, Oxford University Press.
© Open Society Institute (2024). DOI: 10.1093/oso/9780192847089.003.0004

including measurement of the base, should adapt to the current institutional market environment. In addition, tax policy combined with the collection methods should be used to encourage further market development. This means that public education and awareness about market and tax concepts becomes an important element of government policy. Depending on the institutional environment, the linkage between any tax instrument and taxpayer income may be opaque (excise taxes for revenue purposes for instance). Government policy makers should be honest about both motives and institutional constraints, however, so that collection methods can evolve to become more directly linked to taxpayer income.

Emphasis on the individual as the taxpayer will help distinguish the role of those who collect the tax from those who bear the statutory tax burden. This distinction is enhanced by defining advanced payment agents (APAs) as a generalization of withholding agents. It should be clear that APAs are not taxpayers in the same spirit that an employer withholding tax on wages from an employee is not the taxpayer. This distinction becomes important in discussing the basis for advanced tax on capital and the current definition of the taxpayer under most VAT laws.

2.2 Basis of Approach

A frame of reference is helpful for evaluating a tax system, understanding the biases of those proposing to change the tax system, determining the overall usefulness of the reform approach, and weighing potential applications. Some elements are enumerated here that are used as a frame of reference for the development of a collection-driven approach to taxation. These items supplement the discussion in Chapter 1.

2.2.1 The Government Is a Competitor

There are more taxpayers than tax administrators, and most tax administrations have significant budget constraints.[1] Taxpayers and their advisers have an incentive to arbitrage definitions, to take advantage of loopholes, to develop new schemes, and to exploit all legal means to reduce their tax burdens. Thus, the government is at a competitive disadvantage in attempting to implement and administer a tax system.[2] This disadvantage is offset by the ability of the government to collect tax before, or at the time, the taxpayer accrues the income or consumes a good or service; an advantage we exploit.

---

[1] In some economic theories of taxation, the government acts as a monopolist with significant information. The theories of optimal indirect taxation where the government can exploit demand elasticities, and cross-price elasticities, are a case in point (Atkinson & Stiglitz, 2015).
[2] We owe this point to Anne Kruger.

2.2.2 Place Tax Reform in the Context of Overall Reform and Other Revenue Sources

The ability to successfully implement tax changes depends on other developments in the economy. Specific tax changes, within a general approach, need to be based on the current and foreseen evolution of the economy. For example, simple rules and broad-based advanced payments based on accruals to individuals may be preferable relative to attempting to define employees for tax purposes, particularly in situations where much labour is casual labour and more sophisticated taxpayers can restructure their relationships with those demanding labour services to avoid wage withholding (see Chapter 3).

Taxes are not the only source of revenue. Natural resource-rich countries may accrue significant revenues via the ownership of the natural resource reserves (Chapter 6). Some countries may have an active licence fee and toll fee system. The state may hold assets in the form of public enterprises and other public investments. International assistance is also an important revenue source for some countries. While taxes may be the dominant revenue source, placing the tax system in a broader revenue context will provide a better means to evaluate the complementarities and other interactions between tax changes and other revenue sources.

2.2.3 Take Account of Both Tax and Expenditure to Determine the Distributional Implications of Government Policy

Distributional implications will always be an important element of tax reform. It is critical to emphasize, however, the importance of examining the combined effect of tax and expenditures on income distribution.

More generally, it is important to examine the overall income distributional effects of the entire tax system, as opposed to any specific element. If the tax system is designed to achieve revenue objectives with minimal distortions and administrative costs, then some elements of the system can be regressive while the overall effect is progressive.[3]

2.2.4 Keep the System as Simple as Possible

As noted in Chapter 1, there is no such thing as a simple tax system if for no reason other than taxpayers have an incentive to avoid or evade their obligations. In addition, there is the complexity of trying to accommodate economic and institutional

---

[3] Arnold Harberger first noted this point to Conrad.

conditions while taking actions that are consistent with the objectives of the tax system. Simplification can help the processes of administration, compliance, and public education.

2.2.4.1 Keep Definitions to a Minimum and Make Every Attempt to Ensure Clarity

Definitions need to be clear and sufficient to cover needed terms. That said, definitions need to be kept to a minimum. For example, in the sections that follow, there are not separate definitions for taxpayers and/or withholding agents for each tax. There are only taxpayers and APAs. The income tax section does not list income types in the charging sections. Rather, there are only two types of income: income from human capital (the provision of labour services by individuals) and returns to other types of capital. In the case of exemptions, where necessary, a negative listing should clearly state that items or income types not listed are included in the base for either advanced payment or individual reporting. It should be clear that any income accruing to an individual not explicitly defined in the list is taxable.

2.2.4.2 Impose Clear, and Sometimes Clearly Arbitrary, Rules

Numerous decisions and computations must be made, and it is inevitable that there might be ambiguities in attempting to apply methodological concepts in practice. In general, there is no objective test to determine many applications. For example, a resident must be defined for income, VAT, and excise tax purposes. This definition in theory may not depend on physical presence as much as intent. That said, an objective physical presence test (183-day rule) for individuals is recommended because it is objective and can be subject to independent verification.[4] The purpose of clearly arbitrary rules is to reduce the administrative costs for tax administrators and taxpayers, when relevant. Equally important, arbitrary rules are a statement of mutual ignorance because no one knows how to measure the item in a methodologically consistent way that can be independently verified. This approach will enable definitions to evolve with new information and experience while providing a relatively efficient means of allocating resources.

2.2.5 Concentrate Efforts on Objectively Measuring the Bases Given Administrative Capacity and Public Acceptance

All tax bases are measured either ex post or coincident with the taxing event. Even ex post measurement will be made with error relative to the economic definitions. For example, as an economic matter, the basis of the VAT should be the consumption of

---

[4] One important issue is whether incentives are created by the tax system as a whole for taxpayers to become residents.

final goods and services by the resident taxpayers. As a practical matter, the definition of the VAT base is the supply of taxable goods and services to resident individuals. That is, the tax is on market expenditures, not consumption, of domestic residents. Some of these supplies are inputs into the household production of consumption goods and services, such as the purchase of raw food, electricity, pots and pans, and other inputs such as labour in the production of household meals (the consumption good). Other taxable supplies may be inputs into further production of market goods and services, such as inputs employed by persons who are not APAs that are sold in the market or an individual who invests in skill development to increase future market income. For income taxation, the tax base as a matter of method is net market income of the individual. There may be tradeoffs between accurately measuring the tax base and the ability of both taxpayers and tax administrators to apply definitions. Thus, it might be cost effective to define taxable income from human capital as gross compensation from human capital (as is proposed here) less a standard deduction intended to recognize the cost of earning income while relieving taxpayers of document requirements and tax administrators from auditing such derivations.

2.2.6 Accept the Tradeoff between Accuracy and Administrative Costs

Related to the last point, each tax base will be measured with error and effort should be made to increase accuracy. However, increased accuracy can be costly, so there is always a tradeoff between measurement precision and administrative costs, where administrative costs include the costs to the tax administration, the taxpayer, and APAs. The errors can increase or decrease based on the administrative methods employed. For example, advanced payments for income taxes may not be as accurate as individual reporting of income. The total and marginal cost of administration could be higher for personal reporting relative to advanced payments, however. Given that all measures are estimates made with error, policy and administrative choices should be based on these relative tradeoffs and should be part of the public discussion about tax bases.

2.2.7 Depersonalize Compliance to Every Extent Possible

The ability to reduce or to eliminate bargaining and corruption will be enhanced if the tax system is as depersonalized as possible. Depersonalization may be particularly important in emerging economies where corruption is often perceived to be high, tax administrators are sceptical about taxpayer compliance, and trust in government is low. One benefit of using APAs is that tax collection and much, if not all, auditing is at least one step removed from the taxpayer.

2.2.8 Everything Changes, Perhaps Unexpectedly

A government needs to be able to respond to changing economic circumstances. There could be unforeseen changes in prices; adverse or beneficial events; expected changes that accompany economic growth such as economic diversification, increased education, expansion of formal markets, increased integration with international markets; and technological innovations that affect the choice of fiscal instruments. Thus, what is appropriate tax and administrative policy at one point in time, or point in the evolution of the economy, may not be reasonable at other times. There will be changes in rates and relative emphasis in response to unforeseen events. Structures may change both in response to random factors as well as anticipated changes as part of the system's evolution. What is constant in our approach, however, is the framework in which the tax system can evolve.

2.2.9 Learn by Doing

We emphasize learning by doing and a willingness to make changes both considering experience and in response to policy mistakes, of which there will be many. Adjustments in response to experience and errors can be accommodated by maintaining transparent communication with the private sector. While interests are divergent, open communication with the private sector can help evaluate the cost effectiveness of approaches, aid implementation, and avoid mistakes.

2.2.10 Engage in Public Education and Dialogue

The government should enhance public awareness and education. A tax system is complex, so it is important to explain proposals in a way that taxpayers can appreciate both the objectives and the applications. Awareness of the rules and their applications can be an important tool for increasing the integrity of the system because a knowledgeable taxpaying population can hold the tax administration to publicly available standards. Education and understanding of the tax policy and administrative methods can be enhanced by structured public dialogue with all interested parties.

Finally, there are a variety of influences on policy decision making, including domestic interests and international policy changes. Given the increased importance of international trade and economic integration, there may be a natural desire to examine, and adopt, approaches used by other countries. Related to this point, there is a natural risk aversion against trying something that has not been adopted elsewhere. For emerging economies, there is also the potential influence of international donors and advisers. All these sources of information, and financial support for reform, can be important inputs. It is important, however, that the influences and information be placed in context.

2.3 One Economic Basis for the Proposed Structural Framework

Collection-driven taxation is based on three notions:

- When developing the basic policy and changes in policy, focus on the individual;
- When developing the tax mix and implementation, focus on the means of collecting the tax revenue in a way that is cost effective; and
- Economic distortions matter.

2.3.1 Focus on the Individual

The implication of adopting this approach is that the individual is always the taxpayer regardless of how a taxpayer is defined in any statute. It is common for statutes such as the corporate income tax to define the taxpayer as a juridical person, as a drafting matter, or define the taxpayer to be a person other than an individual. In addition, many VAT laws define the taxpayer as the supplier. Policy analysis, however, will always be about how the tax affects individual real income.[5] Thus, policy and policy design questions are always addressed by attempting to understand how public actions affect the welfare of individuals. In this text, we recommend that the taxpayer in any tax statute be defined as the individual to clarify the relationship between policy and implementation, at least through time.

An additional implication of adopting this perspective is that the income distributional implications of the tax mix will clearly be focused on how the tax and expenditure changes affect individual real wealth and incentives. The income distributional implications of policy changes on any entity are not a concern.

Defining the taxpayer as the individual for policy and, hopefully, statutory purposes does not imply that the individual is a resident, is required to register, to complete a tax form, or to pay or be assessed taxes, although individual reporting may be an option. Such decisions may depend on the application of the tax and local conditions.

2.3.2 All Entities Are Flow-Through Entities

If the individual is the taxpayer, then any legal person or entity supplying a good or service is a flow-through entity. These persons or entities retain the services of the primary factors of production and supply goods and services either to other suppliers, to exporters, or to individual consumers. That is, persons or entities supplying goods

---

[5] The individual owner(s) may be several steps removed from a particular policy action under consideration. For example, an emerging economy might consider tax incentives to attract foreign investment. From our perspective, it is the individual owners of the entity making the investment who are the taxpayers, regardless of their residence. The owners' response might be reflected, imperfectly, by the managers who are the owners' agents, and the signals might be further muddled by the self-interest of the manager, resulting in incentives that do not coincide with the owners' objectives.

and services are conduits for individuals who own the primary productive factors (generically speaking, capital and labour) and who determine the allocation of production as well as consumption at various points in time. Entities are the means, not the ends, of economic activity. Entities include, but are not limited to, juridical persons such as corporations, partnerships, all levels of government, political organizations, fraternal organizations, NGOs, trusts, endowments, and individual proprietorships. As the means of economic activity, entities are not taxpayers. Therefore, taxes like the corporation or entity tax are advanced payment systems in a collection-driven framework because the entity is owned, at least ultimately, by individuals whose income is affected by the charge.[6]

2.3.3 Risk Sharing Is an Inherent Part of Any Tax System

Measuring any tax base depends on the results of taxpayer actions. This means that the observed tax base is ex post (or coincident with) the economic results, making risk sharing an inherent part of the process. All taxes have risk sharing elements. For example, ad rem or ad valorem taxes may share variability in production (or consumption) relative to planned actions, and ad valorem taxes are based on realized prices which may differ from the anticipated price when the taxpayer plans.[7] The tax system may affect taxpayer planning and actions, but the observed result will be a combination of actions and random events.

Risk sharing is between individuals and not between taxpayers and the government because government is a flow-through entity in a collection-driven framework. For example, consider a flat rate income tax at a rate of 25%. If a taxpayer's income increases (or decreases) unexpectedly, then the entire population gains (loses) 25% while the taxpayer gains (loses) 75% of the change in taxpayer's income. The entire population gains or loses because the change in tax revenue may result in a change in expenditures, tax rates, or debt.

It is important that risk and risk sharing are explicitly considered in developing policy because the economic results of tax policies might change depending on the presence of risk. For example, output might increase if an ad valorem tax is imposed on the supply of some commodity and the income tax could be more efficient relative to consumption taxes when risks are present (see Annex A1.2). In general, the type of risk sharing depends on the nature of the tax base. Variations in production, for example, might be shared with per unit taxes. Variability in prices and quantities will be reflected in ad valorem consumption taxes. Ad valorem tariffs will reflect

---

[6] We are not naïve enough to believe that individual owners monitor managers to the extent necessary to influence most business decisions. We understand that incentive compatibility issues arise. Taxation may not be able to address such problems, but taxation can influence the distribution of the gains and losses to both managers and owners.

[7] APA managers make decisions under uncertainty as well. Our point is that the APA's actions represent the risk preferences of the owners of the primary inputs, individual taxpayers, as well as risk preferences of individual demanders as reflected in any risk-adjusted demand curve. So, even if managers are risk neutral regarding the rental prices of inputs and the output prices, the project will reflect the risk preferences of individuals, in the aggregate.

the variability of international prices and exchange rates. Income taxes are the most broad-based taxes, in theory, and ex post results represent both direct effects of changes in factor prices as well as indirect effects via the correlation between factor prices that comprise the portfolio of factors owned by the taxpayer.

Explicit consideration of risk sharing also enables policy makers to think of real net worth upon which real income is based as a portfolio of activities. Taxpayers accrue income from the ownership of assets such as capital and labour (human capital), the prices of which are not known with certainty. In addition, some, or all, prices could be correlated, positively or negatively. For example, an exogeneous increase in the price of copper for a producing country that is a small open economy could lead to an appreciation of the exchange rate, which in turn will cause a decrease in the price of importable goods and services as well as a decrease in the domestic price of all exportable goods and services. A per unit or ad valorem tax on copper alone would provide risk sharing via the tax system based on the price of copper. Risks are shared more broadly if a VAT is employed. For example, the unanticipated price increase in copper could result in higher government VAT revenue even if all copper is exported, so there is no direct VAT revenue from copper production. The VAT would also capture the second-order effects resulting from an increase in the demand for imports following the decrease in the domestic price caused by the unanticipated currency appreciation. Finally, a broad-based income tax would further expand the scope of risk sharing by including returns to primary inputs and supplies of goods and services. Continuing with the example of a copper price increase, incomes of the owners might increase. Also, the income of producers of other exportables may decrease. An income tax, by taking both consumption and investing into account, would enable the population to share how the change in one price affects the broader economy.[8]

Of course, no risk-sharing method is perfect in practice, the tax system included. Explicit consideration of risk sharing, however, will provide a broader perspective of the benefits and costs of any set of tax proposals.

2.3.4 Discussion

Some discussion points can be illustrated via the example in Tables 2.1–2.5. Table 2.1 contains a numerical illustration of Haig-Simons income in a manner consistent with Conrad and Alexeev (2021). For simplicity, we assume that the individual is a resident for tax purposes. There are two types of gross income. Income from human capital consists of compensation for labour services in the market regardless of how they are defined (wages, compensation, honoraria, a service-oriented sole

---

[8] As a practical matter, no risk sharing system is comprehensive, in the sense that risk is shared proportionally between the individual taxpayer and other individuals, via risk sharing with government. That said, the income tax, as one instrument, may be more efficient relative to other charges, VAT and wage taxes in particular (see Annex A1.1).

Table 2.1 Individual income—no tax

Row #	Item	Value	Value
1	Gross income		
2	Income from human capital	13,639.65	
3	Income from nonhuman capital		
4	Interest	2,469.33	
5	Accrued income from equity ownership	2,375.01	
6			
7	Total gross income		18,484.00
8			
9	Cost of earning income		
10	Cost attributable to earning human capital	1,832.99	
11	Cost attributable to earning nonhuman capital	651.01	
12	Cost of earning income not attributable to the type of income	869.33	
13			
14	Total cost of earning income		3,353.33
15			
16	Total market income (tax inclusive)		15,130.67

proprietorship, among other definitions). Income from nonhuman capital is divided into two general classifications: interest (the returns to holding market debt) and ownership of equity (shares of corporate entities and equity participation in partnerships, among other possibilities). Net income is computed by reducing gross market income by the costs of earning that income. Like a business, an individual might attempt to separately account for costs attributable to different types of income. Costs of earning a return to human capital include travel costs to and from work, equipment, uniforms, and related costs. Costs of earning a return to nonhuman capital include, but are not limited to, accounting fees, advisory fees, and household expenses related to maintaining or monitoring equity investments. Finally, there are legitimate costs that cannot be attributed to any specific type of gross income. Such costs can include interest expense[9] and the fixed costs of maintaining as well as fostering market interactions. Income (individual profit) is then gross income less all costs of accruing that income.[10]

Suppose there is a consumption tax of 10% and a flat rate income tax of 25% with a personal exemption (zero bracket amount) of 4,200.[11] Suppose further that economic income as defined here is the measured tax base. The taxes on the individual are then computed and reported in Tables 2.2a and 2.2b. The income tax base before the

---

[9] We believe that even debt tied to specific assets (such as housing or machinery) cannot be attributed to any specific activity in an economic sense because of the fungibility of funds. See Chapter 3.

[10] Income is measured on an accrual and accretion basis. See Chapter 3.

[11] See Chapter 3 for how to compute an equivalent individual tax credit equal to 1,050 in this particular case.

Table 2.2a Individual filing, Schedule A: individual income tax

Row #	Item	Value	Value
1	Gross income		
2	Gross wages	13,639.65	
3	Income from nonhuman capital		
4	Interest	2,469.33	
5	Accrued income from equity ownership	2,375.01	
6	Total gross income		18,484.00
7			
8	Cost of earning income		
9	Cost attributable to earning human capital	1,832.99	
10	Cost attributable to earning nonhuman capital	651.01	
11	Cost of earning income not attributable to the type of income	869.33	
12	Total cost of earning income (summation of lines 9 – 11)		3,353.33
13			
14	Total market income (line 6 – line 12)		15,130.67
15	Personal exemption		4,200.00
16	Taxable income (line 14 – line 15)		10,930.67
17	Income tax (25% of line 16)		2,732.67
18	After-tax income (line 14 – line 17)		12,398.00
19	After-tax savings (20% of line 18)		2,479.60
20	After-tax consumption expenditures (line 18 – line 19)		9,918.40

personal exemption is identical to measured income in Table 2.1. Taxable income is computed by reducing net income by the personal exemption as shown in Table 2.2a, line 15. The tax is then computed by taking the product of the result (Table 2.2a, line 16) and the income tax rate. After-tax real income before consumption tax over which the individual has discretion is then simply real income (measured in Table 2.1) less the amount of tax.

Consumption taxes are then computed in two steps. First, consumption needs to be defined. One method is to record all expenditures on consumption goods and services (however defined). A second option is to define saving (the present value of future consumption adjusted for risk) and subtract that value from after-tax income. The result is then the market value of consumption. This computation is shown in lines 19 and 20 of Table 2.2a where a savings rate of 20% of net-of-tax income is assumed. Consumption tax is then the product of measured consumption with the consumption tax rate as shown in Table 2.2b.

Note that the tax results in Tables 2.2a and 2.2b are independent of whether the individual computes the tax and files a return if the base is invariant to the collection method. There is a VAT, so there is no need for the individual to compute personal consumption. In addition, income tax is withheld by APAs. In effect, the tax authorities could compute an assessment after the taxpayer supplies some supplemental

Table 2.2b Individual filing, Schedule B: consumption tax

Row #	Item	Value	Value
21	After-tax income (line 18)	12,398.00	
22	Less after-tax savings (line 19)	2,479.60	
23	After income tax value of consumption expenditures (line 21 – line 22)		9,918.40
24			
25	Consumption tax (10% of line 23)		991.84
26	Net-of-tax consumption expenditures (line 23 – line 24)		8,926.56

information such as family membership. In summary, the policy analysis should be based on how the combined tax system affects both individual income as reported in Table 2.2b and how the tax burden is distributed across individuals.

As a precursor to discussions in subsequent chapters, we note that there are difficulties in computing the tax base defined in Table 2.1.[12] For example, the costs of earning market income may not be observable to the tax authorities, which means that such measures if self-reported are not independently verifiable. For example, some market purchases may be used for either producing consumption or as an input into the production of gross income. Consumables such as paper, personal computers, and electricity are examples. These items combined with the need to record nonmarket time used in the production of market income make it impossible for the tax administration to independently verify these costs. One simplification[13] is for the tax law to provide for a standard deduction in recognition of such costs and have that value be constant across all individuals. This modification is illustrated in Table 2.3a where a standard deduction of 4,000 is assumed. Now the computation of the market-determined taxable income is observable in the sense that gross income arises between the individual and others with the taxable income being computed by reducing gross income by the standard deduction. The resulting tax and net-of-tax real income (Table 2.3a, line 18) differ from the results of Tables 2.2a and 2.2b because the standard deduction is an approximation. This is one cost of simplification with offsetting gains of reduced administrative costs for both taxpayers and tax administrators.

The inability to measure all costs of earning income will affect consumption taxes for two reasons. First, after-tax real income is affected, which will affect both saving and consumption. Thus, consumption taxes could rise or fall depending on how the standard deduction affects income. Second, there is a direct effect on the consumption tax base. Note that saving and consumption in Table 2.1 is based on real income,

[12] The economic effects of simplifications and advanced payments are discussed in detail in subsequent chapters. Our purpose here is to emphasize the importance of the policy focus on the individual.
[13] One important simplification is to disallow some deductions such as some costs of earning market income. This approach is used in most tax systems. Our point, however, is that disallowance of a deduction, while appropriate, needs to be an explicit policy decision relative to the methodological definition of full net income.

including the true costs of earning income in the derivation. The nondeductibility and inability to verify use means that such inputs are reclassified as consumption expenditures as a practical matter.[14] This effect is illustrated in Table 2.3a, line 19, where saving is based on after-tax real income and all costs associated with earning income are assumed to be market expenditures (Table 2.3b). Note that consumption is now equal to total accrued market income less saving because the market cost of earning income is defined to be consumption. Like Tables 2.2a and 2.2b, the results reported in Tables 2.3a and 2.3b can be independent of collection method.

Advanced payments are introduced in Table 2.4, where advanced payments for the income tax are found in Tables 2.4a and 2.4b. In this case, the personal exemption is used to determine the base for withholding on the return to human capital while advanced payments on nonhuman capital are simply the marginal tax rate times the amount of income attributed to the individual.[15] Advanced payment of consumption taxation is based on the VAT as illustrated in Table 2.4c. The issue now is whether the individual is required to report income and reconcile the taxes accrued with the advanced payments or to treat the advanced payments as final

Table 2.3a Individual filing with standard deduction, Schedule A: income tax

Row #	Item	Value	Value
1	Gross income		
2	Income from human capital	13,639.65	
3	Income from nonhuman capital		
4	Interest	2,469.33	
5	Accrued income from equity ownership	2,375.02	
6	Total gross income		18,484.00
7			
8	Standard deduction		4,000.00
9	Taxable income before personal exemption		14,484.00
10			
11	Personal exemption		4,200.00
12			
13	Taxable income (line 9 – line 11)		10,284.00
14			
15	Income tax (25% of line 13)		2,571.00
16			
17	After-tax measured income (line 13 – line 15)		7,713.00
18	Real after-tax income (Table 2.1, line 16 – line 16)		12,599.67
19	After-tax savings (20% of line 18)	2,511.93	
20	After-tax consumption expenditures (line 18 – line 19)	10,047.73	

[14] The standard deduction and reclassification of inputs as consumption can change the allocation of savings from market savings to household saving such as a change in the investment of human capital. See Chapter 4.

[15] A discussion of base measurement for nonhuman capital is found in Chapter 3. We take the advanced payment base as given for current purposes.

Table 2.3b Individual filing with standard deduction, Schedule B: consumption tax

Row #	Item	Value	Value
21	After-income tax income plus personal exemption (lines 17+ 11)	11,913.00	
22	Plus costs of earning income (Table 2.1, line 14)	3,353.33	
23	Less savings (line 19)	2,511.93	
24	Equals total consumption expenditures		12,754.40
25			
26	Consumption tax (10% of line 24)		1,275.44
27	Net-of-tax consumption expenditures (net of expenses) (line 24 – line 26 – line 22)		8,125.63

Table 2.4a Individual filing with advanced payments: wage reporting

Row #	Item	Value	Value
1	Gross income from human capital (Table 2.1, line 2)	13,639.65	
2	Less Personal Exemption (Table 2.2a, line 15)	4,200.00	
3	Basis for advanced payment (line 1 – line 2)		9,439.65
4	Advanced tax on wages (25% of line 3)		2,359.91

Table 2.4b Individual filing with advanced payments: advanced payments on nonhuman capital

Row #	Item	Value	Value
5	Interest income		
6	Gross interest income (Table 2.1, line 4)	2,469.33	
7	Advanced tax (25% of line 6)	617.33	
8			
9	Corporate profits (including accrued capital gain) (Table 2.1, line 5)	2,375.01	
10	Advanced tax (25% of line 9)	593.75	
11			
12	Total advanced tax on nonhuman capital (line 7 + line 10)		1,211.09

Table 2.4c Individual filing with advanced payments: VAT

Row #	Item	Value	Value
13	VAT-inclusive supplies of goods and services	12,754.40	
14	VAT (10% of line 13)		1,275.44

Table 2.4d Individual filing with advanced payments

Row #	Item	Value	Value
15	Gross income		
16	Gross income from human capital	13,639.65	
17	Income from nonhuman capital		
18	Interest	2,469.33	
19	Accrued income from equity ownership	2,375.01	
20	Total gross income		18,484.00
21			
22	Standard deduction		4,000.00
23	Taxable income before personal exemption		14,484.00
24			
25	Personal exemption		4,200.00
26			
27	Taxable income (line 23 − line 25)		10,284.00
28	Income tax (25% of line 27)		2,571.00
29			
30	Less advanced tax (line 4 + line 12)		3,571.00
31	Tax payable (line 28 − line 29)		(1,000.00)
32	After-tax measured income (line 27 − line 30 − line 31)		7,713.00
33	Real VAT-inclusive after-income tax income (Table 2.1, line 16 − line 28)		12,559.67

taxes. If, however, a reconciliation is desired, then the computation is restricted to the income tax alone. This is because computing the individual consumption tax would be redundant given the definition of the base. Thus, there would be only costs and no benefit to require individual reporting of consumption taxes. An income tax reconciliation may be necessary in the current case because the costs of earning income are part of the advanced payment system. This is illustrated in Table 2.4d. A refund is due to the individual because the individual is allowed a standard deduction when the reconciliation is made.[16] This implies that it is possible to eliminate filing (and refunds) for many individuals by including both the personal exemption (for distributional purposes) and the standard deduction in the advanced payment computations. Finally, such computations are exact relative to the definition of taxable income for those individuals whose market incomes are subject to advanced tax. There are other individuals, such as independent professionals, farmers, and other self-employed individuals, with incomes subject to advanced tax

---

[16] The refund arises because the standard deduction is not taken into account. In Chapter 3, we argue the exemption in a collection-based system should include estimates of both the exemption for income distributional purposes and a standard deduction. There are other reasons why a reconciliation might be reasonable as the tax system evolves. See Chapter 3.

Table 2.5 Summary table

Row #	Item	Individual filing (Table 2.2)	Individual filing with standard deduction (Table 2.3)	Individual filing with advanced payments (Table 2.4)	Advanced payments as final tax (Table 2.4)
1	Real income before tax	15,130.67	15,130.67	15,130.67	15,130.67
2	Income tax	2,732.67	2,571.00	2,571.00	3,571.00
3	Consumption tax (VAT)	991.84	1,275.44	1,275.44	1,275.44
4	Real net-of-tax income (Line 1 − line 2 − line 3)	11,406.16	11,284.23	11,284.23	10,284.23

using other methods such as estimated net income who might be required to file annual reconciliations.[17]

Table 2.5 is a summary table that enables a comparison of the different simplifications and advanced payment methods. The effect on real income depends, in general, on the adopted regime holding the rates fixed given both the approximations and the advanced payment system employed. Empirically, the results will depend on the actual market income and expenses of the taxpayers, while the distributional implications will vary based on the distribution of real net income.

2.3.5 Implications

The example supplied has been restricted to consumption and income taxes. As a matter of method, the example can be extended to excises, tariffs, and taxes on real property. Taxes on real property could be relatively straightforward in the sense that the individual could report the current market or appraised value for real property, apply the rate, and remit the tax as part of an additional schedule similar to those in Table 2.1.[18] Alternatively, the administration of the taxing jurisdiction, with sufficient information, could assess the value of real property and then bill the individual as currently practised in a number of countries.[19]

---

[17] One benefit of this approach, however, is that administrative resources can be used to concentrate on a small population.

[18] If an APA pays property tax on behalf of owners, then the property tax accrued would flow through. For example, if XYZ has real property on the balance sheet worth 1,000 and pays 20 in property tax, then net-of-tax income of the owners falls by 20 and would automatically flow through.

[19] Some countries have proposed to use voluntary compliance in the sense that the individual will self-assess the value of the property and report the tax. Compliance would be enforced by requiring the individual to sell the property to any person willing to pay the self-assessed value (Bird & Slack, 2006).

The APAs for tariffs and excises are commonly known by historical practice. Tariffs are collected by the customs department of the taxing jurisdiction and excises may be imposed at the time of importation, production, or sale depending on the type of excise. The individual is still the taxpayer, however, in the sense that these charges are reflected in tax-inclusive prices. It would be difficult, if not impossible, to impose such taxes at the individual level without knowledge of the economy's structure. It would be simple, at least informationally speaking, to have the individual pay tariffs and excises on goods and services directly imported by the individual. It would be difficult, however, to trace the tariff and excises paid by the individual if goods and services subject to tariffs and excises are used as inputs in the production of consumption goods and services supplied domestically.[20] The basic point about APAs is still valid and relevant for policy, however. That is, the APAs (customs in the case of tariffs and customs plus domestic producers in the case of excises) are not taxpayers. The individual is still the taxpayer in an economic sense even if the individual never knows the effect of such taxes on the relative prices charged to them for consumption goods.

The fact that in case of excises and tariffs no individual reporting is required raises some important issues about the administration of comprehensive taxation. It is not a rhetorical question to ask about the utility of requiring both advanced payments and individual reporting. First, the advanced payment system is just that—advanced. The taxing jurisdiction accrues revenue before, or at the time when, the individual either obtains title to consumption goods or accrues income. As noted, there are fewer APAs than individuals. If both APAs and individual reporting are employed, then the tax administration must allocate resources to monitoring both APAs and individual compliance. If the taxing jurisdiction employed only one method, then more resources on a per unit basis could be allocated to compliance activities for individuals not covered by advanced payments, such as small businesses or agriculture, as well as on APA compliance. The management of APAs should be indifferent to acting as an agent for advanced payments if they are compensated for supplying this service.

Finally, the use of APAs without individual filing will result in additional errors. At a minimum, the use of a personal exemption for everyone will result in some taxpayers paying too much tax and some paying too little relative to the individual reporting of correct amounts. The issue is whether the cost associated with either individual filing (or a reconciliation in the case where individuals file but use the advanced payments as credits) is greater than the gains in terms of revenue and efficiency costs. It might be the case that the costs are too great for some economies, particularly those that have low incomes, weak (or corrupt) tax administrations, and

---

[20] Consider imported motor fuel, for example. The individual would have to first report consumption (either in value or quantity) of motor fuel purchased. The individual would have to report the value (or quantity) of motor fuel embedded in the tax-exclusive price of every good and service purchased. This would imply that the individual would have to have information about the structure of the economy to report and pay excises and tariffs attributable to the individual. Exports would be automatically exempted from excise taxes if there is individual reporting and the individual taxpayer is a resident.

populations who are beginning to learn financial and tax concepts and who operate in a cash economy. If the personal exemption is used to eliminate low-income taxpayers from the system, then the error will result in greater revenue to the government. This is because the costs of earning income may increase with income so that higher-income individuals will pay more tax relative to the standard deduction case. The benefit is that tax rates would be lower, holding revenue fixed, administration and compliance costs are lower, and the economy obtains the benefit of broad-based income taxation that can evolve through time.[21]

2.4 Advanced Payment Agents

Advanced payments, for every tax in the tax portfolio, are an essential element of the approach developed here.[22] The use of private sector agents to charge and remit the taxes is already common; we only propose a more intensive use of the preexisting structure. The contribution here is to establish a unified approach to the concept of a withholding agent. If possible, there should be only one definition for an advanced payment agent in law and in practice. As a practical matter, this means replacing the 'taxpayer' concept in VAT and some excise tax laws with an APA and defining the taxpayer to be the individual. The VAT accrued at each point in the chain of value added is then defined as an advanced payment of the tax charged to the individual resident consumer—which in fact it is. For income taxes, instead of wage taxation, we propose expanding advanced payments for all payments for the gross return to the supply of labour. In addition, we redefine the entity tax as an advanced tax to capital owners. We also propose advanced payments for all payments to nonhuman capital, including interest, royalties, rents, and capital gains.

This approach to tax administration and to tax reform can be summarized by stating that the government of an emerging economy should impose advanced tax on all noncapital transactions occurring in the market and on some capital transactions that result in a gain or loss, regardless of how the transactions are defined, with some clear exceptions.

The approach is illustrated in Figure 2.1. APAs interact with taxpayers, individuals, by demanding labour services (human capital) and nonhuman capital services owned by the taxpayers. In return, the APAs pay rentals for each productive factor. For human capital, such payments may be wages, commissions, fees, or honoraria, among other items. For nonhuman capital, the payments include interest, changes in retained earnings and, perhaps, dividends (elements of profit), royalties, rents, and other payments. As an APA, amounts paid to the individual will be on a net-of-tax basis with the tax accruing to the government as a prepayment, or final payment for

---

[21] Note that individuals with no employment income get no personal exemption so those who accrue only income from capital still pay tax. In emerging economies, such individuals are perceived to be in higher income groups so the lack of a personal exemption can approximate the phase out of the exemption.

[22] Advanced payment agents are a generalization of the withholding agent concept described in Conrad & Alexeev (2021).

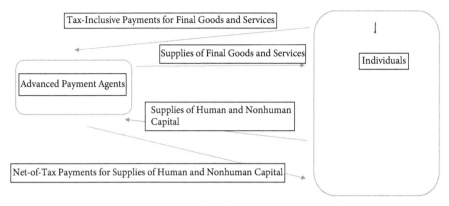

Figure 2.1 Relations between APAs and individuals

the aggregate income tax at the individual level. APAs also supply goods and services to final consumers, to exports, and to other APAs if intermediate goods and services are supplied. Assuming a consumption tax is present, then the APA will include the tax in the price of the final good or service to the individual as an advanced[23] (or final) payment for the aggregate tax at the individual level.[24,25]

The definition of an APA is crucial for the discussions in the subsequent chapters. Thus, we define an APA here.

2.4.1 Who Is an Advanced Payment Agent (APA)?

An APA is any person (individual or legal) who supplies goods and services to another person and/or pays for human and nonhuman capital services. In the case of income taxation, this definition is too broad for practical application, but as a strategy we believe that there are benefits to moving from the general to the specific. An APA must come within the legal scope of the taxing jurisdiction, must be known to the tax administration and, accordingly, should be registered.

2.4.2 Registered APAs

There are two types of registered APAs.

2.4.2.1 APA: Individual

Resident individuals[26] will have a dual role as a taxpayer and an APA if the resident individual:

---

[23] In the case of excises and tariffs, the tax is assumed to increase the cost of production and thus is embedded in the price of the final good or service.

[24] Only interactions with individuals are illustrated. Interactions between APAs can be accommodated by the invoice-credit system of the VAT and for flow-through treatment of income from nonhuman capital in the income tax. These points are discussed in the relevant sections.

[25] What happens at the individual level depends on whether individual reporting is required, or if the amounts withheld are the final tax.

[26] Resident-based taxation is assumed.

- Either makes payments to other individuals in return for the services of any human capital (including employees) or nonhuman capital in excess of a de minimis amount or who charges VAT as an advanced payment to any other person;
- Supplies any good or service to another person in excess of a *de minimis* amount;
- Makes any transfer to related parties;[27]
- Supplies excisable goods of any value; and
- Is not a registered small business taxpayer in the sense that advanced payments are not required for supplies of goods and services to another person.[28]

Alternatively, an individual may voluntarily register as an APA.

The first condition covers situations where individuals retain the services of individuals as household servants and other service providers. Note that the first condition does not include services supplied by entities. The second condition implies that the individual will charge VAT. The third condition covers situations where there are transfers between related individuals subject to the definition of related party (see below), which in general includes relatives and others. This condition may be necessary in situations where there is progressive taxation at the individual level and individuals make transfers to arbitrage the marginal brackets. For example, an individual who works might assign income from nonhuman capital to their spouse if separate individual taxation is the standard.[29] The last condition is the situation where the taxing jurisdiction has a small business tax that is in lieu of other taxes, so the individual will be exempt from advanced payments related to VAT.

Finally, voluntary registration is an option subject to conditions noted in the relevant sections for each specific tax.

2.4.2.2 APA: Entities

For current purposes, an entity is defined as any person or organization, other than a sole proprietorship, which supplies or intends to supply any good or service or who makes, or intends to make, any transfer to other persons. Entities include, but are not limited to, corporations, cooperatives, any level of government, political parties, NGOs, religious organizations, and any organization that supplies goods or services, regardless of whether the supplies are subject to VAT. Again, moving from the general to the specific, an entity will be required to be a registered APA if the entity is:[30]

- A legal person organized under the laws of the taxing jurisdiction;
- Any partnership, joint venture, or other organization under the jurisdiction of the taxing jurisdiction; or

---

[27] Related party is defined in Chapter 3.
[28] See Chapter 5.
[29] Of course, this condition might be modified if joint filing is allowed or required.
[30] There may need to be an exemption for small business entities. It is assumed however, that entities of any kind will not qualify for small business tax status (see Chapter 5).

• Any permanent establishment of any nonresident.

2.4.3 APA Responsibilities

Regardless of whether the APA is an individual or an entity, the APA will be charged with collecting advanced payments on all taxes for which it is eligible, including but not limited to:

1. VAT
2. Excises
3. Tariffs (to the extent that tariffs are collected by banks)
4. All income taxes
   a. Returns to nonhuman capital and capital gains
   b. Returns to all types of human capital, including wages, fringe benefits, service fees, honoraria, etc.
5. Property taxes to the extent relevant.

The base for the advanced payment will be described in the relevant chapters.

APAs will be responsible for periodic reporting, either monthly or quarterly (depending on tax and other factors) and will be compensated for their effort. Compensation may come in two parts. First, the APA will have access to funds during the period between when the advanced tax is collected and the due date. Thus, the APA will be able to accrue interest on the float. Second, a fee structure can be developed based on empirical estimates of costs to the extent that the float is insufficient compensation.

It is important to note two points. First, our recommendation is that APAs that are entities are never considered taxpayers and are not liable for any taxes other than advanced payments. If a separate corporate tax is desired in a country, then the entity would be both an APA and a taxpayer in a manner similar to a sole proprietorship. Second, and related to the first, the fact that advanced payments are taxes paid by others which are held in trust for the government implies there should be personal liability for individuals who are officers of the entity. This approach is similar to the personal liability for withholding taxes under US law.

Responsibilities of APAs become specific for each tax in the portfolio as applied and developed. More specific information is found in Chapters 3 and 4.

2.5 Summary

In summary, our view is that collection-driven taxation means the individual who demands goods and services and supplies productive factors is the focus of economic policy analysis. Because individual choices affect both economic welfare and economic performance, it is natural for the individual to be the taxpayer. Suppliers of goods and services who demand the services of productive factors are conduits to satisfy individual objectives. Accordingly, such suppliers are not taxpayers. There are reasons, however, to exploit the supply and demand relationship to create an effective administrative apparatus. We hope the benefits of this approach become more apparent as each specific taxing instrument is discussed.

References

Atkinson, A. B., & Stiglitz, J. E. (2015). *Lectures on Public Economics: Updated Edition.* Princeton, NJ: Princeton University Press.

Bird, R., & Slack, E. (2006). *Taxing Land and Property in Emerging Economies: Raising Revenue...and More? Unpublished. International Tax Program, Joseph L. Rotman School of Management, University of Toronto.*

Conrad, R. & Alexeev, M. (2021). *Income Tax Reform: A Proposal that Can Be Administered.* Unpublished.

Manhire, J. T. (2015). What Does Voluntary Tax Compliance Mean?: A Government Perspective. *University of Pennsylvania Law Review Online, 164*(11–17).

3
Individual Income Taxation

3.1 Introduction

This chapter is devoted to income taxation. Income taxation is the cornerstone of our approach to longer-term reform, so it is important to examine how income is derived both methodologically and practically.[1] The specific practical structure we propose is based on the use of Advanced Payment Agents (APAs, see Chapter 2) to collect tax on the components of income as they accrue. The extent to which taxable income is aggregated into an empirical measure of comprehensive income with the advanced payments used as a credit will depend on administrative capacity and public awareness. While practical considerations affect the implementation level in any country, the ultimate objective of our approach is to employ an empirical measure of comprehensive income. Thus, it is important for analysts to understand the standard in order to place the current situation in context and to plan for the tax system's evolution. Section 3.2 is devoted to reviewing the derivation of taxable income using the Haig-Simons concept of income and commonly employed tax concepts. Section 3.3 contains the proposed empirical structure based on Comprehensive Market-Determined Income (CMDI) developed by Conrad and Alexeev (2021) as well as a discussion of how the system might evolve. Section 3.4 is devoted to administrative issues. Two appendices, one on tax incentives and one on a proposed depreciation system, complete the discussion.

3.2 Individual Taxable Income: An Introduction via a Tour of a Haig-Simons Tax Form

The Haig-Simons (HS) definition of income is combined with some tax concepts to derive net-of-tax income. Table 3.1 contains a summary of the derivation and concepts. Table 3.1 might be thought of as the basis for a tax return to be completed by an individual on an annual basis.[2] The derivation contains numerous items that

---

[1] We have drafted a separate manuscript about income taxation (Conrad & Alexeev, 2021). A proposed income tax based on Comprehensive Market-Determined Income (CMDI), and its methodological foundation, is contained in the manuscript. This chapter contains a summary as well as some of the analysis contained in Conrad and Alexeev (2021). The interested reader is referred to that document. With some exceptions, this reference should be considered comprehensive for this chapter.

[2] The derivation is made with regard to potentially observable income so that Haig-Simons (HS) full income is not the starting point. Thus, the true starting point of the derivation is one step removed from

Evolutionary Tax Reform in Emerging Economies. Robert F. Conrad and Michael Alexeev, Oxford University Press.

Table 3.1 One derivation of taxable income

Row #	Gross revenue (income)
1	Return to human capital
2	Income from employment
3	Wages and salaries
4	Other cash payments from employment
5	Fringe benefits
6	Pension contributions
7	Medical care and medical insurance
8	Other in cash or in-kind compensation (housing, meals, education, nonmedical insurance)
9	Deferred compensation paid in cash (retirement)
10	
11	Income outside of employment
12	Contracts
13	Sales of goods and services from an unincorporated business
14	
15	Returns to nonhuman capital
16	Interest
17	Dividends
18	Capital gains
19	Rents
20	Royalties
21	Other returns to equity ownership
22	
23	Returns to a mix of human and nonhuman capital
24	Profits from sole proprietorship
25	Returns from equity interests in organizations that are not defined to be legal entities
26	
27	Benefits from government programmes
28	
29	**Equals Total revenue**
30	
31	Less exempt income either via omission or statutory exemption
32	
33	Less gross income accrued this year but deferred
34	Accrued Capital gains
35	Accrued pension benefits
36	
37	**Equals Total taxable gross income**
38	Less expenses of earning income
39	Variable inputs used to produce taxable gross income
40	Variable input expenses will depend on type and composition of gross taxable income
41	Depreciation and amortization
42	Interest expense
43	

Continued

Table 3.1 *Continued*

Row #	Gross revenue (income)
44	Less incentives that are deductible
45	Expensing of capital expenditures that should be capitalized
46	Expenditures seemed socially productive
47	
48	Plus nondeductible expenses
49	
50	**Equals Total deductions**
51	(Standard deduction)
52	(Personal exemptions)
53	**Equals Taxable income**
54	
55	Accrued tax (applicable rates times the line 53)
56	
57	Less credits
58	
59	Accrued tax after credits
60	
61	Less withholding, advanced payments, and carryforwards
62	
63	**Tax due**

might need to be defined either in law or regulation. Some of these issues are noted in the discussion and are summarized in Table 3.2. Our hope is that this discussion will provide a basis for the specific proposals made for the collection-driven income approach presented in the next section.

Three foundational issues are noted. First, the derivation is based on the assumption that the taxpayer is an individual. This means there is no corporate tax or other tax on entities. Personal circumstances such as marital status, dependents, and similar characteristics are not considered. Second, the hypothetical taxpayer is legally subject to tax in the jurisdiction. Thus, there is a presumption that the individual is a resident, a citizen, or otherwise obligated to report comprehensive income in the jurisdiction. Third, for current purposes income has no geographical source. That is, the taxing jurisdiction imposes income tax on a worldwide basis. Each of these issues must be addressed in a tax law. Application may vary, so the items are noted in Table 3.2.

3.2.1 Haig-Simons Income

Simons defined personal income as: 'the algebraic sum of (1) the market value of rights exercised in consumption and (2) the change in the value of the store of

what is derived here as developed in Conrad and Alexeev (2021). Note will be made of the observational and administrative difficulties from this omission as we proceed.

Table 3.2 Policy and administrative issues

    I. Foundational
        a. Who is the taxpayer?
            i. Residence
            ii. Filing Unit
        b. Jurisdictional basis
   II. Income from human capital
        a. Definition and tax treatment of employee and employee compensation
            i. Wages and salaries
            ii. Fringe benefits
                1. Measuring the value of a fringe benefit
                2. Attributing the value of fringe benefits to individual employees
            iii. Pension contributions (deferred compensation) and distributions
                1. Tax treatment (consumption relative to income taxation)
                2. Types of consumption tax treatment
        b. Definition and tax treatment of nonemployee compensation for the supply of labour services
            i. Small business
            ii. Labour services supplied by sole proprietorships partnerships and legal entities
  III. Types of nonhuman capital income and tax treatment of particular items
        a. Interest
        b. Income to equity
            i. Corporate income
                1. Dividends
                2. Retained earnings
            ii. Income from noncorporate activity
            iii. Capital gains
        c. Rents
        d. Royalties
  IV. Treatment of subsidies
   V. Exemptions from gross income
 VI. Definitions and administration of deductions
VII. Other Issues
        a. Real Income taxation and changes in the price level
        b. Where income accrues
        c. Treatment of personal circumstances
        d. Timing

---

property rights' (Simons (1938)).[3] This is known as the uses of income measure and can be stated as:

$$I_{HS} = \text{Consumption} + \text{Change in Net Worth} = \text{Consumption} + \text{Net Saving}.$$

Note that this definition is identical in form to income measures used in business accounting. That is:

$$\text{Business income} = \text{Net Cash Flow to the Business} + \text{Change in Net Worth.}[4]$$

---

[3] Simons (1938): 49.

[4] Economic profit (or rent) is then defined as net cash flow plus the present value of the change in net worth. This measure includes the value of time as a productive input. That is, cash flow is measured during

Individual income may also be measured by reporting the sources of net income. A business income statement is an example of the sources of income and taxable income is generally computed by reference to the sources of income. A business will have income from supplying goods and services from which ordinary and necessary expenses are deducted to measure net income. For individuals there are two general sources of income: income from labour (human capital) and income from nonhuman capital. Several subcategories might be more commonly known as discussed below. The sources of income must equal the uses of income, at least ex ante, so:

I_{HS} = Returns to Labour + Returns to Nonhuman Capital = Consumption + Change in Net Worth.

Two important assumptions about Haig-Simons are noted. First, all values are measured on an accrual and accretion basis. This means that assets are valued at the current market value regardless of whether observable trade takes place. This point is important for computing the change in net worth on the uses side of income and items such as depreciation on the sources side of income. To illustrate, suppose the taxpayer owns shares in an enterprise and the value at the beginning of the period is 100. Suppose further that the value at the end of the period is 125. The change in net worth is 25 regardless of whether the taxpayer sells the shares at the end of the period.

Second, income is a flow between two discrete points in time. Thus, there is an issue about when the flow is measured. Options include the beginning of the time period (a prospective valuation) and the end of the time period (a retrospective evaluation). A prospective valuation implies that consumption, labour supply, and other actions are planned so that income is an estimate. A retrospective valuation (ex post) is a report of the results that accrued during the period. From an economic perspective, the valuation dates would be immaterial if perfect certainty is assumed because what is planned is realized. That is, there would be no difference between the ex-ante and ex-post income measures. Uncertainty, however, will cause the ex-ante and ex-post measures to differ. Uncertainty is an important element of policy discussions and as a practical matter, so we adopt an ex-post perspective. Thus, the HS concept measures the income that results from both actions and random events.

3.2.2 Gross Income

Gross income includes amounts, paid or accrued, in cash or in kind, from all assets in which the individual has a beneficial interest. Gross income in Table 3.1 includes types of income commonly defined either in law or via tax administrative regulations. Note that gross payments to an individual accrue from the ownership of human and

the period, and the change in net worth is the change in the value of assets less liabilities between the end and the beginning of the time period. Thus, either the ending valuation or the beginning valuation (the future value) must be adjusted to account for the passage of time. Note also that net cash flow mixes both sources and uses of funds.

nonhuman capital for reasons discussed below. Enumeration by type of income will facilitate how advanced payments can be used.

3.2.2.1 Returns to Owners of Human Capital

In general, gross income includes all compensation received by an individual in return for the supply of labour used as an input in the production of goods and services.[5] Compensation can be in a number of forms.

a. Income from Employment

Income from employment immediately implies a separation of two types of gross compensation for labour services: payments to employees, however defined, and payments for labour services who are not employees. The difference in classification may not depend on the type of labour supplied but will certainly depend on the definition of employment. For example, an individual might supply labour services in the construction industry under a formal long-term contract and be either a 'contractor' or an 'employee' depending on the contractual terms relative to the definition of employee. The nature of the labour services is identical regardless of classification, but practical differences between employee and nonemployee compensation might arise if the payer is required, as a matter of tax administration, to withhold an advanced tax on employees. Note here that the issue is not with the definition of gross income but whether some administrative accommodation is required. Thus, the definition of employee may determine whether the payer is required to withhold advanced tax on behalf of the recipient. Much then depends on the definition of employee, the information available to the tax administration about individuals supplying labour services, and the administration's ability to monitor transactions. For example, there is the incentive for individuals and potential employers to collude. That is, individuals might be paid in cash on a tax-inclusive basis, but the tax administration may have little means to identify the individual. Those who collude would then be able to share the government's lost tax revenue. Thus, the definition of employee may be important depending on the nature of the withholding system, if any, on both income from employment and compensation received by individuals who are not employed.[6]

Income from employment may be further classified, and defined in some manner, into different categories.

---

[5] Labour supply might be used as an input in the production of either market or nonmarket goods and services. The supply of cleaning services, domestic services, or gardening services may be supplied by or to individuals. Taxable income is restricted to supplies that are potentially observable. Thus, the supply of labour to nonmarket activities is restricted to supplies by nonrelated parties and is a substitute for their own time in the production of nonmarket services. There might be payments between two members of the same household. For example, a parent may compensate children for the supply of certain services. The issue of whether the tax is an individual tax or a joint tax (including family members) where intrahousehold payments cancel out is a question of the taxpaying unit and is discussed below.

[6] The definition may also be important when withholding agents are required to withhold social taxes, such as unemployment insurance, state pensions, and social insurance on those defined to be employees. This issue is described below.

i. Wages and Salaries. Wages and salaries might be defined as any compensation paid or accrued by an employer to the employee that accrues on a tax-inclusive periodic basis. Common examples include payments accruing to employees on a periodic basis (weekly, daily, or monthly).

How wages and salaries are defined, as well as their amounts, might be affected by policies other than tax. There might be minimum wage laws; employee health and safety rules; pension rules (see below); legally required paid days off; maternity leave or leave for military service, where the individual is guaranteed their position after the stipulated period is completed; required days off (either paid or not) for national holidays; paid vacation; and other forms of government regulation of the labour markets.[7] These policies may affect whether the employer and the employee mutually agree to enter a contract, either explicit or implicit. For example, a minimum wage law combined with a mandatory contribution to a state pension might create an incentive for an individual to supply labour as an independent contractor rather than as an employee if the opportunity cost of labour supply is lower than the minimum wage plus the cost of the pension contribution. The importance of interactions between definitions and other legislative policies with the incentives created by taxation can be important in determining the employment status of any individual.

ii. Other Cash Payments from Employment. These payments include, but are not limited to bonuses, awards, other payments in excess of basic wages and salaries, and reimbursement of employee expenses related to employment. All compensation should be included in the gross income of the individual. So, the full value of such benefits and compensation are included as income in Table 3.1.

iii. Fringe Benefits. Fringe benefits have become a component of compensation packages throughout the world, particularly for highly compensated employees. Some fringe benefits might be legally mandated, such as contributions to state pensions. Employer contributions to private pensions may also be part of a package.[8] Other benefits include employer-provided medical care, medical insurance, subsidized (or free) meals, housing, living allowances,[9] transportation (perhaps for personal use), and educational benefits for children.

Such compensation can be classified into two groups. First, there are benefits provided by the employer that might otherwise have to be paid by the employee as a necessary condition for performance. Examples include employer-provided transportation to job sites, the cost of temporary food and housing while working away from home, the cost of tools supplied by the employer, and similar benefits.

---

[7] There may be stipulations via contract in the case of contracts between government and private sector entities. Examples include the requirement to pay the prevailing union wage (the Davis-Bacon Act in the United States) and stipulations in mineral contracts. Such stipulations include but are not limited to minimum numbers of domestic residents to be employed, training requirements, and mandated wages.

[8] In the case of nonnational employees resident in a country, the contribution to pensions and other benefits, such as education, may occur offshore.

[9] Allowances may include provision of servants and security.

Other benefits might be a substitute for an individual's use of wages and salaries, such as health insurance, educational benefits for family members, employer-provided automobiles for personal use, and reimbursed travel expenses for personal reasons (vacations for instance). Finally, some benefits may be available to all employees (contributions to state pensions) or restricted to some employees (use of the executive dining room). Some benefits available to all may be optional (health insurance) with the cost being significantly less than the price of individual purchase. These reduced costs may be due to either subsidy or to the ability of the employee to benefit from being part of a large insurance pool. Other examples of fringe benefits include free parking, life insurance provided by employers,[10] and employer-provided low-interest loans.

Taxation of fringe benefits raises a number of issues. First, it might be difficult to value certain in-kind benefits because the provider of the benefit does not purchase the benefit from a third party. For example, the provider might own housing and provide that housing to management rent free.[11] There may be a difference between the cost of provision, which may be deducted in deriving income to the employer, and the willingness to pay, or at least the market value of the supply to the recipient. This difficulty may also be relevant when the employer provides goods or services that are purchased from independent third parties. Examples include provision of benefits from certain large insurance pools.

Second, some benefits are provided to groups via pooling arrangements, and it might be difficult to attribute the benefit accruing to some individuals. For example, employers may provide cafeteria lunches at subsidized prices, but there may not be records of which individuals take advantage of the benefit and to what extent. Similar examples include access to employee discounts and provision of noncash benefits to family members.

Third, it might be argued that some benefits should be tax free. Some benefits (pooled health insurance) may be deemed socially desirable so the benefit might be excluded from gross income of the individual.[12] Also, the value of the benefit might be deducted in deriving individual income. For example, health insurance might be deducted at the individual level. Thus, exempting the benefit from taxation at the individual level may be equivalent to attributing the value of the benefit to the individual and then allowing the individual to take the deduction if the supplier of the benefit and the recipient are in the same marginal tax bracket. There could also be a net incentive to provide the benefit via exemption even when the benefit's value is deducted from individual income. This is a practical case where some individuals

---

[10] There is also 'key person' insurance that is not a fringe benefit in the sense that the entity is purchasing insurance in case of the death (or loss) of individuals important to the enterprise. This may be an ordinary and necessary cost of accruing income to the enterprise.

[11] In this case, the provider should not be able to deduct either the purchase of the house or the annual depreciation (depending on the depreciation rules in force). The tax revenue consequences of this type of transaction may be nil. The provider forgoes taxable rental revenue and does not get a deduction for expenses, while the individual does not pay tax on the benefit.

[12] The value of the benefit might still be deducted in computing net income of the entity for tax purposes where the tax is imposed either on the entity or included in the gross income of the owner.

do not take deductions either because of the presence of a standard deduction or because taxable income is too low for a positive tax to exist.[13]

b. Deferred Compensation (Pension Income)

Retirement compensation is a type of deferred compensation. The individual for-goes cash compensation at the time the contribution accrues in exchange for such compensation at a later date. If perfect certainty and competition are assumed, then the present value of future consumption is equal to the value of the foregone consumption at the time of the benefit.

Generally, a distribution from a pension contains both the return to invested cap-ital and the accrued gain or loss from the inside buildup during the holding period. This point, however, is simply a statement about any distribution from any finan-cial investment. For example, an individual may make investments in bank deposits or corporate equities and hold the investment for several years while reinvesting the earnings. The individual might make withdrawals years later, with the payment con-sisting of both the initial investment and accumulated interest. Accordingly, what distinguishes a pension payment, as deferred compensation, from otherwise normal savings will depend on the definitions. The definition cannot depend on whether the employer provides the opportunity for deferred compensation because the employer may offer employees convenient savings accounts and options for equity participa-tion in addition to pensions. Generally, the definition of a pension might include some minimum restriction on age in the sense that pension distributions cannot begin before a certain age.

Note is made here of the important point that whether the total savings of the indi-vidual beneficiary increases because they participate in a pension scheme depends on how the beneficiary treats the contributions (and distributions) given their wealth. For example, it is possible that the beneficiary treats the pension as a perfect substi-tute for their private savings, other things equal. Thus, if the employee is offered, or required, to participate in a pension scheme, then the value of every contribution to the pension can result in a decrease in their private individual savings of other types.[14]

Second, how the individual values the deferred compensation may depend on whether participation in a pension is voluntary or mandatory. If participation is vol-untary, then the value of the contribution (either by the employee or the employer) is worth at least as much as the present value of the future benefit adjusted for risk. If contributions have no maximum per time period, then the individual will be able to set the marginal cost of the contribution equal to the risk-adjusted present value of the marginal benefit. If there is a maximum contribution, a common feature of some pension schemes, then the present value, again adjusted for risk, of the marginal

---

[13] We do not support this approach for reasons discussed below.
[14] One important example of such a possibility is Feldstein (Feldstein, 1974). Feldstein provides empir-ical evidence for the perfect substitute hypothesis for, at least, the US Social Security System. Given the pay-as-you-go nature of the system, Feldstein argued that the US capital stock was correspondingly lower as a result. These results generated much new research, some of which calls the perfect substitute hypothesis into question. For one example, see (Leimer & Lesnoy, 1982).

benefit to the employee might exceed the marginal cost of the contribution.[15] If there is a minimum contribution and individuals are required to participate, then pension contributions are forced savings and the marginal value of the benefit might be too small relative to other uses of income.[16] If competition prevails and capital markets are efficient, then the individual affected in this manner may be able to dissave by increasing debt that can be financed by the returns to the excess pension contribution.

Some governments have developed pension rules regardless of taxation, in addition to rules for government-funded pensions for their employees.[17] Governments may allow one of two types of pensions, or both. A defined benefit pension provides an annuity during retirement in exchange for contributions during working years. The amount of the annuity may be based on wages and salaries during working years, so the contributions are based on the value of the annuity combined with a projected return on the accumulated balance. A periodic (usually a year) specific amount accrues in a defined contribution pension plan. A defined contribution pension plan is the second type of pension. An amount, or proportion, of stipulated returns to human capital is determined during the indivdiual's working life, and may be subject to an annual maximum. The amount at retirement may be either converted into an annuity or withdrawn by the individual as a series of periodic payments, perhaps stipulated by law. If nonannuitized withdrawals are chosen, then any remaining value of the defined contribution plan is part of the individual's estate. Regulations may affect the type of pension and how it is funded. For example, employers who offer defined benefit plans may accrue, but not fully fund, the stipulated periodic contributions. Thus, there is the risk that the pension, which is a form of compensation, may not be paid either in whole or in part because of bankruptcy and other situations. Also, the employer may at their discretion be the trustee of the pension funds, if legislation allows. This may create a situation where the pension funds become a source for the employer's capital investment, placing the employer in a potential conflict of interest. Such situations may be addressed by requiring independent trustees to make portfolio decisions and making employer contributions cash contributions, as opposed to accruals.

---

[15] It might be the case that a maximum contribution constraint is not relevant to the extent the contribution to programmes defined as pensions are perfect substitutes for other forms of saving. If the portfolio held by the pension differs from the portfolio desired by the individual, then it might be possible for the individual owner to adjust their personal optimal portfolio by changing the asset composition of the portfolio over which she or he has control. It is important to note that social security systems may have income distributional aspects in the sense that the risk-adjusted expected value of the contribution to one group (generally lower income) is higher than the return to another group (generally higher income) because there is a transfer component built into the system.

[16] There may be an externality in the sense that some members of society obtain a benefit from knowing that those who save too little may have a minimum level of consumption at retirement.

[17] Such legislation may be part of the overall financial legislation that addresses agency and funding issues such as: deposit insurance for individual bank deposits in cases where banks become bankrupt; and regulation of insurance systems and other types of financial instruments by which an individual contributes to or pays for a future good or service that becomes payable either at the individual's discretion, in the case of bank withdrawals or stock sales, or upon the realization of certain events, for example the payment of life insurance benefits to heirs upon an individual's death.

c. Income from the Supply of Labour Services Unrelated to Employment

The terms and definitions of labour supplied to the market in forms other than employment vary from casual unskilled day labour paid in cash to highly skilled professional services of lawyers, doctors, accountants, architects, and other professionals operating as individuals or via entities such as partnerships and corporations owned by the service supplier. The economic substance of the labour supply might be invariant, however, to whether the individual supplier of labour services is an employee as well as to organizational form, but taxes may vary.

The net income from sole proprietorships may be conceived, correctly in our view, as net income because the proprietor is engaged in a business activity and incurs ordinary and necessary business expenses. This means that taxable income should be composed of gross revenues less costs. There may be policy concerns, however, because some sole proprietorships may not have the wherewithal to compute gross and net income on an accrual basis. In addition, some sole proprietorships may be small, according to some definitions, and there may be an issue of the tax treatment of sole proprietorships as small businesses separately from the individual owner. If so, there may be an issue about the separate accounting of small business income of a sole proprietorship. This arises because sole proprietorships may have sources of income other than from the proprietorship. The individual may use capital goods, or the individual could be both an employee for some activities and own a sole proprietorship for other activities. For instance, a government employee (or an employee of any private sector business) may operate a repair service outside of time spent being an employee. Again, the practical question is whether attributing certain revenues and costs of the sole proprietorship to the individual, in general, has any practical effect.

The tax on labour supply could also be affected by the organizational form used by the individual who is not an employee, particularly when there is a separate tax on entities. The potential complexity of imposing tax on the return to human capital is illustrated by the following example. Suppose an individual is an expert in computer repairs and enters a long-term relationship with a large enterprise. The enterprise has several locations and the individual travels between the various locations to service the computers. Assume the returns to human capital for the period are 10,000 and the costs related to travel, including depreciation of a vehicle, depreciation of capital equipment that is combined with labour to complete the repairs, and variable costs are 3000. If comprehensive income concepts are applied, then the individual should be taxed on the 10,000 net return to human capital independently of how the long-term relationship is structured and how the compensation occurs. For example, if the individual is an employee, then on a tax-inclusive basis the individual could be paid 9100 in cash wages and accrue 900 in pension benefits, with the enterprise bearing the costs of transportation and materials. Alternatively, the enterprise could compensate the individual 12,100 in cash and 900 in a pension contribution while requiring the individual to bear all costs related to the provision of the services.

If, however, the individual is a sole proprietor, then the individual could charge the enterprise 13,000 while incurring and deducting all costs. Finally, the individual could create an entity and the entity could enter a long-term relationship with the enterprise. In this case, the entity would charge the enterprise 13,000, take deductions of 3000, and leave a profit of 10,000. Whether the profit is a return to labour or corporate income is a matter of form as opposed to substance. From an economic perspective, the individual accrues 10,000 with the gross value of the services totalling 13,000. Who pays for the cost may simply depend on the nature of the long-term relationship. It could be the case, however, that the tax on labour income could be different depending on the rules. For example, if the individual is an employee and pensions are tax deferred, but employee expenses are not deducted from the individual's return, then the tax base would be 9100 if the employer provides for all related costs or 12,100 if the individual bears the cost. If the individual is a sole proprietor, then the sole proprietor's income would be 10,000 if all 3000 in costs are deducted. If the individual owns a corporation, then the tax base could be 10,000, but the rates could be different if the 10,000 is defined as corporate profit rather than returns to human capital. There are other options.[18] We attempt to address the economic substance in a collection-driven framework so that to the extent possible the individual is taxed on 10,000.

3.2.2.2 Returns to Owners of Nonhuman Capital
Nonhuman capital assets are generally classified into four groups: real property, intangible property, tangible property, and financial assets (see Box 3.1).[19]

Box 3.1 Nonhuman capital assets

Type of nonhuman capital	Gross income associated with type of nonhuman capital
Real property (Land, buildings, mineral deposits)	• Rent (or lease payments) • Mineral royalties • Accrued capital gains and losses from changes in relative asset prices
Intangible property (Patents, copyrights, trade secrets)	• Royalties • Accrued gains and losses from changes in relative asset prices
Tangible property (Machinery and equipment)	• Lease and rental payments • Accrued gains and losses from changes in relative asset prices
Financial assets (Cash, bonds, corporate shares)	• Interest, dividends, profits • Accrued gains and losses from changes in relative asset prices

[18] For example, the individual could be an employee and be paid 8000 in cash and given an interest-free loan of 20,000. If the market interest rate is 10%, then the value of the interest-free loan would be 2000, other things equal. Thus, if interest accrued to individuals is exempt, then 2000 might escape tax.

[19] There are also natural assets such as the atmosphere that have no legal owners and social capital such as language and customs. These assets should accrue economic returns, but the factors are not privately owned. A discussion of these returns is beyond our scope.

Individuals are owners of these primary factors and the returns to ownership are part of income regardless of name and including accrued gains and losses from a change in the relative price of the asset owned. Individuals may use organizational conduits to accrue this income including sole proprietorships, partnerships and corporations, among other structures. These conduits may hold a variety of assets. For instance, a corporation may hold land, buildings, equipment, and intangible assets that are combined with labour to produce goods and services. Such entities are only conduits, however, because all returns accrue to the individual owner(s).

It may be important to distinguish the repayment of capital from income. For instance, a payment on a bank loan may include an interest payment and a principal payment. Only interest should be included in income. The principal payment represents a reduction in the lender's loan balance. An identical result holds for all capital items. For instance, tangible property, mineral deposits, and intangible assets may lose value via depreciation, depletion, and amortization, respectively. Thus, the gross income should include both a return to owning the asset and a payment to reflect its lost value from use.[20]

Note that the value of every return to nonhuman capital should be measured on an accrual and accretion basis for comprehensive income tax purposes. For example, if the corporation declares a dividend in December payable in January, then the income would be attributed to December for a calendar year taxpayer. The same would be true of interest.[21] There are administrative issues with respect to accrued capital gains and losses because the determination of the market value, or any independent value, may be impossible for assets that are not actively traded on markets. For example, mineral deposits and other real property may not be actively traded, making valuation based on methods other than arm's-length trade difficult, if not impossible.

Another issue is that what is interest and what is a dividend is sometimes difficult to determine. One example is the treatment of preferred stock. Such differences would not matter for tax purposes if all income regardless of name is taxed at the same marginal rate. Another example is a lease payment, a financial lease in particular, where the lessor receives a series of periodic payments with title to the asset being transferred to the lessee at the end of the term. Note the identical treatment of

---

[20] The same is true for the definition of dividends. A stockholder may accrue a payment in proportion to their equity ownership in a corporation. It is necessary for the recipient (and payor) to know what part, if any, of the payment represents income from the business, a dividend, as opposed to a reduction in the owner's capital investment. It could be the case that the corporation is partially liquidating in the sense that the investor is being paid a partial return of their capital investment instead of the income. If mark-to-market valuation is not used for corporate accounting, then there are atleast two ways to define a dividend. The traditional approach is to define a dividend as a distribution from accumulated profit. Thus, if accumulated profits are less than the amount of the distribution, then the corporation is partially liquidating in the sense that the book value to capital contributions (as opposed to accumulated earnings) is being reduced. The alternative is to define a dividend as any distribution in proportion to an equity interest except a distribution in complete liquidation of the corporation. Over time, the total value of the distributions might be the same, but what is defined as a dividend (on income to the shareholder) as opposed to basis adjustments via partial liquidations will be different at different points in time.

[21] Interest may accrue but not be paid. Instead, the interest could be capitalized into the loan balance. The capitalized interest is still accrued in the period of accrual and the basis of the loan is adjusted accordingly.

a financial lease with an individual who purchases an asset, uses the asset as collateral to obtain a bank loan for the value of the purchase, and then repays the loan via a set of periodic payments that include both interest and principal. There may be no formal separation of interest from principal repayments in a financial lease, however. Thus, there might be an administrative issue of determining the interest cost each period in order to measure the periodic income relative to the amortization.[22]

An additional administrative issue is whether the basis for any asset should be adjusted for inflation. For example, if the initial basis of an asset is 100 and inflation is 20% per annum, then the market value of the asset would be 120 at the end of the year even if there is no change in relative prices. Thus, a capital gain would be computed to be equal to 20 (120–100) instead of a real gain of 0 (or 120—(100*1.2)) if there is no adjustment for the nominal price level.

3.2.2.3 Benefits from Government Programmes
Government transfer programme payments or subsidies represent gross income for individuals. From an economic perspective, any resource transfer, earned or unearned, that increases individual purchasing power should be included in comprehensive income of the individual recipient.[23] Cash subsidies and other types of income support are examples. Subsidies that change the relative price of some goods and services such as food, education, medical care, and electricity, among others, also increase individual real incomes, other things equal. It might be argued that some programmes are designed to redistribute income. Income distribution, however, should be measured relative to gross and net of tax comprehensive income of which transfers are a part. There may be difficulty in attributing the benefits of government programmes to individuals. Like certain fringe benefits, valuation might be difficult. For example, determining the amount that each individual accrues from gasoline subsidies to be included in taxable income may be difficult.

3.2.2.4 Other Transfers
Transfers (such as income support) are made by organizations, such as NGOs, to individuals. Like government transfers, these transfers increase the consumption potential of the beneficiary and are part of comprehensive income. Also, transfers between individuals who are related parties may not change the wealth of the aggregate group. For example, a parent who gives their dependent child a financial gift does not change the family's net worth. The child's wealth has increased, however, when viewed as an individual and thus should be included as income.[24] There are

---

[22] Tax depreciation might be used to determine the separation between interest and principal for a financial lease. See Chapter 6.

[23] The opposite might be true as well. That is, taxes, such as indirect taxes, reduce purchasing power and thus represent a reduction in income.

[24] Whether the gift is deductible to the parent is a separate issue. It is true that the transfer can be considered a capital transfer that reduces the purchasing power of the parent, when the parent is viewed as an individual. The issue is whether the gift is consumption for the parent in the same sense that a gift to a nonprofit entity is consumption for the giver. Such gifts are defined to be consumption, at least in our

methodological issues with this conclusion, however because there is no difference, in terms of wealth transfer, between a financial transfer and providing benefits such as when the parent pays for the child's college education.

3.2.3 Exemptions from Gross Income

Exemptions from gross income can arise for at least four reasons. First, some gross income is not observable and thus is omitted from income. Farm production used to produce meals by a farmer is one common example. Other types of exemptions, while potentially observable, may be computationally difficult such as subsidies and other transfers.

Second, some types of gross income can be exempted by legislation. As a matter of tax policy, these exemptions should not be allowed from a comprehensive income tax base. There are two types of legislative exemptions: gross income that is permanently exempt and income that is exempt during the current tax period but that might be included in income at some point in the future. The former includes incentives such as interest exemptions on government bonds and post office savings accounts, capital gains, gifts, certain types of returns to labour such as honoraria, some fringe benefits, and employer contributions to medical insurance. In addition, there are tax holidays and investment incentives that flow through to the individual owners. The latter exemption type includes gains that are deferred because they are taxed on a realization basis, such as capital gains, and contributions to certain types of pension funds.[25]

Third, foreign source income might be exempt if source-based taxation is adopted. Finally, there may be mistakes and omissions in either the tax law or administration. For example, if an income tax law contains an explicit list of taxable income with the implication that items not listed are exempted, then items such as the inside buildup of whole life insurance policies could be exempt by omission.[26] It might not be clear

view, in the sense that the giver is no worse off than she would be if she used the funds to purchase consumption goods and services. That is, there is a significant difference between selfishness as commonly defined and economic self-interest in the sense that a gift to a charity is the result of economic self-interest.
    [25] There are items such as a personal exemption that may be a proportion of income, but such exemptions may be with respect to net, not gross, income. That said, if a schedular system combined with withholding is used, then an exemption from withholding tax on wages can be equivalent to an exemption on a particular type of gross income.
    [26] Such methods can be used to reduce taxes even in emerging economies. An individual who owns an entity and supplies services via that entity can purchase a single premium whole life insurance policy and take the deduction for the payment. At some point in the future, the insurance can be redeemed for cash value and the income, if not more, can escape tax. We are aware that this scheme was used in the Dominican Republic, among other places. For example, suppose the entity pays 1000 in t = 1 and gets a deduction, so the net-of-tax cost of the policy is 700 if the marginal tax rate is 30%. Then, if the inside buildup rate is 5%, the cash value of the policy in t = 2 would be equal to 1050. The entity could cash in the policy and receive 1050. At a minimum, the 50 should be subject to tax and whether the 1000 escapes tax depends on whether there is recapture of the earlier deduction. It is common for the inside buildup to be exempt if the benefit is used to pay premiums on whole life insurance policies.

whether such omissions are mistakes or explicit decisions depending on how the statute and administrative rules were drafted.[27]

3.2.4 Expenses of Earning Income

Ordinary and necessary expenses incurred to accrue market income reduce measured gross income in order to derive net income that is subject to tax. Some expenses are not observable and thus cannot be deducted. For example, time spent at home preparing for market work cannot be deducted, even though such time is an input into the production of market income, and a construction worker who supplies their own tools may spend time at home repairing and maintaining their tools.

Observable expenses can be classified into two categories.

3.2.4.1 Expenses Directly Related to the Accrual of Market Income

All ordinary and necessary expenditures directly related to obtaining gross income should be deducted in deriving net income. The expense is deducted regardless of how the taxpayer accrues the income. For example, a particular type of paper used for pleadings is a legal cost that is deductible by an entity if a lawyer is an employee, by the lawyer if the lawyer is a sole proprietor, or by the partnership if the lawyer is a partner. Other examples include transportation costs to work and special clothing. Expenses directly related to the accrual of nonhuman capital income include costs associated with the acquisition and maintenance of the portfolio, including brokerage fees, other transaction costs, reporting, and oversight. Direct expenses also include depreciation, depletion, and amortization of capital assets (such as machinery) used in the production of income.

Administrative issues include measurement of depreciation, depletion and amortization. There are also problems determining costs for sole proprietorships or closely held entities. Basic accounting is one issue. Small business owners may not be familiar with accrual accounting concepts and record keeping may be poor, at least initially. In addition, there may be mixed-use assets. For example, a sole proprietor who owns a retail shop may own (or rent) a building that is part living space and part store. A tailor may produce clothing from home using space, a sewing machine used to produce clothing for sale and for the household, electricity, and other variable inputs.

3.2.4.2 Indirect and Overhead Expenses

These expenses include insurance of various kinds (health, life, and accident (including fire)), interest costs, depreciation of some capital assets, medical expenditures, indirect taxes, and property taxes.

---

[27] Omitted income might include sales in black or grey markets and gross income from criminal activity. For example, an individual may sell illegal drugs on a black market. Such behaviour may be both illegal because of the criminal code and a form of tax avoidance and evasion. Such income is not exempt, however, but should be taxable.

Insurance is a method of sharing risks. The individual pays a premium to be reimbursed the cost of losses associated with risky events if those events occur. Insurance cost is the purchase of an uncertain future claim that is negatively correlated with the value of the insured asset. For example, if an individual purchases accident insurance and there is no accident, then the value of the insured property is preserved and the value of the insurance claim is zero. If, however, there is an accident, then the value of insured property is reduced but the value of the insurance claim is the value of the insurance benefit.[28]

It might be possible to compute the change in net worth from insurance purchases even if the market value of an insured asset is not known. For instance, the market value of a house might not be known if there is no trade. Suppose there is no fire insurance. Then the change in net worth would be equal to V1—V0 if there is no fire, with V0 and V1 being the unknown market value of the house in t = 0 and 1 if there is no fire. If there is a fire and the ending value of the house is equal to Z1, then the change in net worth would be Z1—V1 at the end of the period. If the homeowner purchases fire insurance, then the change in net worth if there is no fire is: V1—V0—Premium and the value if there is a fire is: Z1—V0—Premium + Compensation. The implication is that the insurance premium will be deducted from net income and the net compensation would be included in HS market income if there is a fire because both are observable measures of gains and costs. Accordingly, it is reasonable to deduct the insurance premium because it reduces net worth and to include the value of the benefit, if the adverse event occurs, in taxable income. The same logic applies to uninsured losses, a type of self-insurance,[29] as well as to all types of insurance. The change in net worth attributable to insurance, ex post, would be an allowance for a deduction of the premium and an inclusion of the net benefits. In effect, insurance is equivalent to hedging.

Interest expenses reduce net income because, by definition, net income is a measure of the change in net worth that is equal to the change in the value of total assets less the change in the value of total debt. Accordingly, interest expenses are the cost of carrying debt.

Health care expenditures from the perspective of HS full income as defined by Conrad and Alexeev (2021) are the cost of maintenance and repairs for human capital. There may be attribution, measurement, and administrative issues for health insurance and related expenses. Consistent with the comprehensive income concept, such expenses are made to maintain or to finance assets that may be used exclusively in the household to produce consumption goods and services and have no liquidation value (e.g., a bed). In addition, some assets are held for both investment and production of household consumption, such as owner-occupied housing. Thus, there

---

[28] This is just like an individual who buys an equity position in a firm and then takes a short position in a derivative to hedge the variability of the asset. It is the net return to the total portfolio that matters as opposed to the returns on an asset basis.

[29] The deduction of uninsured losses, including the loss in excess of insurance claims, is consistent with the taxation of the gains because the value of any asset is not known. Deduction of such losses is consistent with the risk sharing property of the income tax more generally. See Conrad and Alexeev (2021).

may be an issue about whether expenses attributable to household production should be deducted, or what proportion should be deducted, because income produced in the household is exempt from tax.

Taxable income is equal to gross revenue less expenses. There are two policy and administrative issues that might result in a difference between comprehensive and taxable income. First, the cost of maintaining records and the compliance costs associated with expenses can be significant. A standard deduction might be introduced in order to address the issue. In some cases, the taxpayer is given the option to take the standard deduction or to report all expenses. The taxpayer will take the standard deduction if either the value of the standard deduction is greater than the value of deductions or the compliance costs of deriving total expenses plus the value of the standard deduction is greater than the value of the deductions. Finally, there may be a deduction related to personal circumstances. For instance, an individual may be allowed a deduction of a fixed amount for herself and a spouse plus additional deductions for dependents such as children. There are alternatives to such deductions, including tax credits and zero bracket amounts, which raise policy and administrative questions about the most efficient method to employ.

3.2.5 Taxable Income, Tax Accrued, Credits, and Net Tax Payable

Tax is equal to the applicable tax rates multiplied by tranches of income, in the case of a multiple-rate structures. Policy issues, therefore, include the determination of the rate structure and how negative taxable income is treated.

At least three types of credits might be applied against the tax. First, advanced payments could have been either paid by the taxpayer or withheld by the person compensating the taxpayer. Advanced payments could be paid on wages, interest, dividends, capital gains, and other types of income from capital. The extent of required advanced payments and amounts credited, including the foreign tax credit, are issues to be determined. There is also an issue about whether advanced payments are the final tax and relieve the individual from reporting some, or all, of their comprehensive income.

Second, it was noted above that credits might be applied as an alternative to personal exemptions or zero bracket amounts. Third, credits may be offered as an incentive. For example, investment tax credits might be used to encourage particular investments and such incentives may apply to the particular investments regardless of entity or proprietorship status. The base upon which the credit is measured (for example, an investment tax credit may be a proportion of defined investment costs) and the treatment of excess credits (refunding or carrying forward for example) are among the issues that need to be addressed.

Finally, tax payable is the last computation and is equal to the total tax liability less applicable credits. After-tax income is then equal to comprehensive income, not taxable income, less tax paid. The difference between taxable income and comprehensive income can be used to measure tax expenditures or excess taxes. That is, comprehensive income, or its estimate, is the basis for determining the size of incentives or disincentives in the tax system.

3.3 A Collection-Based Income Tax that Can Be Administered

The complexities described above, and others, are one basis for the claim that income taxation is difficult to understand, is subject to abuse, and is difficult to adminis-ter. We believe an empirical approximation to Haig-Simons (HS) income restricted to market transactions called Comprehensive Market-Determined Income (Conrad and Alexeev, 2021), can be measured and is administratively feasible. The remainder of this chapter contains one method to simplify the system and to enhance com-pliance. The structure of the income tax is described given the structure of APAs developed in Chapter 2.

The proposal is presented as an objective to be achieved. That is, the proposal is made without regard for administrative setting except for the incorporation of APAs discussed in Chapter 2. Adaption will depend on the institutional and economic con-ditions in a country. We believe it is necessary to understand the desired structure for at least two reasons. First, analysts need a framework in which to develop spe-cific policies. Knowledge of both the current situation and the ultimate objective will enable policy to evolve in a more consistent manner. Second, analytical tools can be improved and new tools can be developed by understanding the desired structure. Tools for the measurement of welfare gains and losses, empirical income distribu-tional analysis, tax expenditure measures, and specific studies, such as measures of economic depreciation, are examples.

Section 3.3.4 is devoted to how a collection-driven income tax might evolve. Initial conditions will vary by country. Specific application will depend on the economy's state, the tax administration's development, and the level of public understanding. There is, however, a path for an emerging economy to develop an income tax compat-ible with a standard developed here that is consistent with what we recommend for the most advanced economies. These issues are discussed here, and we recommend some approaches consistent with the use of APAs.[30]

---

[30] Elements of the proposed structure have been part of our recommendations in countries such as Myanmar, Timor-Leste, Nigeria, Ukraine, and other emerging economies. The latter method has been proposed for the United States and other mature economies where computerization is well developed, tax-payers are identifiable, organized markets dominate the economy, capital markets are well developed, and the tax administration can be used to enhance widespread public awareness and education (see Conrad & Alexeev, 2021).

3.3.1 Foundational Issue: Who Is the Taxpayer?

The first basic decision regarding the income tax's structure is: Who is the taxpayer? We propose that the taxpayer be an individual. Three subsets of taxpayers are proposed: resident taxpayers, registered taxpayers, and registered taxpayers who are required to report reconciliations.

3.3.1.1 Basic Definition

The taxpayer is an individual because all income accrues to individuals from an economic perspective. So, the initial definition of the taxpayer is:

$$\text{Taxpayer} = \text{Any individual.}$$

This definition includes any individual in the world and that is the intended result. Two purposes are served by a general definition. First, form follows economic substance. Individuals accrue income directly and indirectly via conduits such as corporations. If a resident or nonresident individual receives gross income from any domestic person, then domestic tax should be withheld because the tax should be imposed regardless of residence. This treatment is independent of the corporate conduits through which the income flows the individual. For example, a domestic subsidiary of a foreign corporation will impose advanced tax on any interest payment. The recipient may be the parent of the domestic subsidiary, but that parent could be owned by a foreign holding company. The foreign holding company may then be owned by individuals, either resident or nonresident in the jurisdiction. The corporate structure is immaterial for domestic taxation purposes because each entity is a flow-through entity and not subject to tax in the taxing jurisdiction.[31] The individual shareholders bear the statutory incidence of the tax, and the definition reflects that fact. Second, as an administrative matter, APAs will remit advanced payments on all returns to human and nonhuman capital accruing to individuals regardless of residence. Defining the taxpayer as any individual ensures uniform application. To emphasize, APAs will collect advanced payments on income regardless of where the individual is located, their citizenship, or their residence.

3.3.1.2 Discussion of Basic Definition

This approach is no different from current practice for particular types of payments from the collection-driven perspective. Some taxing jurisdictions impose border withholding taxes on certain payments. Any nonresident is subject to withholding tax if payments accrue from domestic sources, and the domestic payer withholds on income accrued in the form of dividends, interest, royalties, and services. The nonresident recipient may be either a legal person or an individual. Legal persons are flow-through entities in the proposed framework so that the individual owners are

---

[31] Some entity or entities in the tier structure may be taxpayers in other jurisdictions, but such a determination is based on the tax law of other jurisdictions.

ultimately the persons on whose behalf the withholding tax is charged. Thus, from a collection-driven perspective, all persons in the world are currently subject to tax for such payments by such taxing jurisdictions. The only issue is what income is subject to tax. If there is domestic source income, then any individual is subject to tax. If, however, the person has no domestic source income, then a nonresident individual, while being a taxpayer, simply has zero tax in the jurisdiction in question according to this approach. We propose extending withholding to all income regardless of residence. Thus, residents and nonresidents are treated in a nondiscriminatory manner. If the resident or nonresident accrues no income, then there is no advanced tax withheld.[32]

This point is illustrated by an example. An APA in Country X might collect an advanced payment on interest accrued to Bank Z (or a legal related party) located in Country Y. The fact that Bank Z is an entity is immaterial from the perspective of the income tax imposed in Country X. Bank Z has individual owners, and those owners are the taxpayers. Whether the tax flows through to the individual owners, some of whom may be citizens or residents of Country X, is an issue for the tax laws in Country Y (and perhaps other countries). From the perspective of Country X, the taxpayer is still an individual. Alternatively, suppose the same APA collects an advanced payment on interest accrued to Bank D, an entity that is also an APA in Country X. In this case, the tax will flow through using a method described below, so that it is clear that the taxpayer is an individual.

The taxpayer concept is completely general, but there can be two restrictions on the taxpayer concept that will help clarify the nature and responsibilities of the taxpayer: residence and registration.

a. Resident Taxpayers

A resident concept is needed for at least three reasons. First, some individuals may be APAs and so it is necessary to define the conditions under which the individual will register as an APA. Residence is one condition. Second, the country may require individual reporting of comprehensive income as defined in the law for at least some individuals. The definition of income is not dependent on whether advanced

---

[32] The definition of taxpayer should be independent of whether the individual has a tax liability in the taxing jurisdiction, otherwise domestic citizens and/or residents with zero income who are not subject to tax would not be taxpayers given the proposed structure. There is a difference between resident taxpayers and nonresident taxpayers (those taxpayers who are not resident) in that a resident taxpayer may be obligated to report comprehensive income and pay tax on that measure because there is worldwide taxation on resident taxpayers. Nonresident taxpayers may voluntarily pay tax on a worldwide basis. This can be achieved by the nonresident becoming a resident or choosing to be treated as a resident. But this option is available to all individuals, resident or not. That is, a resident can choose to become a nonresident and file on a voluntary basis. Of course, most nonresident shareholders of publicly held corporations may not know they are taxpayers in the jurisdiction or even that a tax was withheld on their behalf. That result is fine with us. In addition, whether the affected individuals pay more taxes will depend on the treatment of the advanced payment in their resident countries. If there is a foreign tax credit, then their burden may not increase.

payments exist. Such a requirement is restricted to resident taxpayers. Third, world-wide taxation is proposed and practically speaking such taxation might be limited to residents.[33]

We propose a simple, objective residence rule. A resident taxpayer is defined as an individual who is physically present in the taxing jurisdiction for at least 183 days during any consecutive 365-day period. As noted, the test is objective and potentially can be administered. It might be argued that such an objective test is subject to abuse by individuals. In particular, individuals, presumably high income, can limit their physical presence although their homes for all intents and purposes are in the taxing jurisdiction. While true, the issue is the consequence of an individual being a tax resident. If taxes are lower, administration is even handed, and publicly supplied goods and services are provided in an efficient matter, it might be the case that the individual has a net incentive to become a resident for tax purposes.

Finally, it is important to note that this definition and others noted below do not depend on definitions contained in other legislation. For example, the definition of tax resident may, or may not, be related to the definition of resident used in other statutes such as laws on social spending or for employment purposes. It is important for the tax law to be self-contained in the sense that both those making policy and those administering the law are not subject to changes in rules made in other legislation. Such changes may inadvertently, or intentionally, affect the application of tax law (as well as revenue).

b. Registered Taxpayers

Registration of all resident taxpayers is the ultimate objective, but administrative and other considerations may make universal registration impractical. At the initial reform stages, registration might be limited to individuals who are required to report on an annual basis with expansion as administrative advances continue. One expansion scheme is supplied in Section 3.3.4. Where registration is limited to APAs, no taxpayer needs to be registered.[34] This would be the case if taxable income is restricted to only the portion of comprehensive income that is subject to advanced tax. The approach might be possible if territorial taxation is adopted, and there was the administrative capacity to enforce registration of APAs for all payers of gross income in excess of a *de minimis* amount. For instance, defining the tax base as all payments of income accrued to taxpayers by APAs would make the filing of individual returns redundant if there is a flat rate tax.[35] This would mean, however, that

---

[33] Assisting with enforcement includes entering into exchange of information agreements with other countries to share information about the financial activities of respective residents in other countries.

[34] It is important to note that only individuals are taxpayers. Registration procedures for APAs are different. Some countries have developed registration procedures for entities, for the most part. These procedures, sometimes based on IMF recommendations, include limiting registration to VAT taxpayers and others that populate a large taxpayer unit. It seems reasonable to build on these procedures in developing registration procedures and master tax files for APAs.

[35] Individual characteristics could still be addressed by the APA, at least for some classification of taxpayers.

any income accrued to taxpayers (resident or not) from non-APA payers would be explicitly exempt from income taxation.

There are certain benefits to this approach, particularly for emerging economies. Administrative emphasis would be placed on identifying APAs, ensuring their registration, and ensuring compliance with advanced payments. In effect, the administrative emphasis on income taxation would be identical to the emphasis on suppliers of goods and services under a destination-based VAT. The advanced payment is different, but the administrative emphasis would be the same. Thus, the concept of comprehensive audit is applicable because an APA is responsible for ensuring that every payment for the supply of a primary production factor as well as every supply of a taxable good and service under the VAT is on a tax-inclusive basis, with the APA imposing advanced payments on both supplies of goods and services and the payments for productive factors. Initial information reporting would be potentially simplified because individual taxpayers would not have to be identified and there could be little or no reporting about taxes paid on the taxpayer's behalf. For example, a bank could simply report total interest payments and amounts withheld without attributing the tax to any particular account. In addition, compensation for labour services could be simply the aggregate of payments for labour services to individuals (regardless of employment status) without reporting to each individual taxpayer.

Costs of this approach include the incentive for income taxpayers to seek methods of accruing income from sources other than APAs. This incentive would be present in any system with advanced payments, but there could be a significant difference if income payments accruing from payers other than APAs are legal. The parallel situation of buying goods and services from suppliers who are not VAT taxpayers, as taxpayers are defined in most current VAT laws, is noted. For example, suppliers of taxable goods and services might not be required to collect VAT because they are under some turnover level stated in the law.[36] Thus, there is some potential for buyers and sellers to arbitrage the tax.[37] In addition, like the VAT, taxpayers have an incentive to engage in transactions with persons from abroad if the type of territorial system resulting from the definition of that income is taxable if paid or accrued from an APA. In effect, the taxing jurisdiction is inviting domestic taxpayers to accrue income from abroad.[38] This incentive would be appealing to those with access to international capital markets, those with high net worth in particular. Finally, the APA concept would have to extend to almost all individuals in order to reduce incentives for tax arbitrage.

---

[36] See Chapter 4 for a discussion of this and other examples.

[37] The standard response to this claim is that suppliers must pay VAT on inputs and so the amounts to be arbitraged can be small. In addition, if exempt suppliers supply a small fraction of output, then domestic prices will be determined by the interaction between APAs and taxpayers. In this case, there would be an income transfer to the exempt supplier. While true in theory, goods and services are never perfect substitutes, markets are fragmented (rural and urban markets in emerging economies for example), and uncertainty might affect observed prices (and incidence). See Chapter 4.

[38] There is some safeguard with respect to the destination based VAT because imports are subject to tax.

Registration is a necessary but not a sufficient condition for annual reporting, assessments, or reconciliations. Many registered taxpayers will not be required to complete returns in the most advanced form of the collection-driven tax. The approach adopted here is to require certain taxpayers to register based on conditions foreseen in the economy and to modify the registration provision as conditions change. It is important to emphasize that required registration has little meaning unless administrative resources are devoted to both registration and compliance. Thus, the decision to require registration depends on the capabilities of the tax administration to register individuals, to maintain the registration, as well as to monitor enforcement and compliance. During the initial reform stages, taxpayer registration should include:

- Any taxpayer who is a registered APA or owns a small business (see Chapter 5);
- Resident taxpayers not otherwise registered as APAs or small business owners (see Chapter 5) who accrue gross income from any person other than a registered APA;[39] and
- Any taxpayer, resident or nonresident, who voluntarily registers.

Recall that individuals may be APAs if they own unincorporated businesses supplying goods and services subject to VAT and/or make payments to owners of primary productive factors above a specified amount. Such individuals should be known to the tax administration and should be registered taxpayers. These taxpayers may receive net income from business interests and other payments that might not otherwise be subject to the standard advanced payment methods. For example, an individual owning and operating a retail establishment will accrue net income from the business that is not subject to advanced payments. In addition, there will be the standard concerns about transfer pricing inputs that otherwise would be used for personal use (for example, the rent charged for an owner-occupied building that has both shop space and personal living space).

The second criterion is needed because the definition of taxable income should not be restricted to the income accrued from APAs. One domestic example is individuals who own rental housing properties. The renters will not, in general, be APAs.[40] In addition, individuals may accrue income from persons outside the taxing jurisdiction[41] and the local tax administration will have no control over the payer.[42] An alternative approach would be to state that all taxpayers other than taxpayers whose sole income accrues from APAs are required to register. The intent of the conditions

---

[39] Once registered, the resident taxpayer should be required to keep their registration for a minimum period of at least three years.

[40] A type of reverse charge for income tax purposes might be appropriate in such cases where the owner pays advanced tax based on the same criteria as APAs who withhold on rental payments. Such payments then would be a credit against the final tax due for the individual owner.

[41] There should be international efforts to share information and emerging economies should avail themselves of the opportunity to obtain information about the economic activities of their taxpayers undertaken outside the taxing jurisdiction.

[42] Again, a type of reverse charge can be imposed where the recipient pays the advanced tax in a manner identical to the reverse charge for imported services under the VAT.

above is to achieve this result, but whether practical application of either definition will span the universe of taxpayers may depend on the facts and circumstances.[43]

Any taxpayer should have the right to register. For example, nonresidents may accrue income from residents who are not APAs. Such individuals may choose to become either APAs or registered taxpayers. Some individuals may qualify for refunds depending on the law's overall structure. If refunds are processed, then such individuals may voluntarily register. If any taxpayer chooses to become a registered taxpayer, then there should be a minimum period of at least three years so that the nonresident can exercise such an option on an annual basis.[44]

These requirements might be the basic requirements that evolve through time. For example, if APAs report gross and net payments for primary factors, then such taxpayers might be registered when the tax administration has the ability to create master files and other necessary computer applications for posting, matching, and aggregating the various income payments of the taxpayers. Ultimately, registered taxpayers could include immigrants at the time of immigration, children, or other dependents of other registered taxpayers.

3.3.1.3 Two Exceptions

Taxpayers are individuals, but there are two situations where taxation is effectively imposed on APAs.

a. Treatment of Nongovernmental Organizations (NGOs)

An NGO has no residual claimants if profits accrue. An NGO is an APA, as defined in Chapter 2, and will pay collect tax in a matter identical to a for-profit enterprise. If the NGO has profit, as defined in the law, subject to advanced payments (see below), then such a payment is effectively the final tax on the NGO's income. This is the recommended approach. NGOs would effectively be taxpayers in the sense that NGOs have profits. Such an approach will eliminate the need for rules about imposing tax on unrelated business income. All income is simply aggregated and, if possible, an advanced payment is applied. In addition, it is recommended that donations to NGOs be defined as capital contributions where the individual donating the capital explicitly forgoes any net return (in goods, services, or money) from the donation. This implies that the NGO's capital stock has increased, so the contribution is not revenue and not subject to tax. This means that the taxpayer who contributes to such an organization will not be able to deduct the contribution (see below). Thus, there is no need to treat NGOs with a social purpose any differently from other types of NGOs such as social clubs, endowments, political parties, and others.

---

[43] Remittances can be a significant source of income for residents. As a matter of method, such income should be subject to tax. Such payments might be subject to advanced payments if the funds flow through commercial banks and established entities such as Western Union. Of course, the taxation of these payments may be controversial.

[44] If a nonresident elects to end their registration at the end of the minimum registration period, then there should be a minimum delay before the taxpayer can register again. Three years might be a reasonable period.

Most NGOs will not pay advanced tax on net income (small charities with zero sales and where contributions equal expenses). Large organizations with significant endowments and assets (large charities, various levels of government, religious organizations) might pay tax.

b. Government

The government, being an NGO, will be an APA and will be required to report net income on a comprehensive accrual basis. An advanced payment, if made, would be the final tax. Taxes accrued to the government are defined as capital contributions and so are excluded from revenue for income tax purposes. Thus, a budget surplus, either on a cash or an accrual basis, would not be subject to tax. This means that in most cases the government will have negative income because the taxpayers benefit from government supplies of goods and services. The justification for this treatment is that government is a flow-through entity with the equity participants being taxpayers (both residents and nonresidents) who may benefit from government programmes and policies. The distribution of the benefits is not in proportion to any participant's equity investment (tax payments accumulated through time), however. The net benefits to any taxpayer might then be the basis of any distributional analysis.

The government should provide full reporting to taxpayers on income, as well as the sources and uses of funds, via comprehensive budgeting on an accrual basis as required by the income tax. Such reporting, including equity interests in state enterprises, will be helpful, we believe, in fostering transparency as well as discussions about the net economic benefits of government activities.

3.3.1.4 Individual or Related Parties

It may be reasonable to take personal or economic circumstances into account in determining whether an individual taxpayer is required to pay tax separately or as part of a larger group in which all income is aggregated.[45] Aggregation is based in part on mutual dependence and joint decision making. Kinship or familial relationships are not needed for mutual dependence to exist. For example, two individuals unrelated by kinship may form a business enterprise where joint decisions affect the returns to each individual participant. If income aggregation is considered, then criteria must be developed. As well, if aggregation is allowed or required, then the government must decide about the extent to which income is aggregated. If taxation of the individual is maintained, it still might be the case that the taxpayer provides material support for members of their household.

3.3.1.5 Aggregation into One Unit

Joint reporting occurs when two or more individuals are allowed, or required, to report as one unit by combining their incomes. One economic justification for aggregation is that the observed actions of any group member reflect joint decision making within the group. For example, an individual might reduce labour supply in response

---

[45] The concept of related party is expanded in this proposal.

to a decrease in net-of-tax wages resulting from an increase in the tax rate. If, however, joint decisions are made, then it may not be possible to predict the response to changes in exogenous variables for one individual without taking into account the behavioural changes of other group members. Continuing with the example, if two individuals form a household and both work in the labour market, then an increase in the tax rate on labour income could have any number of possible results. Both individuals could decrease labour supply, one individual could increase labour supply with the other individual reducing labour supply, both could increase labour supply, or even one individual could exit the labour market all together with the other individual keeping labour supply constant. The different results are determined by tradeoffs made within the household, tradeoffs that are not observable, and represent the best decision for the two individuals jointly given their preferences and constraints.

An alternative is for individuals forming a unit to be allowed or required to separately account for individual incomes.[46] For example, suppose that two individuals accrue income from human capital of 1000 and 2000 respectively. In addition, the individuals jointly accrue interest income of 500. While it might be possible to claim that the returns to human capital can be accounted for separately, it is not clear how to allocate the interest income between the two individuals.[47]

The benefit of aggregate reporting is that attribution (and manipulation of the rules) of income to separate individuals in the group is not necessary. In effect, these attribution rules are similar in concept to transfer pricing rules. Whether the benefits of aggregation exceed the costs depends on how income is computed and on the rate structure (or structures). A practical issue with respect to attribution to the individual group members in the case of required individual reporting is whether the aggregate tax of the group would be greater than or less than the summation of the taxes on the individual members. If the tax system is flat rate, then, in general, there is little need for attribution rules unless personal circumstances or standard deductions would affect the total tax bill. For example, if there are no exemptions and the tax is flat rate, then the attribution of taxable income among group members is immaterial. If the tax rate is a flat 15%, then one individual working in the labour market with income of 10,000 would pay tax of 1500, and it would be immaterial if the person working in the labour market compensates a related party for work in the household. If, on the other hand, there is a nonrefundable personal exemption of 1000 per person and there is separate reporting, then the total tax could be affected. For example, if there are intrahousehold transfers, the tax on the sole wage earner would be 1350. If, however, the individual wage earner hires the related party to provide labour services in the household, then the total tax could be reduced to 1200 because the second person could take advantage of the personal exemption.

---

[46] Note the similarity between aggregation for individuals and consolidated reporting for entities.

[47] Note that the issue of joint reporting relative to separate individual reporting is potentially moot if there is a flat rate tax system. That is, the total tax to the two individuals will be independent of whether they report separately or jointly. As well, how the interest income is arbitrarily allocated between the two individuals has no tax consequences in this case.

A 'marriage penalty' might occur in situations where there are variable tax rates and individuals filing joint returns are taxed with a rate schedule that differs from the individual tax schedule. This is the situation in the United States.[48]

The costs of aggregate reporting (or filing) include information costs because there must be an empirical definition of a group and the criteria for membership. These costs may be significant, at least during the evolution of the income tax, so individual reporting is maintained here. Advanced payments might serve as the final tax depending on the definition of taxable income. A personal credit (as an alternative to a personal exemption or standard deduction) is allowed, so there is still the potential for attempts to split market-based income between the members of the group. At some point in the system's evolution, the credit should be refundable. For example, suppose the individual credit is 100 per household member, the flat tax rate is 15%, and there are four individuals who form a household. Suppose only one individual has returns to human capital of 10,000. There is no income from nonhuman capital. The individual tax before credit would be 1500 (or .15*10,000) and the individual would receive a credit of 400 for a net tax of 1100 (or 1500–400). Another example would be a situation where one individual has labour market income of 800 with another member having income of 9200. In this case, the individual with the lower income could take a credit of twelve and the individual with higher income could take a credit of 388. The after-tax credit income of the individual with the lower income would be zero (or .15*80–12) while the after-tax credit income of the member with the higher income would be 1100, so net-of-tax credit income of the group is unaffected by the attribution. An alternative approach is to assign the total credits to the individual with the highest income until the tax is exhausted. This alternative is simply a special case of flexible assignment, however, so it might be easier to allow flexible assignment.

The cost of individual taxation with flexible assignment is that household members must be known to the tax administration. If the tax administration had required registration with information, then the tax administration could perform direct monitoring and computations. Below, a method is proposed for an annual election via the use of APAs who choose to be employers where the APA would perform the net computations as part of a system that makes advanced payments equivalent to the final tax. This approach is amenable to a situation where taxpayers are not registered and will allow the tax information system to evolve.

3.3.1.6 Foundational Issue: Jurisdictional Basis for Tax

Worldwide and territorial (or some mix) are possible bases for taxation. An individual is taxed on their total income under worldwide taxation, so there is no need to determine the geographical place where the income accrues.[49] The income tax base is

---

[48] See 'What Are Marriage Penalties and Bonuses?', Tax Policy Center for a discussion of the various situations in the United States.

[49] There might be special cases. For instance, if a foreign tax credit is provided in the tax law and there is a limitation on the amount of the credit, then the limitation might be with respect to the tax attributable to foreign sources.

restricted to domestic sources under a territorial system.[50] Source rules are required to determine what net income is attributable to the taxing jurisdiction. There are costs and benefits to either approach. The benefit of worldwide taxation is that source rules are not necessary, at least for domestic residents. The cost is that the tax administration may not be able to monitor both sides of a transaction. For example, a resident may accrue interest from a foreign bank, earn wages from the performance of services for a nonresident outside the country, accrue rents from property located in the foreign country, or accrue returns to the equity from an entity operating exclusively in another country. Worldwide taxation may be required, but the tax administration must depend on either voluntary compliance or exchange of information to monitor payments.

Territorial taxation might be preferred given the difficulties of confirming foreign source income, because in the case of territorial taxation, foreign source income is exempt. In addition, there is the potential benefit of taxing the domestic source income of nonresidents. There are at least two costs to this approach. First, source rules must be developed to determine domestic relative to foreign source income. Domestic residents will have an incentive to recharacterize income to foreign sources, given the exemption of foreign source income. Thus, tax administrators may have to monitor transfer prices and other methods to transfer otherwise domestic into foreign source income. Second, there is an incentive for resident taxpayers to accrue income from external sources to the extent that the domestic marginal tax rate exceeds the marginal rate from accruing income overseas.

We believe worldwide taxation is preferred even for emerging economies. Worldwide taxation of individual residents is conceptually superior because individual welfare is increased regardless of where income is attributed. There are practical difficulties to implementing either worldwide or territorial taxation. On balance, however, we believe worldwide taxation is preferred.

The approach developed here is similar to the conventional approach where domestic taxpayers are subject to worldwide net income tax and nonresident taxpayers are subject to tax on gross income 'sourced' in the taxing jurisdiction (depending on the basis for withholding), with the one source rule that the payment is domestic source if the payer is a domestic person. While a complication, there are good policy reasons for adopting such an approach. First, allowing taxpayers to escape taxation via territorial taxation may be politically unacceptable, particularly when the beneficiaries of such an approach are higher net worth resident taxpayers. Second, the taxing jurisdiction might be able to enter into exchange of information agreements without entering into formal tax treaties.[51] Such information exchanges can be helpful in determining who has income accrued from nonresidents; however, such exchanges may be of limited value given international rules. For example, if a resident taxpayer knows that the taxing jurisdiction where they reside has an exchange

---

[50] Some countries, the United States for instance, impose worldwide taxation on its citizens and residents while imposing territorial taxation on nonresidents. That is, nonresidents are taxed only on their income attributable to the United States.

[51] Information exchanges may become cost effective as technological advances are made.

of information agreement with Country X but not Country Y, where Country Y is a tax haven, then the domestic taxpayer can create an entity in Country Y in order to make investments in Country X and neither the taxing jurisdiction nor Country X may know the identity of the beneficial owner.[52] That said, policy consistency is preserved and there is unform application as a matter of law. An implication of the worldwide taxation of domestic residents accruing income from persons other than APAs is that they should be required to register as soon in the system's evolution as possible.[53]

3.3.2 Foundational Issue: What Is the Tax Base?

The Haig-Simons methodological standard is not an achievable objective. The inability to monitor both sides of a transaction, incentives for noncompliance, and difficulty measuring economic values forces a compromise between method and practical considerations. Conrad and Alexeev (2021) developed a practical income tax base, called Comprehensive Market-Determined Income (CMDI), that can be adopted in economies with relatively high income and public awareness as well as advanced administration. A discussion of this base is summarized here. As the ultimate objective, CMDI requires registration of all resident taxpayers, and either annual reconciliations by taxpayers or assessments (with review) by the tax administration, if computerization is extensive and relatively inexpensive. None of these three conditions will be satisfied in emerging economies, so it is important to illustrate evolutionary phases of application consistent with the tax administration and the revenue-driven base of the approach. Knowledge of the standard, however, provides an opportunity for reverse induction. That is, policies can be proposed and implemented consistent with the longer-term objective but with adjustments for current constraints as well as the projected path of the economy.

3.3.2.1 A Practical Comprehensive Tax Base

The tax base is summarized in Table 3.3 with specific provisions found in Table 3.4 (3.4A for gross income of residents, 3.4B for deductions for residents, and 3.4C for nonresidents). A numerical example is found in Table 3.5. Recall that the taxpayer is any individual; registered taxpayers are residents. APAs are used as described in Chapter 2 and advanced payments are made for most types of income.

a. Gross Income

Returns from human capital (or the supply of labour services to the market economy) and returns from nonhuman capital (including financial assets, real property,

---

[52] There should be criminal penalties for such actions given the apparent desire to evade tax. In addition, as noted below, international coordination on beneficial ownership should be encouraged through time as one means to reduce the ability of taxpayers to effectively engage in criminal behaviour.

[53] Estimated payments during the tax year should be required for individuals who accrue income not subject to advanced tax.

Table 3.3 Proposal summary

Summary	
a. Who is the taxpayer?	Individuals, with individual related parties allowed to aggregate income for reporting purposes[a]
b. What is the tax base?	Comprehensive Market-Determined Income CMDI (see Conrad & Alexeev, 2021)
c. What is the tax rate?	One flat rate on all income

Notes on particular provisions

a. Individual credit[b]	A refundable credit per person. A credit is preferred because rates will vary through time as economic circumstances change. Thus, a credit indexed for inflation will ensure that the credit is worth the same amount in terms of tax savings regardless of the tax rate and income, so the credit is not worth more to high-net-worth individuals. The credit will vary depending on the status of the individual in the household (dependent or adult).
b. Taxation of human capital	Any compensation for the market supply of labour services. Administration will be facilitated by extensive withholding, including: i. Wage withholding; ii. Fringe benefit taxation of fringe benefits not attributed to the individual and otherwise subject to wage withholding; iii. Withholding on all supplies of labour services, other than wages, supplied to withholding agents; and iv. Amortization of certain investments in human capital, including medical insurance, significant medical expenditures, and investments in education and training beyond college or the initial education necessary to enter a specified trade or business.
c. Taxation of nonhuman capital	Full taxation of all returns to nonhuman capital regardless of the type or composition. Administration is facilitated using withholding agents who will withhold on: i. Interest income; ii. Returns to equity capital; and iii. Capital gains and losses. 1. Withholding agents with equity traded on an active market will include gains and losses automatically in the computation of the base.

Continued

Table 3.3 *Continued*

Summary
2. Financial intermediaries who hold assets on behalf of individuals will withhold on net capital gains and losses via mark-to-market rules adjusted for inflation to the extent that such tax is not withheld by withholding agents.

[a] One crucial issue is how the personal credit will be measured. The objective will be to design a system where the tax is independent of marital status: two adult individuals with the same combined income would pay the same tax independent of marital status and, to the extent possible, independent of how much of the joint income is attributed to the individual. This is possible only under a flat-rate system. Some empirical work might indicate how to structure the credit so that much of the marriage penalty is reduced. For example, if the credit for an individual is 1000, then the credit for a married couple might be 1800 in order to reduce the penalty. We are not proposing such an approach because we prefer flat-rate taxation. That said, some studies may indicate how to reasonably limit the penalty under multiple-rate systems.
[b] Under accrual and accretion taxation, there would need to be only a final annual return in the year of death with full realization at the time of death, to the extent necessary. See discussion about treatment of estates. There is no need for estate taxes as an anti-abuse device, but estate taxes might be employed for wealth distribution purposes.

machinery and equipment, and intangible property) are the only two types of gross income. As a matter of method, there should be only one definition of gross income: the return from ownership of primary production factors. A practical consideration makes two classifications desirable, however.

i. Returns to the Supply of Human Capital. Returns to market labour are divided into two classifications: returns to employees and returns to nonemployees. Advanced payments are required for both classifications with one exception. As discussed below, advanced payments withheld on returns to employees may be based on personal circumstances (personal exemptions for example). Advanced payments on returns to non-employees will be at a flat rate. The exception is the situation where returns to market labour accrue indirectly via a conduit such as a partnership or corporation. For example, advanced payments will not be withheld on charges of a lawyer with a sole proprietorship, partnership, or corporation if that organization is an APA.[54] Advanced payments will still be required on the accrued income to the lawyer because the APA will withhold on either wages or accrued profits as the case may be.

---

[54] Converting the income from labour supply into corporate income includes any accrued capital gain. For example, it could be argued that individuals in the computer and software industries can convert the returns to their labour (including their intellectual and creative capacity) into a capital gain (or loss) by organizing an entity such as a corporation, keeping some portion of the equity for themselves, and selling shares either to venture capitalists or to the general public. At a minimum, the initial market value of the entity is equal to the market value of the shares held by other than the original owners and the capitalized value of the human capital (less the present value of compensation actually paid to the original owners) is reflected in the share values held by the original owners.

Table 3.4 Summary of proposed individual income tax

Item	Treatment
A. Gross income	
Return to human capital	• Labour services
	○ Individual choice to be an employee for tax purposes; the employer then can withhold appropriate amounts that would account for the individual tax credit.
	○ Withholding at a flat rate on all labour services other than wage income if the individual chooses to be an employee.
	• Return to human capital taxed at the same rate, and on accrual regardless of methodology used to accrue income, including carried interest, incentive stock options, bonuses, and other methods used to compensate individuals for labour services[a]
	• A mixture of labour and nonhuman capital (sole proprietorships for example): treated as full flow-through entity
Return to nonhuman capital	• Full imputation and withholding
	• Full taxation of gains and losses
• Income from equity ownership	○ Mark-to-market with inflation-adjusted basis and withholding by agents.
• Interest income	○ If market value is not known, then treatment will be consistent with accrual accounting where there is full taxation at the time of accrual (realization in this case) less the adjusted basis, capitalized interest expense, and recapture of deferred taxes. Losses from such assets will be limited to gains as is current policy, at least for the transition.
• Capital gains and losses	
Insurance	• Term life insurance: Premiums fully deductible and benefits includable in the income of the beneficiary (life insurance is understood to be a hedge for the present value of future income)
	• Whole life insurance: Inside build-up of whole life insurance taxed and insurance companies will be withholding agents
	• Casualty: Deductible with excess losses deductible (in effect, uninsured losses are fully deductible)
	• Medical insurance and expenses: Medical insurance deductible and expenses in excess of insurance reimbursements are deductible.
Social security	Fully includable and withheld
Pensions	Two options
	• Nondeductible at the time of contribution and income on inside buildup is taxed on a current basis with no tax on distribution **OR**
	• Treat as a current deduction, but as a deferred tax subject to recapture

Continued

Table 3.4 *Continued*

Item	Treatment
Welfare and other government payments (such as individualized subsidies for health insurance, subsidized interest, and all government programmes)	• Fully includable and withheld if individuals can be identified. • Fringe benefit tax imposed on government expenditures for benefits that cannot be attributed to individuals

B. Deductions

Item	Treatment
Interest	Deductible either immediately or capitalized and recoverable at the time of accrual
State and local taxes	Not deductible
Charitable contributions	Not deductible Treated as capital contributions
Other losses	Deductible to the extent not insured above some minimum amount
Fringe benefits	Subject to fringe benefit tax if not included in individual income
Personal circumstances	Refundable personal credit
Standard deduction	A standard deduction is available in lieu of deductions. Amounts to be determined based on revenue estimates.
Aggregate losses	Personal income after refundable credit may be negative and negative tax is refundable up to an absolute maximum adjusted for inflation.

C. Income to nonresidents (either individuals or entities) and other foreign items

Item	Treatment
All income paid to or accrued from resident taxpayers and withholding agents	• Withholding agents withhold on any return to capital. • No second border withholding tax on distributions • Nonresident individuals may choose to become tax residents and if they qualify may be taxed as residents. • The equity participants of entities accruing income from withholding agents may choose to become withholding agents in the United States (for example, the Norwegian State Pension Fund may become a withholding agent, report income to owners, and withhold on individuals)
Foreign tax credit	Allow a foreign tax credit: • The foreign tax credit must flow through to the individual because entities are not taxed. Such computations would be an extension of the gross-up and credit system common for other withholding system such as wage withholding. • There should not be a limitation on the foreign tax credit because there is no definition of foreign source income. Credit would be limited to taxes on income or in lieu of income taxes as currently practiced.

[a] See Conrad (2017) for a discussion of how to tax carried interests, stock options, deferred compensation schemes, and other forms of executive compensation.

Line #	Item	Gross amount	Totals	Tax withheld at source	Assumptions and notes
	Gross income				
1	Return to human capital	102,000.00		13,500.00	Flat tax rate of 25% with individual credit of 12,000. Includes any compensation paid or accrued in exchange for labour services regardless of how it is labelled (wages, fringe benefits, carried interest, various forms of executive compensation such as stock options, some classifications of deferred compensation).
2	Return to nonhuman capital				
3	Assets held in VVV brokerage account	9,544.68		2,386.17	Includes net income, gains and losses from holding any type of asset that is marked-to-market. Interest received is included but dividends as commonly defined are exempt because the underlying income upon which the distribution is based has been taxed.
4	Assets held in employer pension	(11,027.92)		(2,756.98)	The individual is assumed to have an employer-provided pension. Value is the change in the market value of the employee's pension including employer contributions during the year. In this case, there was a net loss for the year.
5	**Adjusted gross income**		100,516.76		
6	Deductions				
7	Interest expense this year	9,625.07			All interest expense is eligible for deduction. Interest expense accrued in any year may be divided into the amount that can be deducted this year and the amount to be capitalized. Deductible amounts equal total interest expense times a ratio. The numerator of the ratio is the total value of assets that are valued on a mark-to-market basis plus the prior year's return to human capital. The denominator is the book value of total assets (both those that are valued on a mark-to-market basis and those that are not) plus one year's return to human capital.
8	Health and disability insurance	1,000.00			Health insurance is deductible as are certain medical expenses. Expenditures on health care are considered expenditures to maintain human capital.
9	**Total deductions**		10,625.07		Line 5 – Line 9
10	Taxable income		89,891.69		.25 * Line 10
11	Tax accrued		22,472.92		Personal CREDIT
12	Personal credit		12,000.00		Line 11 – Line 12
13	Net tax accrued		10,472.92		Summation of total withholding (Line 1 + Line 3 – Line 4)
14	Tax withheld		13,129.19		Tax due (Line 14 – Line 15)
15	Net tax due		(2,656.27)		

Individuals supplying labour but who are not employees will receive compensation net of advanced tax unless the supplier is a registered APA. In many cases, the APA supplying the service will be a VAT taxpayer. Thus, if one APA compensates another APA for any good or service and no advanced payment is made, then no advanced payment will be imposed. This situation applies to the supply of all goods and services and includes labour services.

If, however, the supplier is not an APA, then an advanced payment is withheld.[55] In most cases, the supplier issuing a legal VAT invoice will be a sufficient condition for establishing APA status. Thus, advanced payments will be withheld on payments for all labour services to nonemployee nonresidents (who cannot be APAs) and on domestic residents who are not APAs.[56] For example, if an APA retains the services of day labour or other contractors (either short term or long term) who are not APAs, then the APA will impose the flat rate advanced payment.[57] In addition, if the supply is for delivering goods, such as bricks or other inputs, then an advanced payment will be withheld from the gross charge of the combined provision of the good (the bricks) and services (the delivery) to a particular location.[58,59]

ii. Taxation of the Return to the Market Supply of Labour. The amount of tax on the return to human capital, on a flow and even a present value basis, should be invariant to how the compensation occurs, whether the compensation is in-kind or in-cash, and whether the return is payable directly to the individual supplying the labour or indirectly via an entity on an accrual basis. Returns to labour supply can encompass several commonly used notions of labour compensation including, but not limited to:

- Wages from employment;
- Fringe benefits;

---

[55] This system is equivalent to forming a ring in a manner similar to the system used in sales taxation.
[56] Some entities may not be VAT taxpayers, NGOs for example. Thus, NGOs would not be able to issue VAT invoices. NGOs should be APAs, however, to the extent that the NGO is an entity and makes payments that are returns to either human or nonhuman capital.
[57] If the good or service is subject to VAT and VAT is not charged, then it is possible for the APA to impose a reverse charge and immediately take the credit for the advanced payment on the input. In effect, such supplies would be treated like imported services.
[58] Conrad first encountered this system in Nigeria, and it was labelled reverse withholding at that time. See Conrad (2005) Memorandum on VAT Withholding addressed to Mr G. O. Adesina Acting Director, Tax Policy Research and Development Department. dated 3 March 2005. Conrad borrowed that concept and made a similar proposal in Ukraine. See Conrad (2015). 'Withholding on Payments for Certain Services' Memorandum for Ms Olena Makeive and Members of the Informal Working Group, dated 20 April 2015.
[59] The advanced tax to the supplier of the bricks might be too high because the advanced tax includes both the value of the bricks and the return to human capital. The supplier always has the option to become an APA, however, and perhaps become a VAT taxpayer as well. Also, there could be equity issues involved in the sense that the amounts of advanced tax could impose a regressive burden on low-income individuals such as day labour. This result depends on whether the supplier of the bricks has net income below the zero-bracket amount. If so, then that individual should have the right to become an APA and report either as a small business (if a small business tax is used) or as a sole proprietor. There is still the risk that low-income individuals do not have the means or wherewithal to become registered taxpayers. We believe, however, that the option should be pursued given the high cost of noncompliance, particularly for higher income individuals who do not want to become known to the tax administration.

- Fees, charges, and contractually obligated payments to individuals supplying services but who are not otherwise employed;
- Contributions to pension schemes (a type of fringe benefit);[60] and
- Performance bonuses such as stock options and carried interest.

To emphasize, the issue is not what the compensation is labelled or called. The only issue is whether the payment to the taxpayer is compensation, either directly or indirectly, for the supply of labour. Practical issues include how APAs handle advanced payments and what gaps exist in the coverage of advanced payments.

iii. Compensation for Labour Supplied to the Market: Definition of Employee. As noted, we believe that definitions affecting tax revenue should be contained explicitly in the tax law.[61] The incentive to use the definition of employee to avoid being so defined[62] is mitigated, at least in part, by imposing advanced payments on all labour supplies regardless of definition. If a flat-rate tax is imposed and there is no adjustment for personal circumstances, then the complexity of defining a taxpayer as an employee is resolved, at least in part.

There are situations, however, in which it would be beneficial to have advanced payments incorporate personal credits, exemptions, and standard deductions. The need for annual reconciliations and refunds can be reduced if personal circumstance considerations and standard deductions are incorporated into the advanced payment system. Such incorporation will enable the advanced tax to be the final tax for at least some, if not most, taxpayers, when combined with uniform advanced payments for nonhuman capital income. This potential benefit is exploited by allowing individuals and APAs to choose to be in an 'employer-employee' relationship for tax purposes. The benefit to the taxpayer is that amounts withheld are reduced relative to flat-rate advanced payments for individuals who are not employees. In addition, employee records can be a basis for registration to the extent that registration processes can accommodate taxpayers with wages. Thus, the tax administration has a basis for expanding the number of registered taxpayers along with additional information.

One definition of an employee is: An individual who, by mutual agreement with an APA, enters into a contract, either verbal or written, stipulating that the individual provides labour services in exchange for any type of compensation.

---

[60] Whether distributions from pension systems are subject to tax depends on the tax treatment of contributions.

[61] The definition can be borrowed and cited by reference. For example, an employee could be defined in some other law and included by reference into the tax law. That said, the law should contain a statement that the definition in the tax law does not change if the definition changes in the referenced law. Control over definitions is essential for developing consistent policies.

[62] In some cases, the tax administration is responsible for administering social taxes in addition to the personal income tax on wage income. Advanced payments can be required for both the wage tax and social taxes when an individual is an employee. Relatively high social tax rates can add an additional incentive to arbitrage the definition of an employee. Conrad addressed this issue in Ukraine, among other places including Russia and other central and Eastern European economies, where social tax rates were particularly high. See Conrad (April 2016). 'Merged Social and Personal Income Tax. Memorandum supplied to Small Tax Reform Working Group'.

If a taxpayer and APA agree to an employer-employee relationship for tax purposes, then the advanced payment table will be adjusted for different personal circumstances if such considerations are part of the policy. For example, if the individual credit is 125, the withholding rate is 20%, and the standard deduction is 8000 per annum, then gross wages would have to be 8500 before any advanced payment is made.[63] If, however, the taxpayer is not an employee, then the advanced payment would be equal to 1700. (See the discussion and numerical examples below.)

There should be one, and only one, employer-employee relationship for tax purposes per taxpayer. Taxpayers who receive compensation from more than one APA will benefit from the advanced payment schedule for one relationship while advanced payments at the uniform rate would prevail for all other compensation from APAs.[64,65]

Finally, taxpayers who are not employees and who do not accrue labour income via a formal entity should be deemed to be sole proprietors. Such a designation can be used to allocate administrative resources, once information systems are developed, for registration and compliance.

iv. Fringe Benefits. Gross compensation for labour services might be classified into three groups:

- cash compensation, paid or accrued, that is paid in exchange for the supply of labour services;
- Reimbursement for or direct supply of ordinary and necessary business expenses (transportation to job sites, tools, and related expenses) related to performance (either part of gross compensation and deducted by the taxpayer or the APA may deduct the costs so that the owner gets the deduction); and
- Fringe benefits.

Reimbursement for ordinary and necessary business expenses for employees (or contractors) is includable in gross income of the recipient and deducted. Such payments are not supplements to cash compensation but can be considered substitutes in the sense that the cost of labour supply services includes costs other than direct labour that are necessary for the taxpayer to provide labour services.

[63] See below for how to adjust these amounts for monthly or other periodic advanced payments.

[64] It should be clear that the tax on labour supply to the market is the legal responsibility of the taxpayer. Thus, if there are sources of compensation that are not subject to advanced payments, payments made by any nonresident person for example, then the individual is obligated to report, perhaps through advanced payments, and pay tax on that income. If an APA collects the advanced payment but keeps the funds, then both the government and the taxpayer have legal recourse against the APA. In particular, certain officers of APAs will be liable for the tax and any penalties. In effect, an APA that does not pay the advanced payments to the Government on a timely basis is engaged in theft.

[65] There is a potential problem with the mutually exclusive part of the definition because low net worth individuals may have more than one source of income from labour services. If the income from the supply of labour services to multiple withholding agents is sufficiently small, then the supplier will have too much tax withheld. Some cost-effective alternatives might be developed to address such a potential situation. For example, it might be possible for the tax administration to provide credits for taxes withheld by the second source of the return to human capital against withholding by the employer.

Fringe benefits are supplements to, and substitutes for, cash compensation. As compensation, the costs are deducted from an employer's income and should be included in the gross income of the beneficiary. Benefits might include contributions to pension schemes, employer provision of certain types of insurance, contributions to government programmes on behalf of employees such as unemployment insurance schemes, and other compensation.[66]

In addition, there are benefits designed for specific individuals or groups such as housing, provision of domestic servants, educational benefits for children, and others. Such targeted benefits might be discriminatory in the sense that highly compensated employees are the beneficiaries. An example relevant for many emerging economies is compensation of noncitizens retained (or transferred) to the host country by a foreign investor. These employees may receive housing, automobiles, trips home for vacation, educational expenses for children, gratuities at the end of service in the host country, and other benefits that are provided neither to the employee by the same employer in their home country nor to citizens or longer-term residents of the host country. These benefits can be a significant, perhaps a dominant, portion of the total compensation of such employees. It might be the case that the supply price of labour in a foreign country differs from the supply price of labour in the employee's home country, and the in-kind benefits serve as a substitute wage premium. If, however, these benefits are exempt to the employee while being deducted from income of the APA's owners, then there is an incentive to substitute benefits for cash compensation.

Two types of taxation might be considered. First, there can be an attempt to attribute the benefit to individuals, report those benefits, and impose tax at the individual level via either withholding or annual reporting, depending on the stage of administrative evolution. This approach is identical with comprehensive income concepts. Some benefits can be clearly attributed to an employee. For example, it is possible to attribute payments for a child's education to the employee receiving the benefit. Other cases are not so clear-cut, either conceptually or as an administrative matter. Subsidies to employer-provided cafeterias are one example.

An alternative is to adopt a fringe benefit tax as is used in Australia and New Zealand.[67] In this case, fringe benefits costs (with certain exceptions, such as interest-free loans) are pooled, and the employer makes an advanced payment equal

---

[66] Whether the value of the benefit is also a cost for the recipient depends on the type of compensation. For example, if an employer provides health insurance, then such a benefit might be a deductible cost to the individual recipient if medical expenses are amortized. In this case, the value of the benefit should be included in gross income and then deducted. It might be argued that such an approach can be achieved by granting a deduction to the APA and exempting the income to the employee. Such an approach might be possible, but it is not as transparent as the proposed method. In addition, there could be related incentive issues. For example, profit-seeking firms could still offer tax exempt benefits as a substitute for cash wages in amounts greater than what would be otherwise deducted at the individual level. In addition, there might be an incentive for the government to allow an exemption for benefits that would be otherwise taxable at the individual level. Finally, NGOs and other nonprofits offer such benefits and the deduction by such APAs would result in zero tax revenue in most cases.

[67] See https://www.ato.gov.au/Business/Fringe-benefittax/?=Redirect_URL and New Zealand Inland Revenue. *Fringe Benefit Tax Guide: A Guide to Working with FBT*. IRA 409 (April 2023) for Australia and New Zealand Respectively.

Table 3.6 Fringe benefit tax

Line #	Item	Amount	Notes
1	Subsidized employee food services	60,000.00	Employees receive a 10% discount at company-maintained cafeterias
2	Subsidized parking	80,000.00	Estimated by same methods as those used to provide deduction of travel based on mileage
3	Subsidized sporting events	1,800,000.00	Sky box at NFL Football Stadium plus season ticket purchases
4	Total	1,940,000.00	
5	Fringe benefit tax (via gross up)	646,666.67	(.25/.75) * Line 4

to $t/(1-t)$, where 't' is the advanced tax rate, times the amount in the pool. The gross-up is necessary because the owners of a for-profit entity are allowed to take the deduction for the tax-inclusive expense. In addition, the gross-up ensures neutrality between APAs with owners who seek profit and APAs that are nonprofit entities.[68] If there is flat rate taxation, as proposed here, then the rate will be equal to the taxpayer's marginal tax rate, making both the APA's owner and the individual employee indifferent to the imposition of the tax, other things equal. An example is contained in Table 3.6.

b. Deferred Compensation and Performance Incentives
The income tax base should be determined by accrual accounting to the extent possible. This means that income is measured at the time of accrual even if the cash payment is in the future. Thus, all forms of deferred compensation should be included in taxable income when accrued. Examples of deferred compensation include, but are not limited to: employer contributions to pension plans, gratuities payable at the time the taxpayer leaves an organization, and other deferred income schemes designed to average annual income over time. Performance incentives such as carried interests and stock options are a type of conditional deferred compensation. Pension contributions and the like are based on the wage (defined contribution scheme) or the anticipated benefit (defined benefit scheme) that are based retrospectively on wage payments during certain periods of the taxpayer's working life. Performance incentives, on the other hand, are deferred payments conditional on indicators other than wages. For example, a carried interest is a payment made at the end of a specified period and is based on some measure of returns. A mutual fund manager, or general partner, may be eligible for a payment if the returns are more than a specified amount. That is, a general partner may receive 20% of the profits in

---

[68] If there is a multiple-rate system, then the rate will not exactly match the marginal rate of each taxpayer. Given the predominance of fringe benefits for highly compensated individuals, the rate should be above the unweighted average rate in our view.

excess of a 10% return to equity. On the other hand, a manager of a firm with traded equity may be given the option to purchase shares at a specified price at some point in the future. For example, if the current market value of equity is ten, then the manager may be given the option to purchase equity shares at 12 at some point in the future. If the market value of equity becomes 15, then the manager can exercise the option purchase at 12 and immediately sell at 15, making a gain of 3 per share.[69]

i. Pensions. Employer contributions to pension schemes should be recognized as income at the time of accrual, and the inside buildup in any type of pension programme should be included when accrued. In addition, employee contributions should not be a deduction in deriving taxable income. In short, pensions, although long term, are simply one element of a taxpayer's portfolio of nonhuman assets, so contributions to saving should not be deducted from income and any interest or other income should be recognized at the time of the accrual.

Some countries provide for the consumption tax treatment of pensions by allowing contributions to pensions to reduce the current tax base and to exempt the inside buildup during the accumulation period, with tax being paid at the time of distribution. Under certain conditions, the present value of tax is not changed by this treatment, only the timing is changed. In effect, consumption tax treatment of pensions represents an interest-free loan from the government to the taxpayer. An example will illustrate the point. Suppose a taxpayer contributes 100 to a pension in t = 0 and takes a tax deduction. If the tax rate is 25%, then the taxpayer saves 25 in taxes in t = 0. Suppose the average return is 7% net of tax and the funds are held for 30 years. This means that at the end of 30 years, there will be 761.23 in the account (or $1.07^{30}*100$). If all the funds are distributed in t = 30, then the taxpayer will pay 190.31 in tax (or $.25*761.23$). The present value of the tax, however, is 25 (or $190.31/(1.07^{30})$). Thus, in terms of accrual accounting, the taxpayer should record a deferred tax debt of 25 in t = 0 and the government should record an asset of future taxes equal to 25. The reason such a result is equivalent to a tax-free loan is that if the taxpayer invested 100 in t = 0 in an investment where tax is not deferred, then the tax-inclusive return would have to equal 9.33% in order to have a net-of-tax balance of 761.23 at the end of t = 30. In addition, the taxpayer would be able to invest only 75 from wages if there is no deferral. This means that the future value of after-tax savings outside the deferred pension would be 570.91 (or $76*1.07^{30}$). This is because the taxpayer would have to pay 25% tax on the interest income each year and then reinvest the after-tax return. In effect, the deferred pension scheme simply defers the tax on wage income and leaves the return to saving exempt from tax. Thus, all taxpayers via the government forgo the use of the tax revenue during the period the pension funds are

---

[69] It could be argued that such situations may not be relevant in many emerging markets. Employers in emerging markets learn from others, however, and it has been our experience that if policymakers and administrators are not aware of these situations and, perhaps the income is exempted by lack of understanding, then there is an opportunity for tax avoidance.

invested because the government must reduce expenditures, increase the deficit, or increase tax rates, or some combination, in order to cover the lost expenditures.[70]

Arguments for tax deferral of pensions include an increase in the incentive to save and an incentive for taxpayers to provide for their future by locking savings into a particular account.[71] There might be some incentive to increase saving at the margin, but only if the taxpayer earns more than the average net-of-tax return on investments; an event that should not be expected. In the example, if the investor earns 7%, then she would be indifferent to paying the tax now or later, other things equal.[72] If the investor earns the tax-inclusive rate of 9.33%, then the investor will experience a net gain. If, however, the government must pay 9.33% to finance the debt, then the gain to the taxpayer is identically equal to a loss for all other taxpayers because they have financed the carry on the deferred tax. On the other hand, if the individual makes only 6%, then the present value of the tax is lower, when discounted at 7%, and there is a tax loss. Now all other taxpayers must share both the loss with the taxpayer investing in the deferred scheme and also pay 9.33%. Second, total flows into deferred pension schemes should not be treated as incremental savings. Part, perhaps much if not all, of the contributions may arise from the substitution of savings in other investments.

Third, consumption tax treatment of pensions is difficult to administer. Schemes must be approved and monitored by the Ministry of Finance to ensure that qualifications are satisfied and that distribution rules are followed. Fourth, it is hard to justify different taxes in emerging economies when net-of-tax returns from the inside buildup may be lower than the social value of investment at the margin, particularly if the government must pay higher rates to finance the deferred tax. Finally, and related to the fourth point, the risk-sharing properties of consumption tax treatment may not be as effective as those found with the income tax.[73]

In summary, there is already consumption taxation in this proposal with the use of VAT or another form of indirect tax. There is no need to replicate the features of the consumption tax with income taxes. Thus, if increasing saving is a social objective, then it might be more efficient to increase the relative proportion of current revenue from the VAT instead of converting the income tax base into a consumption tax.

ii. Other Deferred Compensation Schemes and Performance Incentives. Stock options, carried interests, and performance bonuses are conditional compensation forms. The compensation may be structured to address incentive problems such as the principal-agent problem where the owner (the principal) and the agent (the employee) objectives are not aligned. Conditional compensation is still compensation with gains and losses subject to symmetric taxation. For example, if a general

---

[70] There is also a tax prepayment approach to the consumption taxation of pensions. The taxpayer would pay 25 of tax out of 100 of income and invest 75 in t = 0. All future income would be exempt. Given the assumptions, the value of the distribution in t = 30 would be 570.92 (or 761.23 – 190.31). The future value of the balance if there is deferral is less than tax at the time of the distribution under deferral.

[71] The incentive to lock in savings is increased by early withdrawal penalties from qualified accounts.

[72] We believe the adage that 'a tax deferred is a tax avoided', so other things are not equal.

[73] A sample of this literature includes: Easley, Kiefer, & Possen (1993); Nishiyama & Smetters (2005); Athreya & Waddle (2007).

partner is compensated via a carried interest, then such compensation is deducted immediately from the income of the owners. That is, if the general partner gets 1000 in compensation, then there is 1000 less in the net income of the other partners in the period the compensation occurs. Thus, a deduction of 1000 for the other partners should be income (immediately) for the general partner. This point is further reinforced by the fact that capital gains should be taxed on an accrual basis and should be treated as ordinary income to every extent possible. Thus, the issue is how to administer the application of uniform taxation, not whether such compensation should be treated differently. This means that compensation like carried interests should be taxed as current income and be subject to advanced payments at normal rates. Items such as stock options, where there is some timing element and discretion about when to exercise the compensation, should also be treated as ordinary income if a gain is realized.[74] The exact treatment of these gains will depend on administrative capacity. The standard is described below with options developed in the last section.

c. Relationship between Advanced Tax and Social Taxes

Social taxes, including state pensions, health insurance, and other types of social insurance, are typically imposed on wages and are subject to withholding. In at least one sense, these charges are not taxes per se, because the charges are exchanged for a specific benefit such as pensions, unemployment insurance, and other forms of social protection, at least in theory. As a matter of statutory incidence, the charges can be imposed on either the employee, the employer, or both. In addition, the charges are typically imposed on a tax-exclusive basis, particularly on employer contributions. That is, the employer's share of the charge is not part of the wage quoted to the employee as compensation and, in addition, the employee's contribution, if one exists, is not deductible from gross wages in computing the amount of withholding tax. Regardless of the statutory incidence, these charges increase the cost of labour for the employer. Thus, we have found that discussions of personal income taxation revolve around the combined effect of the personal income tax and the various social taxes. This was particularly true in Central and Eastern Europe where there were preexisting mandatory contributions to a variety of social funds (up to four in Russia, for example),[75] each of which were separately administered and sometimes had subtle differences in the definition of the base.

If the social charges are perceived as payments in exchange for specific benefits, such as contributions to privately funded retirement accounts, there would be little reason to discuss wage withholding and social taxes jointly. There are, however, reasons to believe that such charges are indeed taxes to a significant degree in emerging economies. Central and Eastern Europe is a case in point. First, the pension payments are generally a basic flat pension, which is not based on either defined benefit or defined contribution principles. Second, the reform of the economies resulted in

---

[74] A stock option has no value if the option is not exercised because the stock value never exceeds the strike price.

[75] See M. Alexeev and R. Conrad 'A Proposal for Reforming Russia's Social Tax'. Memorandum to Ilya Trunin and Pavel Kadochnikov, dated 1 January 2005.

a real decrease in the value of various types of insurance such as health insurance. For example, it was common to hear about situations where families of hospitalized persons had to make side payments for care, supply their own linens, and perhaps supply much nursing care because of lack of resources in the health sector. Third, the pension system is largely pay-as-you-go and deficits in the pension funds are common. Such deficits result in either an infusion of funds from general revenue accounts or further reductions in benefits. To the extent that there is an overall government deficit, which is the case in most emerging economies, the attribution of a deficit in the social funds is largely a matter of arbitrary accounting with no effect on the overall deficit, or on total government expenditures for that matter, if benefits are paid. In such an environment, it might be reasonable to treat social fund payments as simply part of the overall tax system, with earmarking being largely irrelevant for current purposes.

Thus, discussions of personal income tax inevitably revolve around the combined tax wedge of the personal income tax on wages and the social contributions. In most cases, this will imply that the combined tax rate on labour is higher than the tax rate on the income from capital. For example, the corporate tax rate in Ukraine was 15% in 2016, but the combined rate on wage income was in excess of 40% on low-wage individuals.[76] In Ukraine, among other places, such high rates contributed to the continued informality of the economy via the use of cash payments and schemes such as paying high wages to management who did not have to pay social taxes after a certain threshold, and having management pay cash wages to others. Such schemes then enable the employer to fully deduct the cost of labour while avoiding the high social taxes. In addition, there were examples where individuals were treated as contractors to avoid the combined tax. Computer programming was a case in point.

Funding social insurance and state pensions, as the economies continue to reform, will depend on both the timing and the structure of the reforms to benefit programmes. If the programmes become part of general revenue, then the distinction between social taxes and personal income tax via wage withholding becomes immaterial. If, however, the intent is to have such programmes fully funded, perhaps with subsidies to address income distributional concerns, then revenue streams should be separated. Such a process is really a longer-term issue, to be solved over several years, and has little to do with the current situation or even the transition, when general revenues will be needed for non-income-based subsidies. An awareness of this issue and the effective tax rate on labour is an important element in determining a reasonable tax reform path; we return to the issue below.

3.3.2.2 Income from Nonhuman Capital
Income from all nonhuman capital should be subject to tax regardless of the name and advanced tax should be withheld when possible. In addition, to the extent

---

[76] There is a cap on social contributions so that persons with higher wages pay a lower combined effective social tax and marginal personal income tax rate. See R. Conrad, 'Merged Social and Personal Income Tax'. Memo to Small Tax Reform Working Group dated 26 February 2016.

possible, the base of the advanced tax and the income includable in individual income should be the same. Transparency is increased and administration is more efficient. Regardless of the name, nonhuman capital income is equal to cash distributions to owners during a period plus the change in the value of the assets, or:

$$\text{Nonhuman Capital Income} = \text{Cash Distributions}_t + \text{Asset Value}_t + \text{Asset Value}_{t-1}.$$

where t is a particular period.

Thus, like any income measure, there are two equivalent ways to compute the non-human capital income tax base: the uses side (cash distributions plus the change in asset value during the period) or the sources side with the derivation that varies based on the type of nonhuman capital income. Two points are noted. First, as a practical matter, the values of nonhuman capital are computed on an ex-post basis, like all tax measures. Measured income is then a result of a mixture of interactions with real-ized events that were uncertain at the beginning of the period.[77] Second, the identity above may not hold empirically because of differences in how the sources and uses of income are computed. For example, income to equity is computed by application of accounting standards, standards that are based on historical costs and other factors that might not be adjusted for inflation.

On the uses side of income, cash distributions can be measured accurately if cash is actually distributed or contributed (cash distributions can be negative). There are instances when contributed capital other than cash must be valued, as well as situations where distributions to owners might be in some form other than cash (particularly in closely held enterprises). For example, a shop owner may use some inventory for personal consumption. In addition, the change in the net value of the asset may be computed either by using accounting standards or the market value if there is active trade in the asset. The former case is a situation where the change in the asset value is the change in book value, while the change in market value will be the change in asset value in the latter. Whether the market value and book values are equal depends on whether accounting standards allow, or require, mark-to-market valuations as well as knowing the market value of the assets. There are situations where the change in book value is equal to the change in market value. Time deposits are measured in cash and the values are known, so book values and market values are equal. An inflation adjustment might be needed to measure real income, however.

In most situations, income measured by using the sources is not equal to income measured by using the uses. Thus, the amount of tax may differ depending on which method is used to determine the tax base. Two additional points should be noted. First, there might be a preference for the uses of income to measure the tax base when ex-post market values are known. It is true that the market value measures the

---

[77] Recall from the discussion in Section 3.2 that an ex-ante measure of income will equal the ex-post measure if perfect certainty prevails. This is not the empirical situation, however, so the ex-ante measures, if known, and ex post measures are not equal. In addition, the incentive effects of taxation are analysed using the ex-ante income measure because predictions are made about what will happen if a particular policy is changed.

willingness to pay for the present value of future flows given the information structure and so is considered more consistent with economic principles. That said, market values are measured with error because markets are not complete, and individuals may not value risk in a manner consistent with economic theory.

Second, imposing a tax on income and a separate tax on capital gains results in a type of double taxation as noted by:

$$k(\text{Nonhuman Capital Income}_t) = \text{Cash Distributions}_{t+k}(\text{Asset Value}_t - \text{Asset Value}_{t-1}$$

where k = tax rate.

If there are no cash distributions during the period, then the tax will be twice as high as a single tax on income. In other cases, the double tax is on a portion of income that is reflected in the change in asset value.[78] Our view is that comprehensive income should be taxed once, and the proposed methods of measuring capital income reflect that fact. Given the importance of market valuation, the proposed methods differ depending on the administration's ability to independently observe the value of capital assets.

a. Assets for Which Capital Values Are Known (Time Deposits)

Income from time deposits is inflation-adjusted interest. An example of this approach is found in Table 3.7, where it is assumed that the initial balance is 1000, the real interest rate is 8%, and the advanced tax rate is 25%. Examples are provided for the no-inflation case as well as the 10% inflation case to illustrate the equivalence of the advanced tax in real terms. Note that any withdrawals from the account are immaterial once the interest accrues. That is, cash flow on the uses side of the income equation is not necessarily interest. For example, suppose that the taxpayer withdraws 90 at the end of the period, and before the advanced tax is imposed. The advanced tax (and the taxpayer's income) is not 90. This is because the change in bank account balance is −10 or (990−1000). So, income (and the advanced tax base) is equal to 90 + 990−1000 = 80 if the uses side of the income expression is used. Note that the APA must keep only two values currently: the initial balance and the amount of accumulated interest. The value of inflation can be supplied via public information.

i. Bonds Traded in Markets.

For bonds traded in markets:

Income from Bonds (and basis for advanced tax) = Cash Payments to owners +

(Market Value at the end of the period − Inflation − adjusted initial market value).

---

[78] The intent of a classical system of corporate taxation is to impose a double tax. In this case, the sources of income are taxed at the corporate level while distributions (those defined to be dividends) and capital gains are taxed at the individual level. That is, the individual is taxed on the uses of income. Estonia imposes a corporate tax only on distributions, so in general less than comprehensive income is subject to tax. We oppose that method for reasons explained in Conrad (2016).

Table 3.7 Time deposit

Real rate of return	8.00%	
Inflation rate	10.00%	
Inflation-adjusted nominal return	18.80%	
Advanced tax rate	25.00%	

Row #	Item	Value no inflation	Value 10% inflation
1	Initial value	1,000.00	1,000.00
2	Declared nominal interest	80.00	188.00
3			
4	Ending value	1,080.00	1,188.00
5			
6	Less inflation-adjusted balance: equals inflation rate * Line 1	-	100.00
7	Advanced tax base (Line 4 – Line 1 – Line 6)	80.00	88.00
8	Advanced tax: 25% of Line 7	20.00	22.00
9			
10	Real value of advanced tax base	80.00	80.00
11	Real value of advanced tax	20.00	20.00

An example is found in Table 3.8 for the case where there is a capital gain of 22.25 in real terms. Note again that there is no need to separate computations for 'cash flow' and 'the change in asset value'. Note also that income is computed by using the uses of income. This is necessary for two reasons. First, interest might be accrued and capitalized into the value of the bond (see below for the zero-coupon bond case). Second, cash payments can include repayment of principal. Thus, the change in market value will reflect the amortization of debt. For example, in the case of a simple loan, cash payments would be equal to interest plus principal and the market value of the bond, other things equal, would fall by the amount of principal paid. In this case:

Income from Bonds = Principal plus Interest – Principal = Interest.

Note also that if the bondholder sells the bond before the end of the reporting period, then there is no change in the computation. Only the mark-to-market date changes. This means that the seller will have advanced tax withheld for the period between the initial mark-to-market date and the date of sale, while the purchaser of the bond will have the initial mark-to-market date be the date of purchase. The bond issuer should have records of who owns the bonds, except in cases of bearer bonds, so the computation can be made by the APA. If bearer bonds are legal, then the APA simply does the computation on a standard periodic basis and the allocation of interest income during the period should be reflected in the market price. The bondholder

Table 3.8 Actively traded bond

Assumptions: Same as Table 3.7 except capital gain of 22.25

Row #	Item	Value No Inflation	Value 10% Inflation
1	Initial value of the bond	1,000.00	1,000.00
2	Declared nominal interest	80.00	188.00
3			
4	Ending value	1,102.25	1,212.48
5			
6	Less inflation-adjusted balance: inflation rate * Line 1	1,000.00	1,100.00
7	Advanced tax base: Line 4 – Line 6	102.25	112.48
8	Advanced tax: 25% of Line 7	25.56	28.12
9			
10	Real value of advanced tax base	102.25	102.25
11	Real value of advanced tax	25.56	25.56

at the end of the period will be responsible for the full tax, but the price of the intra-period market price of the bond should reflect the allocation of both interest and tax accumulated to the time of trade.[79]

A special case of an actively traded bond is a zero-coupon bond, and, in this case, income is:

Income for a Zero-Coupon Bond that is traded in the market = Market Value at the end of the period – Inflation-adjusted initial value.

Table 3.9 contains an example of this case. Note that there is literally nothing different between this computation and the computation made for the time deposit.

ii. Returns to Equity. Perhaps the most straightforward way to measure income to equity is the uses side of the HS equation. This approach is possible for corporations that are actively traded as proposed by Toder and Viard (2016). In theory, it is possible to use this approach for all types of equity investments regardless of organizational forms where stock values are not known. So, the approach could be applied to royalties, land rents, and other capital assets. We recommend using the sources side with one adjustment for five reasons.

First, net income to equity will be computed for most business enterprises and the derivation of net income is needed for purposes other than tax. Net income computations, according to the accounting laws perhaps, are demanded by shareholders and equity participants in other entity types to measure performance, to determine distributions, and for regulatory purposes. Thus, equity owners are familiar with net income concepts, if not the detailed accounting rules used in the derivation. Since

[79] Advanced tax should be imposed at the time of trade either by the broker or the owner's agent.

Table 3.9 Zero coupon bond

Assumptions: Same as Table 3.7 except there is an implied capital loss

Row #	Item	Value no inflation	Value 10% inflation
1	Value at the beginning of the period	1,000.00	1,000.00
2			
3	Ending value	1,068.00	1,174.80
4			
5	Less inflation adjusted balance: inflation rate * Line 1	1,000.00	1,100.00
6	Advanced tax base: Line 3 – Line 5	68.00	74.80
7	Advanced tax: 25% of Line 6	17.00	18.70
8			
9	Real value of advanced tax base	68.00	68.00
10	Real value of advanced tax	17.00	17.00

income is derived in practice anyway, there is every reason for taxation to be based on similar concepts.

Second, the adjustment made in the case of market securities is straightforward and eliminates the need for a separate tax on the capital gain. So, the simplicity of using the uses side of the income expression is preserved. A timing adjustment, described below, is required for equity investments for which the market values are not known regardless of whether the sources or uses side of the income expression is used to measure income. The adjustment has desirable properties, but it is not perfect, and owners have direct control of the timing of cash distributions. Thus, there is potential for tax arbitrage. Such an incentive is mitigated, to at least some extent, by using a standard income measure over which the owners have less control.

Third, most countries currently impose a corporate tax that might or might not be partially integrated with the individual tax. Thus, current practice is preserved by using measured income as the tax base. Corporate integration is complete when the system is fully implemented, ensuring more uniform tax treatment of all equity income while building on current practice.

Fourth, the tax authorities might choose one of two methods to measure income attributable to taxpayers. Income can be computed using local or international accounting standards with some transfer pricing adjustments (see Section 3.4.3). This approach may be more convenient and less burdensome on both the APA computing income and the tax administration. We believe a better, although more administratively burdensome approach, is to use economic concepts in deriving income. Some basic rules for the economic income derivation are found in Table 3.10. Local and international accounting standards are based on a specific set of assumptions relative to the treatment of accruals, depreciation methods, treatment of gains and losses, as well as other factors. Economic concepts are intended to derive an estimate of what an entity is worth by using mark-to-market rules, estimated economic depreciation, and no off-balance sheet financing, among other factors. Thus, tax concepts will be more in line with economic concepts, making the tax computation more in accord with HS concepts. In addition, taxpayers will have an additional measure of performance, in addition to income measured using general accounting standards, which is reasonably comparable across entities and sectors. Such information may help investors with evaluations and enhance decision making.

Finally, transparency will be enhanced, at least for entities subject to regulatory oversight. It will be clear that the entity collecting the advanced tax is not a taxpayer. Taxpayers are the individual owners, and they have the right to know exactly how their income is derived. Thus, there should be no confidentiality of tax computations, at least for publicly held entities.[80]

The proposed income measure and advanced tax basis for traded entities is:

Income = Income according to some standard + Change in Goodwill

where the Change in Goodwill = Difference between the sources and uses of income measures.

Recall we claim that income measured by the sources and uses of income will not be equal when there are active asset markets. Accounting rules for depreciation and other computations are used to measure the sources of income. The change in the market value of assets is based on risk-adjusted expectations about future income. Given different approaches, there is no reason to believe that the values will be equal. Adding the difference of the two values to the sources of income will force the equality or:

Nonhuman Capital Income$_t$ – Cash Distribution s$_t$ – Asset Value$_t$ + Asset Value$_{t-1}$ = Change in Goodwill

So:

Nonhuman Capital Income$_t$ + Change in Goodwill = Cash Distribution s$_t$ + Asset Value$_{t-1}$

In effect, the book value reported on the balance sheet is replaced with the market value by making this adjustment. This means there is no need for a separate capital gains tax. In addition, comprehensive income is expanded. This is because the capital gain is positively correlated with income. (The capital gain would be perfectly correlated with income, holding distributions constant, if perfect certainly prevailed.) Thus, replacing book values with market values will eliminate the overlap, leaving income arising from other factors, such as risk taking.

For example, suppose income is 100, there are no distributions, and the initial market value of the asset is 2000. If there is perfect certainty, the market value of the

---

[80] Income derivation for closely held entities should be known by the owners.

Table 3.10 Computation of basis for withholding on income to equity capital
(initial list—not complete)[a]

    I. Option I: Full accrual adjusted for inflation (using the method described in
    Conrad 2017)

Income and expenses	Treatment
Gross Revenue	Full accrual
Interest accrued	Gross-up and credit if withheld
Dividends, capital gains, and other partial liquidations accrued from other withholding agents	Gross-up and flow through of credit
Dividends, capital gains, and other partial liquidations accrued from persons who are not withholding agents	Taxed in full if paid by domestic residents. Gross-up and foreign tax credit, to the extent applicable, if paid by nonresidents.
Capital gains	• Same as individual treatment to the extent assets are not depreciated • Gains and losses automatically included in pool accounts
Foreign exchange gains and losses and other accruals (hedges, forward contracts, derivatives)	Mark to market
Deductions	
Payments to human capital	Fully deductible
Fringe benefits	Fringe benefit tax
Inventories	Either inflation-adjusted LIFO or FIFO
Depreciation	• Open-ended pooled accounting adjusted for inflation for all tangible personal property and intangible property • Separate accounting for real property by asset (including mineral leases, land leases for forest products, and other types of agricultural activity)
Loss carry forward	None—full flow through
Interest expense	Fully deducted
Treatment of certain items	• Exploration and development in mining: capitalization and amortization by property • Research and development: capitalization and amortization via pooled accounting • Pension accruals: current deduction if funded • Reclamation and closure: current deduction on a pooled amortization basis if funded • Bad debt reserves: reserve accounting based on regulatory proportions that are exogenous to entity

Continued

Table 3.10 *Continued*

Income and expenses	Treatment
	• Reserves for insurance: reserve accounting based on regulatory proportions that are exogenous to entities • Training: capitalized and amortized • Regulated utilities: Full flow through accounting to shareholder level
Taxes	Deductible as a cost of doing business unless there is a foreign tax credit
Goodwill	For entities actively traded on any market, the change in the market value of assets (including debt) will be included in income and classified as goodwill
Nongovernmental organizations (NGOs)	• Treated as withholding agents with full public reporting • If no residual claimants, then amounts withheld are final tax
Government	• Same treatment as NGOs
Transition rules	See Annex 2

II. Option II: Use generally accepted accounting principles with adjustments.

Adjustments include:

- Goodwill for entities actively traded on a market, and
- Mark-to-market values for all actively traded assets and liabilities.

---

[a] Omitted items include but are not limited to equity in partnerships, carried interests and stock options.

asset will increase to 2100. The change in goodwill would be zero and there would be one tax imposed on 100. Suppose uncertainty is present, however. The ending market value could be higher or lower than 100 because the market value will reflect the risk-adjusted values of future income. Suppose the ending market value is 2115 or 2095. This means that the change in goodwill will be 15 or −5, respectively, so that the income tax base would be 115 or 95. A nonzero value for the change in goodwill means that either the sources of income are incorrectly measured, or the values reported in the uses of income reflect values that are determined by factors other than income (a change in the macroeconomic environment such as a recession perhaps).

There are advantages to this approach. Income accounting is preserved and all the information contained in both market valuation and accounting standards is used. In effect, the computed value of the change in goodwill is equal to the combined errors in measuring accounting income and from market estimates of the future value of income.[81] If all assets were actively traded, then imposing advanced tax on the uses

---

[81] The change in goodwill = errors in accounting + errors in measuring the risk-adjusted future value of income. These errors could be correlated. For example, book income measures may affect investor

side of the income identity could make standard income accounting irrelevant for income computation purposes. There may be information in computing the sources of income, however. For example, there is information about sales, current costs, and other information that do not require assumptions about historical cost. Thus, the proposed approach provides a basis for investors, as well as the tax authorities, to use all the information available. A second advantage is that one measure of book income can be used to compute advanced tax for both traded and nontraded entities, with the difference being the timing of the measurement of the change in market value. Thus, there is no question about using a separate standard for traded as opposed to nontraded equity. Finally, and as noted above, there is no difference between the derivation of income, as a matter of method, before the adjustment in goodwill, and the application of the corporate tax imposed in many countries. The corporate tax is eliminated, but the use of corporations as APAs remains, so the proposal can be accommodated by most tax administrations.

iii. **Inflation Accounting.** Table 3.11 contains an example of the proposed approach with inflation accounting.[82] Fixed income is computed by subtracting costs (labour and depreciation in this simple case) from sales, all on an accrual basis. Note that sales and labour costs are automatically adjusted for inflation because these values are measured in nominal terms. Depreciation is based on historical cost, however, so it is necessary to adjust depreciation for inflation. If there is more than one asset subject to depreciation and the assets have different lives, then inflation adjustments need to be made on an asset classification basis (see Annex A3.1). Book income before the change in goodwill is found in Line 7. Line 9 contains the value of distributions made to shareholders in cash during the period, and Line 11 contains the change in the market value of equity which is equal to the difference between Line 10 and Line 1. Line 13 is the definition of income, on an ex-post basis, when the change in the market value is known. Of course, this value could be used, and is effectively used, for advanced tax purposes and is equal to income on an ex-post basis. To equate the income tax base using the adjusted book income, the difference between book income and income for tax purposes is computed via Line 17.[83]

Table 3.12 contains an example where inflation adjustments are not made to book income. Note that the lack of inflation adjustments increases book income by more than inflation in Line 8. This is because depreciation is not adjusted for inflation. Thus, other things equal, there would be an increase in the real tax. In the current case, however, the investors know that the advanced tax attributable to book income

expectations about future income, so an error in book income generates an error in the measure of the present value of future income.

[82] The inflation adjustments can be based on either Conrad (1990) or Goldschmidt and Yaron (1991). Detailed rules and computations are included in both documents and are not repeated here.

[83] Inventories may have to be adjusted for inflation regardless of whether LIFO or FIFO is used. The common recommendation for inflation adjustments is to switch from FIFO to LIFO valuation for inventories. The issue, however, is that initial inventories will need to be adjusted for inflation regardless of the valuation choice. The valuation choice determines the timing of any gain or loss on a realization. There are other inflation effects such as the real income gain from borrowing with fixed interest rates.

Table 3.11 Equity investment: inflation indexing

Assumptions: Same as Table 3.7 except there is a partial liquidation of 74 in real
terms during the period

Row #	Item	Value No Inflation	Value 10% Inflation
1	Initial market value of equity	1,000.00	1,100.00
2	Computation of income		
3	Sales	147.00	168.30
4	Labour	40.00	44.00
5	Depreciation (on inflation-adjusted base)	33.00	36.30
6			-
7	Book income before change in goodwill: Line 3 – Line 4 – Line 5	74.00	81.40
8			
9	Partial liquidations (dividends)	61.00	67.10
10	Ending market value of equity: no real gain	1,019.00	1,120.90
11	Change in market value of equity	19.00	20.90
12			
13	Cash flow plus change in market value	80.00	88.00
14			
15	Adjustment in goodwill: Line 13 – Line 7	6.00	6.60
16	CMDI: Line 7 + Line 15	80.00	88.00
17	Advanced tax: 25% of Line 15	20.00	22.00
18			
19	Real value of advanced tax base	80.00	80.00
20	Real value of advanced tax	20.00	20.00

will increase and the change in after-tax income is reflected in a reduction in the
change in the market value of the equity. The result is that there is no change in the
real value of the advanced tax (compare Line 22 of Table 3.12 to Line 20 of Table 3.11).
This result is an example of tax capitalization into market prices and the potential for
markets to offset the effects of inflation. One assumption necessary for this result to
hold is that inflation is fully anticipated. This is a strong assumption. In practice, inflation matters because prices may not automatically adjust to changes in the price level,
inflation is not perfectly measured, and there is uncertainty about the time path of
absolute price changes. For example, nominal wages may not adjust fully to changes
in inflation because of contracts, loans may be denominated in nominal interest rates,
inflation is imperfectly measured, and future inflation is not known with perfect
certainty. The first two points imply that inflation, even if expected, may affect the
income distribution without affecting aggregate real income. The last point implies
that uncertainty about inflation could have adverse effects that can be mitigated at
least in part by inflation adjustments.

Table 3.12 Equity investment: no inflation adjustments

Assumptions: Same as Table 3.7 but market price of capital adjusts to keep real tax-inclusive return at 8%

Row #	Item	Value no inflation	Value 10% inflation
1	Initial market value of equity	1,000.00	1,000.00
2			
3	Computation of income		
4	Sales	147.00	168.30
5	Labour	40.00	44.00
6	Depreciation	33.00	33.00
7			-
8	Book income before change in goodwill: Line 4 – Line 5 – Line 6	74.00	91.30
9			
10			
11	Partial liquidations	61.00	75.26
12	Ending market value of equity	1,019.00	1,012.74
13	Change in market value of equity	19.00	12.74
14			
15	Cash flow plus change in market value	80.00	88.00
16			
17	Adjustment in goodwill: Line 15 – Line 8	6.00	(3.30)
18	CMDI	80.00	88.00
19	Advanced tax: 25% of Line 18	20.00	22.00
20			
21	Real value of advanced tax base	80.00	80.00
22	Real value of advanced tax	20.00	20.00

Two points complete the current discussion. First, if income is negative in any period, then the loss should flow through to the taxpayer. This means there is no need for loss carryforwards at the entity level. The advanced tax will be negative. We recommend, however, that the lower bound on the advanced tax be zero, so there would be no negative tax accruing to the shareholder. This is because the advanced tax is only a prepayment of the total tax that is the aggregate of all income and expenses. Negative income from one income type does not necessarily mean that the individual will have too much advanced tax withheld in total. The taxpayer might still have a positive tax after credits and would have to repay part, if not all, of the negative tax from one income segment. Given the relatively short time lag between the reporting of advanced payments and the annual reconciliation, the additional churning of payments and repayments may be difficult to justify.

Second, there is no definition of dividends. Cash flow to shareholders, not dividends, is recorded on the uses side of the income expression. It is immaterial whether the cash payment is defined to be a dividend, a repayment of capital, or some combination. The definition of a dividend depends on a stacking rule and accounting rules for income measurement. For example, one rule is to define a dividend as a payment from accumulated earnings. This means that payments to shareholders are dividends if accumulated earnings are positive, so the stacking rule is that distributions are dividends first and repayments of capital—partial liquidations—are paid after accumulated earnings are exhausted. Our view is that earnings, if retained, become part of the capital stock and are reflected in the share value. A cash distribution to shareholders lowers the value of the net worth and, accordingly, the share value. Thus, we have used the term partial liquidation for any cash distribution and there is no advanced tax on the distribution.[84] This point is reinforced by noting that cash flow to owners could be negative in the case where shareholders make further capital contributions.

b. Assets for Which Market Values Are Not Known until Liquidation
Income measurement is mechanical when independent observable prices exist, as shown in the previous section. Adjustments are necessary when no independent measure for stock value exists. Individuals hold a variety of investment assets that are not actively traded, including but not limited to: interests in partnerships, sole proprietorships, and other pass-through entities such as closely held corporations. Such entities are relevant for all economies. In addition, some assets are used for both investment and consumption purposes. Owner-occupied housing, collectibles, jewellery, art, and other types of assets are examples.

The absence of independent observable market values on a current basis has two effects. First, it is impossible to measure economic depreciation for the asset. Economic depreciation is defined to be the change in the asset price between two time periods.[85] While related to use and maintenance, economic depreciation can vary for

---

[84] Investors would need to know whether a payment is attributed to accumulated earnings or capital gains are measured on a realization basis. A dividend will not affect the shareholders' capital, but a distribution from capital will reduce the investor's basis for the computation of any gain. Such computations are irrelevant for Haig-Simons income computations and for our policy proposal because gains and losses are accrued when earned, in the case of our proposal, and are taxed at the time of accrual. The initial investment is irrelevant because all values are marked to market and the gain or loss accrues on a periodic basis independent of realization.

[85] Note that this definition is simply the one period capital gain or loss. An alternative definition of depreciation could be the change in the market value of an asset in period 't' after being held for one period, holding all prices constant. (We take it that this is a more common definition employed in empirical studies (Hulten & Wykoff, 1980) and in methodological approaches to the analysis of marginal effective tax rates.) This would facilitate the distinction between the time path of the asset price as it ages from any capital gain or loss resulting from a change in relative prices. This distinction is helpful for some purposes, such as understanding how relative prices of used assets change, but it is not relevant for tax purposes because the only question is: What is the value of the asset at any point in time? While it is interesting to study, or to speculate, about why asset prices change, the only economic issue for tax purposes is what is the value of an asset at a particular point in time and, for income measurement purposes, the difference between the beginning and ending values. Tax depreciation, as opposed to economic depreciation, will be allowed in computing balance sheet values for assets that are used to produce income and for which market prices do not exist. The error in income measure (either positive or negative) will be recaptured using the procedure described here to the extent that such recording is worth the administrative expense. The bottom line is that the objective is to measure 'net income' and not its component parts. Errors from using artificial rules such as tax depreciation and if market prices of used capital goods do not change will be recaptured using the proposed procedures.

Table 3.13 Deferral and proposed treatment

Line #	Time	Totals	0	1	2	3	4	5	6	7	8	9	10
	A. Investment: Annual reporting and reinvestment (Asset A)													
	Balances and accruals													
1														
2	Initial balance	-	-	100.00	106.25	112.89	119.95	127.44	135.41	143.87	152.86	162.42	172.57
3	Interest income			6.25	6.64	7.06	7.50	7.97	8.46	8.99	9.55	10.15	10.79
4	Balance at end of the year		100.00	106.25	112.89	119.95	127.44	135.41	143.87	152.86	162.42	172.57	183.35
	HS income to equity													
6														
7	Gross revenue	-		6.25	6.64	7.06	7.50	7.97	8.46	8.99	9.55	10.15	10.79
8	HS income before tax	83.35	-	6.25	6.64	7.06	7.50	7.97	8.46	8.99	9.55	10.15	10.79
9	Tax	16.67	-	1.25	1.33	1.41	1.50	1.59	1.69	1.80	1.91	2.03	2.16
10	After-tax HS income	66.68	-	5.00	5.31	5.64	6.00	6.37	6.77	7.19	7.64	8.12	8.63
11	Annual effective tax rate			20.00%	20.00%	20.00%	20.00%	20.00%	20.00%	20.00%	20.00%	20.00%	20.00%
	Cash flows													
12														
13	Cash flow to equity	66.68	-100.00	-1.25	-1.33	-1.41	-1.50	-1.59	-1.69	-1.80	-1.91	-2.03	181.20
14	Cash flow to govt	83.35	0.00	6.25	6.64	7.06	7.50	7.97	8.46	8.99	9.55	10.15	10.79
15	Cash flow to the economy	150.04	-100.00	5.00	5.31	5.64	6.00	6.37	6.77	7.19	7.64	8.12	191.98
16	PV of cash flow to equity	0.00	-100.00	-1.19	-1.20	-1.22	-1.23	-1.25	-1.26	-1.28	-1.29	-1.31	111.24
17	PV of cash flow to govt	12.56	0.00	1.19	1.20	1.22	1.23	1.25	1.26	1.28	1.29	1.31	1.32
18	PV of cash flow to the economy	12.56	-100.00	0.00	0.00	0.00	0.00	0.00	0.00	0.00	0.00	0.00	112.56
	B. Asset: No annual reporting and no active market (Asset B)													
19	Discount factors		1.00	1.05	1.10	1.16	1.22	1.28	1.34	1.41	1.48	1.55	1.63
20														
21	Balances and Accruals													
22	Initial balance		-											

Continued

Table 3.13 *Continued*

Line #	Time	Totals	0	1	2	3	4	5	6	7	8	9	10
23	Interest income												
24	Balance at end of the year		100.00										183.35
25	**HS income to equity**												
26	Gross revenue		0.00	0.00	0.00	0.00	0.00	0.00	0.00	0.00	0.00	0.00	183.35
27	HS income before tax	83.35	0.00	0.00	0.00	0.00	0.00	0.00	0.00	0.00	0.00	0.00	83.35
28	Tax before recapture	16.67	0.00	0.00	0.00	0.00	0.00	0.00	0.00	0.00	0.00	0.00	16.67
29	After tax HS income	66.68	0.00	0.00	0.00	0.00	0.00	0.00	0.00	0.00	0.00	0.00	66.68
30	Annual effective tax rate												20.00%
31	**Cash flows**												
32	Cash flow to equity	66.68	−100.00	0.00	0.00	0.00	0.00	0.00	0.00	0.00	0.00	0.00	166.68
33	Cash flow to govt	16.67	–	0.00	0.00	0.00	0.00	0.00	0.00	0.00	0.00	0.00	16.67
34	Cash flow to the economy	83.35	−100.00	0.00	0.00	0.00	0.00	0.00	0.00	0.00	0.00	0.00	183.35
35	PV of cash flow to equity	2.33	−100.00	0.00	0.00	0.00	0.00	0.00	0.00	0.00	0.00	0.00	102.33
36	PV of cash flow to govt	10.23	–	0.00	0.00	0.00	0.00	0.00	0.00	0.00	0.00	0.00	10.23
37	PV of cash flow to the economy	12.56	−100.00	0.00	0.00	0.00	0.00	0.00	0.00	0.00	0.00	0.00	112.56
	C. No inter-period market values												
38	Discount factors		1.00	1.05	1.10	1.16	1.22	1.28	1.34	1.41	1.48	1.55	1.63
39	**Balances and accruals**												
40	Initial balance		–										
41	Interest income												
42	Balance at end of the year		100.00										181.20
43	**HS income to equity**												
44	Gross revenue		–	–	–	–	–	–	–	–	–	–	–

45	HS income before tax	83.35	–	–	–	–	–	–	–	–	–	83.35
46	Tax before recapture	16.67	–	–	–	–	–	–	–	–	–	16.67
47	Recapture	3.79	–	–	–	–	–	–	–	–	–	3.79
48	After tax HS income	62.89	–	–	–	–	–	–	–	–	–	62.89
49	Annual effective tax rate											24.55%

D. Computation of base including recapture

50	What is observable	–	–100.00	–	–	–	–	–	–	–	–	183.35
51	Step 1: Compute return (IRR)	0.0625										
52	Step 2: Compute first year return	6.25										
53	Step 3: Compute imputed annual return		6.25	6.64	7.06	7.50	7.97	8.46	8.99	9.55	10.15	10.79
54	Step 4: Present value	62.82	5.95	6.02	6.09	6.16	6.24	6.31	6.39	6.46	6.54	6.62
55	Step 5: Taxable income including interest											102.32
56	Step 6: Amount recaptured											18.97
57	**Cash flows**											
58	Cash flow to equity	62.89	–100.00	–	–	–	–	–	–	–	–	162.89
59	Cash flow to govt	20.46	–	–	–	–	–	–	–	–	–	20.46
60	Cash flow to the economy	83.35	–100.00	–	–	–	–	–	–	–	–	183.35
61	PV of cash flow to equity	–	–100.00	–	–	–	–	–	–	–	–	100.00
62	PV of cash flow to govt	12.56	–	–	–	–	–	–	–	–	–	12.56
63	PV of cash flow to the economy	12.56	–100.00	–	–	–	–	–	–	–	–	112.56

any number of reasons, including changes in relative prices,[86] expectations, maintenance effort, and other factors. This may not be a significant issue for assets that
are a small part of the overall portfolio of an economy's assets and for which the
price path is generally expected to decrease. The issues may be significant, however,
for real property where there is a probability that the value of the real property will
appreciate (have negative depreciation), but the time path of the appreciation (or
depreciation) is not known. The same statement applies with equal force to equity
interests in closely held entities and related business interests. Second, there are no
objective independent standards for measuring the change in the value of such assets
absent trade. Valuations could be made but are administratively cumbersome and are
subject to dispute.

Taxation of income on a current (or accrual) basis with other income taxed on a
realization basis creates a benefit called deferral that is not available to investors in
assets that can be marked to market. The effect of deferral is illustrated in Table 3.13.
Table 3.13A contains the flow of an investment of 100 invested in a bank deposit
paying 6.25% per annum that is compounded for 10 years. Interest is observable and
taxed at 20%. Table 3.13B contains an investment of 100 in Asset B where the annual
income is not observed[87] and the asset is sold in t = 10. The flow is representative of
an asset such as owner-occupied housing or land.[88] No tax is paid during the holding
period. Reasonable annual taxation is not possible for Asset B. In this case, the change
in the asset value is not known until the end of tax period 10 when the individual
sells Asset B and accrues the income.[89] The change in income for Asset B can be
computed in tax period 10, but the computation itself is identical to the computation

[86] For example, the relative price of a two-year-old energy-efficient automobile may change with a
change in the price of gasoline. The point is to treat all nonhuman capital goods in an identical manner.
That is, bonds are treated no differently from machines, land, or other assets.
[87] That is, there is no attempt to measure the consumption value of a nontraded asset, such as an owner-
occupied house; or the imputed rental value net of expenses from holding the asset (house) for one tax
period and having the owner implicitly charge rent; or the value a miser receives from hoarding cash. Only
the change in the value of the asset, not from its use, is measured. The value added from using the assets is
part of total household income that is not observable. Thus, the flow of services of owner-occupied housing, combined with the value of human capital services and other inputs devoted to household production,
produces a portion of total value added, and real net national income, which is not measurable.
[88] The tax rate is assumed to be 20%. The interest rate is 5.00%, so the tax-inclusive interest rate is 6.25%.
This means that if an individual obtains a tax preference, then the rest of the population must finance that
preference at 5.00% per annum. Risk is absent.
[89] Note the difference between accretion and accrual for Asset B. The individual sells Asset B at the
end of tax period 10, but there is no statement about whether the individual receives cash, a receivable, or
another asset such as real property for the sale. The income accrues at the end of tax period 10 because the
individual has taken an action in the market. Accretion and accrual are equivalent for Asset A. Someone
has taken an action such as posting the interest income to the individual's account. The individual may
not have taken the action, but title to the interest income has been transferred. There is an issue about
exchanges of goods and services relative to cash. If there is an independent value for part, or all, of the
property exchanged, then the deferral period ends. If, however, there is no independent valuation for the
property exchanged, then there will be a trade in the adjusted basis. For example, suppose Individual A
purchased land in 2010 for 100 and Individual B purchased land in 2015 for 150, and there is a like-kind
exchange. For tax purposes, Individual A will have land with a basis of 150 and a deferral period beginning
in 2015 while Individual B will have land with a basis of 100 and a deferral period beginning in 2010. There
may be situations where it might be possible to have constructive realizations and adjust the basis, but the
rule provided above should be the basic approach.

on an annual basis. That is, the tax base is computed by taking the difference in the asset values between the two reporting periods.[90]

Note that the reporting period is one tax period for Asset A and ten tax periods for Asset B.[91] Taxable income for Asset B is equal to the undiscounted summation of the taxable income of Asset A (83.35 in both cases).[92] In addition, the total tax paid on both assets is identical, again in undiscounted terms (16.67 in both cases). The benefit to the owner of Asset B is that the total tax is deferred until period 10 (the disposal date). So, in present value terms, there is a tax advantage to paying the same tax later; thus, the term 'deferral'.[93]

To preserve the neutrality of the income tax across investment types, there must be some adjustment to the taxation of either Asset A or Asset B. One option would be to choose the tax period as the length of time between the purchase of both assets and the sale of Asset B. This makes little sense, however, because the time of disposal is endogenous and defined for each asset transaction. The determination of the tax period needs to be exogenous if the tax system is to be administered. Thus, it is common to choose a tax period of a reasonable but arbitrary length (e.g., one year).

Our proposal is simple and requires a straightforward computation common in many financial transactions; the term 'recapture' is used to define the procedure.[94] Before proceeding with the computations, it is important to note the nature of the problem. If it were possible to measure the change in the value of Asset B each tax period, then tax would be charged. The value of Asset B is not known, however, so neither the owner nor anyone else knows the change in the value. The taxpayer, if she chose, could sell Asset B at the end of any period and then everyone would know the value. If, however, the taxpayer chooses to hold the asset for another period, then she believes, by assumption, that the expected risk-adjusted gain is greater than either investing in risk-free assets or increasing current consumption. Deferring realization means that all taxpayers, via the government, must finance the revenue loss, in the case of the gain (or benefit from deferring the expenditure to compensate the investor for a loss), and the individual forgoes the loss offset in the case of the loss

---

[90] Inflation is assumed to be zero.

[91] Tax periods are commonly assumed to be one year, but in economics there is no reason to have tax periods correspond to a year and, in fact, some countries use tax periods of less than one year. For example, Ukrainian tax periods for profits tax purposes are one calendar quarter and, given the rather contentious flow of taxation under indirect taxes, the VAT tax period is commonly one month. There may be annual reconciliations, but the payment for the month or the quarter is the final payment for the tax period, as opposed to some estimated payment for the tax computed on an annual basis.

[92] A simple savings-type account is used for illustrative purposes. The method is generally applicable in the sense that the comparisons are not path dependent. All that is required is that the value of the two assets is the same at the time the asset subject to deferral is liquidated.

[93] Note that the tax advantages of deferral are not known with certainty. That is, an individual who chooses to make an investment in an asset for which there is not an active market composed of close substitutes does not know whether the value at the end of the holding period will cover their opportunity cost. Increases in real housing and land prices are no sure thing, as evidenced from the financial crisis in 2008 and 2009 and the periodic change in housing prices in particular areas that are subject to factors such as outmigration, increases in unemployment, and other exogenous events.

[94] This procedure is based on William Vickrey (1939), 'Averaging of Income for Income-Tax Purposes', *Journal of Political Economy*, 47(3): 379. https://doi.org/10.1086/255390. Alan Auerbach (1991), 'Retrospective Capital Gains Taxation', *American Economic Review*, 81(1): 167–178. https://www.jstor.org/stable/2006793

(or benefits from deferring the tax on the gain). The cost of the deferral is known, however, and is equal to the interest rate on alternative investments. Accordingly, the solution to the problem is to charge interest on the deferred tax. The interest charge will increase the nominal tax in the case of a gain and increase the nominal refund in the case of a loss in the period of disposal, but the present value of either the gain or the loss will be invariant to the timing of the disposal. Such an approach implies that all other taxpayers will be indifferent to when the investor sells the asset because they will be compensated for carrying costs, at least at the margin.[95]

The steps necessary to determine the interest charge, in general, are:

1. Compute the gain or loss at the time of disposal by subtracting the owner's adjusted basis at the time of disposal, adjusted for inflation, if necessary, from the value of the realization. If the value is zero, then no adjustment is necessary. If there is a gain or loss, then proceed with the computations.
2. Compute the internal rate of return (IRR) from an investment where the adjusted basis is the price paid in the purchase period and the realized value is the price received at the time of sale.
3. Compute the annual imputed interest on an investment equal to the value of the adjusted basis using the IRR as the return.
   a. The initial interest charge is simply the adjusted basis times the interest rate.
   b. The interest charge in each subsequent year is compounded.
4. Compute the future value of the flow of annual compound returns.
5. Impose tax on the summation of the gain plus the interest cost.[96]

For illustration purposes, the steps are reported in Lines 32–37 of Table 3.13B. with the amount of tax on the recapture computed separately to aid the illustration. The

---

[95] If the investment is marginal from the perspective of the investor, then the investor is indifferent (in risk-adjusted terms) to holding the risky asset for one more tax period and investing in a risk-free asset. The proposed approach, however, is intended to ensure that the people of the taxing jurisdiction are compensated given the marginal (or inframarginal) choices of any investor. As a technical matter, the interest rate charged should be the tax-inclusive rate and the individual should be able to deduct the interest expense on the loan and the interest income should be taxable income to the government, as the representative of the people. An alternative would be to charge the net-of-tax rate and disallow the deduction. The net-of-tax rate would be equal to the prevailing interest rate charged for the loan times unity minus the highest marginal tax rate per annum. The determination of the particular 'prevailing' interest rate to be used here is not a straightforward issue. We discuss it briefly at the end of this section.

[96] Note that there are an infinite number of ways to make an investment of 100 in t = 0 and to have a market value of 183.35 at the end of period 10. Given the lack of market data, the actual path is not known, and it would be futile to speculate on the actual period-by-period time path. More important, the actual accrual path is immaterial for tax purposes. That is, there is a type of path independence in this case because the only thing that matters is that the price in t = 0 is 100 and the price in t = 10 is 183.35, not the path. This is true because the present value of the tax would not be affected by the path in this case. If the period-by-period time path were known, then there would be no deferral and the income per tax period would be taxed on a current basis. The internal rate of return is an average, however, that, when compounded per period, yields the desired result. No claim is made that the computation is the ideal solution, but the fact that the ideal solution is not known makes the issue irrelevant given the objectives to reduce or to eliminate the tax benefits of deferral. Thus, the only criterion is whether the present value of the tax is invariant to the individual's choice of when to dispose of the asset given the exogenous definition of the tax period.

recaptured amount at the standard rate is reported (Line 47 of Table 3.13C).[97] Steps are disaggregated for clarity and the future value of the interest cost is computed by taking the present value of the flow and then computing the future value. Again, this is done for illustration purposes.

Note that the present value of the tax for Asset B is the same as the present value of the tax for Asset A. The after-tax net present values are the same because deferral is eliminated. The interest cost eliminates the benefits of deferral because the taxpayer cannot reduce real taxes by delaying payment. In effect, deferred tax is a loan made by all taxpayers to the asset owner and recapture is the balloon repayment. All tax-payers are reimbursed the carrying cost of funding government operations during the deferral period and so are indifferent.[98]

Recapture works in an equivalent manner for losses. That is, given the risk-sharing properties of the income tax, all taxpayers share proportionally in the losses as well as the gains from an individual's income. In the context of deferral, this means that the people of the country should compensate the taxpayer for the deferred interest on forgone tax losses that would have accrued on an annual basis (see Conrad & Alexeev, 2021 for a numerical example).[99] This would be the case in a fully developed income tax because the loss would flow through to the individual and reduce total income.[100]

Tax imposed at the time of realization combined with the interest charge is not a separate capital gains tax. Rather, the tax is equivalent to the annual tax on the flow of returns. The only reason the tax is charged is because zero, or too little, tax accrued during the holding period. Table 3.14 contains an illustration of this point where it is assumed that investors own a closely held enterprise. An investor is assumed to invest 1000 in t = 0 in a corporation and holds the shares for ten years. The corporation uses depreciable assets to produce output for sale. The tax-inclusive return is 13.33% and the tax-exclusive return is 10%. The tax rate is 25% and there is no inflation. These assumptions result in a zero net present value for the investor (discounted at 10% net of tax) if full tax is paid. The advanced tax on the investor's proportional share of income is computed by multiplying the tax rate times the measured tax base. It is assumed that the government uses the international accounting standards as the tax base (shown on Lines 2–7) of Table 3.14. Depreciation is subtracted from gross revenue and the tax rate is applied to yield the advanced tax.[101] This amount is reported to the owner who uses the tax as a credit against total income tax. Depreciation plus

---

[97] There are standard mathematical formulae for making these computations, but interest rates will change through time, so it will probably be more straightforward to compute the total value of the recapture using the rote methods described here.
[98] Like all interest, the interest charge for deferral should be deducted so the interest rate charged is a tax-inclusive interest rate.
[99] Again, advanced tax should be zero if a loss results because the loss will flow through to the owner who will aggregate losses and gains.
[100] An additional benefit from recapture is the elimination of the lock-in effect, or at least it is reduced significantly. Taxing gains and losses on a realization basis has been claimed to create an incentive for taxpayers to defer gains when the proceeds from realization could have been used to make investments in higher returns. The lock-in effect arises because disposals trigger taxation and affect the after-tax return so much that it might not be worth investing in an asset yielding a higher return. See Conrad and Alexeev (2021) to see how our proposal eliminates this effect.
[101] Other costs such as labour are not included here for simplicity.

after-tax income is retained in the entity for investment purposes. The ending book value of the balance sheet is reported in Line 22 of Table 3.14. This process continues until the end of period 10 when the investor disposes of their shares for 2,768.08.

Recall that we propose to set the book value of net worth equal to the market value on an annual basis for actively traded equity. Such a computation is not possible in the case of closely held enterprises because the only time a market value is known is at the date of disposal. In effect, incorporating the change in the market value has been deferred. The steps outlined above are used to compute the tax and interest on deferred amounts and reported in Lines 36–47. Note the following points.

- The gain (435.31 in Line 31 of Table 3.14) is computed by subtracting the book value of the entity from the amount realized. This value is the investor's adjusted basis, not the 1000 initial investment. The initial investment of 1000 has increased in value (at least book value) because earnings were retained and reinvested.[102] Again, there is not a capital gains tax. The investor paid tax each period but in amounts that were insufficient to cover full income. Thus, the tax and interest are imposed to compensate for too little income tax being imposed during the holding period.[103]
- The remaining steps are the same as those discussed in the prior example (Table 3.13).
- Note the present value to the investor (Line 50 of Table 3.14) is positive. This means there are tax-induced rents in the system. Both the return to capital and rents are subject to income tax. This means that the tax and interest charge reduce deferral's benefit while capturing a share of the present value of future rents.[104]

Note that if the realized value and net book values are equal, then there would be no computation for deferral.[105] This means that the present value of the tax is equivalent to the tax that would have been paid if income had been computed according to economic rules. Finally, note the similarity between this result and resource rent taxes used for natural resources. Rent taxes are only imposed if the present value of the

---

[102] The term 'adjusted basis' is used because it is an accurate description of how the investor's equity position changes through time. If there were no reinvestment, then the investor would get cash equal to the retained earnings plus depreciation. The depreciation is a repayment of capital, so the investor has less invested after the repayment, just like repayments of principal reduce the outstanding balance of a loan. Table 3.14 contains the opposite case where all depreciation and earnings are reinvested. The investor gets no cash, but the value of the equity position has increased. Thus, it is necessary to adjust the owner's proportional interest in the entity's net worth.

[103] The example in Table 3.13 is just an extreme case of this point. If some tax had been paid during the holding period, on presumed income perhaps, then amounts reinvested would have been reduced and the amount of tax to compensate for the deferral would have been smaller.

[104] The purchaser's basis is 2768.08 and if the purchaser then sells at a later day for 2768.08 (adjusted for inflation), then there would be no deferral and no tax on the future rents because the rents were capitalized into the market value of the assets. It does not matter how the rents are created. Rents were created here because tax depreciation was greater than economic depreciation, so the investor is making excess profits relative to the economic definition of income.

[105] In the first example, the adjusted basis is 100 because there is no change in the book value (adjusted for inflation). A tax would have been imposed if income was reported.

Table 3.14 Recapture of gains and losses for closely held entity

Line #	Time / Item	0	1	2	3	4	5	6	7	8	9	10
1	**1. Computation of income**											
2	Gross revenue		283.33	315.21	349.96	387.98	429.67	475.47	525.85	581.34	642.49	709.91
3	Tax depreciation		200.00	212.50	227.91	246.21	267.48	291.81	319.36	350.33	384.98	423.61
4	Income before tax		83.33	102.71	122.05	141.76	162.19	183.66	206.50	231.01	257.51	286.31
5												
6	Advanced tax		20.83	25.68	30.51	35.44	40.55	45.91	51.62	57.75	64.38	71.58
7	After tax income		62.50	77.03	91.54	106.32	121.64	137.74	154.87	173.26	193.13	214.73
8												
9	**Nominal cash flow to entity**											
10	Cash in											
11	Cash receipts from operations	1,000.00	283.33	315.21	349.96	387.98	429.67	475.47	525.85	581.34	642.49	709.91
12												
13	**II. Entity cash flow**											
14	Cash out											
15	Advanced tax		20.83	25.68	30.51	35.44	40.55	45.91	51.62	57.75	64.38	71.58
16	Dividends		0.00	0.00	0.00	0.00	0.00	0.00	0.00	0.00	0.00	0.00
17	Distributions to shareholders		0.00	0.00	0.00	0.00	0.00	0.00	0.00	0.00	0.00	0.00
18	**Cash flow to entity (used for reinvestment)**	1,000.00	262.50	289.53	319.45	352.54	389.12	429.55	474.23	523.59	578.11	638.34
19												
20	**III. Relevant balance sheet values**											
21	Entity balance sheet values											
22	End of year net worth (book value at the end of last year—depreciation + cash flow to entity after tax	1,000.00	1,062.50	1,139.53	1,231.07	1,337.39	1,459.03	1,596.78	1,751.65	1,924.91	2,118.04	2,332.77

Continued

Table 3.14 *Continued*

Line #	Item	0	1	2	3	4	5	6	7	8	9	10
23												
24												
25	**IV Computations at realization date**											
26												
27	**A. Capital gain**											
28												
29	Value of liquidation											2,768.08
30	Ending book value of equity											2,332.77
31	Basis of initial tax											435.31
32	Withholding tax on net gain (tax rate * basis for initial tax)*											108.83
33												
34	**B. Computation of recapture**											
35												
36	Capital gain to amortize (cash flow to determine average rate of return)	(2,332.77)	–	–	–	–	–	–	–	–	–	2,768.08
37	Average rate of return (internal rate of return computed from Line 36)	1.72569%										
38	Present value	263.94										
39												
40	Imputed excess return per annum (in t=0 value = Line 37 * Line30)		40.26	40.95	41.66	42.38	43.11	43.85	44.61	45.38	46.16	46.96
41	Excess Return Discounted at Government Interest Rate (Line 40 Discounted at Interest Rate Charged for Deferral		36.60	33.84	31.30	28.94	26.77	24.75	22.89	21.17	19.58	18.10

#	Item	Value
42	Present value of excess return (summation of Line 41)	263.94
43	Future value of excess return (future value of Line 40 at interest rate charged for deferral)	684.60
44	Tax base	249.30
45	Recapture (interest charge for deferral) [tax rate * Line 44]	62.32
46	Total tax on gain	171.15
47	After recapture	
48		

V. Cash flows

48	Cash flow to shareholder	(1,000.00)	-	20.83	25.68	30.51	35.44	40.55	45.91	51.62	57.75	64.38	-	2,596.92
49	Cash flow to government	-											242.73
50	NPV to shareholder	1.23											
51	NPV to government	312.70											
52		313.93											

* For illustration only

project is positive. Under the proposed system, rents are taxed on an annual basis, instead of the deferral of the total tax.[106]

The interest rate to use to determine the amount of accumulated interest is an important parameter. One option is to use an international rate such as LIBOR measured in US dollars, adjusted for inflation. This rate is one minimum return that accrues to the local economy from investing tax funds. This rate may not be appropriate for emerging economies because the cost of government debt may differ from the international rate. Idiosyncratic factors such as country risk may be responsible for the difference. Our view is that the rate should be relatively risk free, and so we believe the use of LIBOR is a reasonable option. The interest rate choice should be determined based on discussions with local policy makers relative to the circumstances in the particular country.

c. Treatment of Incentives

We oppose all investment incentives for reasons discussed in Annex A3.1. If investment incentives are used, however, then there is a question about how to treat the incentives when APAs prepay part, or all, of the tax on return to investments. The issue arises because corporations are not taxpayers so cannot benefit from incentives. This means that any investment incentive given to an entity reduces only the advanced payment, but the effectiveness of the incentive depends on the tax paid by the investor. So, how the tax benefits flow through to owners will determine the net incentive. In the case where securities are traded, an incentive will decrease taxes and increase book income by the amount of the tax saving. Other things equal, the price of the stock will also increase. If capitalization is complete, then there would be no change in the difference between market and book values. So, advanced tax decreases by the value of the incentive. In the case where net worth is not marked to market, book income will increase by the value of the tax decrease created by the incentive, so net income to the owner increases in each incentive year. This increase will reduce the amount of any net gain at the time of realization, other things equal. That is, the gain is equal to the realized price at the time of sale less the adjusted basis (the book value in this case). If the realized price is equal to the change in the book value (perfect capitalization), then the incentive will not be recaptured. The implication is that the incentive is effective to the extent that the advanced tax is used as a final tax.

If the advanced tax is not the final tax, then the net effect depends on what happens at the individual level. If the base of the advanced tax is used to compute taxable income, then the incentive flows through. If, however, book income before tax is used to measure includable income, then the value of the incentive can be lost because the advanced tax will not be sufficient and additional tax will accrue. Consistency would dictate that taxable income at the individual level should be computed using the same methods as the advanced tax, so there should be no issue about negating the incentive.

---

[106] This similarity and the fact that the net present value of income equals the net present value of cash flow is the basis for an accrued rent charge proposed by Alexeev and Conrad (2017).

The issue arises, however, because we advocate the use of taxable income as an alternative measure of investment income. That is, book income using tax concepts can be compared to standard measures of book income. Such a comparison is invalid because the incentive distorts the measure of income. For example, a tax holiday in a time period is equivalent to reporting zero taxable income at the individual level even if there is positive taxable income without the incentive. To increase transparency, we recommend that taxable income with and without the incentive be reported to the individual and that taxable income with the incentive be included into the taxpayer's taxable income. The individual will know the subsidy provided to her because of the incentive. In addition, the differences can be aggregated, once administrative procedures are in place, to compute the revenue losses resulting from the incentive. The information will also be useful in determining the distributional implications of the incentive.[107]

3.3.2.3 Expenses of Deriving Income

APAs will collect advanced payments on gross income except for the advanced tax on employees where individual circumstances might be considered. Expenditures necessary to accrue the gross income should be deducted to derive net taxable income. A discussion of some of those expenses combined with a simplification is presented here. It is important to note that individual reporting, with some exceptions, would be required to derive this measure of net income. Such an approach is not practical in many cases, so an alternative approach is discussed. Again, we believe it is important, for policy analysts to have some familiarity with the notions that provide a foundation for our view of net income so that simplifications and arbitrary decisions can be made in the context of the overall standard.

a. Interest Expense

Net income is the tax base which equals the change in net worth during the period.[108] Thus, interest cost of borrowing should be deducted. The fact that interest income is taxable implies that absent a deduction, this type of capital income would be subject to a double tax.[109] Deductibility by the borrower implies that the aggregate tax revenue from the payments to this type of capital would be zero for payments within the domestic economy, other things equal. Accordingly, only net foreign source interest expense (interest expense paid to nonresidents less interest income accruing to domestic residents from nonresidents) will be taxed in the aggregate.[110]

---

[107] Publication of the subsidy by taxpayer is possible, perhaps limited to publicly traded entities.

[108] If the tax base were personal consumption, then the income to nonhuman capital (savings) would be exempt. Thus, there would be no deduction by the debtor, but the interest income would be exempt for the lender.

[109] The classical corporate tax where corporations are taxed and then the owners of the corporation are taxed is a double tax not because the two persons are subject to the tax on the same income but because the corporation is not allowed to deduct the cost of equity capital from its income tax base. If such a deduction were allowed, then the corporate tax would be converted to a tax on economic rent depending on the assumptions made about the structure of markets and uncertainty.

[110] There are concerns about tax induced excessive leverage being created by the deductibility of interest. Tax induced excessive leverage is not an issue in this proposal for two reasons. First, income from debt

b. Investments in Human Capital

Our approach is to treat investments in human and nonhuman capital the same. The income from human capital accrues to the individual taxpayer who by right owns the benefits accruing from their supply of labour to the market. Investments in human capital, like investments in plant and equipment, can increase both market productivity and consumption. Accordingly, investments in human capital should, as a matter of method, be capitalized and amortized during the taxpayer's life in a manner identical to depreciation of physical capital.

Conrad and Alexeev (2021) recommend the use of open-ended pooled accounts combined with declining balance depreciation tax accounting for the returns to all capital including human capital.[111] Pooled accounting is described in Annex A3.2 and works by establishing an account where capital expenditures are added to the account as accrued, with disposals reducing the account balance. Declining balance depreciation rates are then applied to the adjusted balance. This method is more in accord with economic depreciation concepts and can be easily adjusted for inflation.

Two issues are noted about amortization of human capital. First, the types and amounts of expenditures to be capitalized need to be determined. Two major categories that should be included are education and health care, including expenditure on health insurance. These expenditures increase both the consumption and production capacity of the individual, at least in an expected value sense. Because taxable income measures are limited to market-determined income, it is not reasonable to allow a full deduction for these expenses. It is not possible to accurately attribute the proportion of these expenditures to the accrual of market income, but it should be clear that zero is not reasonable. An arbitrary proportion of 0.3 may be acceptable since that value is the estimated proportion of time spent in market relative to nonmarket activity.

Second, the amortization rate needs to be determined. A modification of declining balance is the unit of production used in natural resources. This method is based on an exogenously given expected life as opposed to a perpetual life under declining balance depreciation with a fixed rate. The annual proportion is then determined by measuring a ratio that has unity in the numerator and the number of years remaining in the amortization period in the denominator.[112] For example, suppose that the amortization period is 10 years. The proportions to be used in this case are found in Table 3.15.

There needs to be a date to begin accumulations and when to begin amortization. Because the tax base is a market measure, the amortization period should not begin

---

and equity are taxed at the same rates, so there is no bias in favour of debt finance. Second, the fact that interest income is taxed offsets any incentive created by the deduction.

[111] Conrad first learned about pooled accounts using declining balance depreciation during the Indonesian Tax Reform and recommended its adoption in several countries since that time, most recently in Myanmar (see Memorandum for: Daw Mya May Oo on Depreciation, dated 18 March 2020).

[112] This approach can result in some cases in a constant amount per annum similar to straight-line depreciation. The advantage of this approach, however, is that the balance can be adjusted each year for additional expenditures as well as subtractions via the use of pooled accounts.

Table 3.15 Proportion of remaining
balance to be amortized each year

Time	Remainder	Proportion
1	10	0.10
2	9	0.11
3	8	0.13
4	7	0.14
5	6	0.17
6	5	0.20
7	4	0.25
8	3	0.33
9	2	0.50
10	1	1.00

until the taxpayer is actively in the labour market. This date varies by individual, however. Simplicity dictates applying an exogenous value to all taxpayers. The average age at which an individual enters the labour force is an arbitrary starting date. The ending date should be the date of death. Retirement age is not the correct date because individuals participate in the market beyond retirement via savings, intergenerational transfers, or government programmes. The numerical values maybe country specific and depend on life expectancy and related factors. An example might be to choose an arbitrary period is recommended of 60 years. If the amortization period begins at age 18 and if an individual lives beyond 78, then additional medical expenditures (no educational expenditures should be allowed at this age) should be immediately expensed. If an individual dies before 78, then the remaining balance is written off in the final tax return (see Section 3.3.3.3).[113]

c. Insurance

As noted, taxation is, among other things, a risk sharing method where the entire population of taxpayers (both resident and nonresident) share risks. Private insurance is also a way for individuals to share risks. Thus, taxation can be complementary to private risk sharing by allowing a deduction for the costs and including the benefits as income. Accordingly, deductions should be allowed for premiums and for losses more than benefits paid. In effect, benefits are added to income. All taxpayers share the cost as well as the benefits of the insurance. Deductions should be available for accident and the term portion of life insurance with the inside buildup of whole life insurance being subject to tax.

---

[113] Final returns and intergenerational transfers are also discussed in Conrad and Alexeev (2021).

d. Other Costs of Earning Market Income

A taxpayer may incur numerous costs to accrue market income, including but not limited to:

- Tools and special clothing necessary for employment;
- Transportation and related employment costs;
- Time spent at home preparing for work and increasing skills;
- Brokerage fees and other costs necessary to maintain, trade, and accrue income from nonhuman capital;
- Childcare; and
- Inputs used to supply goods and services from a taxpayer-owned business.

Some costs are clearly identifiable, but many, if not most, costs have dual purposes. Tools can be used to produce income in the market and income in the household. A taxpayer owner/operator of a taxi service can use the taxi for either personal use or the production of market income. Other costs are clearly identifiable. For example, brokerage fees and settlement costs for financial transactions have only one purpose.

Costs that are clearly identifiable as necessary to produce taxable income should be deducted. Such costs might include:

- Specialized tools related to employment or market activity;
- Childcare supplied by an independent person during working hours;
- Travel expenses related to business;
- Observable compliance costs for those who make annual tax filings; and
- Inputs that are clearly identifiable as market related (for example, food supplied and consumed by others in the case of an individual caterer).

Some inputs are multiple use as noted. In addition, time spent outside the market but used to produce income is costly. For example, time spent complying with the tax laws, preparing for work, or accruing certifications is costly because income is reduced. Practical considerations including the need for independent observability become important in these cases. Clear arbitrary rules for deductibility should provide taxpayers with guidance about these types of deductions.

We recommend the following approach. Items not allowed include, but will not be limited to:

- Own time used for compliance to increase market income (other than time at work to the extent that individuals are compensated for such time);
- Inputs of time by individuals who are related parties to the extent that such individuals do not file returns independently; and
- Certain purchases deemed to have more consumption, or household income, value relative to productive value. Examples include meals shared with clients and deductions for expensive automobiles more than stipulated publicly available amounts.

Note the similarity between the attribution of costs between market and household and transfer pricing rules where the tax administration cannot independently observe both sides of the transaction. So, either transfer pricing or attribution rules might be used for the following items, among others:

- Rental of dual use inputs, housing, equipment, and automobiles; and
- Payments to related parties for labour inputs if the sole proprietorship is an APA and related parties report income separately.

Items that might be fully deductible include but are not limited to:

- Inputs required as a condition of either employment or service provision (tools are an example); and
- Transportation and other market costs that are independently verifiable via third party receipt and are used exclusively as an input into the production of income (brokerage fees, legal expenses related to businesses or assets).

Finally, note that most of these expenses will be incurred by either relatively high-income taxpayers or those who might be subject to a small business tax (see Chapter 5). Limitations on deductions in these cases may increase the overall progressivity of the system.

3.3.3 Methods to Simplify the Deductions and Income Distributional Considerations

As noted in the last section, allowing deductions for taxpayer expenses will require both individual filing and considerable administrative effort. Such deductions also may favour those high-income taxpayers to the extent that the tax rules are too generous.[114] Two adjustments are recommended here that can be used by all countries regardless of their development stage.

3.3.3.1 Allow or Require a Standard Deduction

A fixed amount, adjusted for inflation, can be used to approximate the taxpayer's cost of accruing market income. This deduction would be in lieu of reporting all costs of accruing net income, including insurance, interest, and other costs. The amount might be based on estimates of national averages of individual costs. The standard deduction can be either required or optional. The choice of optional deductions should be limited only to countries that allow or require individual reporting. This

---

[114] If deductions were perfect, then there would be no distributional concerns. This is because the measure of income distribution should be based on net income through time. Thus, if a taxpayer has high gross income but low or negative net income, then the result is not an indicator of an adverse distributional outcome. Some types of economic activity have low margins and the crucial issue is the return to capital. A rational taxpayer would not continue to engage in low return activities unless there are personal benefits in excess of market income measures.

approach has the benefit of being simple and transparent. In addition, there is an element of progressivity in the use of averages because higher income taxpayers would have higher expenses while lower income individuals would have lower expenses, again on average. The final benefit is that mandatory use of a standard deduction would facilitate advanced payments being used as final payments. The elimination of the need for individual filing would reduce administrative costs to both taxpayers and tax administrators and reduce monitoring costs.

3.3.3.2 Employ a Refundable Tax Credit for Personal Circumstances

The second proposal is to use an individual credit in lieu of either a zero-bracket amount or a personal exemption. The credit will be used to provide additional progressivity to the system. Note the different use of the credit relative to the standard deduction. The standard deduction is used to approximate expense deductions while the credit is used to provide additional progressivity. In theory, it might be possible to use either the credit or the standard deduction to achieve both objectives. Separation has the benefit of being able to adjust each approximation independently, however. For example, the amount of the standard deduction can be adjusted through time based on new information about the costs of deriving market income. There should be no distributional considerations to these estimates, other than the distributional consequence inherent in the use of an average for everyone. The individual credit might be adjusted through time as per capita income and the income distribution changes.

An additional feature of the credit is that it can be refundable so that negative taxation for distributional purposes becomes possible. Also, the absolute value of a credit to the taxpayer is independent of the marginal bracket structure. Marginal rates will change over time and the value of the credit is invariant to the change in marginal rates. This property is absent from either the zero-bracket amount or personal exemption. Changing the marginal rates will change the value of the benefit and so these instruments need to be coordinated with the rate structure to achieve desired policy outcomes. Finally, the credit can be expanded to include credits for dependents in cases where aggregation is allowed while providing a means to incorporate such aggregation into advanced tax tables used by APAs. This means that it would still be possible to incorporate individual characteristics without the need for individual reporting. These reasons are sufficient to recommend the use of both the standard deduction and the personal credit.

3.3.3.3 A Note about the Final Return at Death

A decision about whether to enact estate or inheritance taxes should be based on income distributional concerns.[115] Regardless of the choice, we believe that any assets distributed to a deceased taxpayer's estate should be on a net-of-income tax basis. This means that the deceased taxpayer should have paid comprehensive income taxes during their lifetime. In this case, there is no need for a special return in the period

---

[115] We recommend the same approach to gifts. Whether there is a gift tax depends on distributional and tax arbitrage concerns. A gift of assets, however, should be a realization for the donor, and the initial basis for the recipient should be the same as the realization basis for the donor.

that a taxpayer dies. Income accrues until death and is reported in the same manner as for all prior reporting periods. No special form would be required except perhaps with an information return noting the taxpayer's death.

The use of mark-to-market rules for assets held by the taxpayer will ensure that the value of assets at death will be on a net-of-tax basis. There is an issue about unrealized gains and losses from assets for which mark-to-market evaluation is either not possible or costly. There are two options. First, the tax authorities could deem that the unrealized gains and losses are realized at the time of death and use some independent measure of market value to compute both the gain or loss as well as the interest charge on the adjusted basis as described above. The other option is to carry over both the basis and the date of acquisition from the deceased to the beneficiary. In effect, the beneficiary who disposes of the asset would be taxed on the gain or loss for the entire holding period. The latter method might be preferred because no appeal to nonmarket evaluations at the time of death is needed. Disputes and administrative costs might be reduced. Some costs of this latter method, however, are that income recognition is further delayed increasing administrative costs for the tax administration and interest costs for the taxpayer. Our preference is for the former with one proviso. The evaluation at the time of death will be measured with error but the errors should offset. If the valuation was too low, then the tax on the beneficiaries will be higher (or lower, in the case of a loss) when they choose to realize the gain or loss. This is because the initial basis of the beneficiary will be valuation made at the time of death. On the other hand, the tax at the time of death will be decreased (or increased) by a low evaluation. The present value of the revenue gain or loss would be the same, however. The total tax in present value terms will be the same as the present value of the tax under the second option, but the distribution of the tax between the person who died and the beneficiary would be the same.

The proviso is that the total tax could be sufficient to force asset sales.[116] This could result in liquidity problems for potential beneficiaries in countries without well-functioning capital markets. The resolution of the issue should depend on the amount of tax relative to the deceased's net worth. If the tax is relatively high, then it might be prudent to lower the evaluation to the point where zero tax is imposed. Such a result will defer the additional tax, making it the responsibility of the beneficiaries at the time of disposal.

3.3.4 Sequence of Income Tax Reforms

The collection-driven income tax described above is the ultimate objective of the reform process. The income tax is a feasible objective when combined with administration enhancements such as the ability of individuals to have direct access to their records and to make adjusted records without the need to file paper returns.

---

[116] Such an occurrence is not a special case of the computation of tax on aggregate income when accrual and accretion valuation methods are employed. In any time period, a taxpayer with a large accrued capital gain, using mark-to-market rules and relatively small cash income, could be forced to dispose of assets in order to pay tax. The amount of wealth required for such an outcome is sufficient for us to be unconcerned.

This objective might be achievable in economies with relatively high income and education. Each country can benefit from developing their own reform path towards the objective given current conditions, however. Reform implementation will be piecemeal so that timing can accommodate the more general economic reform and enhanced administration.[117] Actual phasing should depend on the facts and circumstances as well as the fact that the income tax reform should be phased as part of the overall evolution of the tax system. One phased approach is suggested here.

3.3.4.1 Basic Structure

The essential elements of the system can be applied, with varying degrees perhaps, in most emerging economies, at least where we have worked.[118] A revenue basis is provided consistent with a phased evolution of the income tax as the administrative capacity, public understanding, and demand for transparency increase through time. There are several essential reform elements that might be among the first actions.

- Modify legislation to clearly define APAs, taxpayers, residents, and other elements necessary to provide a framework in which the administrative and policy framework can evolve.
- Develop initial proposals. Initial proposals may include an individual credit and personal exemption for most, or all taxpayers. Decide whether individual deductions will be allowed or delayed. Implementation of deductions should be deferred until there is experience with the administrative procedures, experience with audits, and taxpayer understanding is enhanced. Restricting deductions will enable advanced payments to serve as final taxes because tax returns are not needed.
- Define the taxpayers that should be required to file returns (entrepreneurs, small businesses, independent professionals). Taxpayers should always have the right to register and to file returns on a voluntary basis.[119] Registration should be required for taxpayers who have income not subject to advanced tax (gross income paid by persons who are not APAs (generally nonresidents) and business income). If individuals operate a business that pays returns to factors (human or nonhuman capital) to other persons, then they will be required to register as APAs.
- Revise registration procedures of APAs so that advanced payments can begin.[120] The foundation of this action already exists because most countries impose

---

[117] Note that the same statement applies with equal force to the implementation of a VAT (or a personal consumption tax) more generally.

[118] Some of these points will be highlighted in the final chapter.

[119] If a taxpayer voluntarily registers and files, then the taxpayer should be required to file for at least three consecutive years.

[120] Two points are noted. First, during the initial stages of the system's evolution, there may be administrative constraints on the ability of the tax administration to issue taxpayer numbers and to otherwise monitor taxpayers or APAs via master tax files and other methods. The number of individuals required to register as APAs might be rather small relative to the total number of taxpayers as well as the number

both VAT and corporate tax. Wage withholding via the use of Pay As You Earn (PAYE) systems is also common. Thus, the tax administration can build on this base while implementing procedures, consistent with VAT, for advanced payments.[121]

- Further develop, and expand, taxpayer registration. There may be no need to register, or to register additional, taxpayers who are employees and those for whom advanced payments will serve as final payments. Expansion of the taxpayer and APA identification systems[122] should proceed incrementally, beginning with individuals who act as APAs, operate small businesses (as defined in a small business statute if one exists), and taxpayers who are not employees, or who have gross income from sources other than employment in excess of *de minimis* amounts. Registration can then proceed to employees via use of the APA records, public education, and other methods. There is no need to issue taxpayer numbers to large groups of individuals until there is the administrative capacity to handle recording and maintenance of the basic files.[123]

- Include an explicit definition of employee as described in Section 3.3.1 and include in the withholding table, to the extent administratively practical, the standard deduction and individual credit. For most emerging economies, the individual credit combined with the standard deduction should be sufficient to limit the application of the income tax to relatively high-income individuals. In some cases, up to 75–90% of the taxpayers should be liable for zero taxes. This level is chosen for both progressivity and administrative reasons. A flat-rate tax restricted to the top 25% of the wealth distribution can be both progressive and revenue productive. The last point is confirmed because most income tax is paid

of individuals who would be required to be APAs because they pay returns to primary factors to others. This group of individuals will include owners of entities that are partnerships or corporations with only a few shareholders, as well as sole proprietorships such as lawyers, doctors, other professionals, and some manufacturing and distribution proprietorships. Second, the tax administration might know the identity of such individuals and should develop means to at least identify resident taxpayers who should be registered. Many countries have relatively small populations so that at least some high-net-worth individuals should be known to the tax authorities. There is the potential for exchange of information, and the tax administration should be able to develop empirical methods that can serve as indicators of wealth for income which is not reported. In summary, given that the ultimate objective of a tax administration includes the ability to register all resident taxpayers under a worldwide taxation approach, there are good reasons to be consistent even at the initial reform stage.

[121] Many countries have implemented taxpayer numbering systems, often beginning with those who are currently defined as VAT taxpayers. Additional APAs can be included in the numbering system once it is clear that the numbering system is for APAs, not taxpayers, at least initially. The need for two numbering systems, such as the Employee Identification Number and the taxpayer number (the Social Security Number) can be determined at a later date. It should be possible to use one numbering system for all persons, APAs and taxpayers, as long as identifiers in the master files exist to classify persons into taxpayers, taxpayers who are APAs, and APAs.

[122] There might be a separate numbering system for APAs other than APAs who are taxpayers. There should be a separate master files for taxpayers and APAs given the different data requirements.

[123] This will mean that the tax administration will depend on APA records during the transition if a standard deduction and individual credit are used in the initial stage.

by those with higher incomes.[124] Make the tax credit refundable at some point in time.

- Begin collecting advanced payments on all income attributable to taxpayers via the introduction of:
  - ○ Revised advanced payments for employees.
  - ○ Extend (to the extent necessary) uniform advanced payments for the supply of services by persons not registered and to individuals supplying labour services. The former group includes all payments to nonresidents if supplies are not imports, residents without proof of taxpayer registration, and APAs where the payments are clearly defined as gross revenue from the provision of services. The latter group includes individuals operating in informal markets and other individuals who are not registered.
  - ○ Impose the Fringe Benefit Advanced Payment, in a relatively simple form that is designed to capture most fringe benefits accruing to higher income individuals.
  - ○ Impose advanced payments on all payments to nonhuman capital at a flat rate (recall there is no border taxation), except capital gains:
    - ▪ Use either local or international accounting standards as the base for advanced payments for the return to equity.
    - ▪ The advanced tax on gross capital gains should be equal to 25% of the flat withholding rate because the tax will be initially a final tax, so the tax will be on gross revenue instead of the net gain or loss.
- Until such time that losses at the entity level can flow through and be deducted in measuring the taxpayer's comprehensive income, carrybacks and carryforwards of losses at the entity level should be allowed.[125]
- Do not allow joint reporting for taxpayers during the initial stage. The taxpayer will be an individual, perhaps with dependents. Allow one member of the defined group to take the standard deduction and credit for the group, to the extent the credit includes related parties. All other related parties will be subject to advanced payments without the benefit of additional credits regardless of their employment status.[126]
- APAs should begin reporting gross compensation, advanced tax paid, and net-of-advanced-tax total income (to human and nonhuman capital) in the case where advanced payments are final taxes. In addition, APAs should report amounts for the income from employment to employees and income to nonhuman capital to the owners of the capital or to other persons who are conduits

---

[124] In the US, the top 25% of taxpayers paid almost 70% of the federal income tax in 2018. See https://taxfoundation.org/data/all/federal/summary-latest-federal-income-tax-data-2023-update/. This value is representative of most countries and might change as the base is expanded and more taxpayers pay nonzero tax.
[125] Carrybacks and carryforwards should be adjusted for inflation and accrue interest. There is an issue about carrybacks in the sense that refunds might be generated. Our preference is to provide for refunds, but if there is resistance to refunding, then carryforwards should be allowed.
[126] There will have to be a means to match related taxpayers.

for the owners (payments to another corporation, for example either a domestic APA or nonresident entity). Such reporting to the tax administration should begin as administrative systems are developed to post advanced payments to taxpayer records in the master tax file.

- Use the advanced tax as the final tax for all taxpayers who are not registered. There should always be an option for taxpayers to register and file returns, but initially the only taxpayers who will file are individuals with excess advanced payments, taxpayers who are not employees, and individuals who operate some type of business enterprise.
- Administrative resources should be used to monitor APAs as well as individuals who have income not subject to advanced tax (a small business that is not an APA and foreign source income). Resources should be used to register sole proprietorships and those operating in informal markets.
- A small business tax could be imposed (see Chapter 5). If a small business tax is imposed, then individuals owning the small business would not be required to file individual returns unless they have income, other than small business income, not subject to advanced payments.
- No reimbursable credits or other negative taxes should be employed.
- Notify treaty partners that border withholding taxes have been eliminated and a new approach to transfer pricing has been adopted (see Section 3.4.3). Seek modifications to existing treaties where emphasis is placed on exchange of information. Do not enter any new tax treaties.

A flat rate tax without consideration of personal circumstances like the system in Georgia might be considered for the proposed system during the initial stages. The approach used in Georgia should be applied only if it is too difficult to have advanced payments for employees including a standard deduction and an individual credit.[127] Another difference between the proposed system and Georgia's policies is that the proposed system is resident based and tax is imposed on net income without regard to source. The use of this method, at least initially, might be based on pragmatic considerations about the ability of the tax administration to manage the taxpayer and APA accounts.

A second option, and one we prefer, is to use advanced taxes as final taxes but to allow both an individual credit and a standard deduction.[128] The standard deduction and the individual credit can be incorporated into withholding tables for APAs who employ taxpayers, so advanced payments for employees would still be a final tax. The difficulty with this approach is that low-income taxpayers who supply labour

---

[127] As noted, the system in Georgia consists of a withholding system without recognition of personal circumstances. Taxation in Georgia (companyformationgeorgia.com)

[128] It is possible to have a combined individual credit and standard deduction until itemized deductions are allowed, but we prefer to keep the two separated because each is a separate function as discussed above. Taxpayers below the threshold would be exempt and the presence of the credit will increase the average tax rate, other things equal. Through time, the individual credit can be made refundable. Maintaining a separate credit from the standard deduction can help clarify that the criteria for determining the distributional effects of the income tax is comprehensive net income, even if it is an approximation.

services but who are not employees would not benefit from the standard deduction and individual credit. Higher income taxpayers would benefit because the two tax reductions would be included for those who are either required to, or voluntarily, report. This group will include professionals as well as those who operate certain business enterprises, among others. Unregistered taxpayers include low-income individuals who are not employees but who will have advanced payments withheld as final tax by APAs. Such low-income individuals would have to register, report, and request refunds to accrue these benefits. An alternative, perhaps burdensome, would be to exempt casual labour from advanced tax. We believe a better approach would be to provide the option for such labourers to become employees. This can be achieved by having the definition of an employee include a voluntary association of any duration.[129]

The tax base will only approximate the comprehensive standard developed here until individual reporting is allowed or required for all taxpayers. This means that it will be possible for taxpayers to have aggregate negative income but still pay tax. For example, an individual may operate a business that has a legitimate loss of −1000 and who accrued interest income of 500. As proposed, there would be no advanced tax on the loss but there would be advanced tax, at the maximum rate, on the interest income. If the advanced tax is the final tax, then the individual will pay tax even though he or she has a tax loss.[130] (This situation might be rare except for high-income professionals operating sole proprietorships that do not qualify for small business status.) In addition, risk sharing is reduced for registered taxpayers as well as nonregistered taxpayers who are simply taxed on gross income.

The intent of the initial reform is to provide the tax administration with expanded advanced payments and to gain from experience while developing a framework for the income tax to evolve. In effect, APAs would be agents for all taxes, except the property tax perhaps. An implication is that income tax and VAT registration thresholds should be the same. In addition, all legal entities should be APAs regardless of any VAT registration level (see Chapter 4).[131]

---

[129] There would still be a problem with individuals claiming the benefit from multiple employers in this case. This problem will be present, however, until such time as all individuals are registered but not required to report.

[130] Note that there is no attempt to separately account for gross income from a sole proprietorship unless the sole proprietorship is also an APA. Expenses of earning business income are deductible because the individual is involved in a trade or business. There is no attribution of the gross revenue, however. In general, there is an inference that gross income from the sole proprietorship would include the gross income for which advanced tax has not been withheld. This may not be the case, however, because advanced tax could be collected on gross revenues from the provision of goods or services supplied to an APA. In addition, there is no need to attribute interest income and other types of income subject to advanced tax.

[131] Tax administration organizational structures might be modified. In particular, there might not be a need for a large taxpayer unit because all APAs would be subject to the same rules. There could be some division relative to 'individual registered taxpayers' and APAs given the fact that APAs are only government agents while individuals are the taxpayers. Hopefully, the number of registered individuals will be relatively small during the initial stage. Most of the affected economies are small enough and the flow of information, at least informally, is sufficient to identify many, if not most, individuals who should be required to register.

3.3.4.2 Evolution

The purpose of the initial phase of the income tax reform is to develop the ability to collect revenue effectively. As stated above, if a country can administer a VAT, then it is possible to administer this administratively based income tax system. The initial system, while not taxing a complete measure of comprehensive income, provides an opportunity for the enhancement of the administrative apparatus and releases scarce administrative resources for other activities such as registration and monitoring of high-risk taxpayers. Resources are released because of the reduction in the need to audit entities for income tax compliance, the elimination of transfer pricing rules, with one exception, the elimination of deductions at the level of the individuals, potential reductions in the number of taxpayers to monitor, and the use of clearly arbitrary rules to facilitate both compliance and administration. That said, it will take years for the system to evolve. The most important perceptual change is the fact that there is no corporate tax and that APAs are not taxpayers. In addition, there will be numerous administrative and regulatory issues that need to be addressed as experience is gained.

The ultimate objective is to have a unified income tax system with optional personal reporting by all taxpayers with a negative tax, to eliminate the VAT (See Chapter 4) perhaps replacing it with a segmented personal consumption tax (see Chapter 4), and to treat asset transactions consistently. The completion of this process may take generations, as is the case with all significant tax reforms. The ordering of the changes will depend on idiosyncratic factors in each economy and the speed of economic growth. One path might include the following actions:

1. Replace the advanced tax (and personal income tax) on gross asset dispositions with an advanced tax on the net capital gain adjusted for inflation. The change in asset prices will be automatically incorporated into the returns for debt and equity for assets that are actively traded and subject to advanced tax as discussed above. Advanced tax will also be applicable on a realization basis to assets that are not actively traded. Once adopted, the system for assets that are not actively traded can be adjusted for interest costs in a manner described above (see Section 3.2.2b).

2. Provide refunds and negative tax payments, subject to an absolute amount adjusted for inflation. This will eliminate the need for any loss carryforwards for individuals. Risk sharing is expanded, and the provision of refunds combined with negative taxes will increase public perceptions that the tax system is progressive and that the tax administration is even handed.

3. Through time, evaluate the public education benefits of refining the definition of net income to equity by including inflation adjustments and adopting economic notions into income derivation.

4. Systematically begin to allow itemized deductions at the individual level, beginning with interest deductions, the cost of maintaining market assets, certain costs associated with acquiring market income, and losses. Refining the use of itemized deductions will be a continuous process based on experience, changes

in technology, and other factors. A standard deduction should always be allowed so taxpayers can determine the relative cost of maintaining necessary books and records.

5. Expand taxpayer registration and payment to the entire resident population. At some point, the advanced payment system should provide information sufficient for the tax administration to compute an initial assessment for each taxpayer. Computer technology and other resources should also be sufficient for individuals to have direct access to their tax accounts in the master tax file. This will allow taxpayers to modify the initial assessment to the extent relevant by providing additional information and documentation.

3.4 Other Administrative Issues

3.4.1 Flow through for Advanced Taxes for APAs

APAs will impose advanced tax on all taxable income accruing to taxpayers. There is an issue, however, about whether APAs should be required to collect advanced payments from other APAs. The issue is similar to the choice between a retail sales tax and a VAT. Exempting advanced tax on payments to APAs is similar to the ring system used in a retail sales tax. Income payments to APAs would be exempt while advanced tax will be collected from all payments to taxpayers, or more appropriately all persons not registered as an APA. If, however, advanced tax is collected on payments made to another APA, then there must be a system to flow through the advanced tax to the ultimate taxpayer. A gross-up and credit[132] is such a system and is commonly used for foreign tax credits and to credit advanced payments for taxpayers who make declarations. Under this system, an APA receiving a payment would include the gross payment into income, just like a taxpayer, and then receive a credit for the advanced tax withheld when the APA makes advanced tax payments. For example, suppose APA 1 is a wholly owned subsidiary of APA 2. APA 1 has taxable income of 100, of which 20 is withheld as advanced tax if the tax rate is 20%. Now suppose that APA 2 has taxable income of 85 after the inclusion of the tax-inclusive income of 100 from APA 1. This could arise in a situation where APA 2 has a loss of 15 from other activities. Advanced tax on APA 2's net income is 17. The advanced tax of 20 has already been paid, so there is no additional advanced tax payable by APA 2. APA 2 reports taxable income of 85 to the taxpayers who own APA 2 and the accumulated advanced tax of 20. Other things equal, the shareholder adds 85 to other income sources and adds the 20 to other advanced taxes. The total advanced tax is then credited against the tax liability.

Note that the flow-through method for advanced payments serves the identical purpose as the invoice-credit system under the VAT. That is, a portion of the taxpayer's final tax is collected at each stage in the APA chain. Accordingly, the taxing

---

[132] This method is used to compute the foreign tax credit in the home country of taxpayers.

jurisdiction receives tax in pieces in cases where income payments flow through APAs. The ability to institute a credit system which functions in the same manner as the invoice-credit system tends to favour adoption of a system where an APA imposes advanced tax on all income payments regardless of the status of the payee.

There may be concerns with this approach, other than understanding the mechanics of the flow-through method. First, an APA may make payments to a person who is not an APA, and that person may then pay income to another person. This situation is similar to the situation where a nonregistered person supplies goods and services subject to VAT to a registered person. Unlike trade in goods and services, this advanced tax is on income, and it is difficult to think of a situation where income payments flow via non-APAs to the ultimate taxpayer. For instance, a bank will withhold tax on interest income payable to an individual. Suppose this payee is an agent for another individual, but not an APA. No gross-up is possible and the payee may not be able to issue the tax credit because, by default, the payee is a taxpayer if the payee is an individual. In this case, the ultimate individual will receive income net of advanced payment. If advanced tax is the final tax, then there is no problem. If, however, the individual reports income, then the net interest will be reported and taxed again. The solution to such situations is for the ultimate owner to eliminate the agent.

Refunds raise a second issue. Two examples illustrate the potential problem. First, there may be an issue with banks and other financial institutions if interest income is subject to advanced tax at the statutory rate. The interest income is gross income from which expenses are deducted, so the bank would be in a perpetual refund position. The story does not end here. The bank is an APA and withholds advanced tax on interest paid to depositors and wages to employees. In cases where gross income of the APA is a return to a factor, the APA should deduct the APA payments made to productive factors in order to determine net factor income to owners. For example, suppose there are no advanced payments, and the bank receives 100 in gross interest, pays interest of 40, wages of 35, and has other costs of 5. Bank profits would be 20. If the tax rate is 25%, then total advanced taxes would be: 10 paid by the bank depositors who receive interest, 8.75 paid by the bank employees, and 5 paid by the bank's shareholders (for a total of 23.75). Now impose advanced tax but allow the bank to credit the advanced tax paid on income paid to inputs. Advanced tax payments now include: 25 charged to the bank on gross interest income, 10 paid by the bank on behalf of depositors, 8.75 paid on behalf of employees, and 5 paid on behalf of the bank owners. The bank would owe 3.75 in advanced tax because of the 20 withheld on gross income. The reason this happens is that income tax should be paid on net income to factors, so the cost of incurring financial intermediation is deducted in deriving net income. Finally, as a practical matter, much interest income to the bank will not be subject to advanced payments because the payors are not APAs. Interest accrues to banks from foreign sources and from individual borrowers who are taxpayers and who will not be responsible for withholding advanced tax.

Second, there is an issue about excess advanced payments more generally, but only at the taxpayer level. Refunds should be paid if advanced payments are greater than the tax payable on the net income of the taxpayer. This situation is like the case where export refunds accrue from VAT. Like export refunds, such excess credits should be paid by the taxing jurisdiction. Refusing refunds would reduce the integrity of the system and promote noncompliance. In addition, payments to the individual are dictated by adopting a negative tax credit. The negative tax credit is for income distributional and risk sharing purposes and is an integral part of the income system. It is true that no refunds are paid during initial implementation if the planned evolution discussed above is adopted. This situation arises because individual reporting is not required, however. Individuals should always have the right to file a return and claim a refund to the extent allowable by law. Furthermore, like the export refund system in the VAT, the presence of a refund is not an indicator of noncompliance. Accordingly, the presence of refunds is not a problem but an indicator of the proper functioning of the system.

3.4.2 Advanced Payments for Employees

It is possible to include personal circumstances in the advanced payment structure for employees. In addition, it is necessary for cumulative advanced payments made during the year to be transferred to another employer should the taxpayer change jobs. A method used in Russia and other Eastern European countries can be adopted to achieve these objectives.[133] The method involves dividing the tax year into subperiods and computing the tax year to date. Advanced tax is then paid on a cumulative basis during the year. For example, if the standard deduction is 1200, then the individual will have a standard deduction in January of 120 and in February of 240 and so on for each month of the year. Advanced tax is then paid on the accumulated income during the year.

Three tables are presented to illustrate the combination of the proposed system with the tax credit. Table 3.16a contains the situation where the individual is paid a constant amount per month during the year. Note that withholding each month is constant because the monthly wage is constant. Table 3.16b contains the situation where the individual gets a raise during the tax year. Such a change can be accurately accommodated via the cumulative system so that the amount of annual withholding is correct. Finally, Table 3.16c illustrates a low-wage individual who receives part of the tax credit each month. Such an approach will help the individual with their monthly cash flow as opposed to getting a one-time payment at the end of the tax year.[134]

There are at least three advantages to this method. First, the taxpayer can switch jobs during the year and, potentially, still have withholding accurately computed.

[133] For example, see Art. 218 of the Russian Tax Code and https://www.garant.ru/news/1554214/ for the method used in Russia.
[134] This method can accommodate situations where the individual's taxable income is positive, negative, or switches from positive to negative (or the other way round) during the tax year.

Table 3.16a Withholding tables for individuals: individual has constant monthly income

Month	Taxable income this month	Taxable income year to date	Tax accrued year to date	Tax credit accrued year to date	Tax withheld this month	Net take home pay this month
January	6,666.67	6,666.67	1,666.67	1,250.00	416.67	6,250.00
February	6,666.67	13,333.33	3,333.33	2,500.00	416.67	6,250.00
March	6,666.67	20,000.00	5,000.00	3,750.00	416.67	6,250.00
April	6,666.67	26,666.67	6,666.67	5,000.00	416.67	6,250.00
May	6,666.67	33,333.33	8,333.33	6,250.00	416.67	6,250.00
June	6,666.67	40,000.00	10,000.00	7,500.00	416.67	6,250.00
July	6,666.67	46,666.67	11,666.67	8,750.00	416.67	6,250.00
August	6,666.67	53,333.33	13,333.33	10,000.00	416.67	6,250.00
September	6,666.67	60,000.00	15,000.00	11,250.00	416.67	6,250.00
October	6,666.67	66,666.67	16,666.67	12,500.00	416.67	6,250.00
November	6,666.67	73,333.33	18,333.33	13,750.00	416.67	6,250.00
December	6,666.67	80,000.00	20,000.00	15,000.00	416.67	6,250.00
Totals	**80,000.00**	**80,000.00**	**20,000.00**	**15,000.00**	**5,000.00**	**75,000.00**

Table 3.16b Withholding tables for individuals: individual gets mid-year raise

Month	Taxable income this month	Taxable income year to date	Tax accrued year to date	Tax credit accrued year to date	Tax withheld this month	Net take home pay this month
January	5,833.33	5,833.33	1,458.33	1,250.00	208.33	5,625.00
February	5,833.33	11,666.67	2,916.67	2,500.00	208.33	5,625.00
March	5,833.33	17,500.00	4,375.00	3,750.00	208.33	5,625.00
April	5,833.33	23,333.33	5,833.33	5,000.00	208.33	5,625.00
May	5,833.33	29,166.67	7,291.67	6,250.00	208.33	5,625.00
June	5,833.33	35,000.00	8,750.00	7,500.00	208.33	5,625.00
July	7,500.00	42,500.00	10,625.00	8,750.00	625.00	6,875.00
August	7,500.00	50,000.00	12,500.00	10,000.00	625.00	6,875.00
September	7,500.00	57,500.00	14,375.00	11,250.00	625.00	6,875.00
October	7,500.00	65,000.00	16,250.00	12,500.00	625.00	6,875.00
November	7,500.00	72,500.00	18,125.00	13,750.00	625.00	6,875.00
December	7,500.00	80,000.00	20,000.00	15,000.00	625.00	6,875.00
Totals	**80,000.00**	**80,000.00**	**20,000.00**	**15,000.00**	**5,000.00**	**75,000.00**

This can be achieved by the first employer (or at a later stage of the system's evolution, the tax administration) providing the new employer with advanced taxes to date. Then the new employer can begin to collect advanced payments on additions to accumulated income. Second, a person who withdraws from the labour force or

Table 3.16c Withholding tables for individuals: individual makes income below credit threshold

Month	Taxable income this month	Taxable income year to date	Tax accrued year to date	Tax credit accrued year to date	Tax withheld this month	Net take home pay this month
January	3,000.00	3,000.00	750.00	1,250.00	(500.00)	3,500.00
February	3,000.00	6,000.00	1,500.00	2,500.00	(500.00)	3,500.00
March	3,000.00	9,000.00	2,250.00	3,750.00	(500.00)	3,500.00
April	3,000.00	12,000.00	3,000.00	5,000.00	(500.00)	3,500.00
May	3,000.00	15,000.00	3,750.00	6,250.00	(500.00)	3,500.00
June	3,000.00	18,000.00	4,500.00	7,500.00	(500.00)	3,500.00
July	3,000.00	21,000.00	5,250.00	8,750.00	(500.00)	3,500.00
August	3,000.00	24,000.00	6,000.00	10,000.00	(500.00)	3,500.00
September	3,000.00	27,000.00	6,750.00	11,250.00	(500.00)	3,500.00
October	3,000.00	30,000.00	7,500.00	12,500.00	(500.00)	3,500.00
November	3,000.00	33,000.00	8,250.00	13,750.00	(500.00)	3,500.00
December	3,000.00	36,000.00	9,000.00	15,000.00	(500.00)	3,500.00
Totals	**36,000.00**	**36,000.00**	**9,000.00**	**15,000.00**	**(6,000.00)**	**42,000.00**

who is unemployed may not have to file a tax return during the year if wages were their only source of income. Third, low-income taxpayers who should benefit from the credit would automatically receive the credit monthly and may not need to file an annual reconciliation if the taxpayer's only income type is wages from employment.

3.4.3 Transfer Pricing

Many related party problems are addressed by universal advanced payments. For example, thin capitalization issues are eliminated, or at least reduced, because any interest payment to another person is subject to advanced tax. Thus, if a foreign entity leverages a domestic related party with debt to transfer price profits to equity out of the country, then the strategy will fail because amounts deductible to the domestic entity increases the amount of advanced tax on the accrued interest paid to the nonresident taxpayer. Furthermore, the nonresident entity receiving the interest will not be able to deduct the costs of supplying and servicing the loan. In effect, the taxing jurisdiction is indifferent to taking the tax as an advanced tax on equity or as an advanced tax on interest income. In addition, the choice about how to finance the domestic investment is tax neutral because there is no corporate tax and the marginal rate on shareholders is the same, at least on a flow basis, and in the long term as owners of debt.[135]

---

[135] Neither nonresident shareholders nor debt owners are allowed to deduct the cost of maintaining either equity or debt; thus, the statement is true to the extent that such costs are approximately equal.

There are still transfer pricing issues, and these issues are related to valuing supplies of goods and services between related parties and other payments that are not classified as either income to debt and equity or, nominally, to the supply of goods and services. For example, a nonresident could supply inputs to a domestic related party and reduce profit subject to advanced tax. It may be in the interest of the nonresident related party to reduce advanced tax to zero if the advanced tax is either not creditable or is in excess of the allowable credit in the country where the nonresident person operates because the nonresident is neither an APA nor a taxpayer in the taxing jurisdiction. In addition, the value of sales by a domestic entity to a nonresident related party can be reduced via transfer pricing, resulting in a similar reduction in advanced tax.

Transfer pricing issues exist in the domestic economy as well. For-profit entities may own nonprofit entities (or at least have an economic interest in nonprofit entities). Individuals who have an economic interest in a for-profit entity may supply inputs that reduce the accounting profits of the entity and accordingly reduce both the advanced tax and the tax due by the individual. Some issues are automatically covered by universal withholding. For example, an equity owner of a business may supply real property for use by the business at an inflated price. Profit subject to advanced tax falls. Rental payments, however, are income to nonhuman capital and are subject to advanced tax. Other transactions might not be so transparent. For example, an equity participant in a business might supply an input at an inflated price and reduce business income accruing to the equity participant. The issue is then whether the supply to the business is income to the owner. For example, the equity owner may be engaged in another business that is losing money, and charging high prices for inputs to the profitable related party would reduce advanced payments and reduce the aggregate loss of the two enterprises.[136] This issue might be addressed automatically by the proposal if individual reporting is allowed but may be a problem during the initial stages of the system's evolution when individual reporting may be only optional. Suffice it to say that the use of purchases and sales between related parties can be a source of potential transfer pricing problems, regardless of whether one party to the transaction is a nonresident. There are also issues with respect to families in situations where each family member is subject to tax as an individual. For example, interest-bearing accounts can be held in the name of the household member in the lowest tax bracket (zero if there is only a flat-rate tax with a personal credit as proposed here). The effective tax on the family unit is reduced. These and other issues provide some basis for expanding the scope of coverage for transfer pricing. The issue is discussed below.

---

[136] This problem may be resolved at the shareholder level because the taxpayer will be taxed on the aggregation of the profits, regardless of the amount of advanced tax. For example, it is possible for the transfer price to simply transfer income from the profitable to the loss-making entity, keeping the summation of the profits the same. The taxpayer will be liable for tax on the summation of the profits regardless of the amount of advanced tax paid. This is true as a matter of method, but it is important to try to make reality conform to the method by ensuring that advanced tax is as close to the total amount of tax payable by the taxpayer as possible.

3.4.3.1 The Problem

We believe that efforts such as the OECD transfer pricing rules, as well as most of the Base Erosion Initiative, are difficult to administer even by the wealthiest OECD countries, and that an alternative, other than formulary apportionment, might be developed, particularly for emerging economies that, individually and collectively, can lead in the evolution of approaches that can be administered.[137] Reasons for this conclusion include, but are not limited to:

- As noted, there are more taxpayers than tax administrators. All taxpayers, many of whom have trained tax advisers, have an incentive to reduce taxes to a minimum (holding constant before-tax profits). It is not possible to monitor, audit, and assess each transaction or set of transactions between related parties, as defined.
- The deterrent effect of audits and publication of settlements is minimal. It is not possible to examine all transfer prices of even one large international firm. Investors know that the probability of an audit is insignificant, at least for particular transactions. Accordingly, even risk-averse investors may have a strong incentive to take aggressive, albeit nonfraudulent, positions.
- Any taxpayer, particularly a foreign investor, has several degrees of freedom that can be used collectively to reduce taxes to a reasonable minimum within a country and globally. These degrees of freedom include:
  - The choice of corporate (or other) organization to employ for any investment in a particular country;
  - The choice of the tier structure of related parties (that is, the ability to create a subsidiary in one country and to have that subsidiary be owned by another subsidiary incorporated in another jurisdiction);
  - The choice of transactions between related parties. For example, a marketing subsidiary in a foreign country purchases the exports from the domestic subsidiary in another country which are then sold either to the parent or to some other subsidiary in a third country;
  - The number and types of transactions (revolving credit agreements, intellectual property, contractual structures to allocate risk, provision of technical services, loan guarantees, rules to allocate overheads, in-kind capital contributions supplied by related parties, and charges for services among others); and
  - The choice about where to source types of income and costs given the source and other rules.
- Transfer pricing rules relate to one set of transactions. There are numerous transfer pricing possibilities, however. So, a government must monitor and perhaps audit every transfer price to reduce potential revenue losses.

---

[137] This material is based on: Conrad, R. 'Comments on Ethiopian Transfer Pricing Documents'. Memorandum for D. Christine Achieng Awiti, United Nations Economic Center for Africa, dated 7 January 2020. There is a more extensive discussion of transfer pricing in Conrad and Alexeev, 2021.

- There is significant asymmetry of information between an investor and tax administrators because tax administrators do not have full information about both sides of a transaction, much less how the transaction affects the profitability of the overall international enterprise. (Exchange of information, joint audits, and programmes such as country-by-country reporting may be helpful but are resource intensive as well as incomplete.)
- Transfer prices, if negotiated, may include a range of values. The range may be sufficient for the investor to pay zero tax when the range is combined with other transfer prices.

To illustrate, suppose a subsidiary of a foreign enterprise is considering making an investment in Country X. There are several ways the potential investment can be organized, including but not limited to:

- Operate as an unincorporated permanent establishment,
- Create a domestic subsidiary that is owned directly by the parent entity, or
- Create a domestic subsidiary that is owned by a subsidiary of the parent corporation that is in a tax haven.

These are not the only options. There could be multiple tiers of ownership and there could be multiple owners. How the domestic investment in Country X is organized is largely beyond the scope of Country X. Country X could require that the investment be made via a domestic corporation with the parent entity owning the shares, directly or indirectly, but what entity, or tier of entities, owns the shares is beyond the control of Country X.

For simplicity, assume that the investment is organized in Country X as a wholly owned local subsidiary. Call the subsidiary Corporation 1. This enterprise is capitalized with inter-firm debt that is a revolving credit arrangement, independent bank financing, some cash, some intangible property owned by another subsidiary, and used property. The parent enterprise guarantees the bank financing for the subsidiary to receive a lower interest rate. The parent charges Corporation 1 for the loan guarantee. Suppose further that Corporation 1 sells output on the local market to distributors at the current market price and sells to a related marketing firm, a subsidiary of the ultimate parent of Corporation 1 located in the Isle of Man under a long-term contract. There is a futures market for some of the goods used in the production of the subsidiary's output and another subsidiary incorporated in Country Y operates a hedging operation on behalf of the global enterprise. The subsidiary in Country X receives services on a fee-for-services basis, receives royalties from the intangible property, pays royalties for the use of a trademark, and obtains inputs manufactured by another subsidiary located in Country Z. Finally, the parent charges the subsidiary an allocated portion of corporate overhead based on a proportion of costs attributed to the subsidiary.[138]

---

[138] We believe that such a fact pattern is not unusual.

For the tax administration to comprehensively audit the firm, it is necessary to determine transfer prices for:

1. The interest rate on the related party loan,
2. The value of the intangible asset that will be subject to amortization in Country X,
3. The value of the property used to capitalize the subsidiary,
4. The value of the loan guarantee,
5. The risk-adjusted value of the contract price between the subsidiary and the marketing company,[139]
6. How to attribute hedging expenses or how to value the inputs used given the hedged positions from the subsidiary in country Y,
7. The value of inputs from related parties used to produce output that is not hedged,
8. The value of the royalty received for the intangible property,
9. The value of the royalty paid for the trademark, and
10. A reasonable percentage charge for corporate overheads.

Even if there are established rules and methods required by regulations in Country X for each general type of transaction, the facts and circumstances related to each computation are unique, and data—including comparables—must be obtained and audited. In addition, the values, and perhaps methods, may change through time in response to economic events.[140] Given the tax administration's access to data, such as country-by-country reporting and other information via exchange of information agreements, the tax administration will always be at an informational disadvantage because there will never be full access to all the internal accounts that might use an entirely different set of prices for management purposes. In summary, determining the transfer price for each of the profit elements imposes a significant burden on a tax administration that is constrained by resources, skills, and information. The prices, if agreed and audited, will be negotiated.

The problem might be traced, at least in part, to traditional efforts to impose taxation on a source basis combined with the definition of a legal entity as a taxable person. Source taxation needs source rules, and the ease of creating unique taxable persons under the laws of different jurisdictions creates the need to allocate or attribute net income to jurisdictions for tax purposes where such allocations and attributions may not be necessary for economic or decision-making purposes. The evolution of the arm's-length standard and transfer pricing rules may have been a natural result because of the intuitive appeal to independent agents acting in their own self-interest to negotiate prices. A subsidiary of a multinational firm is not an

---

[139] The local spot price, if there is such a price, may be used as a starting point, but management will argue that there will be, at the minimum, a risk-sharing component in the long-term contract and may supply arm's-length comparable contracts as evidence of the difference.
[140] For instance, the long-term contract might be renegotiated in light of changes in risk perceptions or overall enterprise profitability.

independent decision maker, however, and the efficient (even tax-inclusive) price to charge for related parties operating in different jurisdictions will not be the same, in general, as the arm's-length price between two independent parties (even if an established arm's-length price that is publicly observable exists), if firm managers even develop such prices for internal decision-making purposes.[141] Accordingly, a series of rules and conventions have evolved that, while not completely arbitrary, are intended to counter the clear incentive for any taxpayer to use every tool at their disposal to reduce their tax bills to a minimum and maximize profit to the individual owners consistent with their risk preferences.

These rules will always lag the ability of tax managers to develop new, and more complex, methods to legally avoid the rules via the use of new instruments and the exploitation of ambiguity in the rules. The private sector has an incentive to reduce taxes, holding other things constant, and has more resources to develop new options relative to tax administrations, individually or collectively.[142] In short, using the arm's-length standard implies that tax administrations are always catching-up because tax administrations are not in a position to determine the next effective method to legally use the rules, and rule changes, in favour of further reducing taxes.[143]

In summary, the objective of a multinational, or domestic, enterprise that operates in more than one line of business or in more than one geographical location is to maximize the present value of owner returns adjusted for risk to the individuals who own the enterprise. Thus, almost by definition, any set of internal prices, if used for management purposes, will not be comparable to arm's-length prices of independent actors.

---

[141] We do not want to imply that enterprises do not use transfer prices for the purposes of internal coordination and to enhance the efficiency of the enterprise. Tax administrators will probably never know these prices because there is no necessary relationship between the transfer prices set relative to profit maximization and the transfer prices used for tax purposes holding profits fixed. In addition, the transfer prices used by the firm may not be set to attribute or allocate income on a geographical basis. For example, an integrated oil company may define divisions (or subsidiaries) into exploration, refining, and marketing. The internal prices charged between divisions is then based on the need to coordinate the activities of the integrated enterprise, regardless of where particular activities take place within each division. Furthermore, it is not clear that tax administrations would want to use the internal prices that maximize the overall profits of the enterprise. The use of such prices may result in losses in one or more divisions, assuming management's objective is to maximize the overall profits. That is, it is not necessary, or perhaps even efficient, for managers to use internal signals that result in the reporting of positive profits for each division when the profits of the overall enterprise are at a maximum adjusted for risk. This would imply that losses would be reported in some countries with profits in others. This is not base shifting in order to avoid tax but efficient signalling.

[142] The recent agreement to impose a minimum tax rate of 15% by each country subject to the agreement is a case in point. First, a 15% rate does not imply that the effective rate will be a 15% minimum for investments in either a particular country or globally. The effective rate will depend on the definition of the base and countries will still have flexibility about how to determine the base. Second, transfer pricing and base shifting rules will still be necessary even at a minimum tax rate. In effect, the transfer pricing problem is not addressed by each country imposing a minimum rate. The range may be affected, but it is not clear whether the range will have 15% as a lower bound.

[143] We also do not want to imply that tax managers of large enterprises are omniscient. Like all agents, they operate with uncertainty and with limited resource constraints. It is true that the evolution of the arm's-length standard has increased the cost of profit shifting, at least to some extent. In addition, tax managers should only engage in tax reduction strategies as long as the expected benefit is greater than the costs adjusted for risk.

3.4.3.2 Ways to Approach the Problem

There are currently some methods other than formulary apportionment to provide simple tools to a tax administration to counter the competitive advantages of a large enterprise.

a. Use Asset-Stripping Rules

The emergence of asset-stripping rules such as the interest limitation as a proportion of taxable income is one method to simplify the system without the use of transfer pricing. The use of this rule could be expanded to include all transfer-priced inputs. There is no reason why the limitation as a proportion of taxable income could not extend to the total of all related party charges. That is, the summation of all charges (interest, purchased inputs, service charges, and other charges) could be subject to a limitation on the proportion of taxable income before the deduction of any related party charge. At a minimum, such a rule would limit the ability of the firm to shift related party interest costs to other related party charges.

The use of such limitations is allowed under international rules for mining contracts, which have tax provisions that are harsher than the limitation on transfer prices. Some mining contracts impose a limitation on all costs as a proportion of total revenue attributable to the operation. Such an approach enables the country to collect some income tax, as well as contractual payments, regardless of the transfer prices used by the firm. Mining, in our view, is no different from other activities as a matter of taxation. Acceptance of such rules for mining thus could imply acceptance of a rule about the limitation on all related party charges.

b. Set Arbitrary Maximums

Another tool is to simply set an arbitrary maximum for any charge. For example, Conrad has argued that head office expenses should be limited to a specified dollar amount with annual adjustments for inflation instead of using a proportion of cost or revenue. The tax administration knows the revenue loss from such a limitation and is spared the cost of determining a proportion and further monitoring costs. This method could be extended to other inter-firm charges. At the extreme, the maximum could be zero, an action that is equivalent to a disallowance of the related party cost.

c. Set Output Prices as a Proportion of the Market Price of Final Output

Zambia imposes a royalty on copper that is a proportion of the LME price of refined copper, eliminating the need to compute the transfer price for copper concentrate under long-term contracts. This value is also used for income tax purposes. Such a rule for output is recommended for all related party sales where a domestic entity sells to a related party. In particular, the transfer price could be equal to a proportion of the first independently observable price for a good or service that the production to be valued is used to produced. Care must be exercised in using this method, but in theory the fraction used should be equal to the share of the output transferred to the related party to total value added (see Conrad and Alexeev 2021).[144] The price and the basis of the computations should be published and applied to all domestic related parties producing similar output.[145] We support this proposal and believe it should be included for valuing output.

d. Impose Withholding Taxes on Related Party Charges

We believe that emerging economies should begin to develop their own rules as an alternative to standards such as the OECD transfer pricing rules. Rules such as the OECD rules reflect a negotiated compromise position of the tax administrations of capital-exporting countries and their investors. At a minimum, the rules reflect the interests of the countries and investors that are exporters of significant foreign investment. The rules are complicated, and we have noted above that the rules are difficult to administer in OECD countries much less in emerging economies where the challenges are significantly greater.

One option is to eliminate formal source rules and treat the corporate tax as an advanced tax as we have proposed. Thus, only individuals are taxpayers. Such a change can be achieved by exempting dividends from taxation regardless of the tax residence of the shareholder. If the advanced corporate tax rate is the same as the maximum rate on labour income, then there is no incentive to re-characterize income for domestic purposes and the income from corporate capital will be taxed once in the taxing jurisdiction.[146] In addition, the absence of formal source rules will enable a country to impose withholding taxes on all related party transactions (both domestic and foreign) at the withholding rate. As an alternative, there could be one source rule stating that income is sourced in the taxing jurisdiction to the extent that the payor is a domestic resident.[147] There will be no discrimination[148] because the withholding tax is imposed on both domestic and nonresident related party payments and the net-of-tax income can be taxed to domestic individual resident owners via a gross-up and credit.[149] The tax administration will not have to monitor any transfer prices on inputs because the total tax payment would be independent of such charges. Revenue lost by increasing the transfer price is gained by the withholding tax. Significant administrative resources will be freed to address more revenue and compliance-enhancing activities such as fraud, evasion, and general compliance activities. Finally, we believe that concerns about double taxation can be addressed.[150] Briefly, double

---

[144] Netback pricing is really a means of computing what proportion of the final output price is attributable to a particular input, such as concentrate.

[145] Conrad and Alexeev (2021) discuss special cases.

[146] There may be an issue about capital gains taxes.

[147] There could be some results that differ from the standard definition. For example, a domestic resident paying rent on land located in another jurisdiction would be subject to advanced tax.

[148] In effect, transfer-priced inputs can be described as a type of disguised dividend. Dividends, however, should be paid out of fully taxed income. Thus, the withholding tax on related party charges combined with a zero tax on dividends will help ensure that dividends are paid out of income that is fully taxed.

[149] The gross-up and credit would be identical to the method used for the foreign tax credit in many countries.

[150] Claims of double taxation should be suspect for two reasons in our view. First, there needs to be a commonly accepted definition of income that is subject to double taxation. Second, it is not clear that

taxation of the integrated corporate enterprise is not an issue if the costs used to produce the good or service that is supplied to the local entity are deducted somewhere, with the 'somewhere' being determined by the management of the global enterprise.

3.4.3.3 Definition of Related Party

The definition of a related party is important because it is used to determine withholding on supplies of goods and services as well as the use of the posted price method for output.

Related Party:

i. With respect to all persons: Any person who owns directly or indirectly any equity in an entity.
ii. With respect to individuals: Any individual who is defined as related by legal or common law status meeting the following conditions:
   a. Dependent: An individual whose measured net income is less than 50% of the value of deemed support supplied, directly or indirectly, by any other individual or individuals. (Such individuals will be required to file consolidated returns with the individual supplying the support.)
   b. Any two or more individuals owning any equity position in any entity, except entities with the equity valued on a mark-to-market basis.[151]

Note that the definition is broad and includes individuals as well as entities. For example, the simple act of owning equity in an entity is sufficient to create a related party relationship. Note, however, that advanced payments are already imposed on income from equity that are based on proportional interests. The related party rule will be used to determine when advanced payments will be made on the supply of goods and services. For example, if an individual owns shares of a retail store and purchases goods and services, then no advanced payment is required because the individual is as long as the shareholder is charge prices that are the same as non-shareholders. Other situations where advanced payments will be required include the distribution of gifts, payments, or supplies to shareholders that are not in proportion to their equity interest. The broad definition is used because of the limitations placed on the application of related party rules by various definitions of control or minimum stock ownership. We believe it is better to eliminate the control and ownership criteria and to develop a specific list of exceptions.

double taxation is inefficient. For example, an enterprise could be subject to taxation only once and pay $10.00 in tax or be taxed twice and pay $8.00 in tax. The issue is the overall tax burden of the enterprise and the marginal effective tax rate faced when investing in any particular country, not the number of times the income is taxed.

[151] The intent here is to make partners in the partnership related parties both to the partnership and to each other within the scope of specific business transactions. In addition, shareholders of closely held entities are defined as related parties for certain purposes. We seek to ensure that side payments between owners that do not flow through the entity but affect the tax position of the individuals are subject to withholding.

3.4.3.4 Summary
In summary, transfer pricing with one exception is effectively eliminated under the proposal. Even in the case of administered prices for sales to nonresident related parties, there will be no individualized pricing, except in unusual circumstances, and there would be transparency with respect to process. Significant highly skilled administrative resources will be freed, and hopefully an entire class of private sector rent seekers will be able to devote their skills to socially productive activities. Our hope is that the freed administrative resources will increase compliance in the important areas of tax avoidance regarding closely held enterprises, the determination of beneficial ownership of individuals, entities using methods (offshore in many cases) to evade tax, and other compliance activities.

3.4.4 A Note about Permanent Establishments

A permanent establishment (PE) is a tax treaty concept used to determine the minimum criteria for a person to be liable for tax, either VAT or income tax, in a jurisdiction other than the country of residence.[152] Using our definitions, the question is whether the economic activity is sufficient for the legal person to be a registered APA. If the activity is sufficient and a PE is established, then some type of separate accounting is necessary to determine the income attributable to the jurisdiction for tax purposes.[153] Source rules are necessary to determine what revenues and costs are attributable to the jurisdiction. This approach differs from corporations chartered in the jurisdiction in this proposal because corporation income is measured on a worldwide basis.[154] The source rules are necessary because the treaty partner will claim that the jurisdiction has no right to tax the nonresident on a worldwide basis. Thus, it is necessary to separately account for income of what is effectively a created entity.

Our view is that emerging economies should not adopt the PE concept. Instead, if a nonresident's economic activity is deemed sufficient to become an APA, then that person should be required to create a domestic subsidiary (or a domestic entity in the country where the nonresident is an individual). Separate accounting would still occur, but the government has some protection because withholding tax would be imposed on all payments for inputs from related parties and the recommended transfer pricing rule can be enforced.

It might be argued that if the level of activity for domestic incorporation is the same or similar to that of the PE rules in a treaty, then our recommendation is really form with little substance and only costs for the nonresident. We disagree. First, one uniform set of standards can be applied to all investors regardless of residence instead

[152] OECD (2019). Model Tax Convention on income and on Capital (2017) (Full Version). OECD publishing, Paris. https://www.oecd.org/ctp/model-tax-convention-on-income-and-on-capital-full-version-9a5b369e-en.htm.
[153] The exercise is similar to a situation where one person owns a grocery store in two locations in the same town and the person is required to report net income for each separately.
[154] Recall there are no formal sources in the collection-driven approach.

of having PE rules differ by treaty. Second, the nonresident is placed in a situation identical to domestic counterparts because registration and reporting requirements are identical. This allows a government to develop accounting and investment rules that can evolve as reform continues. This gain may be offset by the cost of not extending the possibility of PE status to nonresidents resulting in a decrease in investment. That risk may be an acceptable cost given the ample productive uses of scarce administrative resources.

Finally, we have and continue to recommend that emerging economies not enter into tax treaties, at least until such time as the economy's tax structure and administration has evolved to a level compatible with the home countries for foreign investors. Appeal to competent authority for foreign investors can be guaranteed in law rather than treaty and such appeal will be unnecessary as long as a country treats foreign investors in a nondiscriminatory manner, an approach we support. In addition, a country may be able to benefit from exchange of information without formally entering into a full treaty.[155]

This approach is consistent with our proposals for transfer pricing where we believe that emerging economies need not be dependent on concepts and rules developed by advanced economies.

3.4.5 Foreign Tax Credits

We believe a foreign tax credit should be allowed to resident taxpayers given the worldwide basis for taxation. A somewhat different approach to the norm is required, particularly with respect to limitations. A resident taxpayer who pays (or accrues) income tax to foreign governments should be able to credit on an overall basis the foreign taxes paid without limit. This is counter to one common approach which is to limit the credit to the domestic tax on foreign source income.[156] Source rules for determining foreign source income are then necessary. It might be argued that the domestic country will experience revenue losses beyond amounts that would be allowed if there was a limitation. While potentially valid, the cost is measuring foreign source income. This might be simple in the case of bank interest but can be complicated when net income of a PE or other activity must be computed. If a limitation is deemed necessary, then we recommend that the limitation be based on a proportion of the tax on comprehensive income with no carryforward or carryback for excess credits. This approach is more consistent with comprehensive income measures.[157] In effect, foreign taxes below the limitation are then treated as advanced taxes.

---

[155] Alternatively, a tax treaty could be limited to competent authority and exchange of information among a few other issues unrelated to PEs.
[156] The limitation can be computed on an overall basis or by country.
[157] A similar approach is proposed for foreign taxes paid or accrued by APAs who pass through income to taxpayers.

References

Alexeev, M. & Conrad, R. (2017). Income Equivalence and a Proposed Resource Rent Charge. *Energy Economics, 66*(August), 349–359. https://www.ato.gov.au/Business/Fringe-benefittax/?=Redirect_URL

Conrad, R. (1990). *A Proposal to Index the Tax System for Inflation Combined with Foreign Exchange Gains and Loss Provision*. Memorandum Domincian Republic Tax Reform.

Athreya, K. B., & Waddle, A. L. (2007). Implications of Some Alternatives to Capital Income Taxation. *Economic Quarterly, 93*(1), 31–55. Retrieved from https://www.researchgate.net/publication/5053084_Implications_of_some_alternatives_to_capital_income_taxation

Conrad, R. (2005). Memorandum on VAT Withholding addressed to Mr G. O. Adesina Acting Director, Tax Policy Research and Development Department. dated 3 March 2005.

Conrad, R. (2015). 'Withholding on Payments for Certain Services'. Memorandum for Ms Olena Makeive and Members of the Informal Working Group, dated 20 April 2015.

Conrad, R. (2016). *Concerns about the Tax on Certain Distributions*. Memorandum distributed in Ukraine.

Conrad, R. & Alexeev, M. (2021). Income Tax Reform: A Proposal that Can Be Administered. Unpublished Manuscript.

Easley, D., Kiefer, N. M., & Possen, U. M. (1993). An Equilibrium Analysis of Fiscal Policy with Uncertainty and Incomplete Markets. *International Economic Review, 34*(4), 935–952. doi:10.2307/2526973.

Feldstein, M. (1974). Social Security, Induced Retirement, and Aggregate Capital Accumulation. *Journal of Political Economy, 82*(5), 905–926. Retrieved from http://www.jstor.org/stable/1829174.

Goldschmidt, Y. and Yaron, J. (1991). *Inflation Adjustments of Financial Statements: Application of International Accounting Standard 29*. Washington, DC: World Bank Working Paper WPS 670.

Hulten, C. R., & Wykoff, F. C. (1980). Economic Depreciation and the Taxation of Structures in United States Manufacturing Industries: An Empirical Analysis. In D. Usher (ed.), *The Measurement of Capital* (pp. 83–120). Chicago: University of Chicago Press.

Leimer, D. R., & Lesnoy, S. D. (1982). Social Security and Private Saving: New Time-Series Evidence. *Journal of Political Economy, 90*(3), 606–629. Retrieved from https://EconPapers.repec.org/RePEc:ucp:jpolec:v:90:y:1982:i:3:p:606-29.

New Zealand Inland Revenue. *Fringe Benefit Tax Guide: A Guide to Working with FBT.* IRA 409 (April 2023).

Nishiyama, S., & Smetters, K. (2005). Consumption Taxes and Economic Efficiency with Idiosyncratic Wage Shocks. *Journal of Political Economy, 113*(5), 1088–1115. doi:10.1086/432137.

OECD (2019). Model Tax Convention on income and on Capital (2017) (Full Version). OECD publishing, Paris. https://www.oecd.org/ctp/model-tax-convention-on-income-and-on-capital-full-version-9a5b369e-en.htm.

Simons, H.C. (1938). *Personal Income Taxation.* Chicago: The University of Chicago Press.

Tax Foundation (2023). Who Pays Federal Income Taxes? https://taxfoundation.org/data/all/federal/summary-latest-federal-income-tax-data-2023-update/

Tax Policy Center (2020). What are Marriage Penalties and Bonuses. https://www.taxpolicycenter.org/briefing-book/what-are-marriage-penalties-and-bonuses

Toder, E. and Viard, A. *A Proposal to Reform the Taxation of Corporate Income.* Washington: DC, A Joint Publication of the American Enterprise Institute and the Tax Policy Center.

Annex A3.1
Open-Ended Pooled Accounting

A3.1.1 Introduction

We have supported and advocated the use of open-ended pooled asset accounts for a number of years.[1,2] Below some aspects of the system are discussed, along with examples and a proposal for depreciation of tangible personal property (generally machinery and equipment), intangible property, research and development, and pre-production expenses for natural resource projects (oil and gas, mining, and forestry).

A3.1.2 Benefits of Open-Ended Pooled Accounting

Pooled accounting is a method in which assets are classified in groups, the book (or tax) value of the group is reported as the aggregate value of all assets in each classification, and depreciation is computed for the aggregate tax value of the classification. The immediate implication is that there is no need to compute depreciation, or the various remaining balances, on an asset-by-asset basis. For example, traditional vintage accounting requires two depreciation computations for a machine placed in service in 2017 and a machine placed in service in 2018. Open-ended pooled accounting requires only one computation because the two machine values are aggregated through time as assets are placed in service (or subtracted as retired). The method is facilitated by applying declining balance depreciation, a method under which the monetary balance of the pool, is reduced by a constant proportion each tax period. Note that it is not possible to reduce the balance of the pool to zero simply by reducing the value by a constant proportion each year. The balance can be reduced to zero in only two cases: first, if the accrued value of disposals is equal to or greater than the remaining value (adjusted basis) and second, if there are extraordinary disposals such as damage by fire or entity liquidations.

---

[1] This annex is based on R. Conrad, 'Depreciation.' Memorandum dated 18 March 2020, draft for Daw Mya Mya Oo, Government of Myanmar. Conrad originally learned this method from Emil Sunley during the Indonesian Tax Reform.

[2] Conrad learned about the method from Emil Sunley who proposed the method during the Indonesian tax reform.

Evolutionary Tax Reform in Emerging Economies. Robert F. Conrad and Michael Alexeev, Oxford University Press.
© Open Society Institute (2024). DOI: 10.1093/oso/9780192847089.003.0006

Open-ended pooled accounting has a number of benefits, including:

- Declining balance depreciation is more in accord with empirical studies[3] of economic depreciation;
- There is relative computational simplicity;
- Gains and losses from asset disposals are automatically included, making separate computations of capital gains and losses unnecessary for such assets (including automatic recapture in the case of accelerated depreciation);
- Inflation adjustments can be accommodated as needed/required; and
- A tax incentive such as accelerated depreciation can be incorporated as needed.

Some examples of the computations are presented in Tables A3.1.1–A3.1.4. There are seven steps to computing all possibilities for a particular group.[4] Assumptions used to compute each table are: the depreciation rate is 20%, and the initial value of the depreciation pool is 1000. Table A3.1.1 reflects the situation in which an investment of 500 is made and depreciation is computed for the full year. The basis for depreciation this year (Line 5) is equal to the summation of the initial basis and the amount of qualified investment this year, or 1500. A depreciation value of 300 (Line 6) results. The ending basis of the pool (Line 7) is equal to the difference between the basis for depreciation this year (Line 5) and depreciation this year (Line 6). The ending basis becomes the initial basis for depreciation next year.

Table A3.1.2 is based on the assumption that the 500 investment is made during the last half of the year, and a half-year convention is used (see below). The basis for depreciation this year then includes only half of this year's investment value (Line 5) with no change in the subsequent steps.

Disposals are illustrated in Table A3.1.3 where it is assumed that some of the equipment is disposed during the year, for an accrued value of 280. This value reduces the

Table A3.1.1 Asset placed in service during first half of the year

Line #	Item	Amount
1	Adjusted basis of category A at the beginning of the year	1,000.00
2	Asset value placed in service during first half of the year	500.00
3	Asset value placed in service during second half of the year	
4	Accrued receipts from disposals	
5	Basis for depreciation this year (Line 1 + Line 2 + .5 * Line 3 – Line 4)	1,500.00
6	Depreciation this year (0.2 * Line 5)	300.00
7	Adjusted basis of category A at the end of the year (Line 1 + Line 2 + Line 3 – Line 4 – Line 6)	1,200.00

[3] See Hulten & Wykoff (1981a, 1981b).
[4] One additional step would be required to include inflation adjustments into the depreciation system.

Table A3.1.2 Asset placed in service during second half of the year

Line #	Item	Amount
1	Adjusted basis of category A at the beginning of the year	1,000.00
2	Asset value placed in service during first half of the year	-
3	Asset value placed in service during second half of the year	500.00
4	Accrued receipts from disposals	
5	Basis for depreciation this year (Line 1 + Line 2 + 0.5 * Line 3 – Line 4)	1,250.00
6	Depreciation this year (0.2 * Line 5)	250.00
7	Adjusted basis of category A at the end of the year (Line 1 + Line 2 + Line 3 – Line 4 – Line 6)	1,250.00

Table A3.1.3 Disposal at any time during the year

Line #	Item	Amount
1	Adjusted basis of category A at the beginning of the year	1,000.00
2	Asset value placed in service during first half of the year	-
3	Asset value placed in service during second half of the year	
4	Accrued receipts from disposals	280.00
5	Basis for depreciation this year (Line 1 + Line 2 + 0.5 * Line 3 – Line 4)	720.00
6	Depreciation this year (0.2 * Line 5)	144.00
7	Adjusted basis of category A at the end of the year (Line 1 + Line 2 + Line 3 – Line 4 – Line 6)	576.00

Table A3.1.4 Example of new purchase during both halves of the year and a disposal combined

Line #	Item	Amount
1	Adjusted basis of category A at the beginning of the year	1,000.00
2	Asset value placed in service during first half of the year	500.00
3	Asset value placed in service during second half of the year	500.00
4	Accrued receipts from disposals	280.00
5	Basis for depreciation this year (Line 1 + Line 2 + 0.5 * Line 3 – Line 4)	1,470.00
6	Depreciation this year (0.2 * Line 5)	294.00
7	Adjusted basis of category a at the end of the year (Line 1 + Line 2 + Line 3 – Line 4 – Line 6)	1,426.00

basis for depreciation this year. Again, the remaining steps are unaffected. One additional adjustment is necessary in cases where the value of disposals is greater than the initial basis plus any investment this year. For example, suppose the value of Line 4 in Table A3.1.3 was equal to 1155. The resulting value of the basis for depreciation this year (Line 5) would be negative (−155). The procedure in this case is to set the value of the pool to zero for both depreciation purposes and as the ending basis, and then to include 155 in taxable income as a gain.

Finally, Table A3.1.4 is an illustration of the situation where there is an investment in both halves of the year as well as a disposal. As shown, the steps are purely mechanical and yield the correct result given the variety of events.

A3.1.3 Factors to Consider

Some decisions must be made about the design of any depreciation system.

A3.1.3.1 When to Begin Depreciation

There are two options for when to allow a taxpayer to begin depreciation: date of purchase or date placed in service. The date-of-purchase rule simply means that the taxpayer may begin taking depreciation (adding the value of the asset to the pool) at the time when the taxpayer takes possession of the asset. The placed-in-service rule means the taxpayer may not begin to take depreciation until the date the asset is actually used to produce income. An example will illustrate the difference in the rules. Suppose a taxpayer buys a computer for business purposes on 1 August 2019 but does not begin to use the computer until 15 January 2020. Under the date-of-purchase rule, the taxpayer would be allowed to take depreciation in 2019, perhaps with a half-year convention. Under the placed-in-service rule, the taxpayer would have to wait until 2020 to begin depreciation.

Our preference is for the placed-in-service rule, even if application is more administratively burdensome. Invoices, or the date that possession is obtained, may be the major audit document with the date-of-purchase rule. The invoice is also necessary for the placed-in-service rule, in order to verify ownership, but there needs to be an additional record of the date the asset is placed in service. As a practical matter, there may not be much difference for going concerns except at year-end, so administration audits might be concentrated on year-end transactions. A placed-in-service rule, however, is more consistent with standard accrual accounting, particularly for new investments when there is a lag between the time of purchase and the time operations begin. It is preferable to capitalize all expenses and to defer (amortize) preproduction intangible costs such as labour until production begins. We support such capitalization for tax purposes, including for mines as well as oil and gas, so a placed-in-service rule is compatible with this point of view.[5]

---

[5] Capitalization could be accommodated via an exemption with a date-of-purchase rule. Depreciation of assets purchased prior to the date of production would be deferred. Of course, this is simply a placed-in-service rule for this type of situation.

A3.1.3.2 Treatment in the First Depreciation Period

The amount of depreciation taken in the first year should depend on how much the asset is used or how long it is owned. In theory, the amount of depreciation could be a proportion of the number of days, or months, the asset is used during the tax year. Practical considerations have reduced the options to two. The first is to allow a full year's depreciation regardless of the date placed in service or purchased. Thus, there is some incentive for investors to cluster depreciable investments at year-end, particularly when there are incentives that correspond to the timing of investments, such as accelerated depreciation or investment tax credits. A practical alternative is the half-year convention under which assets placed in service, or purchased, during the first half of the year get a full year's depreciation, while those placed in service, or purchased, during the second half of the year get half of the normal depreciation. We prefer the half-year convention because it appears to be a reasonable averaging device and so recommend its adoption.

A3.1.3.3 Optional Depreciation

Some countries, such as Canada, provide for optional depreciation in any tax period. For example, suppose a taxpayer's depreciation for 2020 is 1566. The taxpayer may take any amount from zero to 1566 in 2020. A taxpayer would only take such an option in situations where tax loss carryforwards are constrained.[6] Our view is that tax loss carryforwards, if used, should be long enough to make optional depreciation redundant. In addition, optional depreciation may add further complications to the system. In short, taxpayers should be required to take the full value of depreciation in the period in which it accrues.

A3.1.4 Coverage and Rates

Assets should be classified into groups for tax purposes based on current asset lives. One suggested example is supplied here. Some incentive is provided given that we classified the assets at the lower end of their asset lives. Real property and intangible costs for exploration and development of natural resources should not be aggregated into pools. Separate accounting by property or licence as the case should be maintained for those groups.

---

[6] For example, assuming a FIFO stacking rule for loss carryforwards, suppose there is a remaining tax loss from 2015 of 1000. Suppose further that taxable income before loss carryforwards and depreciation is 1200. In this case, the taxpayer would take the remaining tax loss carryforward from 2015, in order to get the full benefit of the loss carryforward. In addition, the taxpayer would take only 200 of the 1566 in order to have taxable income of zero in 2020. The decision to take only 200, as opposed to the full 1566, depends on the cumulative tax loss carryforward from the remaining prior four years and expectations about future profitability.

A3.1.4.1 Pooled Asset Classifications

A3.1.4.1.1 Three-Year Property
- Computers and office equipment
- Specialized manufacturing tools
- Other equipment with current asset lives of four years or less

A3.1.4.1.2 Five-Year Property
- Automobiles
- Assets with current asset lives of between five and ten years

A3.1.4.1.3 Seven-Year Property
- Research and Development expenditures[7]
- Purchased intangible property

A3.1.4.1.4 Ten-Year Property
- Manufacturing equipment (not otherwise classified)
- Heavy trucks and equipment
- Communication distribution systems
- Specialized heavy industrial equipment such as mining, forestry, and construction
- Assets with current asset lives of greater than nine years under current rules

A3.1.4.2 Separate Classification

A3.1.4.2.1 Real Property
Real property, including buildings and their structural components, can be depreciated over 25 years via either straight-line or declining balance depreciation.

A3.1.4.2.2 Combine Intangible Preproduction Costs for Natural Resource Projects
Our view is that exploration, development, and preproduction expenses should be aggregated into one group for tax purposes.[8] One appropriate method to amortize these expenditures is unit of production, a method that would amortize the expenditures over the productive life of the project. An incentive is provided, however, by

---

[7] It is common to allow expensing of research and development costs. This is bad policy in our view and is a poor incentive for encouraging research. All research and development can be pooled because, like exploration, the joint expenses, both successes and failures, contribute to the risk-adjusted returns from the successes that result.

[8] We understand that it is common to expense such expenditures, but our view is that such expensing is bad policy if the intended tax base is accrued income. The fact that there are significant risks to such expenditures is not a justification, particularly given ring fencing of mining and petroleum projects. Expensing might be provided in the production sharing and mining contracts, but tax policy is applied to all industries. There is no reason, as a tax policy matter, to treat natural resources in anything other than a neutral manner.

amortizing the expenditures over a five-to-seven-year period on a straight-line basis. The amortization should begin at the date of initial production.

References

Conrad, R. 'Depreciation.' Memorandum dated 18 March 2020, draft for Daw Mya Mya Oo, Government of Myanmar.

Hulten, C. R., & Wykoff, F. C. (1981a). The estimation of economic depreciation using vintage asset prices: An application of the Box-Cox power transformation. *Journal of Econometrics, 15*(3), 367–396. doi: https://doi.org/10.1016/0304-4076(81)90101-9.

Hulten, C. R., & Wykoff, F. C. (1981b). The Measurement of Economic Depreciation. In C. R. Hulten (ed.), *Depreciation, Inflation, and the Taxation of Income from Capital*. Washington, DC: Urban Institute Press.

Annex A3.2
Tax Incentives, Exemptions, and Allowances

A3.2.1 Introduction

Almost all countries have used, and still use, tax incentives. We believe tax incentives are popular because of political considerations and not economic criteria. Other than limited accelerated depreciation, we have consistently argued against almost all tax incentives, investment incentives in particular. Our reasons for this opposition are described here. The discussion is divided into two parts. First, some arguments in favour of, and against, tax incentives are discussed, with our view strongly opposed to incentives. Second, a series of standard tax incentives are described, with a discussion of what issues need to be considered. Our hope is that a discussion of what is necessary to design a reasonable tax incentive is so cumbersome that policymakers and administrators will have ample ammunition to defeat interest groups and politicians from granting such incentives.

A3.2.2 Perspectives

A3.2.2.1 Neutrality

Tax neutrality with respect to economic decisions is an essential feature of economic policy design. While deviations from tax neutrality may sometimes be justified on social or political grounds, usually non-neutral taxes increase distortions in the economy, hinder tax administration and compliance, and reduce social welfare.

Tax neutrality is often described by application of a single relatively low rate applied to a broad economic measure of a given tax base. Note that this definition of a uniform tax crucially depends on the definition of the base, which varies by tax. For example, the purpose of a VAT and a sales tax is to impose a tax on domestic consumption. That is, savings and investment are exempt from these taxes.[1] Alternatively, the purpose of a comprehensive income tax is to impose a tax on all income, including the return to saving and the return to human capital. Here, exempting capital

---

[1] Note that certain exemptions such as zero-rating of exports under VAT do not represent deviations from uniform taxation as long as the tax base for VAT is defined as domestic consumption, because exported goods obviously do not belong to this tax base.

Evolutionary Tax Reform in Emerging Economies. Robert F. Conrad and Michael Alexeev, Oxford University Press.
© Open Society Institute (2024). DOI: 10.1093/oso/9780192847089.003.0007

transactions such as a transfer of the principal of a loan does not violate uniformity of taxation, because this transfer does not represent income.

In addition to promoting tax neutrality, uniform taxation is usually less cumbersome to administer. Note, however, that uniform taxation as defined above is not equivalent to tax neutrality, because tax bases may overlap and because certain goods such as leisure cannot be reasonably taxed in principle. Also, administrative simplicity sometimes requires deviations from uniform taxation. Nonetheless, deviations from uniformity serve as a simple and convenient starting point in the analysis of tax neutrality.

While uniform taxes have certain important advantages, there are also some potentially legitimate economic, social, and political arguments for deviations from tax uniformity and even tax neutrality. Below, we discuss the interactions and tradeoffs among these considerations.

A3.2.2.2 Arguments for Incentives / against Tax Uniformity

The following classifications are what might be viewed as arguments for making taxes non-uniform:[2]

(1) *Administrative and compliance simplicity.* Example: standard exemption in the personal income tax (PIT). Generally, the concept of personal income provides for a deduction of the cost of earning that income. These costs, however, are difficult to evaluate properly. The administrative and compliance expenditures on evaluating the cost of earning income for most people might exceed the efficiency gains from correct evaluations. Hence, a standard deduction may represent an efficient tradeoff between social accuracy and administrative complexity. Similarly, minimizing administrative and compliance costs serves as the main argument for a turnover-based VAT exemption and for simplified accounting regimes for small businesses.

(2) *Social and distributional considerations.* Examples: deductions for dependents under the PIT, low VAT rates for food and children's clothing, and profit tax exemptions for businesses hiring handicapped people.

(3) *Externalities and other market failures.* Some economic activities produce positive externalities. Unfettered markets may not provide socially optimal amounts of such activities. A large class of exemptions can be based on the argument that the exempt activity produces a positive externality. In addition, a closely related argument is that some economic activities help start a virtuous cycle of economic growth. Such arguments have been used, for example, to justify investment allowances and tax holidays under the profits tax.

---

[2] We believe that sometimes deviations from uniform taxation are advocated simply to obtain personal gain without any regard for social efficiency. Even in those cases, however, potentially legitimate economic, social, or political arguments are used.

Note that some exemptions may be supported on several grounds. For example, a special tax regime for small businesses has been justified in part on administrative grounds[3] and compliance costs, but there have also been claims that small businesses are particularly good at generating employment and innovation. If that is the case, a special tax regime for small businesses may be justified on the grounds of both social policy and positive externalities.

A3.2.2.2.1 Administrative and Compliance Simplicity

This is perhaps the least controversial argument for non-uniform taxation. Administrative and compliance costs represent a clear social cost and they are relatively easy to calculate and compare to the revenue effects of the corresponding exemptions. It is important to understand, however, that the appropriate comparison is not only to the revenue effects of exemptions, but also to the efficiency losses resulting from non-uniformity of taxation. These efficiency losses are much more difficult to evaluate. For example, a small business tax without a reasonable transition rule to the normal tax system may provide incentives for businesses not to grow beyond the threshold, because the marginal tax rate around the threshold may be quite high. It is unclear how significant these efficiency losses are in any specific case. Nonetheless, in some cases—such as a standard exemption under the PIT and a VAT threshold for turnover—the tradeoff is clearly in favour of these exemptions, at least up to a point.

A3.2.2.2.2 Social and Distributional Considerations

The main issue with respect to these grounds for exemptions is whether the tax system is an appropriate tool for achieving social and distributional goals. Tax exemptions can be poorly targeted and sometimes they significantly complicate administration. Such effects reduce the ability of the tax system to redistribute wealth. Poor targeting of socially motivated tax exemptions can be illustrated by the lower VAT rate for food. High-income people spend more on food in absolute terms and, therefore, receive a greater benefit from this exemption. This problem may be exacerbated if the poor are more likely than the rich to buy domestically produced foodstuffs from the vendors who are below the VAT threshold. In this case, the poor may be able to avoid paying VAT on their food purchases altogether, whatever the VAT rate on foodstuffs, while the rich would be the main beneficiaries of the lower rate. Personal income tax exemptions for medical expenditures provide another example of inadequate targeting, particularly if the deductibility of some of these expenditures is not limited. Clearly, the benefit of this exemption accrues mainly to high-income individuals in any country, including emerging economies.

In addition, socially motivated tax exemptions complicate tax administration and compliance, and the existence of such exemptions creates temptation for abuse. Therefore, taxpayers claiming such exemptions are typically required to provide documentation justifying the use of the exemptions, and the tax administration needs to

---

[3] We hope that the discussion in the chapter on Small Business Taxation is sufficient to convince readers that any small business tax is complex to administer.

audit this documentation, raising both compliance and administrative costs. Some abuse nonetheless occurs, resulting in additional distortions and additional social costs of resources spent on evasion.

Because of the above considerations, we prefer that non-tax instruments be used to achieve social and distributional goals. For example, instead of lower a VAT rate on foodstuffs, a general income subsidy to low-income individuals may achieve the same goal at a lower expense to society. If the tax system is to be used to advance social goals, an effort needs to be made to improve targeting, although such efforts may further complicate tax administration and compliance. Phasing out at high-income levels of certain PIT exemptions such as the exemption for medical expenditures may be an example of improved targeting.

A3.2.2.2.3 Externalities and Other Market Failures

Arguments for these exemptions are often grounded in sound economic theory. Nonetheless, the fact that externalities and other market failures exist does not necessarily justify the use of tax exemptions to correct them.

Tax exemptions to correct for market failures may take the form of tax incentives for investments, although the relationship to investment may not always be direct. Direct investment-related exemptions include investment allowances for solar equipment, accelerated depreciation of certain types of investments in clean energy, tax holidays for alternative fuel projects, and tax-exempt bonds for government finance. Less direct tax incentives include VAT exemptions for certain goods related to investment, such as electricity and steel, and PIT exemptions for capital gains in certain sectors. Some tax incentives attempt to address negative externalities. For example, tax credits under the corporate income tax may be provided for the installation of pollution abatement equipment.

A3.2.2.3 Arguments against Externality-Based Investment Incentives / for Tax Uniformity

While arguments for incentives have a measure of economic validity, they suffer from two major drawbacks. First, considerations other than tax incentives are usually more important in determining the amount and location of investment. Such considerations include the general political, regulatory, and taxation environment in the country, the degree of stability of this environment, the overall quality of tax administration, and, for foreign investors, the potential for profit repatriation and the country's tax treaties with other countries. Second, society's costs of tax incentives for investment are usually significantly higher than the benefits.

A3.2.2.3.1 Economic Arguments

By definition, tax incentives (tax credits, tax holidays, enterprise zones, and other incentives) are discriminatory relative to a low uniform rate system. Such economic discrimination has a number of adverse consequences.

a. Variation in Effective Tax Rates

One intended or unintended result of tax incentives is that the effective tax rates vary either across sectors, across types of investments, or both. Holding the capital stock constant, and other things equal, intersectoral misallocations result. Suppose the general effective tax rate (marginal or average) is t, but a favoured sector receives a tax incentive that lowers the effective tax rate to $t^* < t$. Assuming a fixed real return on capital, r (resulting from being a small open economy, for instance), then the after-tax return on invested capital will be higher for the favoured industry. That is, $r(1-t^*)$ $> r(1-t)$. Thus, capital will flow to the favoured industry from the rest of the economy until $r^*(1-t^*) = r(1-t)$ with $r^* < r$, where r^* is after-tax return on invested capital in the favoured industry. This type of discrimination can be intentional (for instance, incentives for specific industries) or unintentional (for instance, incentives that affect the composition of assets by favouring short-lived assets relative to long-lived assets). Regardless, the marginal product of capital in the favoured sector is lower than in the rest of the economy, implying that capital in the economy is misallocated. That is, 'too much' capital flows to the favoured sector and a dead weight loss (i.e., net loss to the economy) is created because the social value of capital in the favoured sector is lower than the value of an additional unit of capital to the rest of the economy. For instance, the return on the marginal unit of capital might be 2% in the favoured sector while the return in other sectors is 10%. Thus, reducing capital by one dollar in the favoured industry will cost the economy two cents but the economy will gain ten cents if this dollar of investment is employed elsewhere. As a result, the economy gains eight cents (ten cents minus two cents) by the reallocation. Note that the welfare cost is created because investors are responding to the incentives created by the government. That is, income in the favoured sector increases due to the incentives, but total economic income falls.

b. Negative Effective Tax Rates

Negative marginal effective tax rates can result from incentives. That is, the incentive results in a subsidy at the margin instead of simply being a tax reduction (with forgone revenue). The simplest case of a negative effective tax rate is the situation where interest on debt is deductible for profits tax purposes and accelerated depreciation, including expensing, is provided as an incentive.

The effect of negative effective tax rates is similar to the differential rates of return noted above. Capital is misallocated across sectors if the negative marginal effective tax rates are not uniform across industries and assets. The welfare cost might be greater than that which results from intersectoral reallocations, however. This is because investment levels are driven to the margin where what amounts to a direct subsidy is required for that investment. Suppose the return to capital in the absence of incentives is 10%. No investment would be made with an expected return below 10%, if there were no tax incentives or subsidies. If the marginal effective tax rate is −15%, then an investment yielding a social return of −15% can be made by the favoured firm at the margin. Not only is capital misallocated, but the additional capital investment also reduces real income, other things equal. Thus, both intersectoral distortions and negative returns can result from negative marginal rates.

c. Discrimination against Small and New Businesses

Given that a taxpayer must have taxable income in order for the income tax incentive to have any potential effect, tax incentives are either not effective or anti-competitive for taxpayers with no, or small amounts of, tax. For instance, consider a tax holiday. Firms that do not generate any profits at the time and that would otherwise have no tax obligation cannot benefit from this incentive. Alternatively, a firm that would otherwise have a significant tax obligation will have a competitive advantage over the firm that cannot take full advantage of the benefit. The irony of this situation is that it is the small or marginal investors who should be the beneficiaries of the incentive.[4]

Two other economic effects, both counter to competition, result from tax incentives. First, as noted, large firms with significant tax liabilities benefit relative to smaller marginal investors. Second, there is an incentive for greater concentration of assets within larger firms. Large firms can be induced to buy smaller firms in order to arbitrage the differential in tax benefits (large firms can use the benefits while the incentive is of little, or no, benefit to smaller firms).

d. Revenue Losses in Excess of Gains

The government should target incremental investments only in order to avoid revenue losses from incentives for investments that would take place even absent the incentive. Such targeting is difficult because what is marginal or incremental is ambiguous. Thus, revenue costs can be expected to exceed any benefit gains. This is because less than precise targeting results in a reduction in both marginal and average tax on all investments made under the incentive programmes. In effect, the government is providing an income transfer to investors who would have made some of the investments without the incentive. In most cases, unless investment supply is highly elastic, the revenue losses are greater than the investment gains because of the income transfer. Thus, it might be cheaper for the economy to eliminate the incentive and simply make investment grants to attain the desired amount of investments.

A3.2.2.3.2 Administrative Arguments

Tax incentives, regardless of type, increase the administrative complexity of the tax system for at least two reasons. First, tax administrators must monitor different tax regimes depending on the nature of the incentive. Taxable income, or the tax liability, is computed differently for those who benefit from incentives relative to investors taxed under the standard regime. Filing procedures, income derivations, and audit rules all might differ. Transparency is reduced and incentives for corruption are

---

[4] A similar thing happens with small business under a VAT, if the small business is operating under the turnover threshold. Such a small business cannot issue invoices and thus may lose business supplying inputs to VAT taxpayers relative to a larger VAT taxpayer. This is the justification for voluntary registration. Voluntary registration, on the other hand, may lead to more fly-by-night firms. Thus, the government must make a tradeoff between revenue losses due to evasion and discrimination against small business.

increased. Second, anti-abuse rules and other compliance methods must be developed in an attempt to ensure that the incentive is used for the intended function. These rules are generally complex (recapture rules, for instance) and are sometimes arbitrary. The arbitrary nature of the rules results because the government cannot precisely separate desirable from undesirable effects of the incentives.[5] Thus, both the innocent and the guilty might be penalized by the anti-abuse rules.

For an example of these two effects, consider tax holidays. It is imperative that the tax administration audit the business during the tax holiday period in order to avoid transfer pricing from profitable businesses (reducing total tax) to those who operate under the tax holiday and to ensure that income is properly measured. Tax administration resources are diverted from other revenue-productive activities because honest taxpayers, by definition, should pay no tax during the holiday period. In addition, the government must decide whether taxable income should be measured during the tax holiday period or whether to delay application of the tax laws until the holiday period is over. Firms that accrue only losses during the holiday period would not benefit from a tax holiday. Thus, the government needs to decide whether the end of the tax holiday marks the beginning of the time when tax depreciation, cumulative interest expenses, and other deductions are allowed. Complication is increased.

In addition, tax holidays require the development of anti-abuse rules. For example, related party rules are needed to combat the transfer pricing concerns noted above. Recapture rules and reorganization rules are necessary to keep the business from reorganizing into a new business at the end of the tax holiday and effectively get a second holiday.

A3.2.2.3.3 Political Arguments

As noted, tax incentives are discriminatory. Incentives create rent-seeking behaviour by those who do not benefit from the current incentives, and by those who currently benefit, but seek to keep their existing benefits. Such rent seeking increases the welfare cost of the incentives. In addition, if rent seeking is successful, and more incentives are created, then the effective tax base is reduced and economic distortions are increased. The government might have to increase statutory rates in order to compensate for revenue shortfalls, thereby increasing effective rates for those without incentives, generating additional deadweight loss.[6] A counterproductive cycle might be created whereby incentives lead to rate increases, further increasing the demand for special incentives. Such behaviour has been noted in some countries (for instance, Indonesia in the late 1970s and the United States during the early part of the Reagan Administration[7]) and the need for significant tax reforms resulted: tax reforms combined rate reductions with the elimination of tax incentives.

---

[5] For instance, a taxpayer might take advantage of accelerated depreciation to find that the investment is not profitable. This taxpayer might suffer from recapture on disposal of the assets, creating a second cost to the decision made under uncertainty.

[6] The economic loss from taxation often increases disproportionately as tax rates increase.

[7] See R. Conrad, *Essays on the Indonesian Tax Reform*, World Bank, 1987; and *General Explanation to the Tax Equity and Responsibility Act of 1986*, US Congress, 1986.

In summary, tax incentives are politically popular in the short run but economically inefficient in both the short and longer terms. The best tax incentive is a low uniform effective rate across all sectors and investments. This result is achieved, and rent seeking is reduced, only if tax incentives are either eliminated or greatly curtailed.

The next section presents a more detailed discussion of issues raised by specific types of tax incentives.

A3.2.3 Particular Tax Incentives for Investment

A3.2.3.1 Tax Holidays

It might appear that an income tax holiday would be the simplest of all tax incentives; if a tax holiday lasts for five years, then the taxpayer simply does not pay any income tax for five years. The following elements are needed in order to design even a basic tax holiday, however.

A3.2.3.1.1 Is the Tax Holiday a Zero Rate or a Gap in Time?

The first issue is whether the taxpayer must file and compute taxable income during the tax holiday period. That is, the state must decide whether the taxpayer needs to derive all income, report gross income and take all deductions, including interest expense, depreciation, and other deductions. In addition, it is necessary to determine the extent to which any loss carryforwards would be allowed after the holiday period.

A second option is to have the tax holiday be simply a gap in time. For instance, if the tax holiday is for five years, then the taxpayer might not be required to file income tax returns for the five-year period and, at least implicitly, will not take any deductions. Such an approach could be a significant benefit to the taxpayer because assets would not be subject to depreciation or amortization during the tax holiday period, leaving the full balance, perhaps unadjusted for inflation, to be amortized after the tax holiday period is over.

A3.2.3.1.2 What Is the Commencement Date?

The government must determine when in time the tax holiday begins. Given start-up and investment periods, taxpayers prefer to have the commencement date begin at the date when commercial sales (or production) begin. There would be only losses during start-up periods, mitigating the benefit of the holiday.

Some projects, mining projects in particular (see Chapter 6), may have significant accumulated losses during the initial periods of normal operations. The presence of such losses and loss carryforwards may make a tax holiday effectively redundant because no, or few, taxes would be paid during the tax holiday period. Thus, there is an incentive to adjust the commencement date until the time of 'first taxable profits'. This approach should be resisted because the commencement date becomes an endogenous variable for the investor. The investor can attempt to shift expenses to the periods prior to, or after, the tax holiday periods while shifting revenue (and other gains) to the holiday period.

A3.2.3.1.3 What Is the Scope of the Holiday?

In general, a tax holiday applies to the profits tax,[8] but there are questions about whether the holiday extends to capital gains taxes (particularly if the capital gains tax is viewed as a charge separate from the generally applicable tax), property taxes, and withholding taxes. Withholding taxes are legally speaking taxes imposed on the recipients of corporate distributions (either domestic or foreign depending on the laws of the country) as a prepayment of (or final) tax. As such, the corporate entity that benefits from the tax holiday is a separate legal person from the person (either legal or physical) subject to withholding. Thus, we recommend that a tax holiday should not extend to withholding taxes. Some might argue that withholding taxes are ultimately a charge on the same entity, particularly in cases where distributions are made to parent entities (either foreign or domestic). In effect, the argument is that economic substance would imply that for a tax holiday to be effective, the ultimate investor should receive the benefit. While there is some merit to this argument, the argument should be the basis for not allowing a tax holiday in the first instance.

Investors might claim that tax holidays, and other incentives, should extend to contractors and subcontractors, related parties in particular. Again, with respect to related parties, the argument is that business practice may determine corporate structures but that it is necessary to expand the scope of the exemption beyond the single entity in order to be effective. Such extensions should be resisted. Corporate structures may reflect tax as well as general business practice, and there is little economic basis to claim that activities conducted by related parties by necessity need to be conducted in a separate entity. Thus, the taxpayer has a choice by limiting the tax holiday to a single entity. The taxpayer's related parties can be subject to full taxation on gains and losses related to the project, or the taxpayer can conduct the activities of the related party within one single corporate structure, in which case the tax holiday would be effective.

A3.2.3.1.4 What Is the Potential for Abuse?

Some actions can be anticipated which might be forestalled by anti-abuse provisions in a tax holiday.

a. Corporate Transformations

A tax holiday might be granted for a specified period and the law could be drafted so that the tax holiday is available for new investment, with 'new' being defined as a new entity. Such a definition would create an incentive for the following type of abuse. Firm A is a new firm that makes a new investment. At the end of the tax holiday

---

[8] There should be no need for a tax holiday for VAT given the fact that the VAT taxpayer is effectively a withholding agent for the VAT.

period, Firm A is liquidated and the assets are sold to a new Firm B. The question is whether Firm B is granted a new tax holiday.

This type of abuse might be deterred if the tax holiday is granted for a specific project. The project might be new or preexisting. For example, a mine to be rehabilitated and a factory being privatized for the first time might receive one benefit regardless of corporate structure.

b. Existing or New Firm

Defining a tax holiday on a project basis raises the issue of whether tax holidays should be provided to preexisting firms or limited to newly established firms. The simple notion of a tax holiday is a situation where a new investor is making a completely new investment. What is 'new', however, can be difficult to control. For instance, suppose Firm X is an existing firm considering a new investment in a different part of the country (or in a different line of business). If the government allows the existing firm to make the investment, then separate accounting by project must be used in order to segregate revenue and expenses between the new project and the preexisting activities. Such accounting is difficult and there is certainly a strong incentive to transfer price profits from preexisting activities to the new project during the tax holiday. One means to develop separate accounting is to require that the new project be segregated into a new special purpose entity. While clearly a legally defined structure, the transfer of profits between related entities remains a concern.

A direct and indirect ownership test might be necessary in order to define 'new' investors. For instance, Firm C might be a newly created firm otherwise eligible for a tax holiday. Firm C, however, is a wholly owned subsidiary of Firm D, which in turn is owned by two parties, Firm E and Firm F, with Firm E (an established domestic firm) having a majority interest in Firm D. This could mean that Firm C could be eligible for a tax holiday and Firm E could transfer price profits from its other investments to Firm C. In effect, all of Firm E's investments might have lower (or no) taxes because of the tax holiday available to Firm C.

It is also the case that countries might grant tax holidays to foreign investors in a discriminatory fashion. The direct and indirect ownership test applies to this situation as well. For instance, Firm E above is a domestic entity. But Firm D could be incorporated abroad and thus Firm E could effectively control Firm C, which is technically speaking an investment made by a foreign person.

A3.2.3.1.5 What Administrative Incentives Are Created?

Adverse incentives might be created for the tax administration. The tax administration knows that no revenue will accrue during a tax holiday period. Accordingly, there may be no incentive to monitor compliance during the holiday period, particularly in situations where the tax administration operates with various types of revenue targets. Slack administration may lead to poor compliance, which in turn will compound the revenue losses beyond those contemplated when the holiday was granted. For instance, firms have a clear incentive to defer taking deductions during the holiday period.

A3.2.3.2 Tax Credits

Tax credits are used to reduce either the cost of investment or, in the case of employment tax credits, the cost of employees. Like tax holidays, even basic tax credits raise many questions.

A3.2.3.2.1 How Is the Credit Designed?

In cases where taxable income before credits is positive, it can be shown that a credit is equivalent to a deduction. That is, if the tax rate is 'k' and the expenditure qualifying for the credit is Z with a proportion of c, then after-tax income under a credit is:

$$\Pi_A = (1 - k)\,\Pi_B + cZ,$$

where: Π_B = Before Tax Income,
$\quad\quad\quad\Pi_A$ = After Tax Income.

For instance, if Z is 100 and c = .1, then cZ is equal to 10. Suppose before-tax profit is 1,500 and k = .25. This means that the tax before credit would be 375, with the credit reducing the amount to 365 (or 375–10). Thus, after-tax income is equal to 1,135.

Suppose now that instead of a credit the government offers a deduction (or an additional deduction as the case may be) equal to f, which is this case is equal to 40% (or c/k in general). After-tax profit with such a deduction is:

$$\pi_A = (1 - t)(\pi_B - fZ).$$

In order for after-tax income with the credit to be the same as after-tax income with the deduction:

$$cZ = kfZ\ or$$
$$c = kf.$$

Tax credits might be preferable to deductions, however, in cases where tax rates are variable. In this case, the monetary value of the credit is independent of the marginal tax rate. That is, a credit of ten is worth ten regardless of whether the marginal tax rate is 50% or 25%. A deduction of twenty, however, is worth ten if the marginal tax rate is 50%, but only five if the marginal tax rate is 25%.[9]

As noted, credits have been used for encouraging both employment and investment. One difficulty with credits (as well as accelerated deductions) is that the taxpayer may be rewarded for doing nothing. That is, the taxpayer may currently have 60 workers and if a tax credit for employment is provided, without restriction, then the taxpayer could potentially get a credit for the 60 workers without increasing employment at all. To avoid this problem, tax credits tend to be based on 'incremental' effects, or changes in the levels of the desired activity. The problem persists,

---

[9] This is one reason for our preference for personal credits relative to exemptions under a personal income tax.

however, because the taxpayer could be planning to increase the level of the desired activity without the benefit from the incentive. For instance, suppose the tax credit is designed to increase employment and the taxpayer currently employs 60 workers. In addition, the taxpayer plans to hire four new workers during the next tax year absent the credit. If an incremental tax credit were perfectly designed, then the taxpayer would receive the tax credit only for additional workers beyond the original four.[10]

Of course, it is not possible for policymakers or administrators to measure intent before the fact, and so some indicator or proxy is used to approximate incremental effects.[11] For instance, The 'R&D tax credit' (Internal Revenue Code § 41 Research and Experimentation Tax Credit) was introduced in the United States in 1981. The credit is not a permanent part of the IRS Tax Code but has been repeatedly renewed and is still applicable. In general, the tax credit is equal to 20% of the excess of 'qualified research expenses' for the taxable year over the 'base amount', both of which are defined in the section. Taxpayers, however, may elect the incremental credit instead, which equals:

- 3% of so much of the qualified research expenses for the taxable year as exceeds 1% of the average described in the law [the average annual gross receipts of the taxpayer for the four taxable years preceding the taxable year for which the credit is being determined] but does not exceed 1.5% of such average;
- 4% of so much of such expenses as exceeds 1.5% of such average but does not exceed 2% of such average; and
- 5% of so much of such expenses as exceeds 2% of such average (IRC § 41 (c)(4)).

All this makes the incentive more and more complicated to use and administer.

A3.2.3.2.2 How Is the Credit Administered?
A tax credit can be difficult to administer.[12] For instance, in the case of employment credits, there is an incentive for the taxpayer to hire temporary workers to satisfy the

[10] An additional problem with the incremental credit is that taxpayers who, absent the credit, would have reduced employment may not benefit from the credit based on incremental changes. For instance, suppose a taxpayer currently has 30 employees and plans to reduce employment by five during the next tax period. If a tax credit is implemented on an incremental basis, then the taxpayer would still reduce employment by five because the credit does not provide any incentive. If, however, the credit is applied without a definition of incremental, then this taxpayer would benefit and may retain the five workers. This example is illustrative of the problem with incentives based on actions. Such incentives are asymmetric in the sense that the absence of negative actions (or no action because of the incentive) is not sufficient to obtain the benefit.
[11] The art of such approximations is to balance the revenue loss from the incentive against being too rigorous with the definition of incremental, which would reduce (or eliminate) the effectiveness of the incentive. For this reason, we believe that policy makers attempt to err on the side of increasing the effectiveness of the incentive.
[12] Tax credits can be limited, and this provision adds additional complexity. For instance, the credit in any year might be limited to 50% of accrued taxes before the credit.

credit and then reduce the labour force after the benefit ceases.[13] Similar to tax holidays, tax credits increase administrative complexity because of the need to monitor different tax systems.

A3.2.3.2.3 What Is the Potential for Abuse?

Several problems of potential abuse also arise with investment credits.

a. Basis Adjustment

There is an issue about whether the value of the tax credit should reduce the basis for tax depreciation. For instance, if an investment is valued at 1,000 and the tax credit is 10%, then the credit is equivalent to immediately expensing 100 (or 10%) of the investment. If the basis is not reduced, then the taxpayer may deduct 110% of the asset's value and it is possible that marginal effective tax rates could be negative. Thus, it makes sense to reduce the basis, but the computations become burdensome. For instance, if the taxpayer is currently operating with a loss and tax credits cannot be carried forward, then it is not clear ex ante whether the credit has value in present value terms. If the tax credit is not taken, then the taxpayer can deduct more each year because the basis for depreciation is not reduced, thus increasing the carryforward immediately and perhaps into the future. This is an additional reason why the tax credit might not be effective depending on the carryforward limitation and the tax loss carryforward limitation.

b. Churning

There is also abuse potential with investment credits with respect to churning. Suppose that a new machine has a value of 1,000, there is a 20% tax credit, and the taxpayer has a positive tax liability sufficient to absorb the full value of the credit. The government has effectively paid 200 of the investment's value, leaving 800 out of pocket for the investor. This means that the investor can immediately sell the asset for any value greater than 800 and make more money. Such activity is known as 'churning' because, absent enforcement of an anti-abuse rule, taxpayers could in theory trade the same asset and repeatedly take the credit. That is, Taxpayer A could take the tax credit for 200 and sell the asset to Taxpayer B for 900 who would take a credit for 190.

Three design and administrative features are necessary in order to combat such potential abuse. First, tax credits for investment may be limited to 'new' assets and to assets other than real property.[14] Second, 'churning', if proven, may be classified as a prohibited transaction and the tax administration may be given the authority to eliminate the tax benefit for such transactions. Third, the benefit may be recaptured if the

---

[13] There is also the old argument about temporary relative to permanent tax credits that needs to be referenced.

[14] Limiting the credit to new assets may limit the beneficial effects of the incentive because the purchase of used assets may be the most effective investment.

asset is sold before a stipulated time period. For instance, the government might stipulate that the asset must be retained by the investor for five years in order to obtain full benefits. For instance, returning to the 20% credit example, the taxpayer would automatically lose the benefit if that person sold the asset within the first year. Given any asset use by the taxpayer for intended purposes, governments, especially in countries like the United States, attempt to fine tune the recapture by amortizing the lost benefit. This arises because the asset was presumably used for some part of the asset's life and thus the taxpayer is entitled to some benefit. One example of a five-year amortization would be to allow 20% of the investment tax credit for each year the asset is in use. Thus, if the taxpayer sells the asset at the end of the third year, then 40% of the credit is recaptured.

c. Accelerated Depreciation and Expensing

Accelerated depreciation is defined to be any amount in excess of economic depreciation; the extreme being immediate expensing.[15] In general, depreciation is a method to amortize the cost of an asset during its useful life and is accordingly a deduction in the derivation of taxable income on an accrual basis. Accelerated depreciation is then a method to speed cost recovery and thereby increase the present value of the tax deduction.[16]

The equivalence of tax credits and tax deductions was illustrated in Section A3.2.3.2. Thus, accelerated depreciation can have effects identical to an investment tax credit. For instance, if the tax rate is 50% and the amount of excess depreciation is 40, then accelerated depreciation is equivalent to an investment credit of 20 (.5*40) when taxable income is positive.

Given the equivalence with a tax credit, there are similar inefficiencies with accelerated depreciation. In particular, marginal effective tax rates can be negative when accelerated depreciation is combined with interest deductions for debt service. Accelerated depreciation and immediate expensing also share the incentive to create similar types of abuse, churning in particular. Thus, anti-abuse rules are necessary to limit such abuse.

d. Deductions in Excess of Expenses

Another incentive within the accelerated deduction is the situation where more than the expenditure is allowed as a deduction either on a current basis or through time.

---

[15] Immediate expensing might be relatively efficient under what is known as cash-flow taxation. Assets are immediately expensed and debt service is disallowed with this system, among a general movement to cash basis from accrual basis accounting. Cash-flow taxation is discussed in the small business tax chapter (Chapter 5).
[16] One justification for accelerated depreciation is the ability to offset, at least in part, the effects of inflation on the present value of tax deductions. There is some merit to such justifications, but it should be clear that there is only one inflation profile that will offset any particular accelerated depreciation scheme. In addition, the interaction between inflation and accelerated depreciation will not be uniform across asset classifications.

For instance, an incentive might provide for a deduction of 120% of wages in the case of an employment incentive or provide for taking an additional investment allowance equal to 20% of the asset's cost basis in the first year without reducing the basis. In effect, the government is providing a direct cash grant via the tax system equal to the product of the tax rate and the amount of the benefit. For instance, suppose wages are 100 and the tax rate is 25%. A programme to provide a deduction for 150% of the wage bill is equivalent to a direct subsidy equal to 12.5 (or .25*50).

A3.2.3.3 Export Incentives

Export credit schemes and export finance schemes are common types of export subsidies financed by governments. Like direct subsidies, export incentives are some-times employed to encourage increased foreign exchange earnings and to assist with expansion of markets. There are generally two types of export incentives.

A3.2.3.3.1 Incremental Export Revenue Incentives

This incentive is similar in structure to incremental tax credits and expenses except with an opposite sign.[17] That is, the intent is to reduce the tax on incremental export values (or volumes), which in effect reduces taxable revenue attributable to the favoured activity. Like accelerated depreciation and investment credits, such incentives can take one of at least two forms. First, a proportion of incremental export revenues can simply be exempted from income taxes. That is, all the costs can be deducted but revenues are reduced by the amount of the exemption, thus reducing taxable income and tax. The second method is an incremental export credit, which can achieve a similar result. For instance, there might be a credit (such as the one in India) for increasing exports above a threshold. Suppose the credit is equal to 20% of the increased exports, perhaps subject to some quantitative limitation, incremental exports are 100, and the tax rate is 50%. Such a credit is equivalent to an exemption of gross income of 10 (or .2*100*.5).

Potential adverse incentives include inflating f.o.b. export prices to increase the amount of the credit or to obtain the threshold level of exports necessary to obtain credits and re-characterizing domestic sales as exports.

A3.2.3.3.2 Export Processing Zones

Export processing zones were initially developed to reduce the adverse incentives created by import tariffs and to serve as an alternative to duty drawback systems.[18] They are still used to promote exports even though tariffs have been reduced throughout the world. One justification for export zones is that export firms can

---

[17] Another justification for export incentives is the expressed effort to maintain domestic investment relative to having domestic investors make foreign direct investments.

[18] Drawbacks are commonly used in the United States among other countries.

be located in a common space and might be able to trade among themselves while taking advantage of shared facilities (such as infrastructure). Such zones might be seen as particularly useful in situations where a country suffers from lack of infrastructure, including electricity, local transportation, and port facilities. Myanmar is one example where export zones were being developed to offset lack of domestic infrastructure and other facilities.

Those operating in export zones are exempt from all customs duties, and sales of domestic intermediate goods and services are treated as exports for VAT purposes. Thus, the export zone might be perceived as an area where the potentially adverse export incentives created by tariffs and poor VAT administration are eliminated. It is now common, however, for export processing zones to be exempt from domestic income taxation. Thus, with the exception of income taxes imposed on employees of zone businesses, activities in the zone might be considered outside of the country's taxing jurisdiction.[19]

A number of administrative issues arise from such arrangements. First, separate accounting must be maintained to the extent that domestic investors operate both in the zones and in the domestic economy. In effect, the investment in the export processing zone might be treated as an unincorporated foreign branch (or permanent establishment). All of the administrative problems associated with such accounting, including attributions and the like, arise in this situation. Sometimes investors in the zone are required to be special purpose and separate legal entities. This is equivalent to a domestic investor creating a foreign subsidiary. The problems of separate accounting are not resolved for domestic investors because there is a strong incentive for the domestic investor to transfer revenues to the export zone and convert costs, which are tax exempt, to costs to domestic operations, which are taxable. A third option is to place a discriminatory limitation on investors requiring that any investor operating in a zone be foreign. Transfer pricing has no impact on foreign investors for domestic tax purposes because such income is exempt. It is possible, however, for domestic investors to circumvent the foreign investment rule by creating foreign entities which in turn invest in the zone. In such cases, the zone investment is effectively controlled by the domestic investor, and absent look-through anti-abuse rules, may be beyond the power of domestic authorities to monitor.

A final problem with profits tax exemptions for zone investments is the overt discrimination against domestic investors operating in other parts of the country who are attempting to export. In effect, such domestic investors are placed at a competitive disadvantage by their own governments; an adverse outcome in addition to such investors having to overcome infrastructure shortages and domestic regulations.

---

[19] Export Zones can be challenged under WTO procedures and may be discouraged. See https://www.linklaters.com/en/insights/blogs/tradelinks/free-trade-zones-are-they-compliant-with-wto-law.

Export zones may make some sense if the positive pecuniary externalities from clustering can be established. Such demonstrations should be sufficient, however, even absent profits tax exemptions.

References

Conrad, R. (1987) *Essays on the Indonesian Tax Reform*, World Bank.

US Congress. (1986) *General Explanation to the Tax Equity and Responsibility Act of 1986.*

4
Indirect Taxes

General Consumption Taxes

4.1 Introduction

Indirect taxes including general sales taxes (VAT, retail sales tax, turnover tax) are discussed here. Short discussions of selective excise taxes and tariffs are also part of the discussion chapter. Tariffs are included because a tariff will either directly affect the relative price of goods and services subject to tariff or indirectly affect relative prices because the tariff increases the price of inputs. Some context is provided for the discussion relative to the overall approach to tax reform upon which this volume is based.

4.2 Indirect Taxes in Theory

4.2.1 Basis of Consumption Taxation

Recall that the basic framework for the analysis of this volume is Comprehensive Market-Determined Income (CMDI), an empirical measure derived from Haig-Simons income (HS). Conrad and Alexeev (2021) define HS Full Income (HSFI) as the value of goods and services produced by a consumer less the costs of producing the goods and services. Costs include the values of time, both in and outside the market; market goods and services; household goods and services; and services from stocks held in the household. Outputs and inputs are measured either at market prices or at the individual's marginal willingness to pay in the absence of market prices.[1] CMDI is thus only one component of HSFI because independent observability is a necessary condition to include income items in CMDI. Of particular importance is the assumption that consumption is not purchased but produced. For example, the purchase of a restaurant meal is not consumption. Rather, the consumer

---

[1] Marginal willingness to pay is equal to tax-inclusive market prices if market prices exist for market-produced outputs. There are cases where market prices either do not exist or the value in use is greater than the market value. For example, an individual might produce a table in her workshop, the cost of which is much greater than either the market value of an identical table, except for the fact that it was made by the individual, or the summation of the cost of the inputs, including own time valued at market tax-inclusive prices. The table is unique, however, because it was produced by the individual and accordingly the value of the table could be higher, both in total and at the margin, than either the market value of other tables or the total cost of production.

Evolutionary Tax Reform in Emerging Economies. Robert F. Conrad and Michael Alexeev, Oxford University Press.

combines time, the food purchased, and the rental value of space in the restaurant to produce consumption. Continuing with the example, consumption of a meal in the household is produced using food (perhaps purchased or produced by the household), time needed to produce and consume the meal, other purchased goods and services (electricity), and the services of capital goods (pots and pans, stoves, the dwelling, and other capital inputs, some of which could have been produced in the household, e.g., a table or a recipe handed down from relatives).

Note that from an economic perspective there is no difference between capital that is composed of common measures of savings (financial assets and capital goods (both real and intangible)) and capital goods used or produced in the household (a stove, family histories) because the economic function of the capital good is to provide an input into consumption flows in the future. That is, a machine can be used to produce marketable output (along with other factors) for a number of years. In turn, that output produces income used to finance the purchase of consumption goods and services used to produce consumption goods. A stove, however, can be used for a number of years to increase consumption.

Given the fact that CMDI measures the interactions between the household economy and the market economy, Conrad and Alexeev (2021) note that CMDI can be represented in a manner identical to international trade in which labour supplied to the market, among other exports from the household, is tradable. That is, the household consumes by using imports (flows of goods and services purchased on markets) and capital goods either purchased or rented from markets that are combined with labour in the household, goods and services produced in the household (nontradables), and capital goods produced in the household. The imports of capital goods and market goods and services are financed with labour and other tradable goods that are exported from the household to the market plus the income from capital held in the market—all of which are used to earn foreign exchange used to purchase the imports. This means that the trade with the economy (or the elements of CMDI) can be represented via standard balance of payments equations. In particular, the current account is:

Current Account = Returns to market labour + Returns to nonhuman capital held in the market – Purchases of consumption goods and services.

The capital account is:

Capital Account = Change in the value of assets held in the market – Change in the value of debt owed to the market = Savings.

CMDI is then equal to the value of the capital account plus the purchases of consumption goods and services, or:

CMDI = Purchases of market goods and services + Change in the value of the capital account.

This means that the analysis of taxation (consumption or income) is similar to international trade analysis. In particular, an increase in the market wage can be viewed as an increase in the real exchange rate. Accordingly, the value of exports will rise, and the imports of market goods and services will rise, while the change in the quantity of exports is ambiguous. This is because the income effect created by the real exchange appreciation will increase the demand for the exportable (in this case, time in domestic markets) and decrease the demand for exported labour, other things equal. This summary will become important in the discussion that follows.

4.2.2 General Indirect Taxation

Given widespread use of the VAT, it would be easy to assume that this method is the best indirect tax according to some economic criterion. We believe, however, that the discussion of indirect taxation should begin more generally and not with the assumed superiority of the VAT for at least two reasons. First, widespread use, even dominance, of a particular tax instrument does not imply that it is the most economically efficient method in every situation. In our view, there is no a priori economic or administrative reason for the VAT to be the most efficient method of indirect taxation for all countries, or jurisdictions, given the variety of circumstances found throughout the world. The VAT may, or may not, be a relatively efficient tax instrument even in Europe.[2]

Even if the VAT is the most efficient general indirect tax in Europe, there are reasons to be sceptical about adoption in other countries, including the United States. Western Europe, where the VAT was developed, includes a number of relatively high-income countries. Tax administrators are relatively highly trained, but even in this case, it is not clear that highly trained tax administrators have all the tools and capabilities to address advanced, or even some common, evasion and avoidance techniques. In addition, a significant proportion of the European taxpaying population has a basic understanding about the economic intent of the VAT. Finally, the VAT evolved in the context of European integration. Such conditions may not be present in all economies. In particular, some economies may not have many stages of domestic value added, may not have a well-functioning retail sector, at least outside of large cities, and are relatively poor. Finally, what may have been the most effective method seventy years ago may not be the most effective method today, even for high-income, relatively complex economies. Technical, political, and economic change may render what was considered novel or modern in the past ineffective for both current and future economic situations.

---

[2] We do not want to imply that the countries, particularly high-income countries, should switch from the VAT even if, in theory, it would be relatively efficient to do so. A friend and colleague, Mac McCorkle, often reminds economists that such a major change in policy and administration should be really effective in order to justify the fixed costs and time, measured in years, to do the transition.

There are clearly understood problems with an invoice-credit system VAT from both an economic and administrative perspective. In particular, there is ample experience to suggest that the VAT as applied, even in developed economies, is not the VAT as demonstrated by methodological analysis. Exempt goods and services, exempt suppliers (either because they are small or because of the nature of the supplies), and other factors may reduce the scope of the VAT so that it may not be a general consumption tax. These factors and the particular types of fraud that exist may also make the VAT more administratively complex than it might appear.

In summary, the economic standard, including costly administration and compliance, is to pick the general consumption taxation method that raises the needed revenue with a minimum deadweight loss in present value terms. Thus, it makes sense to periodically evaluate the VAT in light of options and given changes in markets, technology, and economic conditions.

4.2.3 Consumption Taxes Are Not Relatively Efficient

One claim made about consumption taxes, in general, is that they are 'efficient', at least relative to income taxes, in the sense that such charges do not distort inter-temporal relative consumption prices. Thus, it is claimed that a general consumption tax, relative to an income tax, does not reduce the incentive to save, which in turn may promote economic growth, where economic growth is some measure of the rate of change in measured GDP, GNP, or NNI, either in the aggregate or on a per capita basis as commonly measured.[3]

No consumption tax method is economically efficient, however; even a flat-rate tax on all market consumption will distort relative consumption prices, both within and between time periods, because any consumption tax base is restricted to the purchase of market consumption and services. That is, only a part of the flow of consumption is taxed. Only a subset of inputs is taxed, which means that general consumption taxes, even if comprehensive in the sense that all consumption goods and services are taxed, are inefficient (Diamond & Mirrlees, 1971). This implies that individuals can avoid the tax by avoiding market consumption.

Reduced consumption might be claimed to increase market saving, but this is not necessarily the case. The imposition of a general consumption tax, at a uniform rate, creates two related incentives. First, the price of market goods imported into the household is increased, which decreases the real exchange rate (price of non-tradables/price of imports). Imports fall, and other things equal, consumption falls. Holding exports of labour constant, savings will rise, but the fall in imports decreases the demand for foreign exchange (individuals supply labour to the market—export—in order to buy market goods and services—imports—that are used to produce

---

[3] Of course, these measures, as commonly computed, may not be indicators of economic welfare as used in economic theory.

consumption). Thus, labour supplied to the market might fall and offset the increase in savings.

In addition, there could be a change in the price of nontradables depending on how substitutable imported market goods and services are for nontradable goods and services produced in the household. For example, the increase in the price of imports will lead to a fall in imports. Thus, there will be an incentive for individuals to increase production of domestic substitutes (growing tomatoes instead of buying tomatoes, making meals at home instead of dining out, doing home repairs instead of hiring help). In addition, there may be an increase in the demand for goods and services used to produce household consumption. For example, the increase in the import price may increase the demand for labour used in the household that can be used to substitute for the reduction in imports. Also, the individual might increase investment in nontradables such as building a garden in order to increase food production.[4] Thus, market savings might fall even if total savings increases (market plus household investment). This analysis is nothing more than the traditional income and substitution effect analysis. In effect, money earned in the market is relatively less valuable when a consumption tax is imposed.

Second, and as an empirical matter, wealth effects need to be considered.[5] If household consumption and market consumption are normal goods both within and across time, then there will be an incentive to reduce both household consumption and market consumption. Thus, the net effect on saving (inter-temporal consumption) and labour supply (within and between time periods as well as the total period of labour force participation) of the imposition of a uniform consumption tax is necessarily ambiguous. Thus, whether a consumption tax is relatively more efficient and results in higher net saving relative to an income tax depends ultimately on the individual preferences given market institutions.

Finally, there are issues of risk sharing. As demonstrated in Annex A1.1 and the references cited therein, income taxes can be more efficient relative to consumption taxes because risk sharing in an income tax is more comprehensive. That is, consumption taxes affect the tax-inclusive variability for intertemporal prices while the income tax affects the variation of both consumption goods and services and returns to capital.

This discussion applies to general consumption taxes regardless of how the consumption tax is administered. Whether one consumption taxation method is relatively more efficient than another will depend on how each tax is administered, in addition to the losses generated by evasion, at least holding administrative effort constant.

---

[4] High net worth individuals might avoid consumption taxation by buying labour services as a substitute for market consumption. For instance, in developed countries individuals might employ household staff, a primary input and not subject to consumption taxation, as opposed to using a commercial service which is subject to VAT.
[5] Economic wealth may not be determined by monetary income. In the simplest model of individual behaviour, a binding constraint on individual choice is time, given market prices, including wages.

4.3 Indirect Taxes in Practice

4.3.1 What Is Taxed and Where

For discussion and comparative purposes, it will be assumed that the government's objective is to impose a tax on consumption expenditures in a particular jurisdiction. Thus, the first two questions to address are the definition of consumption expenditures and the jurisdictional basis for imposing the charge.

4.3.2 Consumption Expenditures: Not Consumption

In economic theory, consumption taxation is imposed at the time of consumption. As a practical matter, this method of taxation is not possible, in part because consumption itself may not be observable, as noted above, and in part because the taxing authority does not know the motivations of the person buying a particular commodity. For instance, the purchase of bottled water might be used to 'save' in the sense that the water is kept in case of a weather emergency, a type of precautionary saving.[6] A pencil might be purchased to do homework, an economic investment, or to draw for pleasure, consumption.

As a practical matter, we have argued that consumption as an empirical matter reduces to some measure of consumption expenditure in an observable market during a particular time interval. Consumption expenditure might be further refined by stating that consumption expenditure is defined as any demand for a good or service by an individual that is not an input into an empirically defined production process, and that is not empirically defined to be either market saving, in the sense that investments are made in certain financial assets, or a means of financial intermediation. Thus, goods and services purchased in the market and used as inputs into a defined production process are not consumption. That is, defining the basis of consumption taxation effectively divides the empirically defined market into two broad categories: final outputs and inputs. In general, final outputs are defined as purchases made by the household sector. Thus, as a practical matter, what is taxed depends on who purchases the commodity as opposed to how the commodity is used. For instance, a lawn mower purchased by a lawn maintenance corporation might not be the object of taxation, while the same lawn mower purchased by a household to mow the family lawn might be defined as a consumption expenditure (certainly a mistaken categorization, at least for anyone who has to mow the grass).

---

[6] All three consumption tax methods (VAT, retails sales tax, turnover tax) might be used to address such deferred consumption by appeal to the 'tax prepayment approach'. If a consumption tax is imposed on water at the time of purchase, then it might be claimed that the risk-adjusted present value of consuming the water at some date in the future is equal to the observed price at the time of purchase.

4.3.3 Jurisdictional Basis for Taxation (Origin and Destination)

A taxing authority may impose a consumption tax on either an origin or a destination basis. Loosely speaking, the difference is whether the statutory intent is to impose a tax on the supply (origin—the physical location of the supplier) as opposed to the demand (destination—either the location of final purchase or consumption by the purchaser or the residence of the purchaser).[7] Assuming that the intent of the tax is to impose a charge on the consumption of domestic residents, the tax should be a destination-based charge. The destination basis will be used in what follows because it is the method most commonly used by governments throughout the world.

4.3.4 Definition of Taxable Goods and Services

In a methodological sense, saving is defined by market purchases that are excluded from the definition of taxable supplies. As both a practical and methodological matter, the empirical definition does not correspond to the methodological standard for a number of reasons. First, the foundation upon which CMDI is based is the production of consumption by the taxpayer. Thus, all supplies of goods and services are inputs, not final consumption. This perspective combined with the need to use labour to produce consumption is one distortion introduced by a broad-based sales tax. Second, purchases by taxpayers of goods and services that last for more than one market period are often defined as consumption. Automobiles, stoves, tools, racks, other consumer durables are examples of the type of capital goods that are taxed by a broad-based consumption tax such as the VAT. It is correctly claimed that such taxation can be relatively efficient because the present value of the tax is equal to the tax on the implicit rental value per unit of time. This tax prepayment, however, is not satisfied in empirical situations. In particular, while it might be true that the risk-adjusted ex ante present value of the implicit rental value is equal to the tax imposed at the time of purchase, the ex-post value is not. This is because the relative price of the stock value of the consumer durables might change for reasons such as a change in exogenous factors such as the interest rate, and the implicit rental value may change with changes in the relative price of other inputs used to produce consumption.[8] Ex ante, taxpayers may realize that the risk-sharing properties of a tax on

---

[7] Note that the purpose of the origin or destination basis for taxation is to determine which government gets the tax revenue as opposed to which government has the authority to impose a tax.

[8] What is saving and consumption will always be problematic as a practical matter. As a methodological matter, saving should include the purchase of any supply that lasts for more than one time period. This is because the decision to purchase the capital good is based on a present value calculation. That is, there is no difference, as a matter of method, between buying corporate equity and buying a stove. The present value of the corporate equity, ultimately, will be equal to the present value of consumption benefits realized by the cash flow, while the present value of the stove is equal to the present value of consumption benefits in the case of traditional consumer models. One result is direct, the purchase of the stove, and one indirect, the purchase of the corporate equity. The result, however, is the same because it is assumed there are no

the flows separately through time and a tax on the present value of a flow are not the same.

Third, there are typically exemptions for goods and services other than saving instruments. Some items may be exempted for distributional reasons (unprocessed food), educational reasons (books), or other administrative reasons (the consumption value of supplies by financial institutions). Fourth, there are supplies that serve both investment and consumption purposes. Automobiles may be one example, where a capital gain or loss could be created by a change in the political conditions of a country (a taxpayer can drive a significant asset out of the country instead of having assets frozen in the banking system) or from a change in exchange rates (or the import regime). Finally, inputs used to produce capital goods in the household might be taxed. For example, a taxpayer who is not an Advanced Payment Agent (APA) might purchase wood and use electricity and labour to produce furniture that is used in the household, which may become family heirlooms, and at some point, may have significant market value as antiques. In summary, like the income tax as a practical matter, there is no reason to expect that a broad-based consumption tax is comprehensive.

4.3.5 Progressive or Regressive

It is claimed that general sales taxes are regressive.[9] The claims are usually based on comparisons of the ratio of expenditures on consumption goods and services to some measure of total income per annum across income distributions. The regressive result is hardly surprising because those with lower income save less, according to empirical definitions of savings. There are two reasons to question such claims, however. First, if there is a comprehensive consumption tax at a flat rate, then over the life cycle, the tax is flat rate in present value terms given that all income is either consumed by the individual or their heirs, at some point in time. Second, and more empirically relevant, a general consumption tax defined relative to observable market criteria and given application can be progressive if the proportion of consumption produced in the household is higher for low-income people relative to high-income people. For example, goods and services, particularly services, which are substitutes for household consumption typically increase with income. Restaurant meals, prepared foods, transportation, consumer durables (TVs, air conditioning, etc.) are examples. Thus, if the proportion of market purchases to total consumption increases with income, then a general consumption tax can be progressive. This tendency can be reinforced by practice in emerging economies where rural populations may buy market goods and services in small markets where suppliers are exempt from some form of general sales tax.

direct consumption benefits from holding corporate equity. That is, both the purchase of the equity and the stove are a means to an end.

[9] For a critical evaluation of this claim, see discussion beginning on p. 106 of Ebrill, Keen, & Perry (2001).

4.4   Three Types of Consumption Taxes

Three types of ad valorem consumption taxes are the most common:[10]

- Turnover Tax (TT)
- Retail Sales Tax (RST)
- Value Added Tax (VAT)

Our intent is to supply a comparison of these three charges from both an efficiency and administrative perspective. Some gains and losses for each charge are summarized in Table 4.1. Tables 4.2 and 4.3 provide an illustration of the basic structure of the VAT, RST, and TT when a good or service is supplied to a domestic resident (the taxpayer as defined in this text) and when it is exported, respectively. The example is structured so that a good or service is either sold to domestic residents or exported after an initial intermediate good is either imported or produced using only primary factors of production (capital and labour). Value added is increased via four production stages. For example, raw ore might be sold to a concentrator (Stage 2), that output is sold to a refiner (Stage 3), which in turn is sold to a fabricator (Stage 4), with final output being sold to a distributor (Stage 5) who either sells to a domestic resident or exports. Given the destination basis nature of the consumption tax, the objective is to impose a tax on domestic residents. This example will serve as the basis for the comparisons to follow.

4.4.1   The Turnover Tax (TT)

4.4.1.1   Structure

A TT is imposed on all market trade of all taxable goods and services. Thus, there is no distinction between inputs and final consumption. APAs (taxpayers in most current statutes) are defined to be any person engaged in the supply of taxable goods and services, perhaps above a *de minimis* amount. In theory, nothing would be exempt, except for exports.

Note that the TT is a transactional tax in the sense that the TT is imposed at the full rate at every stage of domestic value added. The TT thus becomes part of the producers' costs, which in turn will increase the price of the intermediate output at each stage in the chain of value added. In effect, there is a tax on the tax, which has been labelled 'cascading'. The immediate implication is that the effective rate of tax when a commodity is sold to the domestic residents (taxpayers) depends, in part, on the number of stages of domestic value added. In the current example, the effective increase in the price to the nontaxable domestic sector is 10%, even though the

---

[10] Excise taxes are also consumption taxes but are generally not broad based. If excise taxes were broad based, then they might be equivalent to a sales tax, depending on how the tax is administered. Some excises, so-called sin taxes (e.g., on tobacco), are claimed to address negative externalities. Such claims are also made for 'carbon' taxes and other environmental charges.

Table 4.1 Characteristics of various indirect taxes

Item	Turnover tax (TT)	Retails sales tax (RST)	Invoice-credit system VAT (ICV)
Scope	Can extend throughout the economy but may be limited to goods	• Claimed to have limited ability to extend to services • Financial services generally excluded	• In practice, broader application to services relative to RST • Financial services generally excluded
Number of taxpayers	All suppliers of taxable goods and services	All suppliers of taxable goods and services	All suppliers of taxable goods and services
Information requirements	• The value of turnover • Destination of sales	• Value of taxable suppliers • Knowledge of whether purchasers are RST taxpayers • Destination of sales	• Value of taxable supplies • Knowledge of whether suppliers of inputs are VAT taxpayers • Destination of sales
Exemptions	No necessary reason to exempt services, including financial services		
Resale	Taxed		
Treatment of exports	Exempt	Exempt	Zero rated
Rates (holding revenue fixed)	Lower than the VAT rate	Equal to the VAT rate	Equal to the RST rate
Cascading in practice	Cascading	Cascading to the extent that supplies are made to persons other than taxpayers that reenter the market	Cascading to the extent that supplies are made to persons other taxpayers that supply goods further downstream
Theft	• Registered taxpayers do not declare collections • Nonregistered persons charge the tax and keep it	• Registered taxpayers do not declare collections • Nonregistered persons charge the tax and keep it	• Registered taxpayers do not declare collections • Nonregistered persons charge the tax and keep it

Table 4.2 Comparison: VAT, RST, TT

Stage	1	2	3	4	5 Retail sector and purchase by domestic resident defined to be a consumer
A. Value added tax (10.00%)					
Tax-exclusive output price	100.00	250.00	575.00	1,200.00	2,600.00
Tax-exclusive input price		100.00	250.00	575.00	1,200.00
Value added	100.00	150.00	325.00	625.00	1,400.00
Tax-inclusive price	110.00	275.00	632.50	1,320.00	2,860.00
VAT					
VAT on output	10.00	25.00	57.50	120.00	260.00
Credit for VAT on input		10.00	25.00	57.50	120.00
Net VAT	10.00	15.00	32.50	62.50	140.00
Total VAT accrued					260.00
B. Retail sales tax (10.00%)					
Tax-exclusive output price	100.00	250.00	575.00	1,200.00	2,600.00
Tax-exclusive input price	-	100.00	250.00	575.00	1,200.00
Value added	100.00	150.00	325.00	625.00	1,400.00
Tax-inclusive price	100.00	250.00	575.00	1,200.00	2,860.00
RST accrued	0.00	0.00	0.00	0.00	260.00
Total RST accrued					260.00
C. Turnover tax (5.41%)					
Tax-exclusive output price	100.00	255.41	594.24	1251.41	2719.15
Input price accrued	0.00	105.41	269.24	626.41	1319.15
Value added	100.00	150.00	325.00	625.00	1400.00
Tax-inclusive price	105.41	269.24	626.41	1319.15	2866.34
TT accrued	5.41	13.83	32.17	67.74	147.19
Total TT Accrued					266.34

Note: VAT Rate = RST Rate = 10.00%
    TT Rate = 5.41%

statutory rate is 5.41%. Note that the effective increase in prices to the domestic residents would be 5.41% if an imported substitute were sold because there would be no domestic value added.

Cascading is a major drawback of the TT. Absent complete knowledge of the economy's structure, it is not possible to know the effective change in relative prices when goods and services are sold to the resident (or exported). This drawback has some adverse consequences. First, the effective tax rate may become endogenous in the

Table 4.3 VAT, RST, TT Export

Stage	1	2	3	4	5 Export sector and purchase by a nonresident
A. VAT (10.00%)					
Tax-exclusive output price	100.00	250.00	575.00	1,200.00	2,600.00
Tax-exclusive input price		100.00	250.00	575.00	1,200.00
Value added	100.00	150.00	325.00	625.00	1,400.00
Tax-inclusive price	110.00	275.00	632.50	1,320.00	2,600.00
VAT					
VAT on output	10.00	25.00	57.50	120.00	-
Credit for VAT on input		10.00	25.00	57.50	120.00
Net VAT	10.00	15.00	32.50	62.50	(120.00)
Total VAT accrued					-
B. Retail sales tax (10.00%)					
Tax-exclusive output price	100.00	250.00	575.00	1,200.00	2,600.00
Tax-exclusive input price	-	100.00	250.00	575.00	1,200.00
Value added	100.00	150.00	325.00	625.00	1,400.00
Tax-inclusive price	100.00	250.00	575.00	1,200.00	2,600.00
RST accrued	0.00	0.00	0.00	0.00	0.00
Total RST accrued					-
C. Turnover tax (5.41%)					
Tax-exclusive output price	100.00	255.41	594.24	1,251.41	2,719.15
Input price accrued	-	105.41	269.24	626.41	1,319.15
Value added	100.00	150.00	325.00	625.00	1,400.00
Tax-inclusive price	105.41	269.24	626.41	1,319.15	2,719.15
TT accrued	5.41	13.83	32.17	67.74	-
Total TT accrued					119.15

sense that cascading can be mitigated via vertical integration. Such tax-induced vertical integration may be inefficient for the economy. That is, absent the TT, the cost of vertical integration might be too great for the private sector to switch to (or to invest as a new entity in) vertically integrated processes.

A second cost of cascading is that the change in domestic relative prices will be neither uniform nor known. One purported objective of the destination-based consumption tax is to increase all domestic consumption prices by a constant proportion.[11] A uniform TT will not achieve this objective.

---

[11] Whether such an increase in relative domestic prices is efficient, even in a second-best sense, is a theoretical issue and, in general, the answer is no (Atkinson & Stiglitz, 1976).

Finally, negative effective protection can result from imposing a TT. That is, imports of finished domestic substitutes could be encouraged relative to exports, as discussed below. In our example, an imported good that is a substitute for the domestically produced good will have an effective tax of only 5.41% relative to the 10% effective rate for the domestically produced substitute. Negative effective protection will then act to increase imports of domestic substitutes and, accordingly, discriminate against domestic production.

The effect of imposing a TT on exported goods is illustrated in Table 4.3C. The final exported good will generally be free of tax given that the tax is assumed to be on a destination basis. The tax, however, is still imposed at each stage of domestic value added because as a practical matter it is impossible to trace the use of the initial input (Stage 1) through all of the stages of domestic value added. Thus, the tax becomes embedded in the cost structure, absent vertical integration, and tends to reduce the competitiveness of exports produced from more than a single stage production process.[12,13]

4.4.1.2 Administrative and Compliance Considerations

One benefit of a TT is that all suppliers, at least those supplying new goods and services, can be defined as APAs (again, taxpayer in current statutes). The only records required are for turnover and the value of turnover. An APA in any indirect tax system is a person legally responsible for charging the indirect tax to a purchaser as an advanced tax on the payment of the ultimate tax by the resident individual. Accounting might be either on a cash or an accrual basis, but accrual is the preferred method for reasons discussed below. Thus, the TT is well suited for situations where single entry bookkeeping is prevalent, or accounting is otherwise rudimentary, at least relative to the other indirect tax methods.

On the other hand, there is an incentive for suppliers to avoid registration as APAs with a TT because they can sell without charging the tax and gain a tax-induced competitive advantage. A second compliance consideration is that suppliers can evade tax by selling (or transferring) goods to another person free of tax. This can arise in several cases. First, owners can make transfers from the business to themselves; for example, the owners of a retail shop may charge others but not themselves. Second, there may be collusion between otherwise independent persons; for example, the buyer and the seller might agree to make the transaction on a net-of-tax basis (and arbitrage the gain between the tax-inclusive and tax-exclusive price). Finally, other situations of evasion include where the seller either transfers taxable supplies on a

---

[12] Programmes such as duty drawbacks are not effective for a TT because of the practical impossibility of tracing the tax back down the various stages of domestic value added. Special zones might be effective to the extent that the only intermediate goods and services supplied are either imported or produced by a single stage domestic process.

[13] The incentives effects on the balance of payments are clear. There is an incentive to increase the demand for imported domestic substitutes while decreasing the supply of exports (and the supply of foreign exchange), at least relative to a system without cascading. The balance of payments effects relative to a no-tax equilibrium, and holding the exchange rate fixed, will depend on the overall decrease in the demand for foreign exchange resulting from the tax on imported finished goods that are not domestic substitutes.

net-of-tax basis, perhaps in order to gain a competitive advantage, or the supplier transfers taxable goods and services on a tax-inclusive basis and simply keeps the revenue.

Finally, there are problems with the TT that are common to all types of indirect tax (as well as to other types of taxation such the income tax). These problems include difficult-to-tax sectors and transactions, including small business, cash transactions, and barter trade. The number of suppliers that have one or all three characteristics might be significant. These sectors include the retail sector, agriculture, and small business, however defined. The intersection of suppliers with these characteristics arises because of the need for minimal single-entry accounts, at least on turnover, and perhaps inventory, in order to monitor compliance. Accrual accounting is the standard accounting method for general sales taxation and modern sector production and distribution depends on accrual concepts, with receipts, to record transactions and to manage working capital. Minimum books and records may be absent, however, in the sectors cited because of lack of knowledge, the fixed and variable cost of maintaining standardized records, infrequent transactions, lack of access to the banking system (either by choice or by cost) or as a method to avoid detection from the tax authorities.

4.4.2 Retail Sales Tax (RST)

4.4.2.1 Structure

The retail sales tax (RST) is a charge imposed only at the last stage in the chain of measured value added—the point of sale between a supplier (the APA in this text) who collects the advanced tax and the person defined to be the final consumer (the taxpayer). No tax is charged at any point in the chain of value added, so the RST does not cascade, at least in theory. In practice, an attempt is made to eliminate cascading by eliminating the tax on imported inputs and by using a ring system throughout the chain of domestic value added. All domestic persons are divided into two groups in a ring system: members of the ring and persons excluded from membership who are de facto defined to compose the final consumption sector (or foreign purchasers who are effectively defined by exports). Members of the ring are defined to be RST taxpayers (or APAs in this text) in most statutes. These persons are not charged RST on their purchases, but they are responsible for imposing the RST on persons who are not members of the ring. The ring is extended to include exports in a destination-based system so that exports are not taxed as a matter of law. The RST is illustrated in the relevant sections of Tables 4.2 and 4.3. Note there is no cascading as a matter of method.

4.4.2.2 Administration and Compliance Considerations

The RST has been criticized on a number of grounds, at least relative to the VAT, most of which are administrative. First, in order to comply, a RST supplier must know whether the person purchasing a taxable supply is another RST supplier. Purchasers who are members of the ring are exempt while non-ring members are taxable.[14] This need for identification means that an RST is not really a tax only at what are commonly conceived to be retail outlets. In effect, a retail sale is defined to be any sale to a person who is not a member of the ring, other than an export. Thus, like the turnover tax, all suppliers of taxable supplies need to be registered. The purchaser needs to be identified as a ring member and, absent demonstration, the tax should be imposed. In addition, separate accounting needs to be maintained by the APA/taxpayer for taxable supplies to ring members (for which no RST is required) and to non-ring members. Inadvertent cascading can result from charging RST to ring members who are not identified. A second source of inadvertent cascading may result because the tax administration may impose particular requirements for registration. This might occur when there are small business exceptions based on criteria such as turnover.[15] Nonregistration implies that purchases by excluded persons will be subject to tax. Such inadvertent cascading may be reduced by a voluntary registration provision but at the cost of increased administrative and compliance expenses.

An additional concern about the RST, at least in the United States, is the inability to impose tax on services, including legal services, medical services, and general household services such as repairs. These concerns may have both an administrative and a political basis because as a matter of method, services can be included in the RST. Some suppliers provide services to both ring members and non-ring members. Thus, there is a question about the revenue effect given the administrative cost of imposing an RST on such suppliers relative to the administrative costs of determining whether the tax is to be charged on a particular transaction. In addition, many services are provided by small businesses, which might be difficult to monitor relative to the perceived revenue potential. With respect to political factors, lawyers, doctors, architects, economists, and other highly trained service providers may form a potent political lobby to prevent inclusion of their services into an expanded base.

Other administrative and compliance issues are not uniquely RST-related and include the revenue leakage resulting from own consumption by owners, taxable sales made without tax, and theft of the RST by APAs/taxpayers. Note that the revenue leakage is not created by the ring system per se. Rather, the revenue leakage may result from noncompliance. APAs/taxpayers either do not collect the tax or do not remit the tax collected to the government. Thus, the nature of the leakage problem

---

[14] This cost, at least relative to the VAT, may be overstated because VAT invoicing requirements in some countries require that the supplier record the purchaser's VAT identification number (or general tax number) for trade between VAT APAs/taxpayers.
[15] There is generally no small business exemption from sales taxes in US States. For example, any person who supplies taxable goods and services to nonregistered APAs/taxpayers is supposed to register in North Carolina. Accordingly, it is known that tax administrators visit flea markets, art shows, and other places where hobbyists and small APAs/taxpayers sell goods and services. As well, recently large retailers such as Amazon began to impose sales tax on internet sales to NC residents (defined to have an address in NC). So, if a small producer in NC sells to Amazon and that output is sold to an NC resident, then the production is subject to RST.

is the same with either the TT or the RST, although the manifestation may be different.

4.4.3 Value Added Tax (VAT)

4.4.3.1 Structure

A VAT is imposed at every production stage as well as at the time of import and, in the case of the invoice-credit system, the VAT is imposed on every taxable transaction, just like the TT. Cascading is addressed, at least in theory, by attempting to ensure that the tax on inputs is eliminated. There are three methods that might be used to alleviate the adverse effects of cascading:

- The Invoice-Credit System
- The Subtraction Method
- The Addition Method

A numerical example of each method is found in Table 4.4 to facilitate comparison. Given its popularity, the invoice-credit system will be used for comparison with the TT and RST in Tables 4.2 and 4.3.

a. The Invoice-Credit System

As noted, the invoice-credit system is the most popular method; in fact, with the exception of Japan, the invoice-credit system is the default method for administering a VAT. The actions that attempt to ensure that cascading is eliminated include:

- Every taxpayer (APA for our purposes) issues a VAT invoice to the purchaser at the time of the transaction.[16] The VAT is imposed by Customs at the time of importation.
- Periodically (usually monthly) each APA/taxpayer files a VAT return that contains the value of taxable goods and services supplied to other persons, the amount of VAT accrued on those supplies to others, the value of taxable supplies purchased by the APA/taxpayer, and the value of tax either paid or payable by the APA/taxpayer.
- The APA/taxpayer computes the difference between the VAT accrued on taxable supplies from others and the VAT paid or payable.
- The difference between the VAT accrued on supplies to others and the VAT accrued on supplies to the APA/taxpayer becomes payable to the government on a net basis.

---

[16] Note that the VAT is imposed on an accrual basis, as the TT and the RST should be. The reasons for the use of the accrual basis will be discussed below.

b. The Subtraction Method

The subtraction method[17] is an accounts-based system, as opposed to an invoice-based system.[18] Value added, on a current basis,[19] is computed by subtracting the value of all taxable purchases from the value of taxable domestic sales. The difference is the operational definition of domestic value added in the current context, plus any economic rent that might arise.[20] Note that, unlike the invoice-credit system, no tax is imposed, formally speaking, at the time of sale. The implicit assumption of the subtraction method, however, is that the tax-inclusive price of the purchased input is equal to the amount of input VAT that would be paid under the invoice-credit system. Thus, the retail price of the final domestic sale should effectively increase by the full amount of the invoice-credit system VAT or the RST.

Exports, and other zero-rated goods, present no problem as a matter of practice for the subtraction method, as shown in Table 4.4. A difficulty with the subtraction method VAT, like all VAT methods, arises in situations where there is a desire to exempt particular goods and services. Denial of deductions for such purposes would be necessary to reduce the revenue loss created if such deductions were allowed. One benefit of the subtraction method is that it can be applied to all activities. That is, the tax is no longer a tax based on sales but is an entity-based tax. This means that banks and financial institutions as well as nonprofit entities with domestic value added can

---

[17] There can be further refinements of the subtraction method in cases where supplies to a taxpayer (APA) are provided by a person not subject to VAT. In effect, a deduction is denied for such supplies (McLure, 1987).

[18] Japan introduced a subtraction method VAT in 1989 (see p. 12, https://www.gao.gov/assets/ggd-89-87.pdf). We do not believe it has changed yet (https://home.kpmg/xx/en/home/insights/2019/10/japan-indirect-tax-guide.html), but it is under review (https://www.bdo.global/en-gb/microsites/tax-newsletters/indirect-tax-news/issue-2-2019/japan-revision-of-japanese-consumption-tax-system). Michigan and New Hampshire used addition-based VATs since 1976 and 1993, respectively. As described in Kenyon (1996), the Michigan variant is a consumption-type VAT (capital expenditures being deductible in arriving at the definition of profits used in the addition), whereas that in New Hampshire is of the income type (Ebrill et al., 2001).

[19] We prefer to use the term 'current' basis as opposed to 'cash' basis because the VAT is administered on an accrual basis. Thus, a 'current' basis in this context means accrual accounting with immediate deduction of all capital expenditures. That is, the value of taxable supplies will include both cash sales this period and sales on account (accounts receivable). The value of taxable inputs deducted is equal to cash payments for all taxable inputs and those purchased on account, including those financed by debt. Capital assets, at least real and tangible personal property plus some intangible property, should be taxable, as should lease, royalty, and other right-of-use payments. The inclusion of capital assets in the set of taxable commodities and allowance of the immediate credit is called the 'tax prepayment approach', which places the purchase of an asset on par with a lease, at least under certain conditions, which makes the present value of the lease payment equal to the value of the asset. Accordingly, this approach to VAT accounting (and the invoice-credit system as well) is defined as a VAT on a consumption basis. An alternative to the consumption basis is the income basis where the subtraction method is based on accrual accounting combined with amortization of capital assets. Given the standard objective of imposing a consumption, as opposed to an income, tax, we will concentrate on the consumption basis. This distinction and the consumption basis become important when discussing income taxation more generally because a subtraction method VAT on a consumption basis is literally what is commonly called a cash flow tax.

[20] There would be no economic rent if the taxpayer (APA) is operating with constant returns to scale and is competitive. In this case, there may be periods of negative domestic value added, just like under the invoice-credit system. These would be periods when purchases of intermediate goods and services exceed the value of sales. This would be the case during investment periods or periods of inventory build-up (such as prior to a holiday period). In this case, in theory, the taxpayer (APA) should receive a refund or equivalent such as a cumulative loss carryforward at the cost of capital, but the present value of the VAT would be zero except for the final domestic sale at the retail level.

Table 4.4 Options for computing the VAT

Row #	Stage	1	2	3	4	5 Retail sector and purchase by domestic resident defined to be a consumer
A. Invoice-credit system						
1	Tax-exclusive output price	100.00	250.00	575.00	1,200.00	2,600.00
2	Tax-exclusive input price		100.00	250.00	575.00	1,200.00
3	Value added	100.00	150.00	325.00	625.00	1,400.00
4						
5	Tax-inclusive price	110.00	275.00	632.50	1,320.00	2,860.00
6						
7	VAT					
8	VAT on output	10.00	25.00	57.50	120.00	260.00
9	Credit for VAT on input		10.00	25.00	57.50	120.00
10	Net VAT	10.00	15.00	32.50	62.50	140.00
11	Total VAT accrued					260.00
B. Addition method						
1	Wages	80.00	120.00	260.00	500.00	1,120.00
2	Profit	5.00	7.50	16.25	31.25	70.00
3	Returns to non-equity capital	15.00	22.50	48.75	93.75	210.00
4	Value added	100.00	150.00	325.00	625.00	1,400.00
5	Tax	10.00	15.00	32.50	62.50	140.00
6	Total VAT accrued					260.00
C. Subtraction method						
1	Sales	100.00	250.00	575.00	1,200.00	2,600.00
2	Purchases of intermediate goods and services	-	100.00	250.00	575.00	1,200.00
3	Value added	100.00	150.00	325.00	625.00	1,400.00
4	VAT	10.00	15.00	32.50	62.50	140.00
5	Total VAT accrued					260.00

be taxable, at least in theory. In effect, as discussed in Chapter 3 and below, the sub-traction method VAT is effectively a cash flow tax for entity income taxation plus wages with export sales exempt.[21]

---

[21] A cash flow tax might differ from the subtraction method VAT to the extent that the VAT is measured on an accrual basis. It can be difficult to keep the concepts separated. Cash flow taxation is literally record-ing all transactions on a cash basis. The subtraction method VAT is accrual based except that assets are expensed, and debt is ignored, unless the base is explicitly stated to be accrual. There is also a different method to tax value added which is equivalent to profits plus wages. This base is complete accrual plus depreciation and interest deductions.

c. The Addition Method

The addition method VAT arrives at the same answer as the subtraction method. Instead of subtracting the value of intermediate supplies from taxable sales, however, domestic value added is computed directly and is equal to wages plus profit, where profit is measured on a current basis. Again, export sales should be exempt. Of course, the addition method is analytically and for practical purposes identical to the subtraction method because profit, on a current basis, must be computed by subtracting the value of inputs including wages from sales. Accordingly, there is nothing, at least in our view, to distinguish the addition method from the subtraction method, and all the difficulties are identical as shown in Table 4.2.

4.4.3.2 Administration and Compliance Considerations

The invoice-credit system VAT, and the VAT more generally, is claimed to have at least two advantages over the RST. First, the VAT can be imposed on all taxable sales, supposedly, without the need for the taxpayer to know whether the buyer is a member of the ring (or otherwise a VAT taxpayer or APA as defined in this text).[22] Second, to the extent that there is evasion and noncompliance, at least some portion of the VAT may be paid at upstream portions in the chain of value added or at the time of import. In fact, one significant benefit of the VAT is that, unlike the RST, the upstream payments are advanced payments for the tax ultimately charged to the resident, the taxpayer in this text.

These claimed advantages are offset, at least in part, by two drawbacks unique to the VAT. First, unique evasion schemes for the invoice-credit system include false invoicing and fly-by-night firms. False invoicing is a scheme where fictitious invoices are created in order to either increase the VAT credits beyond legitimate amounts or to create fictitious refunds for exports. Fly-by-night firms can be created within the chain of value added as a means to steal the VAT revenue. With this scheme, a supplier subject to VAT is created and the seller, perhaps part of the scheme, transfers goods or services to the related party at a low price in order to reduce the seller's net VAT obligation. The newly created supplier then sells to another person at a high price and charges VAT.[23] The purchaser can then take the credit for the high VAT while the new entity disappears, effectively stealing the net VAT.[24]

---

[22] The subtraction and addition methods may not have this benefit if there are exempt sales to other APAs/taxpayers. In addition, and as noted above, this purported benefit may be mitigated by administrative considerations where suppliers of taxable goods and services are required to identify the purchaser–complete with APA/taxpayer number—if the purchaser is a supplier of taxable goods and services.

[23] There is nothing unique about the related party being the supplier. Purchasers could create fly-by-night related parties. The fly-by-night could buy from unrelated parties and then sell to the related party for a high price, transferring the VAT revenue to the fly-by-night by increasing the purchaser's input credits.

[24] Some governments use cross checking to limit false invoicing. Given computer access, cross checking is facilitated if the suppliers are required to obtain the APA/taxpayer identification numbers of purchasers, which means that suppliers need to know whether purchasers are members of the ring. In effect, one advantage of the VAT is lost. Cross checking has gone to the extreme first in Bulgaria and now in Ukraine where VAT APA/taxpayers are required to maintain special bank accounts which effectively convert the VAT to a cash basis. These schemes will be discussed in due course.

A third practical problem with the invoice-credit system is that export credits, and perhaps refunds, are necessary to ensure that the VAT functions as a destination-based consumption tax. In effect, zero rating is intended to relieve exports of any competitive disadvantage created by taxing goods at upstream stages of value added. Export refunds have been difficult to implement effectively in a number of emerging economies.[25] Administrators appear to be reluctant to provide refunds because of compliance concerns such as false invoicing or false claims of exports. In addition, all VAT receipts can be counted as government revenue, in at least some countries. This is not factually correct, because some revenue collected at the upstream stage in value added should be refunded when the taxable supplies are ultimately exported. Given revenue targeting systems imposed on tax administrations and budget pressures in general, refunds are viewed as increasing the deficit when in fact the failure to delay legitimate VAT refunds on exports is a means to provide interest-free loans to the government. Finally, understanding may be part of the problem with VAT refunds. While simple in concept to economists, in practice the VAT is discussed in terms of a tax on suppliers at each stage of production and the important link between the VAT and RST can be lost. That is, the VAT is essentially a retail sales tax with a different administrative mechanism, but public and even administrators' understanding of this fact might be weak.

Like the RST, the VAT may suffer from inadvertent cascading resulting from excluding particular individuals from registration based on turnover or other criteria, such as exempting goods that are used as inputs further downstream in the chain of value added.[26] Voluntary registration provisions may alleviate the difficulty to some extent but, as noted with respect to the RST, voluntary registration must be traded off against the increased cost of administering compliance for small businesses that might operate on a cash basis to a significant degree.

The invoice-credit system can be more difficult to implement and administer in systems where subnational governments, usually in a federal system, have the right to impose sales taxes. Australia and Canada have developed means to address the issue, and the EU has created a method for dealing with trade among EU countries.

Finally, the invoice-credit system VAT suffers from the same administrative and compliance problems as the TT and RST. To recall, these problems include own consumption by producers who are also consumers (except that some VAT may have been collected at prior stages of value added), charging and collecting VAT by persons who are not VAT APAs/taxpayers, engaging in transactions that are free of VAT (generally related party transactions and transactions in cash), and theft of VAT revenue (again, usually via cash transactions). Cash transactions occur disproportionately at the retail level and so one can expect that much leakage from theft and

---

[25] Conrad has had experience with difficulties with export refunds in a number of countries, including Albania, Guinea, Ghana, Mongolia, Mozambique, Russia, Ukraine, and Zambia.

[26] Exemption in a VAT system means that the supplier of an exempt good cannot take the credit for the VAT accrued on inputs. For instance, banking services are generally exempt from VAT, which means that banks cannot charge VAT. Accordingly, banks will attempt to pass on VAT accrued on inputs because the credit is not available.

noncompliance will occur at this level. The last point may not be as severe under a VAT because of the invoice-credit system. Retailers, who are APAs/taxpayers, would report lower taxable sales relative to input costs if there is leakage. Such reporting may trigger an audit. If, however, there is leakage under the RST, then only sales will be underreported with no reporting of input purchases that serve as a basis for comparison.

4.5 VAT in Emerging Economies: Evaluation and Opinion

It would seem that the invoice-credit system VAT is the consumption tax system of choice given the almost universal adoption of this method throughout the world. In addition, given the significant experience with developing, implementing, and administering the VAT, there may be an expectation that workable solutions to the administrative and compliance difficulties would have been addressed in a reasonable manner. While there is significant evidence that the latter might be true, we have doubts about the former. The fact that governments around the world by and large have imposed a VAT does not imply that the VAT is really the best indirect tax system in all situations. Best practice should not be determined by who uses a particular technique but by the relative economic efficiency of such a method given the current and foreseen economic and institutional environment of any particular country.

If the criterion is relative economic efficiency given the fact that an indirect tax system is to be imposed at all, then the choice should be based on the perceived relevant facts and circumstances at the time of implementation as well as a reasonable projection about the evolution of the economy and future technology.

4.5.1 A Modern Tax?

The VAT is claimed to be a 'modern' tax if for no other reason than it was the latest development in a long line of indirect taxation schemes, including the TT, RST, and manufacturers excise tax (used in Canada among other places). The VAT, however, is not really modern in application. Rather, the invoice-credit system is built on paper-based accounting systems (the invoice), which are possible to employ, at least historically, without standard books of account. The concept is simple enough:[27]

- Create two stacks of receipts: one for sales and one for purchases;
- Charge tax on sales and accrue tax on purchases;
- At the end of the month (or some other period), add up the total tax accrued from the two stacks of receipts;
- Subtract the total tax on purchases from the total tax on receipts; and
- Send the difference to the government.

[27] Conrad is grateful to Emil Sunley, who used this analogy to explain the VAT in Indonesia.

There is nothing modern or even current about the concept. Modern accounting systems, except for those used by small business, are accounts based with computer-generated electronic receipts that provide supporting documentation for the accounts. The VAT, like all tax instruments, has had to accommodate such change. This has made VAT accounting more akin to income accounting, given the evolution in technology, and the relative shift in the composition of economic activity from the production of goods to the production of services as economies evolve.[28]

4.5.2 Economic Circumstances Matter

The VAT was first introduced in France but was not extended to a national basis until 1968 (James, 2011). This occurred at the time of growing European integration, and the VAT might have been a reasonable instrument to employ given the impetus for economic integration and the presence of borders.[29] In emerging economies, the VAT was advocated as a partial solution to tariff issues. Given administrative concerns,[30] there may have been some consensus that the VAT could replace customs tariffs since emerging economy governments would be reluctant to forgo collecting tax at such a convenient choke point (the border). At least substituting VAT for tariffs may have changed the incentives to enforce the VAT on domestic transactions and to reduce the levels of effective protection.

4.5.3 Perceptions Matter

Given the perception that the VAT is a modern tax, it has been our experience that governments in emerging economies have argued that the VAT should be adopted almost as a symbol of economic reform, perhaps before the economy and administration were capable of adopting what is a relatively complex scheme. Central and Eastern Europe liberalization is one case in point. With the break-up of the former Soviet Union, Russia adopted a VAT in 1992 that was a VAT in name only. This policy was made perhaps without regard for the fact that Russia imposed a

---

[28] Earlier in Conrad's career there were discussions about whether the VAT should be administered by the income tax department or the indirect tax and customs department (called Customs and Excises in the UK and former British colonies). There was a recognition that the VAT was an accounts transaction-based tax like the income tax relative to a stand-alone invoice-based charge. In addition, much VAT revenue would be collected at the import stage. Finally, there was usually a pre-existing tax department charged with collecting indirect taxes such as excises and sales or turnover tax. Those discussions are in the past because of the evolution of tax administration into a more unified system based on comprehensive tax accounting. This evolutionary path resulted, at least in part, from the similar, if not identical, methods of income and VAT accounting on an accrual basis.

[29] The relatively recent debates and, what we believe to be, the awkward adaptation of the VAT to the EU without customs borders, may indicate that, absent significant transition costs, the VAT may not be the most appropriate method in the EU now.

[30] The past 30–40 years have also been a time of policy change for many economies. In particular, there has been a trend towards open economy economics with justifiable emphasis, in our view, on the importance of interactions with the world economy. Domestic protection was, and is, being discouraged. The VAT in this context was seen as one means to tax imports (as noted in the text) without domestic protection while potentially relieving exports of any artificial costs created by domestic indirect taxes.

subtraction-based VAT as the basis for the profits tax; a tax which could have been adapted through time to an invoice-credit system VAT. Other Central and Eastern European countries appeared eager to adopt the VAT because of the desire to enter the EU.

4.5.4 Advisers Sell What They Know

Technical assistance in tax policy and administration has become a part of most donor-funded reform programmes. Many advisers, including us, gained initial experience and competence with VAT reform. Thus, given the perception by governments that the VAT is desirable, accommodating that desire was (and is) the path of least resistance for advisers. This is not to say that advisers have uniformly advocated adopting the VAT as part of a reform programme.[31]

4.6 Consumption Tax Reform Going Forward

Given the significant fixed costs and the time, measured in years, necessary to make a major policy change in countries that currently have a VAT, the policy should not change in the foreseeable future. Other countries, including the United States, have the opportunity, however, to evaluate the relative costs and benefits of implementing a particular type of indirect tax regime. In addition, tax administrations in some countries might be tempted to change either to or from a VAT. Thus, it is important to make a candid evaluation of the relative costs and benefits in choosing the best option for a particular country.

What follows is based on the assumption that a type of consumption tax regime imposed on a destination basis is desired.[32] In the context of the overall reform programme, eventually the VAT may be eliminated in favour of comprehensive income taxation, perhaps supplemented with a personal consumption tax described later.

4.6.1 The TT, RST, and VAT Compared Again

In theory, the RST and VAT can generate the same revenue with the same rate and have all of the same desirable properties. The TT's fundamental flaw in theory is cascading. One benefit of the TT, relative to the RST and VAT, is that the same revenue can be collected at a lower rate.[33] In practice, all three taxes will have some elements of cascading, and there will be some elements of the indirect tax in exports for at least some firms because no indirect transaction-based tax will include all market

---

[31] Conrad was part of a group that recommended against implementing a VAT in Puerto Rico in 2011.
[32] We believe policymakers should consider whether an indirect tax, other than selective excises, is desirable at all. See Chapter 2.
[33] The welfare cost of a lower rate might offset the efficiency gains, if any, of a VAT or RST given the higher rate. In addition, the TT can be used to generate revenue to reduce income tax and other rates.

consumption as the base, there will be explicit exemptions, and non-compliance will be part of any system. In addition, rates might vary. Thus, the question is not to pick a method without cascading but to choose a method that can be administered at reasonable cost to both the APA/taxpayer and the tax administration with an acceptable level of compliance while keeping cascading within reasonable bounds.[34] These criteria will depend on a number of practical factors.

4.6.1.1 Some Simple Comparisons
Comparing a TT, RST, and VAT might begin with some simple comparisons about the scope and operation of the tax.

a. Number of APAs
The number of registered APAs for each tax will be the same, other things equal. It is clear that the TT and VAT will have the same number of registered suppliers, other things equal, because the tax is imposed on every taxable transaction. The number of registered RST APAs/taxpayers will also be the same, even if many transactions, and firms, accrue or pay little or no RST. The reason is that the tax administration needs to ensure that leakage is not excessive.

b. Information Requirements
TT APAs/taxpayers do not have to keep records of inputs and do not have to know to whom supplies are made. RST APAs/taxpayers need to know whether the purchaser is a member of the ring. As a practical matter, this is determined by purchasers revealing their status. The purchasers clearly have an incentive to state that they are ring members because then their purchases will be tax free. VAT APAs/taxpayers need to keep records of inputs and outputs with the invoice-credit system. There is no need to know whether the purchaser is a VAT APA/taxpayer, at least in theory. This benefit may not be realized in practice because at least some countries require the suppliers to include the APA/taxpayer identification numbers of purchasers who are VAT APA/taxpayers as part of the invoice. For example, knowledge of the APA/taxpayer status of purchasers is required in Ukraine because of the need to post the credits in the purchaser's VAT account. Other countries such as Korea attempt to cross match invoices, an exercise that is facilitated by the VAT APA/taxpayer supplying the VAT ID number of the purchaser, if one exists. The name and address of the purchaser is required on the VAT invoice on business to business transactions in the EU.[35] In effect, a ring exists at least in form because business-to-business transactions are

---

[34] The famous Diamond-Mirrlees result (Diamond & Mirrlees, 1971) about taxing only output will not be true in practice. In addition, there are practical issues about the relationship between market purchases and consumption, at least in terms of economic theory. Food purchased in the market is not food consumed. A meal is consumed within a household only after a complicated production process, including inputs such as electricity, the service of a stove and refrigerator, as well as household labour. Not all of these inputs will be taxed, household labour in particular, so a uniform tax on market purchases is not equivalent to a tax on total economic value added.

[35] https://stripe.com/guides/invoicing-best-practices-for-germany.

treated differently as an administrative matter, using a different invoice type, relative to business to nonbusiness. Thus, the VAT's advantage over the RST regarding a supplier's ability to treat all purchasers in the same manner may not be as relevant.

c. General Exemptions

A TT does not have to have any exemptions. In fact, there is no reason to have the TT limited to a set of consumption goods and services. If the intent is to have a broad-based tax, all transactions might be taxed, including but not limited to: capital transactions (such as the sale of a business), financial services (including purchases and sales of stock[36]), and even exports. The ability to expand the base is a result of the cascading effect of the TT. The TT is not a consumption tax in any true sense but might be interpreted as a production tax combined with an RST on goods and services going into private consumption. The same might be said for the VAT, as a matter of method, if it is possible to tax financial services and capital transactions (Diamond & Mirrlees, 1971). The VAT, however, is generally intended to impose a tax on the supply of a set of taxable goods and services going to the ultimate taxpayer. Thus, capital transactions and savings transactions, however defined, are exempt. Exports, technically speaking, are zero rated, not exempt, because it is necessary, legally speaking, for exports to be taxable at a zero rate in order for the credit system (and potential refunds) to work. The RST has one large methodological exemption: the exemption for all transactions that do not enter the empirical definition of final consumption. As noted, this is implemented via the ring system where APAs/taxpayers are exempt on their purchases of taxable goods and services to the extent that those goods and services are used as inputs as opposed to own consumption. While the methodological result of the VAT and RST is the same in the sense that no tax should be paid on outputs from one supplier that are used as inputs by another supplier, the exemption is explicit, and perhaps more clearly understood, with the RST.

d. Specific Exemptions

As a methodological matter, the consumption tax base should be as broad as possible. Specific exemptions, however, become an almost inevitable part of the tax system. Common exemptions by commodity include:

- Certain food items (or unprocessed food);
- Certain educational materials (including books and magazines);
- Medical supplies and drugs;
- Certain government services (such as court costs, notary services, and other government services for which a non-zero price is charged such as postal services);
- Public transportation;
- Religious materials; and
- Goods supplied at a zero-market price but for which there is value added.

---

[36] The Tobin Tax is effectively a TT on financial transactions.

The last exemption deserves some explanation. Certain goods and services can be supplied at a zero price even though there is positive value added. For example, concerned citizens might provide meals to the elderly or infirmed at no cost to the beneficiary. Such provision, however, has positive value added because the market value of such provision is probably greater than the cost, at least to the concerned citizens supplying the goods and services. The free transfer of such goods and services is a distributional outcome and the government contributes to the distributional outcome by not charging indirect tax.

Exemptions by supplier commonly include:

- Small scale agriculture, or agriculture more generally, is a special case relative to turnover limits for registration;
- Certain small suppliers, as defined in the law, might be based on annual turnover, employment, or other criteria (see Chapter 5);
- Supplies by religious organizations;
- Supplies by certain nonprofit institutions (perhaps to the extent that the supplies are not competitive with normal suppliers);
- Government;
- The Central Bank; and
- Medical facilities.

All of these exemptions limit the application of any indirect system, including the VAT.

e. Small Business Exemptions

It is common to have some type of small business exemption in a VAT. The standard recommendation is to base the exemption on some measure of annual turnover. Such exemptions are not as common in a TT or RST, with the exception of *de minimis* supplies by individuals. This exemption is sometimes voluntary because small business suppliers can be put at a competitive disadvantage by the cascading of VAT paid on inputs. Purchasers who are part of the stream of value added might avoid exempt suppliers because exempt suppliers cannot issue VAT invoices, making it impossible for purchasers to receive a VAT credit for the purchase of such inputs.

As noted, small business exemptions are less common in an RST and TT. In the case of a TT, the government merely forgoes additional revenue from such exemptions and the small business might enjoy some competitive advantage because no charge on output is required.

f. Cascading

Cascading can be a particularly difficult problem in cases where there are numerous independent stages of domestic value added. Such structures might arise in advanced economies with industries that operate relatively efficiently without vertical integration. This is particularly true when stages of value-added span international borders. Such integration highlights the importance of taxing imports and exempting exports as a means to limit cross-border cascading. Thus, a TT may be a bad choice in such economies. The TT, however, may not be a bad choice in situations where domestic value added is limited, at least initially, and there is the possibility of having exemptions. For instance, in relatively poor economies (e.g., Timor-Leste) where much real, as opposed to measured, GDP arises in agriculture and/or in vertically integrated natural resource production with most output exported, small markets and retailers may be the predominant element of the retail sector. In this case, exempting imported inputs and raw agricultural products may result in an acceptable level of cascading, even relative to a fully implemented VAT which itself will have cascading at least in part. Such economies, also common in Sub-Saharan Africa and Asia, will generally have tax administrations that are constrained with respect to skills and other resources. Thus, such resources could be devoted to administering a tax system in a transparent manner and to gain necessary experience.

g. Technological Change

The invoice-credit system has been adjusted to accommodate computerized accounting systems. Note should be made of the fact that the complementary nature of computerized accounting systems for income measurement may begin to increase the cost-effectiveness of either the addition or subtraction methods for administering a VAT relative to the invoice-credit system. At a minimum, the problems of fly-by-night firms and export refunds are reduced, if not eliminated, by such a change. Thus, the subtraction or addition methods might be a reasonable future option, even relative to an RST. The relative attractiveness of the subtraction or addition methods may be eroded in the inevitable situation where there are exempt supplies used as inputs and there are otherwise taxable supplies made by exempt APAs/taxpayers. Deductions for the value of such inputs should not be allowed in order to maintain the revenue correspondence between the addition or subtraction method and the invoice-credit system.

One complaint about the RST is the need to maintain the ring system and potential revenue losses (or gains) from misclassifications. As noted, this apparent benefit of the VAT may be illusionary in at least some instances. The rapid introduction and the increased use of both credit and debit cards may reduce the cost of such administration. It should be possible to encode a APA/taxpayer number to the extent one exists on the card. Thus, purchases made with such cards that do not have a APA/taxpayer number will attract RST. In addition, the use of such cards at the retail level should limit the leakage inherent in using cash transactions.[37]

---

[37] Conrad recalls some years ago he was in London and wanted a guided tour. He approached one of the wonderful tour guides available in London about pricing. Upon agreeing to the price, he asked if he could pay with a credit card. The response was: 'Of course you may use a credit card, but then I will have to charge you VAT.'

4.6.2 Assessment

The VAT may not be the best indirect tax method in all situations and may be inferior to the RST in the future. Our experience with the VAT has convinced us that there are essentially two benefits from instituting a VAT. First, cascading is reduced (but not eliminated) relative to a TT. Second, and perhaps more importantly, VAT administration is based on a transactional advanced tax, so the government is able to collect some, if not most, revenue either at the time goods and services[38] are imported or at an early point in the chain of domestic value added. This benefit should not be understated. This property is one foundation for the collection-driven approach developed in this volume. It is an essential element of reform in emerging economies and is the basis upon which to build a stable revenue system that can become more efficient through time. So, continued use of the VAT is recommended as part of the general reform system until such time as there is transition to income taxation. Thus, there are numerous benefits from maintaining and improving the VAT as reform proceeds. There are several areas where the performance of the invoice-credit system can be improved.

4.7 Selected Issues Related to the Invoice-Credit System

Some improvements in the VAT as applied may be warranted.

4.7.1 Export Refunds

4.7.1.1 Issue and Case Studies
Export refunds may be the Achilles' Heel (Ebrill et al., 2001) for the Invoice-Credit System VAT (ICV) because of the difficulty many VAT APAs/taxpayers have in obtaining legitimate VAT refunds in a number of countries. Regardless of the rationalization, the inability of legitimate APAs/taxpayers to receive prompt and accurate refunds implies that one of the purported benefits of the VAT, that exports do not contain any element of domestic indirect tax, is negated.[39] Denying refunds or prolonging the repayment of export refunds is essentially a type of interest-free government finance. Another way to make this point is to note that delayed export

---

[38] A reverse charge might be required for implementing a VAT on imported services.
[39] One option to address the issue would be to switch to the origin basis from the destination basis. This option is not realistic for any individual country for at least two reasons. First, exports would be taxed under the origin basis, so there would be no need for export refunds. One country, a small country in particular, would be harmed by switching because most countries with a VAT employ the destination basis. Thus, exporters will complain that exports from the origin country will be subject to a type of double taxation. The exported supplies would be taxed in the country of origin and again in the country of destination. The opposite would be true for imports, which could be free of VAT in both the country of origin and the country of destination. A type of negative effective protection might arise because supplies of domestic substitutes to imports will be taxed. Such an effect may be limited to direct imports because imported supply credits that attract domestic VAT will be zero. Second, given the importance of the VAT on imports for revenue purposes, countries might be reluctant to lose this important revenue source.

refunds should be reported as government debt, so that increases in the balance of export refunds is reported as an increase in the consolidated deficit, which would offset the reported revenue that forms the basis of the excess credit.

We believe that the issue of export refunds is related to the issue of ICV evasion because much of the bureaucratic response to export refunds has tended to be concentrated on the need to protect revenue—either concerns that goods are not being exported, goods are being exported and smuggled back into the country, or revenues have been lost because of the fly-by-night firms, false invoicing, or similar schemes. The former concern is reflected in the attempt by Zambia to implement rules that refunds would be permitted only upon proof that exported goods had arrived in the destination and possession was taken by the importing entity; a set of rules that is difficult, if not impossible, to either administer or to comply with (Conrad, 2014).

The latter issue is reflected by the Bulgarian rule that required firms to substantiate that VAT had been paid at all stages of domestic value added before export refunds could be granted; a substantiation that was impossible for any APA/taxpayer to make, particularly if goods and services went through more than one stage of value added. Of course, a APA/taxpayer could substantiate that they paid their VAT, which is all that should be required. Subsequently, Bulgaria, at the suggestion of business interests, instituted a VAT bank account system (Alexeev, Conrad, & Trunin, 2005). The Bulgarian system effectively converted the VAT to a cash basis by requiring that the VAT be deposited in a special individualized account before a credit could be taken. The accounts had to be cross-matched because a seller who collected the VAT had to deposit the payment before the purchaser could take the credit. In effect, the VAT account system became a type of invoice cross-matching with prior payment because the purchaser had to know that the seller deposited the VAT. In addition, there had to be some type of ordering rule so that the seller could deposit less than total VAT collected in cash from all purchasers. Note that the purpose of the scheme was not to increase VAT revenue, and, in fact, VAT revenue could have been expected to fall through time because the intent was to ensure a means for rapid export refunds. The scheme was quietly disbanded after, we believe, it proved to be cumbersome and ineffective in ensuring compliance.

The Ukrainian version of the VAT bank account system was introduced in 2014 after the discovery of a significant false invoicing operation. This system is claimed to be on an accrual basis so that purchasers can take the credit in the month of supply, regardless of whether they have paid. Such a system, however, is less than full accrual because the seller must have made either cash deposits or have accumulated excess credits in order for the purchaser to obtain an immediate credit.[40] An additional issue with this system is that VAT APA/taxpayers must have both computers and separate bank accounts; requirements that might limit the number

---

[40] Another indicator of the cash basis nature of the VAT is that purchasers appear to withhold payment of the VAT to sellers until they are assured that the VAT paid will be creditable by having their accounts posted for the amounts of VAT related to each particular transaction.

of APAs/taxpayers because of the expensive and cumbersome nature of the procedures. The tax administration believed that full payments had been made and export
refunds were current as of 2016. This may not be true, however. Some large schemes
of false invoicing might be deterred, but there appears to be room for other types of
corruption.[41]

We believe there are two basic problems with the methods used in Zambia, Bulgaria, and Ukraine (as well as other countries) that are intended to attack VAT evasion
of various types and then use the presence of such evasion to increase the cost of
obtaining refunds by honest APAs/taxpayers. First, some evasion may be reduced,
but the cost is borne to a significant degree by honest APAs/taxpayers via the use of
cumbersome schemes, rules that are impossible to apply, and long delays in obtaining
proper refunds. Second, all of these schemes are explicit attempts to shift the administrative burden from the tax authorities to the APAs/taxpayers. The ICV is designed
with the intent of ensuring that if a APA/taxpayer makes a purchase and obtains a
legal invoice, then that APA/taxpayer gets the credit—full stop. The APA's/taxpayer's
job is their own compliance. Compliance of other APAs/taxpayers is the job of the
tax administration.[42]

For example, consider the Zambian system for exports. The government has collected the revenue and so it is the APA's/taxpayer's job to substantiate that the exports
do not reenter the country illegally via some third party and are actually exported
in the first instance. The latter condition is certainly a joint responsibility. That is,
in the case of goods, the APA/taxpayer supplies the documentation and the goods
to the port and the customs department needs to certify that the goods are treated
in the appropriate manner. In addition, it is the customs department and other relevant government bodies that should be responsible for detecting smuggling and
other illegal activities. Two points are important about the Zambian system. First,
export value is irrelevant for VAT.[43] If supplies are exported, then full credit should
be available for VAT paid on inputs. The purchaser, if there is one, is also irrelevant
because the taxable event is the export itself. Second, the Customs Department and
relevant authorities appear to be relieved of the effort required to monitor the flow
of goods and services, at least in part. More importantly, these officials now have a
significant incentive to simply monitor paper because the tracing and monitoring
becomes certification of arrival in another country or its equivalent.

A similar criticism is appropriate for the scheme used in Bulgaria and Ukraine.
Tax administrators now concentrate on monitoring accounts in, we believe, a mistaken belief that compliance is assured via the accounting. In addition, such attention
may divert resources from problems that cannot be addressed by such accounting systems—such as cash transactions at the retail level and other supplies to

---

[41] Corruption and evasion on imports is particularly worrisome.

[42] Of course, honest APAs/taxpayers should be on guard for evasion of others and report it to the extent
appropriate. Our point, however, is that the government should not place such an administrative burden
on APAs/taxpayers.

[43] The export value may be important for income tax purposes, but that point is an issue separate from
VAT.

nonregistered APAs/taxpayers.[44] The accounting systems work only if there is some interest by the purchaser in obtaining an appropriate credit; an incentive absent when supplies are made to nonregistered APAs/taxpayers.

Two approaches (misguided we believe) to address such issues have been attempted that are not related to VAT bank accounts. First, countries use the turnover level for eligibility to get some cash transactions out of the system because of the relationship between supposedly small businesses and VAT noncompliance via cash transactions. The idea appears to be that the administrative problem of cash transactions can be addressed by essentially getting many transactions out of the system. While partially practical, there are costs, including limiting voluntary registration and the forgone revenue that could be obtained by a more reasonable administration. Second, some countries attempt and have instituted a rule that requires businesses to use cash registers. A cash register requirement does not necessarily result in the cash register being used. Tax administrators still have to determine whether reported cash receipts (and VAT) are reasonable. Countries have addressed this issue by surprise audits to determine if the cash register is being used for cash transactions and lotteries based on invoices issued by retailers.

Underlying many of these approaches, at least from the perspective of the APA/taxpayer, is concern about the integrity and competence of the tax administration. APAs/taxpayers may be, and probably are, willing to bear some additional costs if they can get appropriate credits without delay, in order to be relieved of at least some of the burdens imposed on them by corrupt and/or incompetent tax administrators. The price is relatively high, however, for APA/taxpayers, the tax administration, and society as a whole because such measures, while they may be cost effective in the short run, undermine the need to address the fundamental problem, which is to improve the tax administration's competence and integrity.

4.7.1.2 Options for Improvement

We believe that a number of actions can be taken to address delays or unnecessary denials of export refunds. First, the government should be required to pay interest on accumulated refunds at a positive real rate of interest. Some countries provide for such interest charges, such as Ukraine, but it is important that the policy be enforced. Second, there should be some public education, as well as tax administration education, which explains that accumulating a stock of accrued export refunds is equivalent to interest-free debt at a minimum.[45] Third, accounting for refunds should be straightforward and transparent. Refunds can be financed on a current

---

[44] Barter transactions do not go through the banking system; the Ukrainian system addresses this issue by requiring deposits prior to allowing the credit.

[45] Part of the problem with the VAT in general is the lack of public understanding about the VAT's intent. This is particularly true in emerging economies where accounting standards are still evolving. While simple for economists, the equivalence, in theory, of the RST and VAT might be foreign to tax administrators, APAs, and the general public (the taxpayers). Of course, the theoretical equivalence may not translate well to actual practice where there are exempt goods, exempt APAs/taxpayers, turnover limits, and less than timely responses to changes in economic circumstances. Another possible problem is the court system may be corrupt or may favour the government.

basis by simply having all tax revenue flow into a single treasury account with debits for export refunds. Note that VAT cash collections in any month can be lower than cash disbursements for export refunds.[46] Thus, it is important that VAT refunds not be linked to VAT revenues in any particular time period. Fourth, there should be a clear understanding that there is a reticence by most tax administrations (even honest tax administrations) to provide refunds from funds that have been collected in countries where there is no tradition of providing refunds and there may be suspicion about the credibility of the claims.[47]

If it is not possible to establish a reasonable refund system using standard methods, then we believe a reserve should be established to finance refunds. Characteristics of the reserve should include:

- The reserve needs to be in an account with balances published daily (and on a current basis) to ensure transparency;
- Inflows into the account should not be counted as government revenue and refunds should not be treated as government expenditure; and[48]
- Amounts flowing into the account should not be part of any revenue target imposed on the tax administration.

The balance in the fund can be established by either allocating one- or two-months' VAT revenue to the stock to determine the initial balance or by estimating prior refunds.

Other aspects of the refund system may include:

- Expedited refunds for those who are established exporters and who satisfy necessary conditions; and
- Certification of exports by customs. Value of exports does not matter for VAT purposes because exports are, and should be, zero rated if the VAT is a destination-based charge.[49]

Finally, we believe one policy to avoid is either to delay refunds for long periods of time or to allow excess VAT credits as an offset to other taxes such as the income tax. The APA/taxpayer should have the option to carry excess credits forward for some limited time period, excess credits that can be used for the VAT only. Offsets against other taxes can be administratively cumbersome, and ultimately is simply

---

[46] Such situations can occur where much, if not most, revenue accrues from imports, exports are significant, and domestic sales are relatively small. Payment lags could also be a contributing factor. All of these factors are cited to note that VAT collections in any month being less than export refund claims is not a sufficient condition for corruption and noncompliance or excessive refund claims. Of course, over time export refunds should never exceed total VAT accrued.

[47] The lack of symmetry in tax administration has always been an interesting aspect of these types of problems. Once the government has the cash, it is reticent to give it up and questions the honesty of the exporters' claim. On the other hand, evasion may be rampant as long as the APA/taxpayer has a net liability, requiring even more effort on the part of the tax administration.

[48] Ukraine treats (or treated) export refunds as budget expenditures subject to legislative approval.

[49] The value of exports might be important for income tax and balance of payments purposes.

a way for the government to refrain from honouring its obligations. In addition, excess credits can accumulate when there are tax losses from profits (or income) taxes. From a policy perspective, offsetting credits may confuse the economic and political purpose of each tax instrument. More importantly, the VAT is a prepayment for the tax imposed on the consumer (the taxpayer) and APAs are never taxpayers in our framework. Thus, it is inconsistent to allow an APA with excess VAT credits to offset the advanced payments from the income to labour and capital collected on behalf of other taxpayers. In effect, the revenue system may become a series of uncoordinated mixed signals that erode incentives and increase the efforts for compliance. The bottom line is that the government cannot expect compliance by the private sector if policymakers and tax administrators do not abide by the same law.[50]

4.7.1.3 Addressing Evasion

It should be emphasized initially that we believe there are no easy answers to addressing evasion in any tax. There will always be evasion and much of it will go undetected, even in advanced economies. This is a relatively efficient outcome given the tradeoff between reducing evasion and the cost of such reductions, including imposing potentially significant costs on those APAs/taxpayers who seek to comply. In addition, there is no substitute for a direct frontal assault on corruption in the tax administration with a realistic understanding that it will take years and resources to address the fundamental issues. There can be marginal improvements, however, on a more or less constant basis as long as there are clear objectives, public accountability, and constant monitoring.

a. Fly-by-Night Firms

An example of a fly-by-night firm will help illustrate the nature of the scam.[51] Consider Table 4.5. Table 4.5A contains the standard set of legal transactions where Firm A sells directly to Firm C and Firm C sells to a domestic resident consumer. Suppose now that Firms A and C collude by creating a new fly-by-night firm, Firm B. This is illustrated in Table 4.5B. Firm A sells to Firm B for a low price, and, in turn, Firm B sells to Firm C at a high price. Firm A has less VAT to pay to the government and Firm C has a larger credit. Firm B then 'disappears' before paying the VAT and the government loses that revenue. It is also possible for a single entity or group of related parties to create a distributing entity that buys from one related party and sells to another related party, with the distributing entity then disappearing with the VAT. The selling firm pays little or no VAT (and may have excess credits) while the buying firm gets full credit for the high-priced purchase. Finally, it is possible for a

---

[50] We have noted in a number of contexts that APA/taxpayers who do not receive legally obligated refunds will ensure that they capture the refund in another manner, perhaps through decreased compliance. The government needs to demonstrate its own resolve to abide by the law as one important step towards increasing private sector compliance.

[51] Much of the material is taken from Conrad (2004).

Table 4.5 Example of fly-by-night firm

Firm	A	B	C	Purchase by domestic resident defined to be a consumer
A. Honest transactions				
Tax-exclusive output price	1,000.00		2,600.00	2,600.00
Tax-exclusive input price			1,000.00	-
Value added	1,000.00		1,600.00	
Tax-inclusive price	1,100.00		2,860.00	2,860.00
VAT				
VAT on output	100.00		260.00	260.00
Credit for VAT on input			100.00	-
Net VAT	100.00		160.00	
Total VAT accrued				260.00
B. Firm B: Fly-by-night				
Tax-exclusive output price	100.00	2,200.00	2,600.00	2,600.00
Tax-exclusive input price		100.00	2,200.00	
Value added	100.00	2,100.00	400.00	
Tax-inclusive price	110.00	2,420.00	2,860.00	2,860.00
VAT				
VAT on output	10.00	220.00	260.00	260.00
Credit for VAT on input		10.00	220.00	
Net VAT	10.00	210.00	40.00	
Total VAT accrued				50.00

fly-by-night, in collusion with one or more downstream firms, to simply create false invoices which are used as credits by the downstream firms.

The first point in combating this fraud is to note that VAT registration is essential for the fraud to work because sellers to the fly-by-night and purchasers get the credit. That is, it should be possible for an unsuspecting purchaser to get a full credit if they are not involved in the scheme because the VAT invoice is valid. Thus, registration information and procedures are an important first step in combating the fraud. The registration procedure should be reasonable but require information to indicate that the potential registrant is valid. Information should include:

- a fixed place of business, or at least being represented by an established agent such as a known accounting firm;

- ownership structure, and principal officers;[52]
- industry;
- reference to auditor if relevant;
- nature of relationship to other VAT APAs/taxpayers or domestic entities more generally;
- copies of official registration materials, such as corporate documents and business registration; and
- if applicable, require that nonresidents have a domestic agent empowered to address tax matters.

Particular attention might be given to special purpose entities (SPEs) designed for one activity and unincorporated businesses.[53] A site visit may be appropriate to verify documentation. Two functions are served by a site visit. First, some of the information can be verified. Second, an educational function can be served if APAs/taxpayers are supplied with written information about the VAT, reporting procedures, and their responsibilities.

If a potential registrant is seeking voluntary registration because no business has been conducted or because the registrant is below the turnover level, then registration might be delayed until there is a site visit or there might be additional information requirements to ensure that the business is indeed legitimate. Such a procedure might be unnecessary if appropriate corporate documents and business registration have been completed.

Information flows between Customs and domestic tax authorities need to be unimpeded, especially about smuggling. Finally, there should be clear statutory rules about the obligations of individuals listed as officers and accountability of related entities. Ex-post audits of fly-by-night firms might be impossible given the nature of the abuse, so it is important that individuals and related parties can be held accountable.

As an administrative matter, unusually large transactions for one APA/taxpayer or a significant change in the value of transactions (either sales or purchases) might indicate that a particular firm or a firm either immediately prior to or after the indicated firm in the chain of value added might be accumulating, or had accumulated, cash payments in anticipation of stealing the VAT revenue. Of course, such a discovery might be too late except in cases where a relationship between either the purchaser or seller and the dissolved firm can be established.

At the policy level, fly-by-night firms that are known to be related parties might be discouraged by requiring some integrated reporting. For example, transfers from one related party to another should have no revenue consequences. If the transferor charges VAT, then the transferee should get an immediate credit of the VAT

---

[52] Much of this information can be cross checked with business registration procedures common in many countries. No VAT registration should be issued to any person either not properly registered to do business in the country or in the process of obtaining such registration.

[53] The registration rules need to be balanced so that legitimate APAs/taxpayers are not unduly burdened with requirements.

on accrual. Thus, one approach, particularly for smaller economies where the number of firms is not too large, is simply to either deny registration for related parties or otherwise require consolidation.[54]

b. False Invoicing

False invoicing[55] is a second common abusive practice unique to the VAT and the problem is worldwide. Given the ICV, the invoice can be the key document for obtaining a credit. As such, the invoice can be effectively as good as cash because the person who holds the invoice has a claim against the government for either reduction in their net VAT obligation or a refund (Bird, 1993). False invoicing can be particularly difficult to monitor because invoices can be generated by the APA/taxpayer for their own use, particularly by computer, in addition to organized efforts to develop a market for the sale of false invoices.[56] As long as the APA/taxpayer is not too greedy, false invoicing can be difficult to monitor. For example, if a APA/taxpayer would otherwise have a net VAT obligation of 10,000 and generates false invoices that reduce the liability to 9,750, then detecting repeated abuse might be difficult except in cases where audits are extensive or there is independent evidence that the fraud is taking place.[57] Large false invoicing either relative to a APA's/taxpayer's own business or in terms or organized fraudulent activity is generally the objective of enforcement efforts.[58]

False invoicing has been attacked using a number of methods, including invoice lotteries, cross-checking (prominent in Korea), and VAT bank accounts (Ukraine and Bulgaria). None have been completely successful, but all impose significant administrative costs. The Korean cross-checking system is probably the most famous and now extends to credit cards (Lee, 2016). A cross-checking system is one where APAs/taxpayers are required to supply invoices for both supplies and purchases. The Government then attempts to match the purchase invoice with the

---

[54] There have been situations, in Russia for example, where branches of the same corporate entity have been required to register separately. The justification for the approach was, in part, geographical separation. Goods produced in one part of the country might be shipped to another part of the country for further processing and/or distribution. Potential VAT at the time of shipment might be lost if goods in transit are lost via illegal distribution channels. The perceived need for such reporting in places like Russia may be an indicator of the level of corruption and noncompliance; an issue not addressed well by such reporting requirements.

[55] Our debt to Smith and Keen (2007) is noted.

[56] The market might also extend to otherwise legitimate invoices that are of no value to the owner, if that APA/taxpayer has excess credits and is not able to obtain refunds. Such trade, while illegal, is one means for those who are not able to obtain legitimate export refunds to effectively obtain some value for what is owed by the Government.

[57] There is a parallel between such behaviour in the VAT and deductions under the income tax, particularly in countries such as the United States where individual filing is prominent. For example, fake deductions for things such as charitable contributions have historically been a problem in the United States. The extent of the problem has been deemed sufficient to warrant required information reporting by organizations that receive such donations. Another example is fake receipts for expenses, particularly for individuals engaged in unincorporated business. Some abuse is deemed tolerable; for example, some individuals overstate the amount paid for taxis related to travel and taxi drivers in the United States might supply receipts that are official but otherwise blank.

[58] False invoicing is not restricted to VAT and can be used in transfer pricing, money laundering, and other schemes. It has been discovered that false invoicing resulted in significant overstatements of exports and imports in China. http://www.china-briefing.com/news/2014/03/21/minimizing-risk-falsely-issued-invoices-china.html.

sales invoice. One criticism of this system is the administrative cost relative to the increase in compliance. Such costs have been reduced and will probably continue to fall with the advent of increased computer capacity and power combined with electronic invoicing systems (González & Velásquez, 2013). While such systems might be feasible for larger diversified economies, one significant drawback of these systems for emerging economies is the expense of using computers for VAT APAs/taxpayers and the significant initial costs for the tax administration. Some have argued that reducing the number of VAT APAs/taxpayers is a net benefit in such economies (Harrison & Krelove, 2005). We are sceptical. In particular, limiting the number of APAs/taxpayers (even given administrative constraints) probably reduces the economic efficiency of the VAT, may reduce revenue, and may increase evasion via both false invoicing by unregistered APA/taxpayers and by other means. Thus, a decision to limit the number of APA/taxpayers or, more appropriately, how to limit the number of APA/taxpayers, needs to be placed in the context of the VAT's overall objectives and the tax system in which it is developed.

Other difficulties with cross-checking include false positives. Legitimate invoices might fail to match either because one pair is missing or there were errors in entry. Other problems may be related to the specific programme adopted in a country. For example, if a country does not require small VAT APAs/taxpayers to be part of the computer system, then there will be the potential for evasion via false invoicing by such groups. In addition, if there is an exemption for invoices below a certain amount, then evasion can continue by issuing numerous false invoices below the stipulated amount.

4.7.2 VAT Accounting

VAT accounting should be on an accrual basis. Standard VAT language includes time of supply as the earlier of:

- The time the goods are available for the purchaser's use;
- The issuance of the invoice;
- The removal of the goods; or
- The payment of cash.

For services, the time of the supply is the time the services are supplied.

The conceptual basis for the ICV is transfer of title as we understand it and little to do with the time the invoice is issued. That is, if goods are shipped to the purchaser and become part of the purchaser's inventory, then the VAT arises regardless of whether a VAT invoice has been issued. The same is true with the provision of services. That is, the provision of the service is when the VAT accrues. As a practical matter, the time the invoice is issued may be the time of supply and when a paper trail is established.

There are three points of note about VAT on accrual. First, the APA supplying the good or service has an incentive to collect the tax. That is, the supplier is liable for tax, usually within the month of the charge, regardless of if the purchaser actually paid. Second, the government is able to collect revenue a bit faster because there may be a lag between the time of sale and the time of cash payments if the goods are shipped (or delivered) prior to the time of payment. For example, the term for receivables may be thirty to ninety days under many commercial contracts.

This VAT on accrual has been claimed to adversely affect working capital levels, but such a result is doubtful. Working capital is defined as cash plus accounts receivable less accounts payable plus inventories. Accounts receivable will include the VAT due from the purchaser and accounts payable will include the VAT due to the government if the APA/taxpayer does not pay the VAT until cash is received. Thus, the VAT in accounts receivable should offset the payable through time. If the APA/taxpayer pays the VAT to the government, accounts receivable do not change but accounts payable fall by the amount of the VAT payment, resulting in no change to working capital. For example, consider Table 4.6. Column I is a representation of total working capital in the absence of VAT. Suppose, however, that nothing changes except that a VAT is imposed, and the supplier has an outstanding receivable of 114 in VAT that the purchaser has not paid by the end of the taxable period. Column II contains measured working capital in the case where the VAT is on a cash basis. The supplier is not required to pay VAT to the government until the purchaser pays. Accounts receivable increase by 114. However, accounts payable also increase by 114, which implies that the total value of working capital remains unchanged. Consider now the case where the VAT is charged on an accrual basis (Column III). In this case, the supplier is required to pay the VAT charged to the purchaser even though the purchaser has not paid. Thus, accounts receivable increase by 114 relative to the no-VAT situation (or the same as the cash-based VAT situation), and the cash balance is reduced by 114 (the amount of the VAT paid to government) but accounts payable is the same as the no-VAT situation (or is reduced by 114 relative to the cash-based VAT situation). Thus, working capital is unaffected. The cash balance is adversely affected by the use of accrual accounting, but total working capital should not be affected.[59]

Finally, VAT on accrual means that the purchaser who is a VAT APA/taxpayer is able to take the credit even though they have not paid the VAT on their purchases. This results in an identical result to the situation where the seller has to pay on an accrual basis: no change in working capital.

More importantly, there is an administrative reason for requiring the ICV to be on an accrual basis. Under the accrual method, only invoices need to be tracked. Under the cash method, VAT invoices may also have to be matched with cash receipts if there is a timing difference between the time of sale and the time the cash is paid. That is,

---

[59] There are situations where working capital is adversely affected, such as when the government denies export credits and refunds. For example, inventory build-up periods prior to holidays may affect working capital to some extent if there are periods of excess credits. This should be only a temporary result, however, and, in theory, may have no effect if the excess credit is treated as part of accounts receivable, or a negative account payable, from the government.

Table 4.6 VAT and working capital

Situation	I No VAT	II VAT on cash basis	III VAT on accrual
Cash	1,000.00	1,000.00	886.00
Accounts receivable	1,489.00	1,603.00	1,603.00
Accounts payable	899.00	1,013.00	899.00
Inventories	25,871.00	25,871.00	25,871.00
Total working capital	27,461.00	27,461.00	27,461.00

two sets of documents must be maintained and matched using the cash basis: one set of documents to confirm transfer of title and a second to match the payment. Such complications lead to errors, matches of payments and sales get misclassified or lost, and manipulation by APAs/taxpayers. The most famous example of a scheme created because of the cash method of VAT accounting occurred in Russia during the early reform period. The scheme worked as follows: (1) a VAT APA/taxpayer sold taxable supplies to another domestic person, creating a receivable for the supplier; (2) the purchaser did not pay for the supply and thus there was no VAT payable to the government; (3) the purchaser would make a 'loan' to the seller (perhaps in the amount of the net-of-tax value of the transaction); (4) the purchaser then transferred the loan to an offshore related party; and (5) the seller either repaid the loan or cancelled the receivable to the purchaser. None of the last transactions were subject to VAT because financial transactions are exempt. In effect, the buyer and seller were able to create a series of capital transactions which were not subject to VAT and the seller never paid VAT to the government because there was no cash payment in exchange for the goods. The government should have declared the transactions as shams and imposed the VAT plus penalties and interest on both APAs/taxpayers. Instead, the Russian Government imposed VAT on all loans; a situation that took years to rectify.[60]

One final issue is the selective use of the cash method. Of course, the cash method is common for small businesses, particularly in the retail sector. In this case, cash accounting is simply a special case of accrual with the payment and the issuance of an invoice occurring at the same time. There have been situations, however, where governments grant, or are lobbied to allow, cash accounting for particular APAs/taxpayers or industries. The most prominent cases are large state-owned public utilities such as gas and electricity companies.[61] Two factors contributed to this unique situation. First, prices may be controlled by the state; in some cases, prices are below cost, creating the need for state subsidies. Second, consumers, who may be other large state enterprises as well as final consumers, either do not pay or are slow

[60] In some cases, it became impossible to trace whether the loan was made by the purchaser because a banking intermediary could have made the loan via a series of back-to-back transactions.
[61] Such proposals were common in the former Soviet Union and were one basis for overall cash basis accounting in Russia where there were still a number of large state enterprises operating at the time the VAT was implemented.

to pay their bills. Given this situation, it was argued that allowing cash accounting will relieve the utilities of cash flow pressure.

Such proposals should be resisted in our view. Switching to the cash method fails to provide an incentive for the enterprises to collect arrears (VAT in particular) and decreases transparency by providing a form of interest-free finance to the state enterprises. It is better to have accrual accounting combined with explicit subsidies for state enterprises to the extent that prices are controlled. At a minimum, explicit subsidies are part of the normal budgetary process so that decision makers may be forced to explicitly consider the economic cost of both state ownership and the adverse effects of pricing.

4.7.3   Used Assets and Real Property

Used assets are not an issue for sales between APAs. The seller got a credit when the asset was purchased and imposed VAT on the sale at a later date. There is also no problem with supplies between nonregistered purchasers because of the tax prepayment property of the VAT. The first purchaser pays the full VAT in present value terms and then subsequent sales, while exempt, will include the VAT remaining on the asset's useful life.

A problem might arise, however, with trade between nonregistered and registered persons, trade in long-term assets in particular. Real property is a case in point. If VAT is imposed on real property and sold to a nonregistered person then, in theory, the person prepays the present value of the VAT. If a subsequent sale is made to another nonregistered person, then there should be no problem.[62] The issue arises when the nonregistered person sells the property to a registered person who cannot take a credit for the embedded VAT. This is one difficulty with the VAT treatment of housing and some countries exempt housing from the VAT. Exemption is not correct in our view because real property is a mixed-use asset. It is a store of wealth and has consumption value. Thus, the consumption value of the asset during the holding period should be subject to VAT in order to be comprehensive.

Conrad and Grozav (2008) propose a scheme where VAT is imposed on each transaction of real property. The administration is based on closing documents where VAT is charged to the purchaser and the seller takes a credit for the inflation-adjusted value of the VAT paid at the time of purchase. Successful implementation depends on the ability to maintain property records in a market with clearly established titles. Thus, the proposal can be implemented when these criteria are established. This method can be adopted once there are formal titles and can be imposed when the transfer is concluded via a formal closing.

Finally, there are other types of long-lived assets (jewellery, works of art, used automobiles) with both consumption and investment characteristics that are a significant

---

[62] Note that any income accruing to the nonregistered seller will be subject to recapture under our proposed income tax.

portion of a country's capital stock. Trade between nonregistered persons is not a problem, but in some markets such as artwork and antiques, potential purchasers are registered resellers. In this case, methods such as the 'margin' method used in the UK might be reasonable. Using the scheme, the reseller charges VAT only on the difference between the purchase and selling price. In effect, the reseller is treated as an agent or a service provider such as a tailor.[63]

4.7.4 An Additional Improvement — Financial Services

Personal savings and investments should be exempt from VAT given the consumption tax objective. Financial services, however, should be included in the VAT base. Historically, it has been difficult to separate financial services from savings, or the return to savings, for banks and other financial services. Poddar and English (1997) proposed a way to compute the value added from financial services using the addition method. That proposal has proven robust through time. Adopting this proposal requires a separate technique relative to the invoice-credit system (as shown above). The benefits should be worth the adoption costs once the VAT administration has matured.

4.8 Summary: The Role of General Consumption Taxation in the Overall Reform

The widespread adoption of the VAT including the adoption in most emerging economies can be justified because of the limitations of turnover tax systems that it replaced, the inevitable use of the border as a collection point for taxes, and the need for revenue to finance reforms that take perhaps a generation to implement, even if well planned. Thus, the VAT is an essential element of a collection-based system. Through time, perhaps another generation, the relative importance of the VAT should decline at least from the perspective of the reform adopted here as the income tax becomes more prominent. It is important to note that a flat-rate VAT combined with a flat-rate income tax (with extensive use of APAs) may have two characteristics that are desirable. First, the income tax with a credit, perhaps refundable, can add progressivity to the system. Second, as noted in Chapter 3, the income tax should become relatively more important as growth increases. Observed savings should increase as income increases, and the income tax with an exemption, or refundable credit, should be relatively more income elastic relative to the general consumption tax.

---

[63] A tailor may produce a suit for a customer using the customer's cloth. That is, the cloth is never sold to the tailor and so the tailor charges only for the service. This is one example of a more general classification of transactions known as 'tolling'. For example, a smelter may refine another person's ore or concentrate and the input might even be imported. VAT should be charged only on the service provided (by the smelter in this case), but there can be significant administrative issues such as the situation in Russia where Russian smelters process imported raw materials from nonresidents.

If there are concerns about the detrimental effect of the income tax on savings, then from the perspective of the taxpayer, the effective tax on consumption (measured relative to CMDI) is higher than on savings across all income groups for which the income tax is positive when combined with the VAT. That is, from the perspective of the taxpayer, the marginal tax on the savings is the individual marginal rate while the effective tax on consumption is the marginal tax rate on income plus the general consumption tax rate.

Our view is that through time, far beyond our lifetimes, the general consumption tax will wither away to be replaced by a more comprehensive income tax. There are two reasons for this view. First, economic growth and technological change may increase the administrative advantages of the income tax and therefore reduce the need for APAs to collect advanced payments to both primary factors and on the supply of goods and services. These changes may also be complemented by increased public understanding about the nature of consumption taxes as an advanced payment on particular income measures through time as well as the potential for the income tax to be a more efficient risk-sharing device. Finally, the administrative advantages of the VAT, as commonly applied, may decline over time. This has already begun to happen in certain circumstances with regard to low-bulk high-value goods such as cell phones and with respect to services. In particular, some goods and services are now treated under the VAT in a manner similar to the RST, so it may be the case that expansion of the RST component may erode any VAT advantages through time.

4.9 Excise Taxation

Excise taxation is a consumption tax on a relatively small set of goods and services. Recommendations about including excise taxes in a reformed system are supplied here.[64]

4.9.1 Purpose of Tax

The methodology for excise taxation depends on the issue being addressed. If the principal purpose of the tax is to correct a negative externality, then a per unit charge is appropriate. Alternatively, an ad valorem tax may be reasonable if the main purpose of the tax is to collect revenue. The primary advantage of excise taxation is that collection can be either at the point of importation or manufacture. Thus, an ad valorem approach must be tempered with the administrative costs of determining the basis for the ad valorem tax.

4.9.1.1 Externality Correction
A charge imposed to correct a negative externality should be a per unit charge adjusted for inflation. The purpose of the charge is to change relative prices so that

---

[64] This section is based on a 16 September 2019, Memorandum for Dr Vera Songwe from Robert Conrad entitled: Excise Taxation in Ethiopia.

market participants incorporate the social cost of the externality when they make private decisions. The charge is per unit because the externality is generally assumed to be unrelated to the price of output (other than the underpricing for the externality). For instance, the quantity of secondhand smoke is generally assumed to be independent of whether the smoke is created by cheap or expensive cigarettes. From our perspective, the charge is not a tax because the purpose of the charge is to establish an efficient market price so that the payment is made in exchange for a specific benefit. The specific benefit is the right to use the good or service that creates the externality by paying the full market price. Thus, the charge is not for revenue but is effectively a charge in exchange for an unpriced (or underpriced) property right. For example, secondhand smoke is created by using the atmosphere to transport smoke. Absent the correction, the price of using the atmosphere is zero at the margin.

Revenue to the government may be a significant by-product of the use of the excise as an incentive to incorporate the negative externalities. As a matter of method, the tax should be imposed on the specific ingredients that causes the externality. For example, the charge for alcoholic beverages should be based on alcoholic content of the product. Thus, other things equal, the charge per unit volume for beer and wine should be lower relative to spirits. In the case of motor fuel, the tax should be based on the amount of lead, particulate matter, unburned hydrocarbons, and other ingredients that affect air quality.[65]

4.9.1.2 Revenue Collection

Excise taxes, as a sub-classification of general consumption taxes, designed for revenue purposes can be ad valorem, in general, and flat rate within a commodity classification. This revenue objective can be achieved, within the product classification, by imposing a charge that does not affect relative prices, again within the product classification.[66] In theory, the tax should be charged to the consumer, in the same manner as a VAT. Ad valorem excises are discriminatory consumption taxes and in many countries are designed to exploit inelastic demand while discouraging consumption.

Retail ad valorem excise taxes are not the norm, however, for at least four reasons. First, excise tax rates are so high that governments in some countries are concerned that quoting the tax as a percentage of the net-of-tax price would be politically unacceptable.[67] Tax-exclusive rates in excess of 500% on tobacco products are common, and politicians may be concerned about public resistance to such rates.

---

[65] The value of the per unit charge might be changed through time in response to changes in the marginal value of the negative externality. For example, if fossil fuel use is reduced and other efforts to reduce air pollution are successful, then the marginal value of the negative externality may be reduced. Note that the change in the per unit charge through time is not for revenue purposes. Revenue could increase or decrease as a result of the changes.

[66] Differential rates may be optimal in a world with costless administration and with knowledge of own—and cross-price elasticities. In addition, imposing an ad valorem excise on tobacco products discourages the use of tobacco products relative to consumption of other commodities. It is possible, however, to exploit the relatively inelastic nature of demand (and the lack of close substitutes) by imposing such a differential excise in order to raise revenue.

[67] We report this argument but do not support it. Anyone can compute the ad valorem equivalent of a per unit tax.

262 Evolutionary Tax Reform in Emerging Economies

Second, evasion might be significant if taxes at such high rates are collected at the retail level. Governments may resort to collection methods using tax stamps that are placed on the tobacco product at the manufacturing level (usually inside the protective wrapping). Per unit charges are preferred in this situation because the same stamps, or other control methods, can be used for any excisable product, regardless of quality and price.[68]

Third, one advantage of excise taxes is that there are fewer manufacturers and importers relative to distributors and retailers. Administration is simplified because the bulk of the excise can be collected from fewer registered persons (APAs in this volume). In short, the major administrative advantage of excise taxation is physical control of the goods[69] by treating the manufacturer as a type of bonded warehouse where the tax is imposed at the time taxable goods leave the facility (similar to the relatively few chokepoints used for collecting import tariffs). This advantage is lost if the collection point is moved to the retail level. The number of collection points increases, and it may not be possible to monitor all points of sale, including small shopkeepers and street distribution. It is important to note that administration at the retail (or wholesale) level is still necessary. Site visits and periodic checks are necessary in order to ensure that supplies have been taxed.

Fourth, if the excise tax is collected at a point other than the retail level, the ad valorem tax is easier to evade by manipulating the reported prices. At a minimum, administrative costs are increased.

Finally, it should be noted that the primary function served by excises is that the Government can collect significant revenue with minor behavioural modifications, at least in the short run, because of the inelastic nature of the commodities being taxed. Public acceptance, even of gasoline taxes, is relatively high with the major political opposition arising from producers, who while vocal are relatively small in number.

4.9.2 A Proposal: Two Options

4.9.2.1 Combined per Unit and Ad Valorem Rates

Taxing jurisdictions might consider a two-pronged approach by using a combination of a per unit and ad valorem rate. Regardless of the rate choice, we believe the excise tax should be restricted to four commodity types: alcoholic beverages, tobacco products, petroleum products, and automobiles. A fifth group might be cell phone service if reasonable administration is possible. Finally, the gasoline tax can be supplemented

---

[68] There is a question about the use of tax stamps. Stamps can be, and are, forged. The stamp has value, just like the VAT invoice, and, absent enforcement, the price of stamps on a black market can reach the value of the tax. Thus, the tax administration must spend resources enforcing compliance and monitoring the stamps.

[69] Taxable services such as cell phone services are a different matter because there is no physical control. Most phone service is regulated, however, so there are few suppliers and administration is facilitated by suppliers charging the tax as part of their billing process, like the VAT.

by a general carbon charge on the use of fossil fuels in general. Revenue from the other excises is minimal, and the revenue losses can be more than compensated for by devoting administrative resources to the restricted set of commodities.[70]

a. The Per Unit Charge

The per unit charge, as noted, should be based on components of the taxable good responsible for the externalities or other health effects. Specifically,

- Alcoholic content for any type of alcoholic beverages;
- Tobacco, by weight, for tobacco products;
- Either simple volume of motor fuel at the most elementary level or a carbon-specific charge based on international scientific data;
- Engine size for automobiles; and
- Minutes of cell phone use.

The per unit amount should be adjusted automatically for inflation. The amounts, to the extent possible, should be related to the value of the negative externality produced. Like carbon values, the values for particular goods can be based on current estimates found in the scientific literature.

b. The Ad Valorem Rate

The ad valorem rate should be based on the price at either the factory gate or at the last point of trade between related parties. For example, if a local producer owns or is otherwise related to wholesalers and distributors (such as private branders), the excise should be imposed at the point of sale between the producer/distributor and any independent party.[71]

The rate should be as high as the market will bear in order to exploit the low demand elasticities. Rates are constrained, however, by rates in other countries. Most excisable goods are high value, low volume, and are susceptible to smuggling. This issue is particularly relevant in countries with porous borders. In these situations, maximum rates should be competitive with neighbouring jurisdictions to reduce smuggling until such time as borders are controlled.

4.9.2.2 Market Netback Pricing

A reasonable compromise between the advantages of collection from a few APAs/taxpayers and the use of the ad valorem tax is to collect the tax at the time

---

[70] This does not mean that externality correction is inappropriate for other goods and services. Many negative externalities can be addressed, efficiently, by regulation. Noise ordinances and toxic chemicals are examples.

[71] VAT and income tax records can be used to determine if a manufacturer has a related distributor or private brander.

of manufacture or importation but base the tax on some measure of market value.[72] The system can be developed by using the following steps:

1. Use market surveys to compute the average market prices of excisable products.[73] Product differentiation, Irish whiskey and vodka for example, can be taken into account, but differentiation should be limited to 'high' quality and 'low' quality, for cigarettes and other taxable commodities, at least initially. It is important to get the system operational, to begin to accrue significant revenue, and to gain experience before there is any attempt to fine tune the system.
2. Stipulate an ad valorem rate in the law.
3. Stipulate that the base of the tax is the retail price with netbacks for VAT and the existing excise.[74] The netback then is a straightforward computation.
4. Convert the ad valorem tax to a per unit equivalent by multiplying the measure of the base by the ad valorem rate.
5. Collect the per unit equivalent either at the factory or at the time of importation.
6. Make all computations at most on a quarterly basis.

For instance, suppose the measured average market price before VAT is 100 and the existing tax is 30 at the retail level. The retail tax base is equal to 70. A tax rate of 42.8% would preserve the tax of 30. That rate would then be used through time so that the excise would vary with the observed average price.[75] This per unit value would be accrued at the time of shipment or the time of importation regardless of the declared value of the commodity.

Administration is simplified because there are fewer taxpayers. Valuation problems are reduced. Values are based on arm's-length market surveys and thus neither transfer pricing rules nor cost accounting are required. The government also gets the funds at an earlier date relative to a retail tax. There are still incentives to evade, smuggling in particular, but overall compliance should be greater with this system relative to a retail tax.[76] Finally, there is no need to make inflation adjustments, and changes in relative prices, at least between excisable goods and other goods and services, are automatically taken into account by using an ad valorem basis.

---

[72] Fernando Cossio introduced Conrad to this method and Conrad made this proposal in a number of countries, including the Dominican Republic, Russia, and Ethiopia.

[73] The statistics offices should be contacted to determine the extent to which market surveys are used.

[74] The VAT should be based on the excise-inclusive price of the commodity.

[75] Alternatively, the tax-exclusive rate could be converted to a tax-inclusive base by making stipulations (either assumed or empirically determined) about mark-ups and other costs. It might be possible for the base to be negative using the method described in the text if smuggling is significant and markets are competitive.

[76] There also may be incentives to increase the quality of the product, a result known from the imposition of a per unit charge.

We recognize that the proposed approach, in its simplest form, would affect the relative demand for different types of products within a class. For example, the effective tax rate per unit on lower quality excisable goods will be higher relative to higher quality products, unless the surveys are finely tuned. As stated above, it is possible to take into account product differentiation by computing average prices for different classes or qualities. In our opinion, however, such differentiation is unwarranted initially and can be added as experience is gained.

4.10 Uniform Tariff

We have recommended, and continue to recommend, that taxing jurisdictions impose a uniform tariff as one initial reform action. Our view is that a uniform tariff can help to stabilize revenues and to lay the foundation for the tax system's evolution.[77] Some justifications for this recommendation are offered in the next section. This discussion is followed by a discussion of implementation steps. A summary of the overall proposal for a uniform tariff is contained in Box 4.1.

4.10.1 Justifications for a Uniform Tariff

There are a number of advantages to imposing a uniform tariff.

Box 4.1 Summary of uniform tariff proposal

1. Establish a rate between 6% to 10%.
2. Provide for a short list of exempt goods. Only goods on the list will be exempt.
3. Ensure that imports financed under gratuitous assistance and imports by foreign governments are exempt.
4. Impose excise taxes on tobacco products, cars, and perhaps petroleum products. If excise taxes are ad valorem, impose on the tax-inclusive price. If excise taxes are per unit, then increase the amount of tax by the tariff rate to ensure that excises are based on the tariff-inclusive price.
5. Use the official exchange rate to compute all import and tariff values.
6. Develop a system to monitor transshipments and to limit the use of unofficial re-exports.

---

[77] This material is based on: 18 August 2002 Memorandum for Mr Ashraf Ghani Minister of Finance Islamic State of Afghanistan Subject Uniform Tariff: Supplemental Comments, by Robert Conrad

4.10.1.1 Simplicity

A uniform tariff is relatively simple to administer.[78] Tax administrators do not waste resources to determine classifications and can use resources for revenue-productive activities. In addition, this type of simplification can be a step towards limiting corruption and evasion. Tax administrators cannot use variation in the rates to obtain bribes from reclassifying imports to low-tariff categories. Importers cannot try to reclassify goods in order to reduce tariffs.[79]

Simplification can enhance compliance, and revenues, because it is easier for both the tax administration and the importer to understand the rules. Simplification in some countries is important because revenues are needed while the customs administration is reformed. Finally, simplification is a device that can be used to demonstrate to the public that government is committed to reform and to establishing a tax system that is transparent.

4.10.1.2 Revenue

Tariffs can be used for protection on a selective basis in addition to generating revenues. In general, there is a tradeoff between tax revenue and protection because of the rate variation necessary to generate protection. High tariff rates are designed to retard imports, and thus tariff revenues are reduced, other things equal. In addition, exemptions, or zero rating, for certain tariff classifications, of course yields zero revenue. Smuggling and corruption are an inevitable result in some cases. Variation in tariff rates, however, is necessary for selective protection and thus, in general, revenue yields can be low relative to a small uniform tariff. Corruption and smuggling, rent seeking at a minimum, can be an inevitable result.

4.10.1.3 Uniform Protection

A uniform tariff gives equal protection to all domestic production of import substitutes and the amount of protection is known. Effective protection is 10% if the uniform tariff rate is 10%. No one can predict how the economy will evolve during a transition, the government cannot be engaged in picking winners for domestic investment, and thus uniform protection is a reasonable policy.

4.10.1.4 Consistent with Longer-Term Reform Strategy

A uniform tariff can help reinforce the VAT because of the importance of VAT taxation at the import stage. In addition, the move to a uniform tariff from a variable rate structure can further stabilize revenue as VAT procedures evolve.

---

[78] We note again that no tax is easy to administer. Customs is relatively easy to administer because it is possible to get taxpayers to pay the tax before they get the goods. In addition, complete evasion is difficult for large importers who must use the major ports for large shipments.

[79] Tax administrators and importers can still reclassify goods to the short list that attract zero tariff, and valuation is still a source of abuse. The important point being made here is that the degrees of freedom for corruption are reduced.

4.10.1.5 Relatively Efficient

A uniform tariff may not be efficient under most economic conditions. Efficiency costs, however, can be offset by two important aspects of a uniform tariff. First, administrative costs might be reduced by making compliance costs lower and speeding the flow of goods through customs. Second, the government will accrue additional revenues at a crucial time. These revenues can be used to stabilize the economy and provide the infrastructure that will accommodate enhanced economic activity.

4.10.2 Implementation Steps

The following steps should be taken to develop and implement the uniform tariff proposal.

1. Decide on the short list of exemptions.[80]

Exemptions should be limited to a short list of goods including:

- Medical supplies, and
- Basic food items consumed by the poor.

2. Reduce or eliminate nontariff trade barriers.
3. Decide on the rate and speed of implementation.

Revenues can increase significantly in many countries if a rate between 6% and 10% is chosen. It is necessary to consider whether to move to a uniform tariff in one action if the existing structure is significantly variable. One option is to implement a radical reduction of the tariffs. This is a procedure where low rates are increased, and high rates are reduced, in a series of two or three steps to arrive at the desired uniform rate. Such actions, if publicly known and with a firm government commitment, may help ease the transition to a simplified uniform structure.

4. Be clear that payment of a uniform tariff will be imposed on all government purchases as part of a tax-inclusive budget concept. It is essential that the government pay the tariff on all imports in order to eliminate negative protection created by customs exemptions for government purchases.
5. Prepare and implement a public awareness campaign. Elements of this campaign should include:

[80] It could be better in our view to have no exemptions and to provide subsidies. For example, providing subsidies for health care to low-income individuals could be more effective than a general exemption.

- The policy to be implemented (including the law and explanation).
- The context of the policy (in particular the fact that policy is being implemented along with a tax on domestic services).
- The short-term objectives (revenue and transparency in particular);
- The fact that all government levels will pay the tariff on its own purchases; and
- The medium-term objectives (the need to build the capacity and the compliance base necessary to develop other tax instruments as the economy responds).

References

Alexeev, M., Conrad, R., & Trunin, I. (2005). *VAT Accounts: Methodology and Experience.*

Atkinson, A., & Stiglitz, J. (1976). The Design of Tax Structure: Direct versus Indirect Taxation. *Journal of Public Economics, 6*(1–2), 55–75. Retrieved from https://EconPapers. repec.org/RePEc:eee:pubeco:v:6:y:1976:i:1-2:p:55-75.

Bird, R. M. (1993). Review of Principles and Practice of Value Added Taxation: Lessons for developing countries. *Canadian Tax Journal, 41*(6), 1222–1225.

Conrad, R. (2004, 5 September). [Valuation and Transfer Pricing: Memo #1 to Sergey Shatalov].

Conrad, R. & Alexeev, M. (2021). Income Tax Reform: A Proposal that Can Be Administered. Unpublished manuscript.

Conrad, R. F. (2014). Rule 18: Analysis and Recommendation (Zambia). Memorandum prepared under auspices of the World Bank.

Conrad, R. F. and Grozav, (2008). Real Property and VAT. In Krever, R. editor *VAT in Africa.* Petoria, South Africa: The Petoria University Law Press.

Diamond, P. A., & Mirrlees, J. A. (1971). Optimal Taxation and Public Production I: Production Efficiency. *The American Economic Review, 61*(1), 8–27. Retrieved from http:// www.jstor.org/stable/1910538,

Ebrill, L. P., Keen, M., & Perry, V. J. (2001). *The Modern VAT*: International Monetary Fund.

González, P. C., & Velásquez, J. D. (2013). Characterization and Detection of Taxpayers with False Invoices Using Data Mining Techniques. *Expert Systems with Applications, 40*(5), 1427–1436.

Harrison, M. G., & Krelove, R. (2005). *VAT Refunds: A Review of Country Experience (EPub)*: International Monetary Fund.

Kenyon, D. (1996). A New State VAT? Lessons from New Hampshire. *National Tax Journal, 49*(3), 381–399.

James, K. (2011). Exploring the Origins and Global Rise of VAT. *The VAT Reader (Tax Analysts)*, 15–22. doi: http://dx.doi.org/10.2139/ssrn.2291281.

Lee, H. C. (2016). Can Electronic Tax Invoicing Improve Tax Compliance? A Case Study of the Republic of Korea's Electronic Tax Invoicing for Value-Added Tax. *A Case Study of the Republic of Korea's Electronic Tax Invoicing for Value-Added Tax (March 7, 2016).* World Bank Policy Research Working Paper (7592).

McLure, C. (1987). *The Value-Added Tax: Key to Deficit Reduction?*: American Enterprise Institute.

Poddar, S. and English, M. (1997). Taxation of Financial Services Under a Value Added Tax: Applying the Cash-Flow Approach. *National Tax Journal, 50*(1), 89–111.

5
Small Business Tax

5.1 Introduction

A small business tax may be a necessary evil in the context of a collection-based tax system, at least initially. Through time we have developed a view that a country might be better served by not implementing such a charge, or at least should evaluate the option of doing nothing. We believe the supposed administrative gains from having a small business tax are either low or nonexistent, at least on a net basis. In addition, the supposed revenue gain, as well as compliance gains, from the small business tax may be offset by reduced revenue and compliance from the other parts of the tax system. Those who would not otherwise qualify may manipulate definitions to their personal benefit. At a minimum, we do not believe the imposition of a small business tax is a simplification, for the reasons described in Section 5.2.

Small business taxes are used throughout the world.[1] The most common types of small business tax, particularly in emerging economies, are patents (fixed fees) and a charge based on turnover. Our concerns about these systems are described in Sections 5.3 and 5.4. We have worked on small business taxes in a number of countries: Ukraine, Russia, and Egypt in particular. Ukraine and Russia adopted particularly bad small business taxes in our view, for reasons elucidated in Section 5.4, and these taxes are still applicable in 2021. Both of us had the opportunity to devote some effort to reformulating how a small business tax might be developed to meet at least part of our concerns; this chapter is based on that effort. We believe the small business tax as proposed might serve as a model for how a separate special small business tax might be accommodated into a tax system that is evolving.

There is a question about whether a small business tax is necessary within the framework of the collection-based system proposed in this volume. The corporate tax is eliminated and there is much emphasis on advanced payments. Thus, the crucial issue for the proposed reform is whether a business is required to register as an Advanced Payment Agent (APA). If not, then all administrative emphasis is shifted to the individual owner who might be required to report income from business. Then the issue is whether the individual exemption is sufficient to require positive tax. In effect, there should be no small business tax, only an individual exemption. In addition, if the individual credit is refundable, as recommended in later stages of

[1] See https://openknowledge.worldbank.org/entities/publication/9ea0fe5f-6c1a-5aa7-b6d9-2d96e17d2615 and https://www.oecd.org/publications/taxation-of-smes-in-oecd-and-g20-countries-9789264243507-en.htm.

Evolutionary Tax Reform in Emerging Economies. Robert F. Conrad and Michael Alexeev, Oxford University Press.
© Open Society Institute (2024). DOI: 10.1093/oso/9780192847089.003.0009

development, then the individual has a clear incentive to be registered, so the only issue is accounting for business income. The responsibility for proving the deductions should be the individual's, so the taxpayer should have a reasonable incentive to keep records, if expenses are greater than the standard deduction (as proposed in this volume). Thus, the common administrative issue is collecting information on gross revenue, particularly when there are cash transactions. The issue is addressed in part by APAs withholding on the supply of services and the definition of related parties. Therefore, the remaining issue revolves around sales that are not covered by advanced payments. That said, we do not expect countries to accept our proposals in toto. Accordingly, we believe that it is possible to improve the structure of small business taxes within existing tax reform frameworks.

5.2 Purpose of a Small Business Tax

The small business sector can be the most vibrant sector of any economy, accounting for significant domestic value added and job creation.[2] The sector is less formal than the large business sector in any economy (including large, diversified economies like the United States). Public reporting is less common, because the businesses are either family businesses or closely held firms. Accounting is not as rigorous, in the sense that outside audits are not as common and valuations may be more subjective,[3] except perhaps in cases where the owners are attempting to attract outside capital, relative to large publicly held firms. Some small businesses open and close rapidly depending on economic circumstances, others last for generations without becoming large, while some businesses evolve into large, sometimes publicly held, enterprises.

5.2.1 Justifications for Small Business Taxation

One objective of tax policy and administrative design is economic neutrality. That is, effective tax rates, including administrative costs, should be the same across sectors and activities, at least at the margin. Relative to this objective, small businesses should not be given any competitive advantage or disadvantage compared to large enterprises. The best way to achieve this result may be to include small business into the generally applicable tax system. In addition, the tax system should, to the extent possible, neither impede nor encourage the dynamic process noted above. There are some reasons to believe, however, that even a well-designed tax system might discriminate, inadvertently, against small business and thus a special tax regime might be justified for at least three reasons.

---

[2] Based on working memos (Conrad, 2005, 2006, 2015). Conrad (2006) contains a comparative survey of small business taxes throughout the world. The interested reader is referred to this document for one set of comparisons by country.

[3] The going concern value of closely held businesses or proprietorships is difficult to measure because there are neither stock market values nor comparable accounts (across businesses) upon which to base valuations.

One justification for a small business tax (SBT) is that it may decrease compliance costs for small (and medium) sized businesses, however defined. The costs of maintaining complete accounting records on an accrual basis, combined with other tax requirements, can be large relative to net income for small businesses. These costs, representing a type of significant fixed cost as well as a variable cost of maintaining reasonable records, may place a small business at a competitive disadvantage relative to large enterprises, with the result that small business investment is lower than the efficient level.

Second, a small business tax with lower compliance costs may encourage owners to move from the grey economy.[4] Third, a small business tax might be justified on administrative grounds. There may be a perception that tax revenue from small business is relatively minor and that administrative resources might be better utilized to monitor larger taxpayers. Thus, it might be preferable to reduce the administrative burden by developing simplified structures that require less administrative skill and compliance activity.

5.2.2 Arguments against Small Business Taxation

All three justifications might be questioned. It is true that advanced accounting and reporting standards may impose a relatively large burden on some small business activities, such as small shops holding inventories that are self-financed, but the purported difficulty is neither uniform nor universal across the sector. The issue may be identifying and defining small business in the first instance because it may be possible to construct books and records relatively cheaply. Some small businesses may have employees subject to wage withholding, are voluntary VAT APAs/taxpayers, are legal entities that are required to comply with stated financial regulations, have access to foreign exchange, and are able to get financing from the banking sector. Being required to file and report taxable turnover for VAT and taxable income for income tax purposes is, of course, an additional burden, but the burden may not be onerous in the context of the existing business. Businesses incapable of maintaining books of account may operate below particular thresholds to be in the tax system.[5]

Providing an incentive to shift to the formal sector may be a desirable outcome, but there are problems with using a small business tax for this purpose. First, firms operate in the grey economy for a number of reasons, including compliance costs. The total costs of taxation include the tax payment, compliance costs, and potential costs imposed by unscrupulous tax officials (or a general lack of regard by the

---

[4] The discussion is based on the assumption that there is no intention to lower effective taxes, however defined, for the sector. That is, the sector, again however defined, should pay its fair share of taxes.

[5] There is relatively cheap accounting software that can be used by small businesses. Of course, cheap is a relative concept and depends greatly on how a small business is defined. In countries where per capita income is relatively low, a computer costs multiples of per capita income. Thus, small traders, including street vendors and the like, may not be able to afford either a computer or the accounting software. In such cases, the tax administration might devote resources to helping small businesses develop simple accounts that can be used for finance as well as tax purposes.

government for taxpayer rights). Thus, one should not expect that small businesses will begin complying with the tax laws if only compliance costs are reduced, even significantly, by a small business tax. Second, large enterprises also operate in the grey economy or engage in transactions that reduce their exposure to the tax system. Thus, there is no reason to create a small business tax if the objective is to encourage market participation by all parties. Third, there may be particular benefits from moving to the formal sector, including access to finance, exposure to a broader market, and legitimacy. In addition, some potential entrepreneurs may be willing to operate in formal markets but do not have the information and training to begin the transition. That is, avoiding taxes and costly compliance is not the only reason to remain or to establish a business in the informal sector. Criminal activity in general, tradition, lack of information, poverty, lack of financial infrastructure, limited market access, and inconsistent or emerging standards may be additional complicating factors.

With regard to the allocation of administrative resources, it is true that large taxpayers account for most tax revenue.[6] The fact that most revenue accrues from large taxpayers does not imply, however, that the sector will be the source of the largest marginal increase in tax revenue from application of reasonably well-managed additional administrative resources. Nor may the large business sector be the source of the largest revenue gains in the reformed system proposed here. In our proposed collection-based system, the corporate tax is eliminated, and emphasis is placed on income at the taxpayer level (the individual level). At least at the initial stages, the issue for revenue generation is defining APAs, given the emphasis on advanced payments, and it might be the case that revenue gains by having small businesses become APAs would be significant. Once again, the issue is defining the extent of the small business sector in the context of both the particular economy and the current tax system.

The last point raises the issue of what might be wrong with the existing tax system that may be responsible for the need to create a special small business regime. It could be the case that overall improvements in policy and administration will enhance compliance for most taxpayers, including the small business sector. In addition, particular policies could reduce the need for a separate tax. For instance, a personal exemption in the personal income tax that eliminates 90% of the population from tax, combined with extensive withholding on nonwage payments, would eliminate a portion of the potential small business taxpayer groups from the tax regime, such as smallholder agriculture and informal rural markets, where the business has no employees other than family members. In addition, a targeted public education programme of tax administrators with no collection or auditing authority might begin working with small businesses to develop basic accounts that can be used to enhance personal decision making, access to capital, and tax compliance. Thus, it may be important to examine the structure and administration of the existing

---

[6] This is true for developed economies such as the US as well. For example, in 2018, 351 out of 508,473 active corporations paid 68.61% of total corporate tax. See Table 4 'Returns with Total Income after credits other than 11202, 1120-REIT and 1120-RIC' (Statistics of Income, 2018).

tax regime before imposing a separate regime with additional, sometimes cumbersome, procedures when removal of preexisting structural impediments may be more efficient.

5.3 Types of Small Business Taxes

The purpose of the SBT may be to serve as a substitute for individuals paying business taxes as part of their individual income tax or to reduce the compliance cost for small entities paying the enterprise profits tax if a separate profits tax is maintained.[7] This tax should not be designed as a tax incentive, however. That is, there should be minimal incentives for taxpayers to change organizational structure (to become a small business rather than employees or to become small corporate entities rather than large entities) in order to take advantage of lower taxes. To the extent possible, effective tax rates (both total and marginal) should be equal on the income of taxpayers who own the small business. The only purpose of the tax is to reduce accounting and compliance costs. Thus, it is important to coordinate the small business tax with the enterprise profits tax, again if this tax is maintained, or with its elimination, and the personal income tax, as well as the VAT, in order to ensure that adverse incentives are minimized.

Three common types of small business taxation are discussed below.[8]

5.3.1 Patents (Fixed Fees)

A patent is a type of fixed fee paid on a periodic basis (monthly, quarterly, or annually) in lieu of one or more other taxes. A patent system could be designed as a required minimum tax, with additional income taxes levied if income is greater than a specified threshold. Alternatively, the taxpayer might be subject to only the patent with no attempt to enforce compliance beyond the simple payment.

The primary advantage of this system is perceived simplicity. Taxpayers make a minimum contribution to the tax system and administrative costs are supposedly reduced for both the tax collector and the taxpayer.

There are some disadvantages to the system.

5.3.1.1 Regressive Impact
The tax can be perceived as regressive. As long as the taxpayer qualifies for the patent, the same amount of tax is paid regardless of income level. That is, the marginal tax rate is zero and the average rate falls as income increases. In addition, the taxpayer must pay the patent even if there are real economic losses. This fact is illustrated in

---

[7] Based on report written for Egypt (Conrad, 2006).

[8] A fourth option, presumptive measures based on physical or presumed indicators, is no longer widely used. For example, prior to 2006, Egypt determined the presumptive tax on bakeries based on the quantity of flour used. Problems with presumptive measures include: (1) the need for measures to be industry or activity specific; (2) a lack of comparability across sectors; (3) the potential for abuse and negotiations; and (4) alternative measures are preferable.

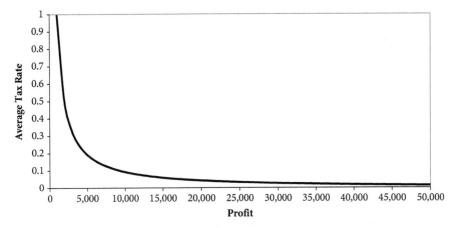

Figure 5.1 Regressive nature of a patent (fixed fee)

Figure 5.1 where the average tax rate for a patent is graphed as a function of profits. The regressive nature of the tax within the small business sector is clear.

5.3.1.2 Discriminatory Treatment

With a patent system, the same tax might be paid regardless of industry. Thus, the tax can be discriminatory across sectors due to economic differences. This may not be a particular problem when the patent is to serve as a substitute for the individual tax. In that case, industrial classification should not matter given the stated objective of individual taxation. Countries (such as the Kyrgyz Republic and Israel) have attempted to offset intersectoral discrimination (and the regressive impact to some extent) by creating sector-specific payments and payments that vary with some measure of activity. For instance, restaurants might pay one fee, small shops a different fee, and petrol stations a third fee. In addition, small shops might be taxed on measured physical area of the facility, cafes on the number of tables, and petrol stations on the size of their storage facility. This type of rate and base differentiation complicates administration. Tax administrators must be physically present in the establishment, monitor the measures to record changes, and apply different standards depending on the facts and circumstances.

5.3.1.3 Cumbersome Administration

A patent system is not easy to administer. The only administrative relief is the absence of income accounting or otherwise measuring the generally applicable tax base. It is still necessary to measure turnover (or gross proceeds) if qualification is based on turnover, to register taxpayers, to monitor activities, and to reduce evasion. In addition, there are incentives for large taxpayers to become small taxpayers if the patent is small relative to other payments. Anti-abuse rules are necessary, and these rules must be enforced. Finally, the transition to a normal tax regime may be difficult if the average tax rate for normal business is greater than the tax rate for the small business prior to moving into the normal regime.

In short, compliance activities are reduced only at the margin and there may be little reason to expect compliance increases without consistent application of administrative procedures for registration and monitoring. If monitoring procedures are not improved, incentives for corruption are not reduced. An unscrupulous tax administrator can accept bribes up to the patent amount to enable taxpayers to avoid either the tax or even larger bribes to continue in the patent system when the business otherwise does not qualify. Therefore, much of the tax revenue might be paid in cash, which means the tax administration needs to issue receipts and track cash payments. Use of the banking system may be one means to reduce corruption in this case.

5.3.2 Gross Proceeds (Turnover)

A second small business tax base is a measure of gross proceeds (or turnover).[9] The tax is measured as a fixed proportion of gross proceeds, or other measure of turnover values, and thus the tax level changes with that measure. Despite the benefit of taxes increasing with the measured base, a gross proceeds tax has similar drawbacks to the patent system. First, proceeds and profitability are not necessarily correlated and thus enterprises could be paying tax in periods when income is negative. A regressive impact could also result if costs are not proportional to proceeds.

Second, there is discrimination across industries because profit margins vary. For instance, the profit margin for a small store could be 20% because of the need to maintain space and inventories whereas the margin for a translating service could be 80% because of its labour-intensive nature. The effective tax rate (on average) will thus be four times greater for the store relative to the translating service. That is, the tax may have no relation to profitability.

Finally, administration is still cumbersome with a gross proceeds tax. The only administrative benefit is the absence of a need to compute net profit. The tax administration must still audit turnover and undertake compliance activities.

5.3.3 Net Cash Flow

Net cash flow is an alternative to accrual accounting for income purposes. Double entry bookkeeping is not required. Simple cash accounting is sufficient and can be used to measure receipts and expenses.[10] The most efficient measure of net cash flow includes immediate expensing of all asset purchases (full depreciation in the period of payment), no accruals of any kind (deferred compensation, receivables, or

---

[9] The measure should be 'gross proceeds', not turnover. Interest income and payments other than repayment of capital should be included in the measure in order to avoid taxpayers either using a small business to shelter taxable income or re-characterizing sales as other types of income.

[10] This method is used in Poland, in the United States for individuals and some smaller enterprises, and in a number of other countries, particularly countries in transition.

payables), and elimination of debt from the base. Debt can be eliminated in one of two ways: either interest expenses are disallowed, or loan proceeds are included in income with loan repayments and interest expenses deducted. The first method is more commonly used because excluding loan proceeds and repayments is more in accord with standard income accounting.[11]

This method is neither regressive in impact nor discriminatory because the base is a measure of income. There are timing differences relative to accrual accounting, accounting differences that can affect the present value of taxes. For instance, immediate expensing of assets in periods when the tax base is otherwise positive would decrease the present value of taxes relative to other conventional depreciation even though the total tax bill in undiscounted terms might be the same. That said, cash flow accounting is generally superior on economic grounds to either the gross proceeds base or the patent. The method is more complicated relative to the other methods, however, because both revenues and expenses must be measured and monitored. Thus, the administrative costs are greater.

Cash flow accounting may be easier to administer relative to accrual accounting only in certain situations, when the timing of trade and cash exchange coincide. Cash flow accounting, however, may become cumbersome to monitor when there is debt as well as working capital other than cash. In this case, two documents are necessary to substantiate an audit: first, there needs to be some record of the transaction, and second the cash receipt or payment matching that transaction must be recorded.[12] See Table 5.1 for a summary of the different options for small business taxation.

5.4 Experience in Two Countries

5.4.1 Russia

Elements of the small business tax in Russia are found in Table 5.2. When enacted, the purported benefits of the system included the three points cited above in Section 5.2. Given these limited objectives, the Russian system leaves much to be desired. Concerns include:

5.4.1.1 Optional Base
The taxpayer may choose to be taxed either based on gross proceeds at 6% or net cash flow at 15%.[13] Taxpayers with average profit margins, measured in terms of cash flow, would be indifferent between either system, other things equal. Those with greater margins would switch to the gross receipts system and those with

---

[11] It is necessary to eliminate debt elements in cash flow accounting in order to ensure that the marginal effective tax rates are zero. Effective tax rates can be negative with leverage when cash flow is used because of the double counting for capital that is possible when assets are expensed and debt is used. In addition, the incentive for thin capitalization is reduced.
[12] We believe the VAT is an accrual-based charge at least in part for this reason. That is, the VAT accrues at the time of supply regardless of when the cash is paid (see Chapter 4).
[13] Regions may have the option to reduce the rate from 15% to 5% in some cases.

Table 5.1 Summary of different options for small business taxation

Type	Potential Benefits	Potential Costs
Physical indicators	• Not accounts based (similar to physical controls for excises) • Tax is known per indicator	• While indicators may be industry specific, effective tax rates will not be uniform (except by chance) • Impact of the tax (progressive, regressive or proportional) is not known • Eligibility must be monitored • Difficult transition to a normal system
Fixed fee (patent)	• Tax is fixed and known • No audits needed for verification • Collection costs relatively low	• System is regressive (taxpayers with lower profits pay a higher effective tax rate) • Eligibility must be monitored (accounts must still be maintained and monitored) • Difficult transition to normal system (may retard enterprise growth)
Turnover (gross proceeds)	• Auditing is reduced because taxes are not related to costs	• It is a turnover tax • Impact on taxpayers is not known • Tax is proportional to gross proceeds, but effective tax could be progressive, proportional, or regressive depending on production structure • Discriminates in favour of services and low overhead operations (manufacturing and more capital-intensive industries suffer relative to services) • Eligibility must be monitored • Difficult transition if effective tax rates increase when there is a shift to the normal system
Net cash flow (using single entry accounts)	• Auditing is less complicated relative to accrual-based accounting • Tax is neutral across industries (at the margin) • No need for special rates—Statutory rate structure can be employed • Transition to normal tax accounting less onerous	• More complex relative to other systems • Eligibility must be monitored

Table 5.2 Russian simplified tax system (STS)

Topic	Description
Eligibility requirements	• Revenue threshold: company revenue must not exceed RUB 112.5 million in nine months of the year before STS is adopted • No branches or representative offices • Cannot be a bank, insurance company, nongovernmental pension fund, investment fund, security market participant, pawnbroker, organization involved in the production of excisable goods, organization involved in the mining and sale of raw materials (except 'common commercial minerals'), gaming industry, or privately practicing notaries or lawyers. • Ineligible if more than 25% of company's charter capital was contributed by other legal entities. • No state-financed companies • Must be registered in Russia. • Must employ less than 100 employees during the fiscal period • Depreciated book value of fixed assets and intangible assets must be less than RUB 150 million • Must not be involved in a production sharing agreement (PSA) • Must not have previously chosen to be part of agricultural tax system (see below)
Election/disqualification	STS may be adopted at the beginning of the fiscal period, if the company qualifies. Applications are submitted to the tax authorities from 1 Oct.–30 Nov. of the year preceding adoption. If, during the course of the accounting (fiscal) period, the company does not meet one of the eligibility requirements, it is disqualified from using STS for one year and must adjust its books accordingly beginning from the quarter in which the infraction took place. This often means incurring fines and penalties.
Accounting	• Federal Law does not require companies using STS to maintain accounting records. In practice, however, it is necessary. • Annual reporting and payment
Simplified taxation	Pay a single tax. Exempt from profits tax (except tax due on dividends and interest on securities), property tax, and VAT (except on imports). As of 1 January 2011, pay social contributions at same rate as regular regime.

Continued

Table 5.2 *Continued*

Topic	Description
Tax rate/base	• Choose to be taxed on aggregate income (6%), or income minus expenses (regions set rates from 5 to 15%) • Can change this choice annually • Income determined on a cash basis • Some expenses that are deductible in the regular regime are not deductible under STS, including expenses on: consultation services, entertainment, current market research, prior year losses, and unrecoverable debts • Assets acquired under STS are written off as expenses as a lump sum at the moment the fixed assets come into service or at the moment immaterial assets are entered into the accounting records (there are rules for how to expense assets which were acquired before the transition to STS)

Note: Russia Rubles 1 RUB = 0.013 USD (27 January 2022) http://www.xe.com/.
Source: Russian Tax Code, Chapter 26.

lower margins would prefer the net cash flow system. Thus, effective rates will vary across small business sectors based on regime choice. Those with high margins, including services, may have overall lower average and perhaps marginal effective rates.

5.4.1.2 Ownership Requirements
A direct ownership test limits another legal entity to owning 25% of a small business. Thus, a large entity, a steel company for instance, can take advantage of the benefits for small business by direct ownership. There is not an indirect ownership test. The steel company could set up a number of subsidiaries, each of which owns 20% of a series of small businesses, and in effect can own and control a small business. This might not be considered an important issue except for the other requirements for small business status.

5.4.1.3 Other Requirements
The turnover limit of 150 million rubles, adjusted for inflation (or almost 2 million dollars at the exchange rate in early 2022) creates an incentive to split into small businesses. For instance, a series of retail stores might split into separate entities under common control and be taxed under the small business tax.

The employee requirement is also problematic. Given the rates, it is possible that persons who would otherwise be employees will shift to service providers in order to take advantage of the lower effective rate (6% below 150 million as opposed to the marginal 13% personal income tax rate). Employers would prefer this system because of the social tax contributions in addition to the ability to arbitrage the personal income tax. The less than 100 employee requirement provides an additional incentive to convert employees into independent contractors.[14]

Other requirements are reasonable in the sense that an attempt is made to ensure that large taxpayers do not attempt to abuse the system. For example, mining operations and financial business are excluded.

5.4.1.4 Questionable Compliance

One supposed benefit of a small business tax is an incentive for increased compliance and reduced administrative costs. Both of these are questionable assumptions in general and in Russia in particular. A separate administration is required to monitor small business. Turnover must be verified as well as ownership structures, value of fixed capital, and the number of employees. Audit rules differ from normal profits tax so it may be necessary to develop some specialized skills in the tax administration. With regard to compliance, taxpayers who do not pay tax under the normal regime have little incentive to pay it under the small business regime. A reduction in marginal rates still results in a positive rate, and if the cost of noncompliance is not increased, then taxpayers may have an incentive sufficient to stay out of the system.[15] Incentives for corruption are not eliminated, particularly for those near the upper limits for qualification.

5.4.1.5 Transition Out

There is generally the expectation that some small businesses will become large businesses. Thus, there needs to be a reasonable transition out of the system. This transition is not present in Russian law. For instance, if a business crosses the turnover threshold, then the marginal tax at the switch point could be in excess of 1,000% given the facts and circumstances. For example, a taxpayer paying 6% of 150,000,000 would pay 9,000,000 in tax. If the taxpayer collects one additional ruble, then there is a regime change, and the profits tax could be 10,000,000 if taxable profit is 50,000,000. Thus, a one ruble increase in turnover results in a 1,000,000 ruble increase in tax. This is a strong incentive to underreport or to otherwise stay small.

5.4.1.6 Summary

In summary, the benefits of the Russian small business tax in its current form are questionable at best. In addition, it is not clear that reporting and increased administrative requirements for the general tax regime are all that onerous relative to a SBT, particularly for taxpayers with a number of employees (so withholding is required),

---

[14] The definition of employee and the incentive to arbitrage taxes including social taxes is a common problem throughout the world. In addition, it is known that the small business tax in Ukraine resulted in some shift from employees to contractors.

[15] There may also be concerns with becoming identified. Once in the system, the taxpayer will be known and will have to respond to changes in the tax laws. One might prefer to stay in the informal sector given the risk of eventually higher taxes.

that are legal entities (and thus have to file minimum corporate reports), and have turnover of 150,000,000 rubles. The net effect of the small business tax may be that tax revenues fall.

5.4.2 Ukraine

Two types of taxes are imposed by the current regime as reflected in the Presidential Decree of June 1999, which has been modified from time to time.

5.4.2.1 Fixed Fee (or Patent)
A patent system is available to taxpayers meeting the following criteria:

  a. The business must be owned by a physical person (is not a legal entity); and
  b. The business has:
- less than ten employees, and
- turnover of less than 500,000 hryvnia (UAH) (about 14,000 US dollars at the exchange rate in 2023) per annum.

The patent ranges from 20 to 200 UAH per month depending on a determination by the local council. The patent increases with the number of employees (by 50% per employee).

5.4.2.2 Proportion of Gross Revenues
A tax on sales (or turnover, however defined) is available to taxpayers meeting the following criteria:

  a. Legal entities and entrepreneurs; and
  b. Businesses which have:
- less than 50 employees, and
- turnover less than 1,000,000 UAH per annum.

The tax rate is 6% for taxpayers required (or choosing) to pay value added tax (VAT) and 10% for taxpayers not paying VAT.

5.4.2.3 Other Provisions
Other provisions of the Ukrainian system include:

  a. Taxpayers have the right to choose the regime. (Presumably physical persons who qualify for the patent may choose the proportion of gross revenue regime.)
  b. Taxpayers are required to maintain income and expense records, although the form of record keeping is not clear.

c. Taxpayers are exempt from:
- VAT (to the extent relevant),
- Profits tax, if applicable,
- Personal income tax for the owner, if applicable, and
- A variety of other taxes and fees.

5.4.2.4 Problem 1: Uncertain Tax Reduction and Uneven Impact

As noted above, lower taxation might be one benefit of an SBT. Whether a particular business in Ukraine pays lower taxes with the SBT of either form depends on the facts and circumstances of a particular taxpayer, however. For instance, it is clear that a new business operating with a loss would opt for the normal tax regime, all other things equal,[16] if that business qualified for the SBT.

Some indicators about the uncertain nature of the tax reduction and uneven tax burden are provided in Table 5.3.[17] Table entries contain the percentage of costs to revenues which make a taxpayer indifferent between paying a profits tax of 25% and paying the turnover tax of either 6% or 10%. The individual tax rate has been computed as a tax-inclusive rate, including the social tax and the enterprise profits tax of 25%. Results for both a 6% and 10% SBT rate are reported. A value greater than the reported entries will result in the taxpayer favouring the normal tax regime, other things equal, while any value less than the reported entries will favour the SBT regime. For instance, a value of 60% is reported in the case where the SBT rate is 10% and the small business is a legal entity (and thus subject to the enterprise profits tax). A firm qualifying for the SBT will opt for the small business tax if the ratio computed for that enterprise is less than 60%. Alternatively, the normal tax system will be favoured if the computed value is greater than 60%. That is, the tax under the normal regime is lower if the ratio of cost to revenues is higher than 60%.[18]

Note should also be made of the fact that the effective tax rate (measured in terms of the proportion of tax payable to tax-inclusive profit) is not uniform across firms or industries.[19] This is illustrated in Figure 5.2 where the effective rate is computed as a function of the ratio of revenue to profit (for both the 10% and 6% turnover tax rate). The statutory rate is equal to the effective rate when the ratio of revenue to profit is unity (costs are zero, not including the value of the owner's time) and increases as costs become larger as a proportion of revenue. The effective tax rate becomes infinite when costs are equal to revenue (profits are zero). Businesses with low costs relative

---

[16] We examine one issue at a time in this section. Thus, it is important to keep the concept of 'other things held constant' in mind during the discussions. For instance, a loss-making enterprise may opt for the SBT regime if compliance costs are lower, bribes to tax officials are lower, audit costs are lower, or for any other number of reasons. In addition, a loss-making enterprise may opt for the small business tax regime if taxes unrelated to income such as land rent are lower under the SBT regime.

[17] Similar results can be obtained for the fixed fee except that the fixed fee comparison would be based on total profit. For instance, suppose a small business had no employees and could choose the patent system. An enterprise profits taxpayer with profit less than 9,600 UAH would favour the normal tax system, while an individual would prefer the normal tax regime if profits were less than 5,926 UAH. Comparisons could also be made for SBT regime choice (either patent or turnover tax).

[18] Again, no profits tax should be paid if the ratio of cost to revenues is 1.0 or greater.

[19] Effective tax rates are measured either as a proportion of tax-inclusive income or as a proportion of the tax-inclusive (or tax-exclusive) return to invested capital. The proportion of tax-inclusive income is used in this chapter.

Table 5.3 Turnover tax relative to tax on profit: percentage of cost to turnover required to pay the same amount of tax

| | Normal tax regime | |
	Individual	Enterprise
SBT rate	40.5%	25%
10%	75.31%	60.00%
6%	85.19%	76.00%

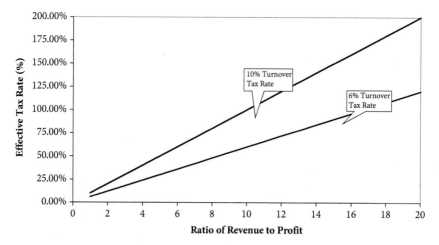

Figure 5.2 Effective tax as a function of ratio of revenue to profit: turnover tax ratio of cost to profit assumed to be 50%

to revenues (and thus high accounting profits) have lower effective rates and are thus favoured under the SBT regime. For instance, services (professional services or other types of labour services) typically have high ratios of revenue to costs. Such sectors will be favoured relative to retail trade (where inventories are important, and margins are generally lower) or manufacturing (where the ratio of revenues to cost could be near unity because of the high capital-to-labour ratio relative to service sectors).

Profit in this case is the return to the owner's human capital. To illustrate, suppose a small business owner operates a retail business and the owner adds 20 to the value of output. Suppose further that the cost of goods sold is 200. Competition would lead to the owner selling for 220 (200 cost of goods and 20 cost of time) in order to have zero economic profit. If the SBT rate is 6% on gross turnover, then the tax would be equal to (220 * 0.06 = 13.20). Profit in this case is the return to the owner's human capital. To illustrate, suppose a small business owner operates a retail business. Suppose further that the cost of goods sold is 200 and the owner adds 20 to the value of output. Competition will lead the owner to sell output for 220. If the SBT rate is 5% on gross turnover, then the tax would be equal to (or 220*0.06 = 13.20). If the profits tax is 25% for the SBT, then the tax would be 5 (or [220 – 200]*.25). The owner's

Table 5.4 Tax savings from small business tax (100,000 profit—costs 50% of revenues: income tax savings only)

Absolute tax savings	Percentage tax savings	Situation
20,500	50.62%	10% SBT rate: physical person
28,500	70.37%	6% SBT rate: physical person
38,100	94.07%	Patent: physical person: no employees
5,000	20.00%	10% SBT rate: juridical person
13,000	52.00%	6% SBT rate: juridical person

after-tax return would be either 6.8 or 15 under each regime. If, however, the small business was consulting with no costs, then revenue would be 20 and the tax would be 1.2 (20*.06) and 5 (20*.25).

Finally, any realized tax reduction can be significant for those favoured small businesses with profits. For instance, consider an enterprise with 100,000 UAH in profit. Tax savings are reported in Table 5.4 under a variety of taxpayer situations. It is clear that significant tax savings can be created by the SBT if the taxpayer is in a position to take advantage of the benefits.[20]

Two types of discrimination are created by the pattern of benefits. First, certain industries are favoured relative to others for taxpayers qualifying for the SBT. As noted, services will tend to be favoured relative to manufacturing because the ratio of cost to profits is smaller. Second, small business can be favoured relative to employment. This can be particularly important with respect to services and employment income. For instance, a person making 100,000 on a tax-inclusive basis as an employee might pay twenty times more tax than a person who is a consultant and pays the fixed fee. Both vertical and horizontal equity are violated as a result. It is important to note that such inequities arise because of the legitimate application of the SBT. Abusive practices and corruption might increase the inequities, a point noted below.

5.4.2.5 Problem 2: Complications

It has been claimed that the SBT in Ukraine is a simplification. Taxpayers will have to pay only a fixed fee or report gross income. While this is a relative simplification, the following points need to be included in any evaluation:

- Taxpayers under the normal tax regime are not required to report costs. It is sometimes argued that reporting revenues is simpler than reporting revenues and costs. This is true for any profits-based tax regime, however. There is no statutory requirement that taxpayers report costs, and taxpayers can simply report taxable revenue.[21]

---

[20] Taxpayers with a higher ratio of cost to revenue will have lower tax savings.
[21] It is true that the tax bill will increase, but the amount of increase is not clear. It depends on the amount of costs. The tax bill for service providers may not increase much; thus, it may be in the taxpayer's

- There is a statutory requirement that income and expense statements be maintained. Thus, there is little simplification for taxpayers to the extent that they obey the statute, and the statute is enforced.
- SBT taxpayers must withhold personal income tax and pay social taxes for any employees. In addition, taxpayers might have to pay VAT. Thus, much of the basis for profit accounting is already required by these statutes. Again, there is no simplification resulting from the SBT if taxpayers comply.
- The introduction of an SBT complicates tax administration and the tax system. Incentives for evasion and avoidance are created, tax administrators must monitor additional criteria, and indicators of compliance differ across taxpayer categories (SBT relative to normal taxpayer). In effect, the tax administration is being asked to administer two tax systems (see also Figure 5.3).
- Legal entities are required to maintain and to report specific activities according to the corporate law. Thus, SBT entities may have to engage in three types of compliance activities:

1. Statutory (or public) reporting,
2. SBT reporting, and
3. Standard tax reporting (in order to verify that the taxpayer qualifies for SBT).

In summary, it is not clear whether a patent system (or turnover tax) is simpler in a situation where eligibility criteria must be monitored, additional avoidance and evasion incentives are created, and reporting requirements are enforced.

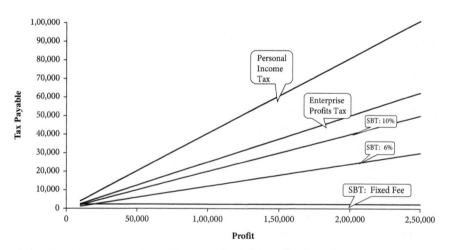

Figure 5.3 Comparison of small business tax and normal tax regime tax burden assumption: costs = 50% of turnover

interest to pay a profits tax on a gross income basis. Our other point is that there is a tradeoff between simplification, rates, and the size of the tax bill. Reporting gross revenue may be simpler, but the tax bill may be higher, holding rates fixed, relative to reporting profits.

5.4.2.6 Problem 3: Uncertainty about Increased Participation

Proponents claim two elements of the SBT create incentives for small businesses to increase their participation in the formal economy and to officially register as taxpayers: (1) lower taxes and (2) reduced compliance costs.

Such incentives, however, might not be realized for a number of reasons. Tax reductions and reduced administrative burdens may affect taxpayers at the margin but may have little total effect without increased compliance activities. That is, taxpayers who are not registered will have no incentive to pay reduced taxes if they can pay zero tax by continuing to be non-registered.

Non-registered taxpayers may also be concerned about their tax obligations through time if they become registered. Once registered, taxpayers become formally known to the tax administration. Legal tax obligations might change through time either by changes in the law or changes in taxpayer status. Thus, non-registered taxpayers may determine that any short-term gains from paying relatively low taxes in the short run are not sufficient to compensate for the increased scrutiny and, perhaps, taxes that result through time from registration. In summary, the taxpayer is making an evaluation between being registered and perhaps paying lower taxes with an SBT relative to the normal regime versus attempting to avoid taxes altogether and running the risk of being caught with an obligation to pay the normal tax plus penalties. As long as the risk-adjusted present value of avoiding registration is higher than the present value of either paying under the normal or the small business regime, then the taxpayer will not register.

5.4.2.7 Problem 4: New Incentives for Corruption and Evasion

It is claimed that corruption may be reduced by introducing small business taxes and that voluntary compliance will increase. These benefits may arise because taxpayers register and comply with the law. It was shown above, however, that the introduction of a SBT is not sufficient to even create a relative incentive for taxpayers to comply with the system. In addition, the SBT may create offsetting incentives for evasion and corruption as was illustrated in the case of the Russian SBT.

Other SBT evasion and avoidance techniques include:

- Business Splitting: One large firm might split into a number of smaller legal entities in order for each separate business to qualify for the SBT.[22]
- Abuse of Ownership Rules: The 25% corporate ownership rule can be avoided by creating a shell corporation that owns various percentages of different corporations. It is possible to establish different entities for specific transactions in order to ensure that the value of the transactions fall below the turnover limit.
- Shift from Employment: Employers and employees have an incentive for the employee to become a consultant or independent contractor in order to arbitrage the difference between the social tax plus personal income tax and the SBT.

---

[22] We understand that some retail stores in other countries organize small businesses based on cash registers. That is, each cash register is a separate small business for SBT purposes even if the cash registers are physically in the same store.

- Change in Form: A corporation (or other legal entity) might dissolve and make the employees independent contractors in order for each individual to take advantage of the SBT. Total taxes might be reduced, while the cost of running the business increases.
- Otherwise Fraudulent Transactions: We understand that the SBT is generally on a cash basis. Thus, it is possible for related legal entities to engage in the following type of transaction. Firm A (a small business) sells to Firm B for the value of 1,000. Firm B does not pay Firm A. No turnover is reported. Instead, either Firm B makes a loan to Firm A for 1,000 or Firm A sells the receivable to Firm C (a related party) for 1,000. These transactions would not be subject to SBT because the additional transactions are characterized as capital transactions and not turnover.[23]
- Increased Domestic Transfer Pricing Incentives: Related parties will have an incentive to transfer price goods and services domestically (in addition to internationally) because of the tax differential created by the SBT relative to normal taxation. For instance, a large firm could establish a group of interrelated small businesses under current rules (by using indirect ownership to avoid the 25% ownership requirement). In addition, there appears to be nothing to keep small businesses from having interests in other small businesses. The large firm could buy inputs from the small firms at high prices, thereby reducing the large firm's profits taxes, and reducing total taxes because of the rate differences.

5.4.2.8 Problem 5: Economic Distortions
Profits taxes are generally neutral with respect to input choices, given investment, but other things equal, a turnover tax induces the firm to employ less of all inputs. In addition, turnover taxes are known to cascade.[24]

Finally, the SBT might contribute to the bifurcation of the economy. Legitimate large taxpayers might avoid transactions with SBT taxpayers who sell inputs because of the cascading, even if the SBT taxpayer is a VAT taxpayer. Differential taxation combined with the uncertainty about the benefits of getting small businesses to participate in the formal economy may lead to further segmentation of the economy, a result opposite of the desired outcome.

5.5 Policy Elements of a Small Business Tax

The SBT is neither an easy tax to develop nor to administer as demonstrated by the previous discussion and the two case studies. If an SBT is contemplated, then a number of factors should be considered. First, the intent of the charge should be to serve as a substitute for individuals paying business taxes as part of their individual income

[23] Such schemes abound whenever there is a significant difference in taxation between business enterprises such as exists under the SBT.
[24] The VAT was developed as one means to reduce cascading.

tax or to reduce the compliance cost for small entities paying the enterprise profits tax. Only the former case applies in this text because the enterprise tax is eliminated. Thus, the issue is whether the small business should be an APA. Second, there should be minimal incentives for taxpayers to change organizational structure (to become a small business rather than employees or to become small corporate entities rather than large entities) in order to take advantage of any lower taxes. To the extent possible, effective tax rates (both total and marginal) should be equal. The only purpose of the tax is to reduce accounting and compliance costs. Thus, it is important to coordinate the small business tax with the enterprise profits, if it is retained, and the personal income tax, as well as the VAT, in order to ensure that adverse incentives are minimized. Third, there needs to be a reasonable method to transition from the small business regime to the generally applicable system. It is important that the tax not be an impediment for relatively efficient growth, and thus it is imperative that transitions into and out of the tax regime be structured to reduce any inhibition from changing regimes. Finally, simplified accounting is reasonable for business tax purposes in any tax system. Note that if the overall reform strategy is adopted, then there are only two issues. First, is the business going to be an APA? Second, if the business is an APA, then what is the relationship between the advanced payments and the total tax of the individual? Some notes about these issues are discussed below.

There are also a number of technical issues that need to be defined.

5.5.1 Definition of Small Business

The basic criterion for defining a small business is generally some measure of turnover. That criterion might be reasonable, but turnover should not be the basis for determining eligibility because it creates incentives for splitting businesses and shifting profit.

5.5.2 Definition of Gross Proceeds

Gross proceeds should be broadly defined to include all cash receipts except capital contributions and repayments. Qualification should not be based on the number of employees because of administrative reasons (it is difficult to define and to monitor any definition of full-time equivalent employees).

5.5.3 No Related Parties

A small business should not be owned by a large business, a group of large businesses, a wealthy individual, a group of wealthy individuals, or any combination of such persons. In addition, a group of small businesses should not be related by common ownership (or control). For instance, a husband and wife should not be allowed to treat two separate stores as separate small businesses. There need to be clear (and somewhat arbitrary) aggregation requirements and rules to ensure that the small business tax is not used as a tax shelter, that operations are not split into multiple organizations, and that large taxpayers (either individual or corporate) cannot own small businesses. The same definitions for related parties that are used for determining transfer pricing and other rules should be applied to small businesses.

5.5.4 Activities Covered by the Charge

Qualifications should be further restricted. The following persons should not qualify for the SBT:

1. Producers of excisable goods;
2. Producers of certain services (e.g., electricity and financial services);
3. Persons with large charter capital (or capital listed on stock exchanges) or large assets (such as a manufacturing plant); and
4. Persons engaged in certain activities (insurance, recipients of foreign exchange from export, professionals such as doctors, lawyers, architects, engineers, or those engaged in other specified activities).[25]

5.5.5 Bookkeeping Requirement

Books of account should be maintained and should be sufficient for determining eligibility (both initial and continuing). The books should include asset values, at least the initial purchase price or contribution value, ownership information, and gross receipts, among other information.

5.5.6 Registration

All small business taxpayers should be registered and issued taxpayer numbers. Information sufficient for monitoring should be required, including ownership structure, address of business, addresses of owners, type of organization, and other statutory information.

---

[25] It might be beneficial, as a drafting strategy, to list only those sectors and enterprise types that are to be eligible for the SBT.

5.5.7 Coordination with Other Taxes and Tax Provisions

It is important that the SBT be coordinated with other taxes in order to reduce arbitrage incentives and to reduce administrative costs. Some particular elements of coordination are noted here.

5.5.7.1 Definition of Employee
The definition of employee should be in the income tax law, not in the small business tax law. The definition of an employee is important for determining requirements for withholding and perhaps the payment of social taxes. Employees should not be eligible for small business taxation.[26]

5.5.7.2 Definition of Related Party
The same definitions for related parties that are used for determining transfer pricing and other rules should be applied to small businesses.

5.5.7.3 Rates
Tax rates should be coordinated to the extent possible to reduce arbitrage incentives, particularly when there is no individual reporting. For instance, the income tax rate and the small business tax rate should be the same, assuming the cash flow tax is employed. Coordinating rates is more difficult if the small business tax base is gross proceeds, but some rate approximating the rate on net income is desirable. If the proposed overall reform is adopted, then the APA withholding rate should be uniform across sectors.

5.5.7.4 Turnover Levels
The gross proceeds level and the exemption levels for certain taxes should be coordinated in order to provide consistent signals, to reduce complexity, and to provide a more comprehensive view of a small business. For instance, the gross proceeds level should be equal to the turnover level necessary for mandatory VAT registration. Thus, a small business would automatically be exempt from VAT.

5.5.7.5 Provision for a Tax Credit
One objective of income tax policy as it evolves is to create a unified tax system. In cases where a person has other income sources, a credit might be appropriate, and is proposed here. For instance, an individual might have wage income and small business income measured on cash flow. Both types of income should be combined into a measure of the comprehensive base and to allow a credit for the small business tax paid against total taxes due.

---

[26] The definition of an employee is difficult and all countries, including the United States, have significant problems determining whether a physical person is an employee. We believe the definition should be clear and based on objective standards in order to encourage compliance.

5.5.8 Optional Registration

Persons that otherwise qualify for small business status should have the right to be taxed under the normal system. Such a provision will ensure that persons with legitimate losses are not unduly harmed by the SBT and that persons have the option to become VAT taxpayers. A minimum duration (three years, for instance) is required for optional registration, however. This is necessary in order to keep taxpayers from coming into (or out of) the system based on current circumstances.

5.5.9 Exempt Taxes

Small business taxpayers should be exempt from other income taxes on small business income and VAT. Small business taxpayers should not be exempt from property tax, or other sales taxes or fees. Small business taxpayers also should be required to pay withholding and other taxes on behalf of employees. It is not clear how to treat the social taxes of a small business owner, however. Some countries exempt small business tax owners from social tax. A powerful incentive is created to arbitrage the tax system in this case, particularly when the exempt person qualifies for benefits. Thus, policymakers must decide whether to exempt social taxes and, if they do, they must set the small business tax rates relative to the combined rates of the exempt taxes.

5.6 A Practical Proposal

The elements necessary for a reasonable SBT are illustrated in Table 5.5.[27] Two types of small business are defined: microenterprises, basically individuals (physical persons) with gross receipts above some multiple of the exempt amount for the personal income tax;[28] and small businesses, individuals and simple partnerships, with turnover above the maximum amount required for microenterprise status but less than or equal to the turnover threshold for the VAT. Microenterprises pay a patent while small businesses pay tax calculated by applying the individual income tax rate to the cash flow base. In effect, the small business becomes an APA if the system proposed in this volume is adopted. If, however, a separate corporate tax is maintained, then individual income tax rates are applied because legal entities, other than simple partnerships, should not be allowed to register as small businesses. In effect, the small business is treated as an individual for tax purposes and no additional individual tax is required of the owner.[29]

---

[27] Again, the proposal is presented for those countries that choose to continue the practice.
[28] The multiple could be unity if micro-business is determined to be essentially labour services.
[29] At some point in the future, small business income can be integrated with the personal tax to form a more comprehensive tax base. Whether there are any revenue or efficiency consequences to treating small business separately depends on the individual rate structure. For instance, if the tax is flat rate, as we generally support (see Chapter 3) then few consequences might arise as long as the small business income plus other types of income is greater than the exemption level. It is important to note that audit rules need to be developed for personal use of business property, a necessity regardless of the tax regime.

Table 5.5 A practical proposal (based on proposal developed for Egypt in 2006)

Legislation Section	Language
Part I: Intent	In general, the legislative intent (regulatory intent) of this tax is to provide a simplified tax regime for two types of businesses, as defined in this law: micro-enterprises and small business.
Part II: Definitions	The following definitions will be used for the purposes of this law. a. Business: A business is any economic activity, profit seeking or not, with gross receipts other than wages attributable to that activity. 　i. Personal investment exemption: A capital investment, including all types of gains and losses attributable to that investment, made by a physical person who does not take an active interest in managing the object of the investment, is not a business. Examples of such an exemption include but are not limited to purchase of a personal residence, investments in equity shares of any publicly traded entity in which the physical person owns less than a 1% interest, investments in bank deposits, insurance instruments, and other financial market instruments.[a] 　ii. Personal lending and borrowing exemption: Borrowing and lending (as well as the income from borrowing or lending) for personal purposes by a physical person is not a business. Examples of such excluded activities include but are not limited to borrowing for the purposes of activities related to the personal investment exemption and lending to immediate family members and other lending to physical persons that occurs from time to time on an irregular basis.[b] b. Sole proprietorship: A sole proprietorship is defined to be the aggregation of all businesses totally owned by one physical person or collectively owned by the members of a physical person's immediate family. For the purposes of this law, immediate family is limited to spouses, and parents and their children, all of whom are residents. Immediate family does not include siblings. c. Simple Partnership: Any business organized according to the laws of the country that: 　i. Is not a legal person or a corporation, or a cooperative, or a permanent establishment, or a sole proprietorship, or a state organization, or a not–for–profit. 　ii. Includes no more than three co–owners, all of whom are resident physical persons. 　iii. Satisfies the requirement that gains and losses are shared in proportion to capital contributions. d. Small business entity: A small business entity is any legal entity other than a sole proprietorship or partnership that satisfies the following requirements: 　i. Has only one classification of stock in the case of joint stock companies; and 　ii. Has less than, or equal to, five owners all of whom are resident physical persons.

Continued

Table 5.5 *Continued*

Legislation Section	Language
	e. Cash receipts: The value, either in cash or in-kind, received in exchange for any good or service supplied by the business, including the disposal of any capital asset (tangible or intangible) attributable to business without regard to source. Cash receipts also include payments, either in cash or in-kind, from all types of capital, including interest, dividends, and royalties as well as all proceeds from loans attributable to the business except any payment received from owners in exchange for a specified good or service. Payments received from owners that are not included in cash receipts include capital contributions, loan repayments, and interest receipts.
	f. Cash expenses: The value, either in cash or in-kind, paid in exchange for the purchase of any good or service including the purchase of any capital asset (tangible or intangible) attributable to the business without regard to source. Cash expenses also include payments, either in cash or in-kind, for all types of capital expenses including interest, principal, and royalties except any payments to the equity owners other than those payments in exchange for a specified good or service. Payments to owners that are not included in cash expenses include but are not limited to: dividends (or payments that are constructive dividends), interest payments, principal repayments, a loan to the owner, and repayments of capital contribution to the owner of equity capital.
	g. Cash flow: The difference between cash receipts and cash expenses.
	h. Value of turnover: Cash receipts less any capital payment.
Part III: Effective date	1 January 2XXX
Part IV: Tax provisions	**Micro-enterprises**
I. Who is the taxpayer?	The owners of the micro-enterprise who satisfy the eligibility requirements.
a. Eligibility requirements: (Note: Eligibility requirements pertain to the taxpayer's business).	Qualify if all the following conditions are satisfied: any sole proprietorship or simple partnership with cash receipts for the previous tax year that are greater than MINIMUM and less than or equal to MAXIMUM.
	Small business
	The person if that person is a legal entity who satisfies the eligibility requirements. The physical person or persons who own the business if that business is not organized as a legal entity.
	Qualify if all the following conditions are satisfied: any sole proprietorship, simple partnership, or small business entity with cash receipts for the previous tax year greater than MINIMUM but less than or equal to MAXIMUM.

b. Exclusions: No business, entity, or person other than a sole proprietorship, a simple partnership, or a small business entity shall be eligible for either micro-enterprise or small business status. Such persons or entities include, but are not limited to:

1. Non-resident physical persons, non-resident entities (including partnerships), agents of any non-resident person, and permanent establishments of foreign enterprises and domestic legal entities.
2. Any resident physical person, simple partnership, or entity that has an economic interest, directly or indirectly, in a business or entity that is not a small business if that economic interest is greater than 1% of the total equity value of that business.
3. Any resident physical person who manufactures excisable goods (or goods subject to the highest VAT/GST rate).
4. Any resident physical person, simple partnership, or entity that chooses to be taxed under the normal regime or who chooses to be a VAT/GST taxpayer.
5. Any producer of petroleum or other mineral resources; and
6. Any person engaged in a business providing financial services (including but not limited to banks, brokers, and insurance companies).

Any sole proprietorship or simple partnership that has employees (as defined in the income tax law) is subject to wage withholding.

Any entity with any equity owned, directly or indirectly, by another entity, other than a small business entity as defined above, or any nonresident person.

Any state entity or any entity with state equity participation (where state is understood to be any level of government (national or local)) or any state-owned organization or combination of states.

c. Election:

1. Any person eligible for micro-enterprise tax status may elect either normal tax status or small business tax status.
2. The election may be made prior to the tax year in which the election becomes effective but in no case later than the end of the first quarter of the tax year.
3. The taxpayer must not have any tax arrears or outstanding tax debts in order to take advantage of the election.
4. The tax authority should grant the taxpayer's election if the taxpayer is otherwise qualified.
5. The election is binding for a period of three years unless the taxpayer becomes ineligible for micro-enterprise status.

1. Any person eligible for small business status may elect normal tax status.
2. The election may be made prior to the tax year in which the election becomes effective but in no case later than the end of the first quarter of the tax year.
3. The taxpayer must not have any tax arrears or outstanding tax debts in order to take advantage of the election.
4. The tax authority should grant the taxpayer's election if the taxpayer is otherwise qualified.
5. The election is binding for a period of three years unless the taxpayer becomes ineligible for small business status.

Continued

Table 5.5 *Continued*

Legislation Section	Language
II. What is the tax base?	No tax base.
	Cash flow as defined in regulations, including loss carryforwards to the extent applicable. Loss carryforwards:
	1. In the case of sole proprietorships and simple partnerships: None. 2. In the case of legal entities: If cash flow is negative in any tax year, then such negative amounts may be carried forward and deducted from cash flow in succeeding tax years without limitation.
III. What is the tax rate or tax?	$X per annum.
a. In lieu of taxes:	The income tax rate on all cash flow in excess of zero.
	The micro-enterprise tax is paid in lieu of all value added (general sales) taxes and income taxes attributable to the business.	The small business tax is paid in lieu of all value added (general sales) taxes attributable to the business.
b. Tax credit:	None.
		i. Sole proprietorship and/or simple partnerships: The small business tax may be credited against the personal income tax of the owner, or owners, of a sole proprietorship or simple partnership. The credit may be taken only if the income attributable to the small business (or the allocated share of the income attributable to the small business in the case of a simple partnership) is included in the gross income of that taxpayer. ii. All other persons: None.
IV. Other provisions:	
a. Registration	i. Taxpayers who qualify for either micro-enterprise or small business taxation shall be registered taxpayers and must comply with all registration requirements in the relevant tax law, tax administration law, or instructions. Registration is necessary prior to, or concurrent with, registration under this law.

ii. Taxpayers who qualify for either regime shall register for the appropriate regime with the tax administration.

1. Registration is necessary prior to obtaining any benefits available under this law.
2. The taxpayer may register by completing the necessary forms prescribed either in regulation or instruction.
3. Notwithstanding the prior provision, the registration form must contain:
   a. The name of the business.
   b. The address of the business.
   c. The location of books and records.
   d. The names, addresses, and taxpayer identification numbers of all owners as well as each owner's proportional ownership share; and
   e. Cash receipts for the tax year prior to the date of registration.
4. Registration remains valid as long as the taxpayer's status has not changed, and the business is in full compliance with the tax laws.
5. Taxpayers shall notify the appropriate authority of any change in ownership at the time ownership changes. Failure to notify the appropriate authority in a timely manner may result in revocation of the taxpayer status under this law as well as fines defined in the tax administration statute.

b. Books and records

In the case of all businesses subject to this law:
Taxpayers should keep accurate books and records as prescribed in various instructions and regulations.
Books and records shall be kept in domestic currency.
Notwithstanding the prior provision, books and records must include:

i. A single account entity book containing cash receipts.
ii. The value of turnover recorded in aggregate on a daily basis.

i. A single accounts journal with three columns. One column shall be designated for cash receipts, the second column shall be for cash expenditures. The third column shall be designated as the cash flow.
ii. The value of all other cash receipts and all cash expenses recorded at the time of either receipt or payment.

Continued

Table 5.5 *Continued*

Legislation Section	Language
	iii. Cash flow computed on a daily (weekly, monthly) basis. iv. The accounts journal may be maintained on a computer if all requirements for computerized record keeping are satisfied. iii. The value of other cash receipts recorded at the time of receipt (or constructive receipt). iv. The ledger book is supported by sales receipts, invoices and other documentation, such as the change in cash register or simple cash balances, as required in regulations. v. The ledger may be kept on a computer if the requirements for computerized record keeping are satisfied.
c. Movement between micro-enterprise and small business taxation	a. If a business registered as a micro-enterprise becomes ineligible for micro-enterprise status and eligible for small business taxation (or elects small business taxation even if a business is still eligible for micro-enterprise status), then the taxpayer shall notify the appropriate tax authority within 30 days of the change in eligibility. b. The taxpayer shall seek registration for small business taxation status concurrently with notification to the appropriate tax authority. c. Taxation under the small business taxation regisme commences on 1 January of the tax year immediately following the date when eligibility changed. d. The business will maintain the new status as long as the taxpayer remains eligible for that status, but in no case shall the taxpayer return to micro-enterprise status within four years of the date when eligibility changed. e. The tax liability for the transition period may, at the taxpayer's election, be equal to one-half (50%) of the tax computed with reference to each regime. f. If a taxpayer registered as a small business becomes eligible for micro-enterprise status and wants to exercise that election to become a micro-enterprise, the taxpayer shall notify the appropriate tax authority of the change in eligibility and the desire to make that election. The small business taxpayer may become a micro-enterprise, with permission of the tax department, provided the taxpayer did not have micro-enterprise status for at least four years prior to the year when the taxpayer becomes eligible for micro-enterprise status. The taxpayer may implement the change of his status only as of 1 January of the tax year immediately following the year when he becomes eligible for micro-enterprise status.

d. Movement from either micro-enterprise or small business taxation to the normal tax regime	a. If a business registered as a micro-enterprise or as a small business becomes ineligible for its current status and eligible for the normal tax regime (or elects to be taxed under the normal tax regime even if the business is still eligible for its current status), then the taxpayer shall notify the appropriate tax authority within 30 days of the change in eligibility or within 40 business days of 31 December of the desire to elect to be taxed under the normal regime.[c]
	b. The taxpayer shall seek registration for the normal tax regime concurrently with notification to the appropriate tax authority.
	c. Taxation under the normal taxation regime will commence on 1 January of the tax year immediately following the date when eligibility changed.
	d. The business will maintain the normal taxpayer status as long as the taxpayer remains eligible for that status, but in no case shall the taxpayer return to prior or other taxpayer status within four years of the date when eligibility changed.
	e. The tax liability for the transition period may, at the taxpayer's election, be equal to one-half (50%) of the tax computed with reference to each regime.
	f. If a taxpayer registered as a normal taxpayer (or has elected to be taxed under the normal tax regime) becomes eligible for either small business or micro-enterprise status and desires to make that election, then the taxpayer shall notify the appropriate tax authority of the change in eligibility and the desire to make the election. The election may be exercised, with permission of the tax department, provided the taxpayer did maintain normal taxpayer status for at least four years prior to the year when the taxpayer becomes eligible for and expresses the desire to change the status. The taxpayer may implement the change in his status only as of 1 January of the tax year immediately following the year when he becomes eligible for either micro-enterprise or small business status and expresses the desire to change his status.
e. Administrative provisions	Services for small and micro-enterprise taxpayers:
	i. A special taxpayer services division shall be established within the tax administration to provide educational and other services to persons who qualify or may qualify for either micro-enterprise or small business taxation.
	ii. Services shall include, but are not limited to:
	1. Maintenance of registration records,
	2. Assistance with registration,
	3. Taxpayer education, and
	4. Assistance with compliance.
	iii. Notwithstanding the previous provision, staff of the special taxpayer services division may engage in neither audit nor collection activities with respect to small nor micro-enterprise businesses.
f. Tax year:	1 January until 31 December of each year.

Table 5.5 *Continued*

Legislation Section	Language
Payments	Fifty per cent (50%) of the fixed amount is due and payable on 30 June and 31 December.	Small business taxpayers shall make quarterly payments equal to the cumulative tax due based on cumulative cash flow during that quarter. The net amount payable will be the cumulative tax to date less credit for any prior payments. In no case shall refunds be made during the calendar year. Tax is due and payable on: 31 March, 30 June, 30 September, and 31 December
Annual reconciliation	None.	The fourth quarter payment shall be deemed the final payment for the calendar year, representing the annual reconciliation for the tax year. Payments will be accompanied by appropriate reporting forms as prescribed in regulations.
Audits[d]		
g. Mergers, acquisitions or re-organizations		a. Taxpayers shall notify the tax authority within 30 days of any merger, acquisition or reorganization of the business. b. Taxpayer status must be determined with respect to the merged business or each separate reorganized business. There is no presumption that the taxpayer status of the preexisting business will be maintained. c. Any outstanding tax liability becomes the legal liability of the successor entity or jointly for the reorganized entities.
h. Liquidations or cessation of business activity	Cessation without liquidation: The tax administration shall be notified of the cessation of activities within 30 days of the date of cessation. 1. The semi-annual fixed fee for the period when the closure occurred is due and payable at the date of closure. 2. Owners must report on the continued status of the business.	No effect.

i. Liquidations and other permanent closures:	The tax administration shall be notified of the permanent closure or of the intent to liquidate within 30 days of the cessation of the business. Any outstanding tax liability becomes the legal responsibility of the owners.
	The fixed fee for the relevant semi-annual period shall be due and payable at the time operations cease.
	1. The cumulative tax for the year is due and payable within thirty days of the time operations cease.
	2. A final return shall be filed within thirty days after operations cease.
j. Anti-abuse provisions	a. Disguised wages: Physical persons who provide labour services and who would otherwise qualify as an employee under the tax law are prohibited from qualifying for either the small business or the micro-enterprise tax regime with respect to those labour services.
	b. Forced aggregation: The Head of the Tax Authority has the right to aggregate businesses for the purposes of either the micro-enterprise or small business tax if, after taking into account relevant facts and circumstances, it is deemed that the disaggregated businesses were organized for the purpose of qualifying for either the micro-enterprise or small business tax regime.
	c. Certain abusive transactions: The Head of the Tax Authority has the right to change certain transactions if, after taking into account relevant facts and circumstances, it is deemed that transactions were made (or recorded) for either the purpose of reducing the tax liability or maintaining a particular status. Such transactions include, but are not limited to:
	i. Year-end straddles,
	ii. Deferred payments schemes, and
	iii. Excessive acceleration of expenses.[e]
	d. Other anti-abuse provisions as provided in the general tax laws apply.
k. Violations:	All general tax violations should apply (including but not limited to failure to file, failure to register, late payments, under reporting, and criminal violations).

Continued

Table 5.5 *Continued*

Legislation Section	Language
l. Miscellaneous provisions	a. All amounts stated in domestic currency shall be adjusted each year for inflation. The minister shall determine the method of indexation and the method shall be publicly known. b. Activities, businesses, and enterprises exempt under the income tax law are exempt from either special regime. c. Types of income exempt under the income tax law are exempt under the small business tax. The types of expenses that correspond to the above types of income are not included in cash receipts.

m. Transition Provisions	a. Taxpayers taxed under special regimes: No transition rules.
	b. Taxpayers currently subject to normal taxation:
	  i. Simplified books of account shall begin on 1 January 2XXX.
	  ii. Accruals of either revenues or expenses reported for the tax year 2XXX-1 shall be deducted from cash flow for 2XXX if realized in 2XXX. Such accruals will be ignored if not realized after 31-12-2XXX.
	  iii. Repayments of loans outstanding (either owned or owed) as of 31-12- 2XXX-1 and for debt service on such loans paid or received after 1-1-2XXX will be taken into consideration for cash flow purposes in the tax period realized.
	  iv. The book value of any, and all, assets as of 31-12-2XXX-1 will be ignored for the purposes of computing cash flow in 2XXX and beyond.

[a] Regulations are not supplied but will be a necessary part of implementation. Footnotes will be used to indicate the need for particular regulations.
[b] May need a bright-line test elucidated in a regulation and instructions.
[c] A different election procedure may be necessary if this provision becomes too complicated.
[d] To be supplied by a tax administrator with legal training.
[e] A regulation will be necessary as well as, perhaps, a bright-line test.

5.7 Summary

Policymakers considering adopting a small business tax or modifying the existing tax should first ask about the limitations of the existing income and indirect tax regime before adopting what can be in effect a separate regime that is not coordinated with the rest of the system. It might be better to have no special treatment of small business and simply work on productive margins to increase administrative capacity of both the tax administration and the taxpayer slowly through time.

Second, policymakers should be aware of the need for public education about the nature of the tax system and how to comply. It is now common for tax administrations to be organized by establishing a large taxpayer unit. Some of the staff not in the large taxpayer unit might be organized into a cadre of trainers who have no authority to collect taxes but who are charged with working with small businesses to establish books and records necessary for determining profit for both individual and tax purposes.

Third, and consistent with one theme of this volume, is a need to begin developing a systematic data system, which, although simple or rough, can provide indicative information about the state of a small business tax system and the system more generally. Some of that information is illustrated in Box 5.1.

Box 5.1 Helpful Information

1. Number of registered SBT taxpayers by industry and year of registration.
2. Number of SBT taxpayers who have graduated to the regular tax system.
3. Number of SBT taxpayers who were formerly registered as regular taxpayers.
4. Tax revenues by fee.
5. Tax revenues by industry.
6. Number of audits performed on SBT taxpayers.
7. Profits and losses of SBT taxpayers.[30]
8. Ratio of cost to revenues for industries in (both SBT taxpayers and others).
9. Employees in the SBT sector by industry.
10. Number of SBT taxpayers who are juridical persons.
11. Number of SBT taxpayers who are physical persons.
12. Number of SBT taxpayers who were VAT taxpayers prior to the SBT registration but who are no longer VAT taxpayers.
13. Number of SBT taxpayers (by industry) who are VAT taxpayers.
14. Number of SBT taxpayers who are APAs under the system proposed in this volume.

---

[30] It should be possible to obtain such information because the law clearly states that accounts must be kept.

References

https://openknowledge.worldbank.org/entities/publication/9ea0fe5f-6c1a-5aa7-b6d9-2d96e17d2615.

https://www.oecd.org/publications/taxation-of-smes-in-oecd-and-g20-countries-9789264243507-en.htm.

Conrad, R. (2005). [Memorandum: Small Business Taxation (Ukraine)].

Conrad, R. (2006). Proposals for a Micro and Small Business Tax Regime.

Conrad, R. (2015). *Small Business Tax Proposal*.

Statistics of Income. (2018). *Corporation Income Tax Returns*. Washington, DC

6
Mining and Natural Resources

6.1 Introduction

There is an argument for not having a separate chapter devoted to mining contractual payments in a volume on general tax reform. Our view is that mining should be treated like any other industry. Mining operations should be APAs, and the owners of the entities engaged in mining should be taxed on the net income from mining as part of CMDI. In addition, owners of mining assets should include the contractual payments accrued from a producer into CMDI and should be taxed. In most cases, this means that mineral revenue should be included in the government's tax return because the resources are held in trust for the population. Again, this objective is achieved by having government, like any other pass-through entity, be a registered APA as well as a taxpayer, like nonprofit organizations in general.

There are three reasons why we included this chapter. First, Conrad began his career working on what has been labelled mineral taxation and reexamining the issues has been a constant part of his professional life. The countries where he worked on mining issues include: Indonesia, Russia, Mongolia, Zambia, Mozambique, the Dominican Republic, Timor-Leste, Ukraine, Nigeria, Guinea, Tanzania, Sierra Leone, Liberia, Saudi Arabia, the United States (Alaska and the Navaho Nation), China, Romania, Afghanistan, Ecuador, Myanmar, Albania, the Kyrgyz Republic, Kazakhstan, Niger, Iraq, Canada, Ireland, and Jamaica, among others.

Second, mineral revenues, including taxes and contractual payments, are a significant proportion of total revenue in a number of emerging economies. Such economies may be poorly diversified, so changes in mineral prices have significant effects on tax payments from other sectors. Accordingly, the structure of mining contracts, both revenue and risk structure, can be important elements in the evolution of a collection-based tax system.

Third, from the beginning of our careers, we have been bothered by the claims that a significant amount of natural resource revenue consists of economic rent. We did note in our early work the distortionary effects of ad valorem charges, often called royalties. But as an American where significant mineral rights are vested in private hands, Conrad noted that the analysis of distortions presents a situation where the government is imposing a tax, because the government has no property interest in the resource base, leaving private arrangements between the individual resource owner and the producer opaque. That is, in the United States, the US federal government (or state governments) do not typically own reserves on land that is privately owned,

Evolutionary Tax Reform in Emerging Economies. Robert F. Conrad and Michael Alexeev, Oxford University Press.

so there are no contracts between the government and the producer for such properties.[1] The contract is a private transaction, and the US federal government imposes tax on the income of both parties to the contract: the individual resource owner and the individuals who own the entity that produces the reserves. In addition, natural resources are part of an economy's capital stock. It may be a gift from nature, but that truism does not imply that the opportunity cost of extracting the reserves at any point in time, if at all, or the cost of risk bearing evident in contracts, is zero. These are real costs, and the owner should receive a risk-adjusted competitive return to invested capital before there is any discussion of rents or surplus. Mineral rights are vested in the state in most other countries, however, so it seemed to us that claims made to justify the Resource Rent Tax (RRT)[2] assume that the government is effectively giving away title to the reserves and certainly any fiscal responsibility from resource ownership in exchange for the possiblity that some empirical measure of surplus exists.[3]

Conrad's early advice in the natural resource area was certainly mainstream, however. In Indonesia, for instance, he supported a reduction in royalties and increased use of income instruments. This recommendation was not based on the supposed methodological superiority of income-based charges, but on the fact that the form of the charge could be legally described as an income-type tax and thus creditable for foreign tax credit purposes.[4] Conrad gained more confidence in his thinking through time, and so began to change both his approach to reform and his advice to include royalties as a fundamental element in developing mineral policy. The arguments for high-grading and other distortions from royalties seem to him to ignore the real costs borne by a resource owner, either individually or in the aggregate, including the forgone value of the future use of the remaining reserves, the opportunity cost of using the land and water for other purposes, and the cost of bearing risk.[5] The fact that resources are both gifts from nature and held by the state are irrelevant to the efficiency analysis of mineral extraction from this point of view. Treating a royalty as a tax is equivalent, in our view, to referring to electricity prices or water prices charged by a state-owned utility as distortionary taxes.

This perspective implies that there should be a separation of 'taxes' from 'returns to factors of production'. For example, countries that have national electric companies

---

[1] There are contracts for offshore oil properties and for properties on federal and state lands. The rules for federal lands are contained in the Mining Law of 1872. The federal government essentially gives away the resources based on the Mining Law of 1872, creating a significant redistribution of income from the people of the United States to investors in properties covered by the law.

[2] Garnaut & Clunies-Ross (1983).

[3] The implicit assumption is the belief that all the payments for the reserves are rent. Thus, there are no opportunity costs to the resource owner in total, on average, or at the margin. In effect, the government owning a marginal deposit with 100,000,000 tons of crude oil, can let the marginal deposit be developed, and gets zero in return because the wealth of the economy is not reduced.

[4] While legally a creditable tax, economically speaking such income-based charges are not taxes in our view. The state holds the mineral rights and forms a joint venture with the investor. Thus, the balance sheet of the joint venture is equal to the capital value of the investment plus the value of the mineral rights. For example, if the income sharing rate is 25%, then by assumption 25% of the initial investment is in the value of mineral rights.

[5] For a formal presentation of the approach, see Conrad, Hool, & Nekipelov (2018).

do not, and should not, include the price of electricity as a distortionary tax, and public finance experts devote considerable effort to public sector pricing of such flows. Flows from mineral deposits are no different from our economic perspective. The fact that the quantity of reserves is unknown, the government does not 'produce' mineral resources above the ground, and has, if any, only a passive equity interest in the assets of the entity that extracts, processes, and markets those reserves is relevant for the computation of the efficient flow price, but that per unit price is not distortionary. This approach and the recommendations that are implied are discussed here.

6.2 Terminology

The vocabulary for particular mining charges, such as royalties and windfall charges, is not uniform, so knowing the name (e.g., royalty) does not necessarily explain how the charge is computed (the base). Thus, it is important to account for these differences in the discussion that follows. For the purposes of this chapter, the following definitions will be used, in addition to the more commonly known concepts of income taxes, withholding taxes, and equity participation, among others:

> Royalty: A payment to the owner of the reserves (usually some level of government)[6] that is the indicator of the purchase price (or relative price) of a natural resource at the time of extraction.
> Excess or Windfall Charge: A charge in addition to (or perhaps as a substitute for) a royalty and all generally applicable taxes. Application of the charge will depend on some legislatively defined trigger related to the specified base.

6.3 Fiscal Analysis Framework

A government of a country endowed with mineral assets might perform five different economic functions, four of which have direct financial consequences:

- Manage the resource on behalf of the population;
- Impose and administer the general tax regime;
- Take equity positions in some, or all, mining operations;
- Use state enterprises as operating companies; and
- Regulate the mining industry (health and safety, environmental, and other regulatory functions).

Payment stream elements, the total cash flow to government, and the risks borne by the economy will be affected by how many functions are undertaken and the choice of instruments. The payment streams are only a partial measure of the gross

---

[6] The differentiation of payments into royalties and taxes will be explained below, in addition to how property rights allocation differs around the world.

benefit to government, however. That is, total gross economic benefits to the country could be greater than the financial gain to the government because the financial gain to the government is a measure only of the distributional benefit created by sharing the total revenue accrued from production and sale. For instance, a government might forego tax revenue in order to require a mining company to purchase inputs from domestic sources.[7] Such a requirement might benefit domestic suppliers, on a net basis, if the value of supplying the goods and services is greater than their opportunity costs. Economic costs are imposed as well and thus it is essential that the gross benefit be balanced against the real costs in order to ensure positive economic returns, including the growth of the economy.

Some benefits and costs of each of the four revenue-generating functions are summarized in Table 6.1 and a description is provided below.

Table 6.1 Summary of potential government functions in the natural resource sector

Function	Financial payments to government	Financial and opportunity costs
Ownership function (stewardship of the reserve base)	Financial returns to ownership • Bonus • Auction bids • Royalties (including variable royalties) • Excess profit schemes	• Reduction in wealth via accumulated depletion • Lost diversification
General tax function	• Personal income tax • Profits tax • VAT • Tariffs • Property tax	• Distortions in private sector decision making • Administrative and compliance costs
Passive investment function	• Dividends • Capital gains • Interest (if passive investment is via loans) • Price participation agreements	• Less diversification (both domestic and international) given investment budgets • Foregone current government expenditures (such as debt reduction or education)
Operating company	• Returns to management (in addition to dividends and capital gains)	• Further losses in diversification • Lost efficiency in public sector enterprises

[7] In addition, fiscal revenue losses might be direct or indirect. A direct revenue loss would result if a government explicitly reduced a payment in return for domestic sourcing. The loss might be indirect if the government simply required domestic sourcing; since costs to the firm are higher than without the rule,

6.3.1 Manage the Resource on Behalf of the Population: Returns to Ownership

A country must determine how mineral ownership rights are allocated. State ownership of subsurface rights is common in most countries. Ownership may be at the national level (Zambia) or at the subnational level (Canada). Mineral ownership means that a government's assets (or balance sheet) will include the value of the subsurface rights in addition to other assets, such as assets of state enterprises, government buildings, and the power to tax (an intangible asset). If a deposit is developed, then the government may receive financial flows from a variety of sources, including but not limited to:[8]

- Land rents;
- Bonus payments;
- Auction values;
- Royalties; and
- Resource rent charges (often called resource rent taxes).

The type of payment, the timing, and the amounts will depend on a country's legal framework, how extraction rights are awarded, the quantity and quality of the deposit, and other factors. It is important to note that the government is responsible for the speed with which resources are exhausted[9] and thus can use these instruments, along with production quotas to the extent quotas are not redundant, to influence how much operators develop and determine extraction within and between time periods.

Resource extraction is not costless to any economy. At a basic level, the wealth of the economy is reduced with cumulative depletion. In addition, the government closes off options for different contractual forms or methods for awarding contracts to different investors by determining a particular contract form and choosing a particular operator (either public or private sector entity). The government, and society more generally, foregoes the use of surface rights and other rights resulting from the need for such assets in the production of subsurface minerals. Finally, the government must administer the fiscal regime as well as monitor, and hopefully actively husband, the resource base.

---

profits taxes paid by the mine would be reduced by more than the increase in taxes paid by the supplier. See Gaddy and Ickers (2006).

[8] The value of the reserve base might change even if the deposit is not developed. For instance, governments should expect a competitive return from holding reserves because, at a minimum, reserves are assets from an economic perspective. Thus, a government holding assets in the ground is foregoing selling those assets or converting them into cash or other tangible (or intangible) assets that accrue cash income. Therefore, a government needs to be aware of this opportunity cost of developing deposits and should hold reserves as long as the returns are at least as great as those foregone benefits.

[9] The reserves belong to the people of the country and part of that property right includes the rate of depletion. The government can unbundle the property right and give that right to a contractor (or someone else). The right has value, however, so there should be gains to the country in exchange for relinquishing that right.

At an aggregate level, extraction may change the diversification of the economy's asset base. A resource discovery increases the variety of assets in the economy, which is reversed as the reserves are depleted. Significant resource discoveries can affect domestic relative prices, which can have adverse impacts on nonresource sectors. For instance, the price of nontradables may rise because, at least in the short run, the stock of nontradable assets may have to be reallocated between preexisting economic activities and new mining activities resulting from an appreciation of the real exchange rate. Although overall wealth in the economy may increase due to a resource discovery, sector-specific losses may result, in traditional export sectors in particular, and such costs are part of the real cost of resource development (and to the extent they occur, should be part of any mineral evaluation and policy).

6.3.2 Impose and Administer the General Tax Regime: Return for Rights to Taxation

The right to tax is vested in the state. This asset enables governments to accrue economic resources from the private sector without directly supplying goods and services in exchange. That is, unlike the private sector, the government does not have to supply a specific good or service to in order to generate revenue. Most governments choose alternative means to collect tax revenues, including:

- Direct taxes, such as profits and personal income taxes;[10]
- Indirect taxes, such as VAT, excises, and tariffs; and
- Property taxes.

With the exception of certain discriminatory taxes such as excises (fuel, tobacco products, and alcoholic beverages) and selective tariffs, taxes (direct taxes and VAT in particular) are generally applicable. That is, tax policy is (and should be) designed to accommodate economy-wide effects. Thus, mining should be treated like any other sector with respect to overall tax policy, particularly with respect to the use of direct taxes and VAT.

Three elements of the income tax are particular to mining: the treatment of expenses for exploration, development, and reclamation. All three elements, however, have similar counterparts in nonmining industries: exploration is effectively searching and is similar to research and development; development is a type of self-constructed asset; and reclamation is similar to expenses related to plant closure (disposal of hazardous waste, restoration, and other issues). A significant issue in the VAT treatment of mining is related to the export nature of production and the use of imported inputs, particularly during the initial investment stage. VAT refunds

[10] Capital gains taxes are really income taxes and are defined as such for current purposes. The treatment of capital gains, particularly for trade in mining licences, is becoming an important issue.

would be significant if standard VAT treatment is afforded to the mineral sector. These problems, however, are similar to any new investment where imported inputs are required, and the output is designed for export. In emerging economies, this is relatively common with manufacturing in general.

The costs of developing a generally applicable tax system include administration and compliance costs. Such costs are complicated by the asymmetric nature of the information structure. Taxpayers have access to information about revenues and costs while tax administrations may have little or no means to independently verify that information. In addition, incentive compatibility is absent in a tax system because there is not a direct transfer of goods or services in exchange for tax payments. An additional cost of a generally applicable tax system is the adverse economic incentives created by lack of direct exchange. Incentives are created to change investment and labour supply decisions, which may reduce real net national income.

6.3.3 May Take Equity Positions in Some, or All, Mining Operations

Some countries, such as Zambia, have chosen to take equity positions in particular mining enterprises. Potential financial gains include dividends from shares and capital gains.

Such gains are not costless, even if shares are so-called free equity. The government as a minority shareholder may be adversely affected by decisions made by those with majority positions, particularly in countries where transparent corporate governance is lacking, and shareholder protection is weak. The government and economy more generally may bear two additional costs. First, the government now owns rights to physical capital and intangible assets held by the mining company in addition to holding the reserves. Thus, the government is taking a longer position in mining and there will be a higher correlation between overall government revenues and mineral prices (or returns to mining more generally), unless the government pursues an active risk diversification strategy. Second, the economy will be less diversified, all else equal. Funds used to invest in mining enterprises could have been used to invest in other domestic and international assets (with perhaps higher marginal returns) in addition to reducing the society's exposure to mineral price risk.

Finally, there is an additional cost that is common to both passive and active equity positions. The government may be placing itself in a direct conflict of interest. Taxes reduce profits and environmental standards may reduce profits. Thus, the government must actively trade off implementing effective tax and regulatory policies with reduced financial gains from asset ownership.[11]

---

[11] It is sometimes claimed that the ability to influence corporate decisions via board membership afforded by share ownership is a benefit for government. Influence is limited, however, when the government is a minority shareholder. It should also be noted that the government is a sovereign state and has the power to regulate and influence corporate decisions directly by government action. This power,

6.3.4 May Use State Enterprises as Operating Companies

State enterprises may take a majority interest in mining enterprises and may themselves become operating companies. Potential dividends and capital gains increase with larger equity interests and the government can directly affect the operating decision of the enterprise, which in turn may affect both the level of financial benefits and their distribution.

The costs of using state enterprises as operating companies include greater financial costs (relative to passive equity ownership), making the economy even more dependent on mineral production for government revenues. That is, this strategy increases risk bearing in minerals, unless mitigated by other means, and decreases the diversification of the economy. Potential conflicts of interest are greater relative to passive equity participation. In addition, there is the risk that state-operated companies will be less efficient relative to private sector counterparts unless those enterprises are placed in competitive situations in both the output and input markets.

6.3.5 Summary

In summary, governments may accrue financial benefits from mining in different ways.[12] If form follows function, then the structure and levels of the financial flows will depend on the different types of functions undertaken by the government. This implies that concentrating on the 'total take' may be inappropriate because the economic objective is to maximize the net social benefit from mining (or any other activity), and the 'total take' is a measure of the gross financial benefit without regard for the structure of the costs required to accrue various components of the gross benefits.

In addition, cross-country comparisons of total take may be misleading unless adjustments are made for the number and structure of functions undertaken by the government. For instance, the US federal government does not hold mineral rights on private land and therefore does not collect mineral factor payments. In addition, there are no state-owned mining enterprises in the United States. Chile, on the other hand, has both a state mining enterprise and state ownership of reserves. Thus, comparing the gross benefits (or total take) between the United States and Chile would be misleading absent adjustments for the payment streams which flow to private parties in the US (royalties and returns to ownership of mineral enterprises) but to the state in Chile. That is, the total take to the economy could be the same in the US as it is in Chile, but the distribution of that revenue is different, resulting in a different measure of government revenues.

Countries vary with respect to their fiscal regimes and these differences in function may reflect social choices, such as mineral ownership patterns, policy choices,

---

if properly and appropriately applied, may be more important relative to the benefits of holding minority positions.

[12] Some international comparisons are found in Conrad (2014).

and administrative constraints. For instance, the United States federal government does not impose royalties except when minerals are held by the federal government.[13] Given these differences, one might conclude, as we have, that there is no international 'best practice' for treatment across the range of potential instruments used by governments. Governments appear to choose to undertake different functions, which lead to differences in both the type of instrument employed and the risk borne by the state.

6.4 Principles for the Design of a Fiscal Regime

In terms of project finance and financial returns, the five elements of the framework discussed in the last section can be achieved using three general fiscal structures:[1415]

- Returns to ownership,
- Generally applicable taxes and fees; and
- Returns to equity participation.

The economic function and basis for evaluating each instrument is summarized below.

6.4.1 Royalties: Returns to Ownership

These payments are returns, risk adjusted, for the ownership of mineral resources and include royalties or perhaps some type of implied equity participation.[16] These returns are in effect factor payments for an input into the production process and, if set reasonably, are not taxes in any sense of the term. In general, royalties are based on some measure of output value (usually via a netback price, measured output value, or on a net smelter return basis in the case of some nonfuel minerals) or some measure of output value less what are effectively short-run costs.

For instance, it is common for royalties to be paid to private landowners in the United States and overriding royalties are paid to investors who retain an economic interest in production once production rights are sold. In addition, ad valorem charges are used in contracts between miners and downstream producers (smelters and other refiners) and are understood to be mutually advantageous 'price

---

[13] The standard example is offshore petroleum. The US federal government imposes a royalty equal to 16 2/3% of the measured price as compensation for extracting the reserves.

[14] This material is based on Conrad (2008).

[15] It is common to structure economic analysis via targets and instruments. If there are three targets, then there need to be three instruments to solve the problem unless two or more instruments are perfectly correlated. In addition, if there are three targets and only two instruments, then mathematically the system is under-identified and cannot be solved. Under-identification is not a problem here. Rather, there are a variety of instruments within each of the three groups, such as income taxes, the RRT, and direct equity participation.

[16] The RRT is effectively a carried interest. The accrued rent charge (ARC) discussed in Section 6.5.2.4.c.i is a type of equity ownership (Alexeev & Conrad, 2017).

participation' provisions. Thus, royalties might include some risk-sharing elements in addition to capturing the return to a scarce production factor.

Royalties have been criticized (Otto, 2006; Conrad et al., 2018) because of the incentive to high grade, to inter-temporally reallocate extraction, and to reduce total recovery from the mine. Such criticisms have been one impetus for the development of profits-based factor returns such as the RRT (Garnaut & Clunies-Ross, 1983) and production sharing.[17] Being profit or net present value (NPV) based, the investor has an incentive to use reserves until the value of their marginal productivity is zero. Such conditions have been used to justify a shift from extraction-based royalties to excess—or profits-based charges. These perceived gains are offset by the cost of shifting resource factor payments until later in the life of the mine and of shifting more risk, relatively speaking, onto the resource owner. The latter effect results because the resource owner risks supplying their reserves to the producer while receiving a lower or zero payment in present value terms relative to the royalty.

The use of net short-term profits-based royalties, such as those employed in the United States for offshore petroleum and in the British Columbian royalty system, or excess profits charges like the RRT, might be claimed to be reasonable from an investor perspective, however. In effect, a net short-term profits charge is proportional to the value of extraction at the margin. Thus, if the value of extraction is low or zero, then little or no payment is made. This is a demand-based notion with little or no regard for supply because the opportunity cost to the resource owner is either low or nonexistent. In the extreme case, a marginal mine can be exhausted without any payment to the resource owner.

It is important to note that the emphasis on high grading and reduced total yield is viewed as a loss either from the investor's perspective or from the perspective of both the investor and the resource owner. The mistake is that tax analysis is used to derive the results (Conrad & Hool, 1981). In effect, the party who collects the royalty has no opportunity costs; the government is simply a tax collector with no economic interest in the property. In addition, most analyses, including the one presented here, begins with the use of present value maximization from extracting the reserves. One objective of using this perspective is that the willingness to pay for reserves, both in total and at the margin, is obtained. That is, part of the present value, and all of the present value in the case of constant returns to scale, can be attributed to an unpaid factor: the resource in the ground. Thus, if reserves are not physically scarce from the demander's point of view, and it appears that they are not physically scarce, then the demander will demand reserves until the value of the marginal product of reserves is zero. Any per unit charge will lead to high grading and premature mine closure from this perspective.

---

[17] It is perhaps ironic that ad valorem royalties are claimed to be inefficient when imposed by government, but such claims are rare in the private sector. There is, of course, the intermediate microeconomics assignment problem demonstrating that an author who receives a royalty for book sales prefers sales maximization to the publisher's objective of profit maximization. There is also the famous share cropping result initially noted by Marshall. The latter result can be shown to be misleading, at a minimum, if the value of the land is endogenous (subject to depletion with use). There are also principal-agent issues with the author-publisher arrangement, making a royalty a reasonable second-best approach.

As noted, the above description is a demand notion and has nothing to do with the minimum amount the owner needs to be paid to cover their opportunity costs. This view needs to be balanced with the opportunity costs of supply, however, even in the case where inputs are not physically scarce. That is, resource owners might have opportunity costs, both in total and at the margin, relative to standard measures of user cost. To illustrate, suppose a country is endowed with a photocopy machine, instead of a mineral deposit. Suppose photocopy machines can be produced with constant returns to scale, so no scarcity rents (or natural resource rents) are present. The fact that the photocopy machine is a gift from nature is immaterial for the efficient use of this resource.[18] The owner can either sell the machine outright or use the machine to produce photocopies. If the owner sells photocopies, then a charge will be made on a per unit basis. In a competitive market, this charge will be based on the market value of new and used photocopy machines, depreciation rates, and interest rates. In effect, the per unit charge for the photocopy includes a user cost for retaining an economic interest in the machine and the dynamic reduction in the value of the machine resulting from use. Even a used photocopy machine has scrap value, and it is unlikely that 100% of the maximum number of photocopies (the reserves) are ever produced, so the potential is not exhausted.

There is no economic difference between photocopy machines (payments to real estate agents or payments to authors) and minerals in the ground. Private resource owners can sell title to the land and minerals or retain an economic interest in the property. If the owner retains an economic interest, then a per unit charge might be appropriate if the owner's opportunity cost is not zero. Countries that vest mineral rights in the state face the identical problem. Selling land and mineral rights is the exception for countries, so countries tend to retain an economic interest in both the minerals and the land. Thus, it might be reasonable for a country to charge a basic royalty for extraction.

The determination of the charge is really a public-sector pricing problem. That is, the government needs to consider such factors as the direct user cost of extraction, any externalities, risks, administrative costs, and perhaps general equilibrium effects when making such a determination. If the risk-adjusted marginal opportunity cost is zero for these resource owners, then a royalty is inefficient. If the opportunity cost is not zero, then economic efficiency may be increased if such a charge is imposed. That is, it may be economically efficient to high grade (or to extract less than all reserves). A fee based on extraction, either per unit or ad valorem, is in effect a wage for the resource, and might be appropriate if opportunity costs are nonzero at the margin and administrative capacity is constrained. This interaction of the supply price with the investor's demand will determine the ultimate level of extraction and recovery as well as some relative risks to be shared by the two parties.[19]

---

[18] Alternatively, to say that 100% of the value of the photocopy machine can be taxed away is immaterial to its efficient use.

[19] If demanders were not charged a marginal wage for labour, then firms would either drive the value of the marginal product of labour to zero or demand labour to the point where supply becomes inelastic. If workers charged for labour on a per unit basis, then less labour would be demanded relative to the zero marginal opportunity cost case. This is effectively high grading and premature mine closure in the labour market.

6.4.2 Generally Applicable Taxes and Fees

Profits, withholding, and other taxes are generally applicable taxes and provide part of the institutional background for all investments, including minerals. Thus, there is little justification for special treatment of the mining industry with regard to these taxes. The question is not whether mineral investments might increase (or be more efficient) if taxes were lower. Rather, the economic issue is whether the social value of investment at the margin, including taxes, is higher or lower relative to investments in other sectors. That is, general tax policy should be designed to be economically neutral, or as neutral as possible, between all economic activities at the margin. Lack of special treatment, however, does not mean industry-specific provisions are unnecessary.

6.4.2.1 Taxes on Returns to Invested Capital

In most countries, taxes on the return to invested capital currently include profits taxes on entities as well as dividends and capital gains at the shareholder level. If our perspective is adopted then the profits charge is an advanced tax. The economic intent of the either charge is to capture part of the return from invested capital for the state. For instance, if the profits tax (or advanced tax) is 20% and the gross-of-tax return is 10%, then the state should accrue 2%, leaving a net-of-tax return to the investor of 8%. In effect, taxes on the return to invested capital are analytically equivalent to free equity on a gross-of-tax basis. This profit is what creates the risk-sharing properties of the income tax. While equivalent to free equity in a mathematical sense, this tax has a different economic intent from free equity. The government has no residual interest in the invested capital, does not vote, and does not directly influence decisions. Rather, the government chooses the tax policy, rates, and base to determine revenues as well as to affect the inter-sectoral allocation of resources. Economic neutrality is one efficiency objective for these taxes in combination with the tax on the return to human capital. Other things equal and restricting the analysis to one firm, the government's and the shareholders' interest coincide because the greater the profits, the greater the returns to the government and to the shareholders. Neutrality is an economy-wide notion, however, because appropriate rate and base selection will lead to higher returns to the overall economy given the government's constraints. The effective tax should be the same at the margin regardless of the economic sector in which the capital is invested. That is, the effective tax should not be 20% in the mining sector, 10% in the textile industry, and −2% in general manufacturing. Therefore, reducing the profits of one firm may increase the overall economic return to the economy. The function of the profits tax as a matter of policy design may differ from the returns to free equity.

Given the general applicability of taxes on net profit and the accrual basis of the tax, specific provisions will be contained in the tax laws for particular industries (mining, banks, insurance, agriculture, forestry, and other sectors for instance). The purpose of the industry-specific provisions is to recognize the special circumstances in that industry. Neutrality should still be a consideration in the design of these industry-specific rules. Four specific items might be addressed in the generally applicable tax law for the mining industry.

a. Exploration

Exploration expenditures are capital expenditures with an uncertain outcome and should be treated like others in a similar category (research and development in the drug industry, for instance). These expenses should be capitalized during the exploration period if the intent is to measure economic income. The capitalized expense can then either be written off if the expenditure proves worthless or amortized during some period of the mine's life if exploration is successful. A more general option, and one more in line with economic method, is to pool all exploration expenditures made by the investor across properties and to amortize the failures against the income of the successes. The theory behind this approach is based on the fact that all exploration yields information that has value. Exploration is effectively a search process and all the costs associated with the search are amortized with the discoveries. This approach would require that ring-fencing be eliminated (see Section 6.5.2.1.b) because one reason to have ring fencing is the losses created by expensing exploration and development. Such losses would not be created if such expenses are capitalized as recommended here.

b. Development

Development is essentially a self-constructed asset. That is, labour and other factors are used to build an operation that may last many years or fail. Thus, development in mining should be treated like any self-constructed asset, such as a building. Again, capitalization is required if economic income is the intended base. The capitalized basis will then be amortized during some part of the asset's productive life, perhaps using unit-of-production amortization methods.

c. Depletion

Depletion is the equivalent of depreciation for the value of the reserve base. Private investors should not get depletion for the reserves simply because title to the reserve base remains with the property owner (the state) in most instances.[20] There are, however, organizational expenses, bonuses, and other pre-production payments that are not directly related to exploration and development but that are designed to retain the investor's interest in the particular property. Such payments should be capitalized and amortized (on a cost basis).

d. Reclamation

The investor might be responsible for future reclamation payments when production ends. In effect, a future expenditure is accrued when extraction occurs during the production period. Thus, recognition of this expense should be made during the production period under accrual-based systems. There should be some estimate (which

---

[20] As a matter of policy, the government should keep depletion accounts.

might be revised) of the amount of the reclamation expense. Once the level is determined, the annual amount can be amortized by one of two methods. First, there can be consumption tax treatment where the cash contributions to a reclamation fund are deducted in the period of the contribution. The inside build-up of interest is not taxed. Any surplus over expenditures at the time of reclamation should be taxed and any deficit deducted. The second method is to employ accrual methods (or income methods). The amount is deducted at the time of accrual (regardless of the level of the cash contribution), like bad debt reserves for banks. Interest income is taxed as long as the investor holds title to the funds. No gain is recognized at the time of disbursement in this case.

The choice of the appropriate system, assuming an accrual-based approach, may depend on how the contributions are treated on the investor's balance sheet. If the liability is offset by a fund on the investor's balance sheet, then interest should be taxed. If, however, the payments are not transfers on the balance sheet but are contributions to a fund that is not carried on the investor's balance sheet, then interest should not be taxed to the investor. The investor no longer owns the asset in this case.

6.4.2.2 Border Withholding Taxes

Withholding taxes are based on gross income from domestic sources paid to nonresidents. It is not possible to require nonresidents with domestic source income to file a return and report net income. Thus, withholding on a gross basis might be considered an approximation of the net tax. Given the approximate nature, the tax rates are generally lower than the corporate tax rate (unless there is some type of corporate integration for dividends). In addition, rates might vary depending on the nature of the payment. Interest withholding on a gross basis might attract a lower rate relative to management fees and dividends, for instance. Rate variation might result in transfer pricing incentives if various payments are made to related parties or particular payments can be restructured to attract a lower rate. Finally, withholding rates might be modified by tax treaty, which might create an incentive for investors to 'treaty shop' by investing in the host country via an affiliated firm resident in a country with low withholding rates. Mining investments should not get any special treatment in the withholding regime and should be subject to the generally applicable charges and rates.[21]

6.4.2.3 Indirect Consumption Taxes

Consumption taxes, usually VAT, are intended to impose a tax on domestic final consumption. As such, mining should not be harmed or benefit, on a relative basis, from this regime. There are some administrative issues with mining, however. Under a VAT, imports are taxed, and exports are zero-rated. This treatment is consistent with the intent to tax domestic consumption. Mining investors incur large expenses during the years of the mining cycle before receipts are positive. In addition, when receipts do accrue, they are from exports in many cases. Thus, the tax administration must be

---

[21] We note that if our approach is adopted then there would be no border withholding taxes because there would be universal withholding via the use of APAs.

prepared to provide refunds for excess credits during the production period and to supply refunds for input taxes during the pre-production period. Investment in mining will be adversely affected otherwise. Some countries have provided exemptions for mining in an effort to reduce the administrative burden of refunds and to ensure that investors are not unduly harmed. There is a tradeoff, however, because there is the incentive for the miner to sell on the domestic market tax free (either production or imports) if the exemption is too broad. Thus, governments generally restrict the exemption to imports of goods used in investment or production and attempt to ensure that all domestic sales are taxed.[22]

6.4.2.4 Tariffs

Tariffs might be used for both revenue and domestic protection. There is little need to protect the inputs used in mining if there are no domestic suppliers and thus exemptions for capital goods are common. In addition, such exemptions relieve the government of the need to develop duty rebate systems when production is exported. If tariffs are used for revenue, as in the case of a low uniform tariff, then exempting mining is more difficult to justify.[23]

6.4.3 Returns to Equity Participation

Governments with ownership rights to minerals already own one important input into the mineral production process—the minerals in the ground. Equity participation by government in the mining venture expands that ownership to include the value of machinery and equipment used to extract those minerals. Therefore, it should be clear that equity participation in the mining venture reduces the returns to the investor, other things equal, unless that equity participation is financed fully by the government.

It appears that governments have two reasons for seeking equity participation. First, there is a desire to affect the investment and development plans. Second, there is the perception of additional financial gain. There is a question about the first motivation given that the mineral owner is a government and has regulatory powers. There may be little gain from equity ownership given that the resource owner should be able to determine jointly with the producer the extraction profile and the appropriate role of the state to enforce reasonable disclosure.

Financial gains include dividends and capital gains. These financial gains will be in addition to the factor payments (royalties and excess profits charges) as well as generally applicable taxes. These incremental gains should be weighed against the costs. Costs include:

---

[22] A more extensive discussion of these issues is supplied below.
[23] This statement does not imply that free trade is inferior to a uniform tariff. Rather, a low uniform tariff, such as the one introduced in Chile during its economic reforms, may be an effective, and relatively efficient, revenue device if the government cannot administer other taxes effectively.

- Forgone opportunities to invest in other sectors or abroad to diversify the economy,
- The increased risk incurred by assuming a greater proportion of the mine-specific risks,
- The economic effects resulting from having less diversification, and
- The direct (or indirect) costs incurred from the asset purchase.

Many natural resource-rich economies are relatively poor in other assets, and it might be important for the country to attempt to diversify its asset base which will result in more economic stability over the longer run. Thus, investing in domestic subsidiaries of foreign operations may not be in the country's long-term interest. The government can affect company decisions by buying an ownership interest in the international firm on the open market to the extent that such investments are reasonable.

6.5 Recommendations

Consistent with our perspective, we do not believe there is a one-size-fits-all policy. The best policy for a particular economy depends on the relative importance of minerals in that economy, per capita income, the expected time path of per capita income growth, the cost of access to international capital markets, attitudes towards risk, administrative capacities, and other factors. What follows is our approach to the essential elements of a transparent and relatively efficient minerals policy.

6.5.1 General Background

Minerals policy should be based on the principles of economic efficiency, compatibility with the country's laws, stability for the economy, revenue productivity, and administrative feasibility.

6.5.1.1 Need to Measure Opportunity Costs of Mineral Extraction

The fact that minerals are a gift from nature is largely an economically meaningless statement. Like labour, capital, and other assets, minerals are present, they are finite at any point in time, somebody owns them, and their value needs to be determined. As noted, determining the value is really a public-sector pricing problem when the government owns the reserves. We believe, however, that reasonable estimates of the opportunity cost of mineral extraction can be developed.[24] Developing the minimum government revenue requirement from resource ownership is practically impossible

---

[24] Estimates of the social opportunity costs of reserves and of extraction are needed. The fact that these values are estimates and depend on prices should not be a major concern. All asset values (even those in highly developed financial markets) change daily and reflect the interaction of estimates of the future combined with preferences towards risk. Valuing in-situ reserves and the opportunity cost of extraction will be subject to the same forces. Methods are available (National Research Council, 1999).

without such estimates. For instance, consider the potential tradeoff between ad valorem royalties and surplus charges such as the RRT. It is generally not possible to evaluate risks unless the expected value is held constant, but, in turn, the expected value of use should be the resource owner's opportunity costs. Some measure of economic opportunity cost would also be helpful to determine efficient policy instruments. An ad valorem royalty based on price or a per unit charge will be inefficient if the economic cost of extraction in the country is zero at the margin, for example. Thus, such measures would be helpful in framing the debate about efficient factor payments.[25]

6.5.1.2 Contracts Should Invoke Statutes

Contract negotiators should be constrained by generally applicable law. If no desired investment is forthcoming, then there is ample justification for a public debate about the overall economic policy. Factor payment structures should be defined in the mineral law because they are not taxes.[26] Treatment of mining under generally applicable taxes should be stated explicitly in the relevant tax laws. Discretion to change rates and bases, if allowed, should be restricted to mineral factor payments and equity participation, if any. No discretion should be allowed with respect to generally applicable taxes unless there is a transparent process with public notification, including legislative amendments. Generally applicable taxes should be developed based on policy considerations beyond the scope of mining contracts.

Another issue may be the nature of the contracting process itself. Governments should have laws, regulations, and procedures for negotiating, reviewing, and administering contracts. In some cases, government contracts in other sectors may have stated values higher than mineral contracts (defence contracting in the US, for instance). Mineral contracts should be subject to the same due diligence and procedures as other government contracts.

It might be the case that the generally applicable tax laws and regulations are silent on specific topics (treatment of hedging, for instance). One strategy in such cases is to list the issues where legislative or regulatory attention is required, develop the policy, and include specific language in the contracts. The contracting process can then be used as one way to assist the evaluation of overall policy.

6.5.1.3 Stabilization

Stabilization, if necessary, should be restricted to financial provisions and for a limited time period. For instance, the period could be limited by the jointly determined

---

[25] We believe some estimates of scarcity value are based on the value of extraction from the perspective of the producer (Adelman, 1990). This measure is not what is needed because it is derived from demand. Thus, in a competitive market, if the supplier charges a fixed price, then the demander of reserves, an oil company, should treat the supply of reserves as perfectly elastic and set the value of the marginal product of reserves equal to the input price. Measured rents would then be zero. What is needed is a measure of the supply function of reserves into the production process by the owners of reserves.

[26] In general, public-sector prices for electricity and other inputs are not contained in the tax law. This is more than semantics from our point of view. The fact that royalties and charges such as the RRT are defined to be taxes has led to notions such as tax-induced high grading, which may or may not be appropriate given the marginal opportunity cost of a country permanently losing reserves. Form following function in this case may lead to better framing of issues and tradeoffs.

discounted payback period (or an approximation). Our preference would be to stabilize only factor payments and equity participation rules, but we appreciate the need to stabilize tax rules. It should be noted that stabilization is a two-way street. In particular, the government needs to be informed about any changes in ownership structure and other matters related to corporate management. In addition, investors should not be allowed to arbitrarily change computations of certain items (attributions for inter-affiliate costs) without prior notification.

6.5.14 Basis for Framing Recommendations

- Investors expect a reasonable risk-adjusted ex-ante return from their investments.
- That said, the government may have something of value to sell and it should not provide unnecessary incentives for investment. It might be better to wait than to enter into a poorly structured deal or one with unclear implications.
- The major, and perhaps only, benefit from mineral investments is revenue. Employment is a minor factor given the fact that mining is the such a capital-intensive industry. Transfer of specialized training and technology is relatively minor and can be expensive for a government to obtain. The need to invest in such transfers depends on the long-term prospects for mineral development and the ability to support a labour force with such specialized skills.
- Any regime must be administered. We assume that the administrative capacity in developing countries is constrained. Thus, compromises must be made in order to ensure that provisions can be administered.[27]

6.5.2 Generally Applicable Taxes

Recommendations for generally applicable taxes are summarized in Table 6.2. These recommendations supplement those associated with the recommended approach to reform proposed in this volume. If the proposed approach is taken, then the mining firm should become an APA and make advanced payments for all generally applicable taxes. The base of the advanced payment should include the mining-specific provisions noted here. If, however, the approach advocated in the volume is not adopted, then the application of traditional profits tax and withholding taxes are relevant. Finally, the proposed approach to transfer pricing should be adopted regardless of the overall policy application in the jurisdiction.

Generally applicable taxes, along with the regulatory environment and other factors, provide part of the economic environment in which all investors operate. These taxes should be designed with respect to overall policy objectives, of which mineral investments may be an important part. It is important that the generally applicable

---

[27] As an aside, we believe that governments should retain the outside expertise necessary to monitor contract compliance until administrative constraints are relaxed. Such skilled resources are available, and the gains can be worth the considerable costs.

taxes be reasonable, or all investment will suffer. In the case of mineral investments, the issues with respect to generally applicable taxes are the total tax burden on the industry and the burden relative to other sectors. Given a reasonable overall burden, inter-sectoral considerations might be more important for the longer-term stability of the tax system.

6.5.2.1 Profits Taxes (or basis for advanced payments): Taxes on Return to Invested Capital

Again, if the approach advocated in this manuscript is not adopted, then taxes on enterprise profits should apply in the mining industry as in any other industry.

Table 6.2 Recommendations for generally applicable taxes

Instrument	Recommendation
Profits tax (or bases for advanced tax)	1. Capitalize all pre-production expenses (exploration and development) into one pool and amortize over a fixed number of years using a straight-line amortization schedule. 2. Allow deductions for reclamation expenses on either an accrual or cash basis. Do not tax interest income if cash basis accounting is used, but tax surplus of receipts over expenditures at the time of reclamation. Tax interest income if accrual methods are used but only if the fund is carried on the investor's balance sheet. Do not tax any surplus at the time of use if receipts are greater than expenditures. 3. General income tax provisions: • Transfer pricing: Thin capitalization using 50% of taxable profits on net interest method. Restrict head office expenses and other expenses such as hedging via reasonable but arbitrary limitation. Use OECD Guidelines to the extent that they can be reasonably administered. • Use advanced pricing agreements. • Depreciation: Pooled accounting might be preferred. Rates should provide for marginal accelerated depreciation (such as double declining balance). No expensing should be allowed. • Source rules should be developed and allowed to evolve with administrative capacity. • Allow ring fencing. • Withholding taxes: Establish uniform withholding taxes on all payments to nonresidents with the possible exception of arm's-length interest.
Indirect taxes	I. See Section 6.5.2.2.
Tariffs	II. Explicitly exempt (or zero rate) major industrial goods, including mining equipment, if the tariff is designed for protection. An exemption may not be needed if policy intent is revenue, not protection, and there is a low uniform tariff.

a. Mineral-Specific Provisions

In spite of the general applicability, there are some provisions that are specific to the mining industry, such as exploration and development expenses, other pre-production expenses, and reclamation and closure expenses.

i. Exploration and Development Expenses. Both exploration and development expenses should be capitalized as noted earlier. In addition, we recommend that all pre-production expenses be pooled and amortized in the same group. This would eliminate the need to separate exploration from development for administrative purposes, a distinction that might be arbitrary. Using one date, the date that commercial production begins, will enable a rather clean separation between the investment and production periods for policy purposes. It might be claimed that exploration expenses should be favoured relative to development because of risks and the inability to finance such expenditures with debt. The former may be largely irrelevant if ring fencing is applied because the present value of the expensing provision may be reduced significantly. In addition, discriminatory treatment of one type of risk via the tax system may not be efficient. It is not clear that, at least with respect to returns in the capital market, risks associated with exploration are greater than risks from research, developing new products, developing a new product line, or even making a passive investment in an emerging economy. Exploration is a capital expenditure from an economic perspective, just like the construction of a building. The latter justification for expensing, inability to finance with debt, may be largely irrelevant for international firms. The ability of an integrated multinational firm to finance its activities will depend on the numerous factors responsible for determining that firm's overall debt capacity. Attribution of debt to specific activities, even if that debt is collateralized to particular assets, may be arbitrary from an economic perspective.

There are two choices for the amortization schedule. First, the assets can be amortized using a unit of production methodology. This method has a long history and is consistent with depreciating assets over their expected useful life. This is the preferred option. The second method is to use some form of arbitrarily determined accelerated depreciation over a specified time period, such as straight line over five years. Given the general tendency in tax laws to provide some form of accelerated depreciation, the latter option might be used because the present value of the benefits will be greater.

ii. Other Bonus Payments, Organizational, and Other Pre-Production Expenses. Expenses not directly related to exploration and development might be pooled with other production expenses and amortized in one pool. This may be the simplest approach. Alternatively, such expenses might be amortized according to the general tax rules for organizational expenses.

iii. Funding Reclamation and Environmental Damages. It was noted earlier that two methods exist for the treatment of reclamation and environmental damage expenses. First, reserves can be created and perhaps funded. If funded, consumption tax treatment might be applied so that the interest on the inside build-up of the fund accrues tax free. In this case, surpluses would be taxed if unspent at the end of the project's life.

The alternative, and we believe economically correct, method for income accounting is to employ standard accrual accounting. The liability for reclamation accrues as extraction continues. Thus, it is reasonable to recognize the accrued expense at the time it arises.

The more difficult question is the treatment of the build-up, if any, from the reserve. This is really an issue of who carries the fund on their balance sheet. If the fund is carried on the investor's balance sheet, then the interest should be taxed. If the fund is carried on the balance sheet of another entity (a joint-lock box account for instance), then the firm should not be taxed on the interest unless that interest is distributed to the firm. Title to the reserves is effectively transferred to the other entity and thus the interest income does not belong to the firm.[28] We believe, however, that the interest should be taxed as part of a general tax-inclusive budget process. Thus, the interest income accumulated in any lock box or fiduciary account should accumulate at the net-of-tax interest rate. Regardless of the method, expenditures in excess of fund balances should be immediately deducted if the investor is liable for the expenditure.

b. Other Provisions

Other provisions and procedures have implications for mining contracts but should be applicable to all taxpayers. Some particular provisions and regulations are noted here. Again, it is emphasized that this discussion is about generally applicable provisions and should not be unique to mining.

i. Ring Fencing the Profits Tax. Ring fencing is a generic tax term that is not restricted to natural resource extraction.[29] Ring fencing is a term applied to any set of activities that are taxed separately, either under special rules or by segregating a particular activity, or set of activities. One example of ring fencing outside the natural resource sector is the segregation of income from electricity generation between the production and transmission of electricity.

Within natural resources in general and mining in particular, ring fencing is used to segregate certain activities and tax, or at least attempt to tax, those segregated activities independently from other activities in which an investor might engage. Ring fencing might be achieved in two ways. Horizontal ring fencing is a situation where the same, or similar, activities (such as mineral extraction from two different physical locations/tracts/licence areas) are taxed separately. That is, the taxpayer will compute a separate tax for each property instead of computing a single tax for the aggregation of interests. Vertical ring fencing is a situation where downstream

---

[28] Contract provisions may interact with this tax provision. A contract might provide for accrual of unfunded reserves if there are sufficient guarantees or there may be a full funding requirement. The tax provision may affect how the contracting parties structure funding reclamation and environmental damages.

[29] This section is based on Conrad's work in Zambia (Conrad, 2011) and Mozambique (Conrad, 2012).

activities, or a particular set of downstream activities, are segregated from upstream activities. This type of ring fencing might be achieved by administrative definition in some instances. For instance, concentrating, smelting, refining (in the case of oil and gas) and other downstream activities, such as distribution and marketing, might be defined as 'manufacturing' as opposed to 'mining' in the tax law, thus potentially separating activities for tax or other regulatory purposes.[30] Regardless of the type of ring fencing, some type of separate accounting is required to compute the tax base attributable to the different activities when ring fencing is imposed. Thus, one important practical issue is the ability to measure the tax base attributable to segregated activities.[31]

An example will illustrate the point. Suppose an organization has three mines in different parts of the country, two concentrators, and one smelter. All smelter output is exported. All production from Mine 1 goes to Concentrator 1 for processing while production from Mines 2 and 3 goes to Concentrator 2 for processing. All output from Concentrators 1 and 2 goes to the smelter for processing and the smelter does not use throughput from any source other than Concentrators 1 and 2.

There are a number of ways this organization can be ring fenced, including:

- Vertical Ring Fencing between Mining and Processing: Mines 1, 2, and 3 would be treated as one group, while the two concentrators and the smelter would be taxed together as a separate unit.
- Horizontal Ring Fencing for Mining and Vertical Ring Fencing for Mining and Processing: In this case, Mines 1, 2, and 3 would be treated as separate units under horizontal ring fencing, while the two concentrators and the smelter would be taxed as in Part 1.
- Complete Horizontal and Vertical Ring Fencing: Each mine, each concentrator, and the smelter would be taxed as separate units in this case.

These three examples are not exhaustive for the assumed facts but illustrate the different combinations of activities that might or might not be aggregated into one unit.[32]

ii. Taxes and Charges to Which Ring Fencing Might Apply. Ring fencing can be applied to a number of taxes and charges:

---

[30] This distinction is maintained in the United States, and Conrad was informed that Mozambique has a similar policy. This could have implications for policy applications in Mozambique. For instance, the law on fiscal incentives for mining and petroleum contains mineral incentives, while general investment tax credits and other incentives apply to manufacturing under the general tax law.

[31] It might be thought that the whole should be equal to the summation of the parts. For instance, if the total profit from two deposits is 100, then one might expect that separate accounting for each project should total 100, perhaps −10 to Property A and 110 to Property B. Such a result might not be achieved in practice, however, because the rules applied to the computation of each separate property may differ from the rules applied to the aggregate (or the consolidated) profit in addition to the differential costs of maintaining different accounting regimes. Such limitations should be kept in mind when evaluating different ring-fencing schemes.

[32] Ring fencing may be the result of corporate structures, either required or allowed. For instance, one investor might be allowed, or required, to establish separate special purpose entities by tract or activity. The creation of subsidiaries and reporting on a separate company basis can be equivalent to ring fencing.

- Profits and Income Tax: Ring fencing is most commonly applied to income taxes where separate accounting by ring-fenced activities is required. In effect, the intent is to treat each separate activity as a distinct, independent taxpayer even though one investor owns all of the activities.
- Value Added Tax (VAT): Ring fencing might apply to VAT and in this case each separate activity is effectively a separate VAT taxpayer (or APA). In general, ring fencing for VAT purposes might be inefficient or ineffective because trade between the separate segments will cancel out (no revenue effect) and the total VAT on trade with third parties should be independent of whether the investor's activities are ring fenced or combined, at least other things equal. Situations where ring fencing might be justified for VAT purposes include:

  ○ If firms produce both taxed and exempt activities (a firm could produce both taxed and exempt supplies in different locations or in different operations); and

  ○ If investors engage in different types of activity (one investor could engage in both leasing and other financial transactions and production of goods like autos).

- Royalty: Ring fencing may be a de facto outcome of the payment's function, which is to compensate the resource owner (the government) for the sale of reserves when they are extracted. If the royalty is based on production of ore and the rate is either per unit or ad valorem, then there is ring fencing by definition. Ring fencing may not be the result, however, if the royalty is imposed on the sale of concentrate, or the transfer of oil at the end of a joint pipeline) from more than one deposit.
- Excess Profits Tax: An excess profits tax, such as the Resource Rent Tax, might be ring fenced by property if the policy intent is to capture some proportion of excess profits, however defined, attributable to a particular property. The property might be a lease, an aggregation of adjacent leases, or a single mine (or well) depending on the legislation and regulations.

iii. Gains and Losses from Ring Fencing. Two advantages are noted for ring fencing (either horizontal or vertical). First, tax losses from exploration, development, and other start-up expenses cannot be used to offset income from either other production operations or downstream activities. Second, and related to the first, is that the ability to offset income with losses from another set of activities might create a competitive advantage for preexisting profitable firms relative to new entrants. The revenue loss and competitive advantage implications from aggregation of interests results in mining in part because exploration and development expenses may be immediately expensed or benefit from accelerated amortization. The need for ring fencing in this case can be reduced by replacing expensing with capitalization and amortization more in accord with economic principles as recommended in this chapter. Exploration and development are capital expenditures and income accounting should reflect the capital nature of the expenditure by treating the expenditures like other expenditures on capital goods (either tangible or intangible).[33]

There are also costs to ring fencing. The most obvious cost is the administrative need to separately account for net income (or cash flow) or other measure of the base attributable to the separate activities.[34] Attributions of revenue (in cases where there are transfers from upstream to downstream activities, both of which operate domestically) and expenses must be made when an investor has two activities that are segregated, either horizontally or vertically. Transfer pricing rules may have to be applied or formulary methods used to attribute expenses and sales in such cases. Absent reasonable administration, an investor can use transfer pricing to offset, at least in part, the expected revenue gain created by the inability to use losses more rapidly. For instance, the investor might reduce losses attributable to a mine by shifting some expenses otherwise attributable to a loss-making mine to a profitable upstream processing operation. In effect, transfer pricing may become a domestic as well as a cross-border issue. The rule developed in Chapter 3 is to impose an advanced payment on all related party transactions. Thus, transfer pricing problems for inputs are largely irrelevant either domestically or internationally. Accordingly, we recommend adoption of this approach, regardless of ring-fencing rules.

iv. Deciding the Best Policy. In our view, like almost all policies, there is no best practice for ring fencing. As noted, the need for ring fencing can be reduced significantly if exploration and development expenses are capitalized more in accord with economic principles. That said, there are still tradeoffs between administering ring-fenced systems relative to systems with aggregated interests, even when significant upfront capital expenditures are expensed. Some important issues to consider before making an informed decision include:

- To what extent is ring fencing a practical issue? For instance, if a country maintains a policy under which separate deposits are held by separate unrelated parties, then the issue is irrelevant. On the other hand, if the same foreign or domestic investor is able to hold more than one mining licence as well as engage in downstream and even unrelated activities, then policymakers will need to make an informed judgment about the need for ring fencing.[35]
- How will ring fencing be administered? If ring fencing is adopted, then clear administrative guidelines will be necessary to segregate the interests to be taxed

---

[33] It might be claimed that expensing exploration and development is beneficial to the investor because risks are offset, at least to some degree. There is an economic question about whether expensing such costs is efficient.

[34] For discussion purposes, we are assuming that ring fencing is used to measure income.

[35] Ring fencing may be implied by statute. For example, there can be only one mining licence held by a legal entity in Indonesia. That is, a separate corporation must be created for each mining licence, usually some type of special purpose vehicle. There is no need for ring fencing by contract with this statutory requirement. The costs of ring fencing noted in the text still arise if one entity owns two or more special purpose entities required by the statute.

separately. For instance, there might be an issue of ring fencing adjacent licences or determining at what point in the chain of value added to separate upstream and downstream activities.

- What methods will be used to separately account for income between ring-fenced activities? In addition, what accounting rules (both tax and financial) might be necessary to measure the tax base when interests are aggregated? There is no practical standard for determining certain attributions. For instance, two separate properties might share a purchasing office for inputs. Costs of the purchasing office could be attributed to each separate property based on the ratio of input values supplied to each property, by the proportion of orders of each separate entity, or some other reasonable method.
- What are the revenue effects? Potential revenue effects relative to changes in administrative costs should also be considered.

Ring fencing is a common feature of mineral contracts. We believe, however, that aggregation of interests is the best approach as a matter of methodology. The issues of tax shields from losses may be irrelevant, as noted above, if exploration and development expenditures are capitalized, and perhaps pooled, across interests. In addition, the competitive advantage of a preexisting entity with income to shield is reduced. Finally, the incentives of domestic transfer pricing and other attribution rules are largely eliminated.[36] This approach will help preserve the neutrality of government policy across all sectors, sectors where ring fencing is not required.

6.5.2.2 Oil and Gas and Mining
Two characteristics of oil and gas production, and natural resource production more generally,[37] may create administrative difficulties under a VAT:

- Long periods, including exploration and development before the time that production begins; and
- The fact that most, if not all, production is exported.

While the characteristics occur at different stages in the production cycle and arise for different reasons, when combined they create the problem of large refund claims that are due long after the VAT was paid.

a. Long Investment Periods
It can be many years between the time exploration begins and production commences. During this period, the investor makes expenditures only. If the investor is a VAT registered APA, then a net credit position will occur during every taxable period. For example, suppose a producer's costs during a month are $10,000, of which

---

[36] Again, VAT issues are not discussed here. See Chapter 4.
[37] The material here is based on advice supplied to the Governments of Timor-Leste, Mongolia, and Guinea, among others. See Chapter 4 for a further discussion of natural resource taxation. The VAT issues are discussed here so the VAT discussion might be self-contained.

$8,000 are purchases of inputs subject to VAT. If the VAT is 10%, then the producer would have accrued, and must pay, $800 in VAT either to suppliers who are VAT APAs/taxpayers or at the time of import. This fact pattern would result in the producer reporting net VAT due of -$800 (or 0–800) for the tax period. It is common in VAT regimes to provide for a carryforward of excess VAT until the next tax period, like a loss carryforward, and to allow the credit against future income withheld by the producer on sales. The problem is, of course, that sales are not anticipated for years.[38]

b. Exports
The policy intent of a destination-based consumption tax is to impose a tax on final consumption expenditures in the domestic economy, so exports are zero rated. To illustrate, assume that the producer's costs during the period were $10,000, of which $8,000 were purchases for goods and services subject to VAT (either imports or domestic supplies). The producer, like in the example above, would accrue VAT of $800 if the VAT rate is 10%. Suppose, however, the field is producing but all supplies are exported. Such a fact pattern would imply that the producer would have a net position of -$800 (or 0*value of export—.1*8,000); a result identical to the net VAT that arises during the preproduction period.

Thus, these two characteristics result in a situation where an oil and gas producer will never have a positive liability and should be in a net refund position for the entire life of the project, as long as the preponderance of production is exported. It is important to note that such a result is the correct answer because the producer either has no domestic value added during the investment period, or none of the domestic value added is actually consumed domestically.

c. Potential Solutions
There are at least four potential ways to address the problem.

i. Subject the Producer to VAT but Provide for Expedited Refunds. The first, and conceptually best, approach is for the domestic producer to be a registered VAT APA/taxpayer, pay VAT, and file for refunds. It is necessary, however, for there to be an expedited refund procedure, in order for the producer's financial results to be unaffected by having capital tied up unnecessarily, and often with zero interest. There

---

[38] It should be noted that much imported equipment used in natural resource projects (oil and gas exploration, in particular) is leased. Thus, there should be no VAT on the imported equipment itself because the equipment is not purchased. Rather, the equipment will be re-exported at the end of the term, with title remaining with another entity. Such an arrangement should not impose a problem under a VAT, at least conceptually. If the lessor is foreign and so is not a domestic VAT APA/taxpayer, then VAT should be imposed on lease payments themselves because the lease payments are the measure of the value of the equipment services during any taxable period. Such a tax can be imposed via a 'reverse charge', where the domestic investor imposes the VAT and immediately takes the credit, or perhaps might be imposed by a special customs regime for imported services. Regardless of the method, the VAT on the lease should be available for immediate credit by the producer. If the lessor is a domestic VAT APA/taxpayer, then the VAT system should work as designed. The lessor pays VAT at the time the equipment is imported, receives a credit for that VAT, and charges VAT on the lease to the lessee.

are approaches to address the refund issue (see above), but the question naturally arises about the expense and inefficiency created by collecting money simply to have it refunded more or less immediately. Thus, other alternatives might be available.

ii. Exempt Imports to Operations from VAT. The greatest proportion of input values subject to VAT arises from imports of goods and services. Thus, it is possible to exempt imported inputs used by the producer. This approach eliminates (or reduces) the churning created by imposing VAT with immediate refund but creates two additional problems. First, VAT on domestic supplies is not exempt by this scheme and so an artificial import bias is created by exempting imports only. In effect, domestic suppliers are placed at a competitive disadvantage because of the import exemption. Such negative protection may hamper efforts to use oil and gas production to create domestic linkages. Second, an exemption for imports can be a source of leakage and fraud. Oil and gas producers and their employees import consumer and other goods not used in oil production, and such imports should be subject to full VAT. In addition, if there is an exemption, there is an incentive to use the exemption to import goods that are resold into the domestic market free of VAT. Thus, the administrative requirements for monitoring an exemption system are largely the same as those required for monitoring the VAT in general, which may nullify the benefits of this approach.

iii. Ring Fence Oil and Gas Operations for VAT Purposes. A third option is to treat oil and gas operations as outside the taxing jurisdiction for VAT purposes. That is, domestic supplies to oil and gas operations are treated as exports and zero rated while direct imports are exempt because they are treated as not entering the country. In effect, the upstream oil and gas operation is treated as an export processing zone. An immediate consequence of this approach is that any domestic supply of oil and gas or any other good or service subject to VAT is immediately subject to VAT. This type of regime has all of the costs associated with export processing zones. Imports and domestic supplies into the ring-fenced operation must be monitored and treated as if they were in a bonded warehouse and outputs have to be monitored to ensure that the goods are either exported or taxed if they flow into the domestic market. Thus, all of the requirements of a standard customs regime are necessary for the ring-fenced activity. This approach could be particularly costly if areas are geographically diverse and otherwise difficult to control.

iv. Exempt the Producer from VAT. A final option is to exempt oil and gas producers from VAT. A VAT exemption results, however, in treating the operator as a domestic consumer so that supplies to the operator are treated as sales of final consumption. Full VAT is charged and there is no possibility for refunds. While potentially the least costly to administer, this option is the costliest in economic terms. The VAT simply increases the producer's cost by the amount of the VAT and lowers margins and overall profitability. Such a result is the inefficiency the invoice-credit system was designed to eliminate. If such a policy is enacted, then the producer may require modification in other contractual payments to offset the inefficient charge; a revenue tradeoff that is difficult to adequately predict ex ante. At a minimum, a VAT exemption will make the investment less attractive. We believe that this approach is basically flawed and recommend that it be eliminated from consideration.

6.5.2.3 Tariffs

Whether mineral investments and other large-scale investments should be exempt for part or all of import tariffs depends, in part, on the policy intent of the tariff. If the tariff is designed for domestic protection and outputs are exported, then an exemption is appropriate if a duty rebate system is not employed. Domestic substitutes for mining equipment and other significant investments may be nonexistent. Taxing imported inputs may deter exports and provide a justification for explicit exemptions.

Exemptions are more problematic if the purpose of the tariff is for revenue and the tariff is designed to be a uniform tariff at a relatively low rate (such as in Chile). The uniform tariff is equivalent to a devaluation of the currency in this case with the proceeds going to government revenue. Using a uniform tariff might provide needed government revenues in emerging economies with limited administrative capacity. Such revenues might enhance stability which is necessary for a good investment climate. Thus, exemptions for major investments, including mining, may not be effective in such cases. That said, we prefer exempting imports of significant industrial inputs, including mining, given our understanding of the tariff systems in most emerging countries.

6.5.2.4 Capital Gains

The transfer of mineral interests outside the taxing jurisdiction of a country has often been a problem for mineral-producing countries. In 2012, Conrad developed the proposal discussed here. While not perfect, the proposal makes it difficult for any entity through a number of tiers to escape domestic taxation for what is effectively a sale, either complete or partial. This is achieved by defining the source of the transaction as domestic to the extent that the sale is related to a mineral property in the taxing jurisdiction, almost regardless of the nature of transaction. The statute was adopted in Guinea, and we believe it has been recommended in other countries. The proposal is contained in Annex A6.1.

6.5.2.5 Factor Payments

Recommendations for factor payments are summarized in Table 6.3. No recommendation is made about rates because the rates must be determined relative to the structure selected, as will be discussed below, and perceptions of opportunity costs.

a. Basic Royalty

Table 6.4 is supplied to illustrate some of the basic notions that may provide a framework for the recommendations to follow. A stylized example of the production and downstream processing of a (nonfuel) mineral is provided with the accompanying netback computations. Assuming competition, constant returns to scale, economic accounting (perfect accrual accounting), and perfect certainty, the netback computation will yield the producer's willingness to pay for ten tons of reserves. Columns 1–5 contain the computations necessary for 10 tons of ore (with a grade of 0.1) to yield 0.951 tons of final output given production ratios and production losses (plus internal consumption, if any).

Columns 6–7 illustrate the netback process assuming that the London Metal Exchange (LME) price is 500. In this case, the value of final output is 475.5, which is reported as the last entry of column 6. Repeated reductions for processing costs (Column 7) yield the f.o.b. (freight on board) values of inputs (ore, concentrate, etc.) at each stage in the chain of value added. The residual of 5 is the maximum amount the firm is willing to pay for the reserves. The resource owner must now compare this value to the opportunity cost of selling that ton to the producer. If the resource owner's opportunity cost is 5 or below, then the owner is willing to sell for 5. Thus, the resource owner can charge a royalty of 5 per ton. Alternatively, the resource owner can charge an ad valorem royalty at different stages in the chain of value added.[39] These computations are found in Column 10 of the table. Given the assumptions, the producer and resource owner are indifferent between the per unit charge of 5 and the royalty at any stage of production, assuming timing differences are minor.

While stylized, three points are noted about this example:

- A royalty is related to the value of reserves in the ground before extraction;
- A royalty can be structured so that it can be imposed at various stages in the chain of value added; and
- The ad valorem rate falls, holding the royalty amount fixed, as the imposition point approaches the price of final output.

Table 6.3 Summary recommendations for factor payments

Instrument	Description
Base royalty	Impose ad valorem-based royalties on value that can be reasonably measured and audited. Vary rate inversely with the point in the chain of value added used as the base. For instance, the rate should be higher for the value of concentrate than for the value of ingot in order to keep the royalty constant when measured as a proportion of the valuable material.
Surplus payments	1. A fixed RRT based on overall corporate cash flow using a market-determined discount rate. 2. Variable royalty designed to capture a proportion of profit.

[39] The timing of title transfer is ignored for present purposes.

Table 6.4 Example: Production and downstream processing of a nonfuel mineral

	1 Proportion of valuable content	2 Production losses and internal consumption	3 Tons of valuable content	4 Tons of waste	5 Total tons
Reserves	0.100		1.000	9.000	10.000
Ore	0.100	0.010	0.990	8.010	9.000
Concentrate	0.500	0.020	0.970	0.970	1.940
Final product	1.000	0.020	0.951	0.000	0.951

	6 F.O.B. netback value	7 Processing costs	8 Value of input	9 Royalty	10 Royalty rate
Reserves	35.00	30.00	5.00	5.00	14.29%
Ore	135.00	100.00	35.00	5.00	3.70%
Concentrate	285.00	150.00	135.00	5.00	1.75%
Final Product	475.39*	325.39	285.00	5.00	1.05%

Note: LME price = 500 per ton
10 tons of reserves extracted
* This is the c.i.f. (cost insurance freight) price at LME (London Metal Exchange), which is the same as the f.o.b. (freight on board) price depending on whether the person is a buyer or a seller.

Reality differs from the stylized example in a number of ways.

- Netback valuations are based on accounting data, not economic data, and there must be an agreed methodology for computing any netback (even a net smelter return).
- Markets are not perfectly competitive, information is not perfect, and production may not exhibit constant returns to scale.
- LME prices may be uncertain and processing costs are also uncertain even if ex post accounting is perfect. Thus, the value of the netback is uncertain ex ante.
- The choice of a per unit or ad valorem royalty will thus have different risk-sharing properties. For instance, an ad valorem royalty at any stage in the chain of value added will have a price participation component that is lacking in a per unit charge. On the other hand, a per unit charge increases the downside risk of the producer, regardless of price. The resource owner's risk is that the producer will stop buying by closing the mine.

Given uncertainty, administrative constraints, and lack of perfect accounting, tradeoffs are inevitable. In particular, it is not clear whether charging a low royalty rate on the LME price is more accurate, or more efficient, than charging a higher rate on the measured f.o.b. border price or net smelter return given errors in measurement and the administrative costs to both parties. It is clear, however, that the LME price (or other market price) is an arm's-length price and may not be manipulated by either party.

Finally, basic economics applies via the 'no free lunch' assumption because opportunity costs are positive. Thus, some payment for the scarce production factor is warranted. The issue is how to determine a practical means to measure this payment given administrative constraints that might be significant in emerging economies. Some options are provided below, which might be considered given administrative capacity and risk preferences.

b. Ad Valorem Royalty

A basic ad valorem royalty should be part of any factor payment system. This payment serves as a signal of the resource owner's (the government's) opportunity cost and ensures that the country will accrue some cash payment for the permanent reduction in wealth resulting from extraction. Price risks are shared by ad valorem royalties for major minerals if this type of risk sharing is mutually desirable. A fixed per ton royalty might be reasonable for minor minerals and industrial minerals if that rate is adjusted automatically for inflation and the economic environment is monitored.

The base should be determined with regard to administrative capacity and the presence of arm's-length transactions at various stages in the chain of value added. Rates should vary inversely with the stage in the chain of value added at which the royalty is applied (rates should be higher at the extraction stage, other things equal).[40] The rate should be fixed for the basic royalty and the rate should be set in conjunction with the degree of equity participation, if any, and the presence of supplemental charges such as the RRT.

One extreme might be the situation where the royalty is imposed on value less short-run production costs, as is the case for offshore petroleum in the United States. Short-run costs should be defined so that the computed value is an approximation of the cost that must be covered to keep the plant operational. That is, output values below this cost measure will result in mine closure, other things equal.[41] The other extreme might be represented by a royalty imposed on the LME price adjusted for quality of ore (or the quality of exported output). This would be easier to administer, and the rate would be determined relative to published materials about costs at various production stages.

Our preference is to compute the royalty at the point nearest to extraction as possible given administrative constraints. Some additional study by the governments

---

[40] There may be a separation of the value of the royalty and the point of title transfer. For instance, domestic law might state that title to minerals is transferred at the time of export, but the base of the royalty might be the LME price. The royalty rate is adjusted, however, to account for this fact and is lower when applied to the LME price. In effect, the royalty payable approximates the value of the commodity at the point of sale.

[41] The fact that the rate in practice will not be 100% after costs are deducted can be interpreted as the return necessary to induce investment over the longer term. That is, the charge should be 100% if measured costs are deducted and long-run marginal costs and output values are accurately measured.

themselves might be warranted to determine the best valuation point (and rate) given the particular tradeoffs they face.

c. Additional Charges

There are additional charges that might be part of a comprehensive mineral taxation regime.

i. Resource Rent Tax (RRT). The use of the RRT or an 'R-Factor' charge might be considered depending on the ability of a country to bear risks relative to an investor.[42] Mining has risks, particularly in emerging economies. The risks from any one project are idiosyncratic, however, and can be mitigated via diversification. Thus, the questions should be who has the lower costs of risk bearing and whether the payment structure can be arranged so that the marginal cost of risk bearing is approximately equal. We believe there are indicators that the stockholders of large multinational firms may have a lower cost of risk bearing relative to the citizens of an emerging economy. Stockholders of such firms probably earn per capita incomes many times higher than those in emerging economies and have cheap access to diversification via international capital markets. This might be in marked contrast to citizens of emerging economies who have low income, are generally poorly diversified, and have costly access to international capital markets.[43]

Additional charges like the RRT and 'R-Factor' may not be required if the royalty is reasonable, there is no equity participation, and the generally applicable income tax can be applied and administered. Having the tax system fixed, it will be inevitable, we believe, for royalty reductions or reductions in other profits-based charges to be traded for additional profits-based charges. It might be possible to impose a reasonable present value-based charge if the government is aware of the change in risk structures and can use policies outside the contract to diversify any additional risks resulting from using such profits-based charges. In addition, an excess profits charge can be justified in situations where mineral deposits are known (exploration has been completed) and there are other pre-existing investments. The presence of pre-existing assets will increase the present value to the investor unless the government explicitly sells those assets for some measure of market value at the beginning of the contract.

There are additional reasons why an RRT might be beneficial. For example, the government will capture part of any extraordinary gain, however defined. In addition, if royalties are reduced on marginal projects, then overall government revenues might increase because of additional investment. These benefits must be weighed

---

[42] The RRT was first proposed by Garnaut and Clunies-Ross (1983). An 'R-factor' charge is similar in the sense that the r-factor is the minimum internal rate of return (IRR). If the charge is progressive, then rates depend on higher returns. For example, if the IRR is 10%, then the rate might be 25%; if the RRT increases to 15%, then the rate may increase to 35%.

[43] There also may be moral hazard for the government negotiating the contract. For example, there is a risk for both the existing government and the contractor that the contract will be voided if a new government is installed. The existing government may be in a better position to reduce that risk than the contractor.

against the risks of having a profits-based charge in addition to the profits tax. Government revenues will become more dependent on such charges (if the RRT is ever paid). If an RRT is introduced while royalties are decreased, then the present value of overall government revenue could fall for two reasons. First, the RRT might never be paid on marginal projects. Second, the royalty reduction will result in lower revenues from all mines. Thus, balancing the costs and benefits is required with respect to this instrument in a manner similar to any fiscal policy tool.

The RRT and 'R-Factor' charges can be made equivalent. The discounted payback periods will be the same if the uplift factor for the R-factor charge is the same as the discount rate used for the RRT, the respective measures of the base are the same, and the 'R-factor' becomes effective when the discounted benefit-cost ratio is greater than 1. We prefer the RRT to the 'R-factor' charge because it is more straightforward, and it is not based on internal rates of return as might be the case with progressive 'R-factor' charges.

A well-designed RRT might be reasonable, given the above qualifications, and some recommendations are offered about how to structure the charge. These recommendations are based on the view that the purpose of the investment in a particular country is to increase the overall wealth of the international firm.[44] Thus, the cash flows attributable to the mine used to compute the base and discount rate to employ should reflect to some degree the effect on overall profits. Given this perspective, the RRT might be structured to include:

- Nominal cash flow attributable to the entire project (no debt),
- No deduction for any inter-affiliate costs,
- The surplus charge should be deductible from profits taxes,
- Use of either the international firm's nominal cost of equity capital or the nominal industry average cost of equity capital if the investor's stock is not traded, and
- A fixed rate.

The first two points are consistent with the overall maximization of corporate wealth. The use of debt for a particular project will depend on the overall debt capacity of the international enterprise, and how that debt is attributed may have a limited effect on the overall corporate results. Inter-affiliate costs are not cash flows out for the overall enterprise.

Deductibility of the RRT from the profits tax is consistent with the fact that the RRT is literally not a tax, but a factor payment combined with a risk-sharing scheme. Thus, it becomes an ordinary and necessary business expense for the investor.

---

[44] It is possible that the net present value of a mine in a country can be negative on a standalone basis, even ex ante, and the investor will undertake the project because the wealth of the overall corporation is increased.

Market-determined costs of capital can be measured via the capital asset pricing model (CAPM) commonly used in finance.[45] Some computations for selected mineral industries, on average, are supplied in Table 6.5.[46] Using the firm's cost of capital has a number of advantages:

- It is easy to compute and is not subject to negotiation.[47]
- It is market determined, publicly available, and transparent.[48]
- It varies with market conditions. All prices, including interest rates, change and are uncertain. Thus, there is no reason to use a fixed discount rate when a market-determined rate is available.
- It is a nominal value.

Using a nominal value with nominal cash flow is consistent and inflation is automatically taken into account.[49] The law or regulations will have to define some parameters if the approach is taken. Particular definitions include: any smoothing rules (such as a three-year moving average), which publicly available reports to use, and which financial indices to employ. Once determined, anyone should be able to compute the return.

One potential criticism of CAPM is that the return is an average, not a marginal, return. This is really a question about the size of the investment in a particular mine relative to overall corporate investments and the degree to which the corporation is diversified. There could be no marginal effect (the marginal is equal to the average) for large, diversified firms. For other firms, the market will react to the announcement of the contract and to operational results for the investment. Thus, the

Table 6.5 Industry average risk-adjusted cost of capital

Item	Bauxite	Copper	Diamonds	Gold	Iron	Oil & gas
Risk-free rate (LIBOR)	3.08%	3.08%	3.08%	3.08%	3.08%	3.08%
Market return	15.8%	27.8%	29.70%	8.60%	23.6%	21.00%
Beta	0.828	0.828	0.648	0.648	0.828	0.601
Risk adjusted cost of capital	13.61%	23.55%	20.33%	6.66%	20.07%	13.85%

Note: The betas used are the average industry beta between 1998 and 2002.

[45] For one standard reference for the development of CAPM, see (Brealey, Myers, & Allen, 2006).
[46] The CAPM equation is: $E(r) = r_0 + \beta_L [E(r_L) - r_0]$ where $E(r)$ is the expected return, r_0 is the risk-free rate (taken as short-term LIBOR in the examples), r_L is the market return, and β_L is a reported value for the co-variability with the market of the asset in question.
[47] Obtaining the investor's cost of capital should be a standard part of any due diligence for mineral negotiations and evaluating the qualifications of the investor.
[48] The value may also adjust to the specific contract in the country.
[49] This is not double indexing. Rather, the unit of account, dollars during a period, is used to measure both the base and the rate.

marginal influence of changes in the project being developed is reflected by market participants.[50]

Finally, it is important to note that the RRT applies only after a number of years have passed—if at all—and the investment is fully recovered. Thus, there is a significant risk that the present value of RRT is small, particularly when traded off against a reasonable royalty. Alexeev and Conrad (2017) developed an income-based excess profits charge, called the Accrued Rent Charge (ARC), to address the long lag before any payment is realized. The proposal has the following elements:

1. Create one pooled account for all preproduction expenses and a second account for all capital expenses after production commences.[51]
2. Impose a 'placed-in-service' rule combined with capitalized interest. All capital expenses will be amortized during the production period. Accrued expenditures during the preproduction period plus accrued interest on the entire balance will be added to the balance of the unified mineral expenditure account.
3. Use the unit-of-production method (or a declining balance method for a specified time period) once production begins to amortize the balance of the unified mineral expenditure account.
4. Disallow any additional accumulated interest on the capital balance once production begins.
5. Reduce the balance of the unified mineral expenditure account by the amount of the accrued depreciation and increase the account by any additional accrued capital expenditure made during the accounting period. (Effectively, assume that the placed-in-service date is equivalent to the date capital expenses accrue once production begins.)
6. Compute profit during the accounting period, the basis for the charge, as accrued revenue less the following:
   a. accrued cost,
   b. depreciation,
   c. royalties,
   d. the investor's capital cost (capital costs are derived as the product of the investor's nominal cost of capital and the current asset basis), and
   e. any compounded accumulated loss carryforward.
7. Disallow a deduction for loan interest expense because such a deduction would be double counting. The full cost of capital is deducted in step 6.
8. If the base of the charge is greater than zero, then impose and collect the charge.

---

[50] There is an option to use a variable royalty which is an approximation of profit, not present value. We can develop this option as desired but have chosen to restrict ourselves to commonly proposed structures.
[51] Alternatively, all tangible personal property and real assets could be grouped into different asset accounts with different depreciation rates. The present value of the error resulting from using one pooled account will depend on the differences between the economic asset lives of the property relative to the asset life of the pool.

9. If the base of the charge is negative, then allow unlimited accumulated loss carryforwards multiplied by the nominal return on equity capital.

10. Use the market-determined cost of equity capital for investors who have shares traded on markets. Use the industry average cost of equity capital for investors who do not have shares traded on markets.[52]

11. Compute all values in nominal terms, including the investor's cost of capital. Thus, there is no need for additional inflation adjustments during the investment period.[53]

Adjust for inflation in the pooled depreciation accounts during the production period by multiplying the ending balance of the pooled account by a measure of inflation (such as the US GDP Deflator, if accounts are measured in dollars). No other inflation adjustments should be necessary because there is no interest deduction and the value used to measure the cost of equity capital should be nominal.

Simulations in Conrad and Alexeev (2017) illustrate that the ARC compares well relative to the RRT and other rent schemes, accrues revenue faster, and exhibits more symmetric risk sharing. Note should be made of the fact that the derivation of the ARC is similar to the derivation of economic income that is proposed in this volume and above with respect to mineral expenses. Thus, the charge, adjusted for the cost of equity capital, can be built on the policy proposals developed here.

ii. Equity Participation. Finally, we believe countries should not take equity positions in any mining enterprises. There may be two reasons to take equity. First, there is the expectation of additional financial gains. Second, the government can have additional influence over the investor's decisions. The latter point may not be relevant because the government can use appropriate regulatory power to influence firm decisions and to obtain reasonable disclosures. In addition, the government would obtain an equity position in a subsidiary (or joint venture) of a generally larger enterprise. Ultimately, the management of the parent enterprise will make decisions about domestic operations and thus owning equity in the domestic firm will have little or no effect on the government's ability to influence these decisions.

As for the former point, additional revenue comes with additional costs. First, equity positions are riskier than royalties (which might have to be reduced in order to purchase 'free equity'). Second, the government already owns the reserves in the ground. Taking an additional equity position in the capital equipment and organization used to extract those reserves may reduce economic diversification. Further concentration of the economy's dependence on one or two international prices might be contrary to the country's need for diversification, unless there are compensating

---

[52] Some averaging over a number of years might be necessary to smooth the observed returns.

[53] This is one of at least two methods to adjust income for inflation over a time period. One alternative is to adjust the asset basis for inflation each period and then apply a real capital charge. The present value of either approach is the same, but 'income' accrues sooner under the proposed method.

adjustments made in the budget and other means. The need for compensating adjustments, however, raises the issue of why the equity position was taken in the first instance.

References

Adelman, M. A. (1990). Mineral Depletion, with Special Reference to Petroleum. *The Review of Economics and Statistics, 72*(1), 1–10. https://www.jstor.org/stable/2109733.

Alexeev, M., & Conrad, R. (2017). Income Equivalence and a Proposed Resource Rent Charge. *Energy Economics, 66.* doi: 10.1016/j.eneco.2017.07.003.

Brealey, R., Myers, S., & Allen, F. (2006). *Principles of Corporate Finance.* New York: McGraw-Hill.

Conrad, R. (2008). *A Comparative Analysis of the Mining Fiscal Regimes in Guinea, Liberia and Sierra Leone.* Washington, DC: The World Bank.

Conrad, R. (2011). [Memorandum: Ring Fencing (Zambia)]. Drafted under the auspices of the International Growth Center.

Conrad, R. (2012). [Memorandum: Ring Fencing (Mozambique)]. Drafted under the auspices of the International Growth Center.

Conrad, R. (2014). Mineral Taxation in Zambia. In C. S. Adam, P. Collier, & M. Gondwe (eds), *Zambia: Building Prosperity from Resource Wealth* (pp. 82–109). Oxford: Oxford University Press.

Conrad, R. and Alexeev, M. (2017). Income Equivalence and a Proposed Resource Rent Charge. *Energy Economics, 66,* 349–359.

Conrad, R. F., & Hool, B. (1981). Resource Taxation with Heterogeneous Quality and Endogenous Reserves. *Journal of Public Economics, 16*(1), 17–33.

Conrad, R. F., Hool, B., & Nekipelov, D. (2018). The Role of Royalties in Resource Extraction Contracts. *Land Economics, 94*(3), 340–353. Retrieved from https://EconPapers.repec.org/RePEc:uwp:landec:v:94:y:2018:i:3:p:340-353.

Gaddy, C. and Ickes, B. (2006). Resource Rents and the Russian Economy. *Eurasian Geography and Economics, 46*(8), 559–583.

Garnaut, R., & Clunies-Ross, A. (1983). *Taxation of Mineral Rents.* New York: Oxford University Press.

National Research Council. (1999). *Nature's Numbers: Expanding the National Economic Accounts to Include the Environment.* Washington, DC: The National Academies Press.

Otto, J. (2006). Mining Royalties: A Global Study of Their Impact on Investors, Government and Civil Society.

Annex A6.1
Proposed Capital Gains Statute

The purpose of this statute is to impose a capital gains tax on transfers, either direct or indirect, of any mining title or licence.[1] Steps necessary to implement such a procedure are outlined here. Examples are supplied to illustrate particular situations.

A6.1.1 Intent

The intent is to impose a tax on the capital gain (or loss) resulting from the transfer of exploration, development, mining, and any other licence related to minerals and mineral development sourced in Country X. There are two types of transfers.

a. The mining licence itself can be transferred by the person or persons holding the licence; this is called a 'direct transfer'.
b. The owners, either resident or nonresident, of the entity (or entities) of the domestically incorporated entity (or entities) holding the licence can transfer ownership of the domestic entity. This is an 'indirect transfer'. Indirect transfers can be of two types:
   i. Type 1: Indirect transfers made by domestic persons. That is, the person holding any ownership interest, either direct or indirect, of the domestic person holding the licence related to mineral interests in Country X and who transfers all or part of that interest is also a domestic person.
   ii. Type 2: Indirect transfers made by a person that is not organized under the laws of Country X (a domestic person for present purposes), is not a physical person liable for income tax in Country X, and does not have a permanent establishment in Country X. That is, the person holding any ownership interest, either direct or indirect, of the domestic person holding the licence related to mineral interests in Country X and who transfers all or part of that interest is not an entity organized under the laws of Country X, is not a physical person liable for income tax in Country X, and does not have a permanent establishment in Country X.

A capital gains tax should be imposed on both the direct transfer of a mining licence and on the transfer of any equity interest in the domestic entities holding a mining

[1] Conrad developed this proposal during an IMF mission to Guinea in 2011.

Evolutionary Tax Reform in Emerging Economies. Robert F. Conrad and Michael Alexeev, Oxford University Press.
© Open Society Institute (2024). DOI: 10.1093/oso/9780192847089.003.0011

licence (Type 1 indirect transfer).[2] A withholding tax should be imposed on Type 2 indirect transfers. Such distinctions are necessary because it is important to identify whether the transferor of any interest is subject to the country's income tax and, if not, to ensure that the proper person withholds tax on the gain from the transfer made by a nonresident person. Type 2 indirect transfers will be made by persons who are not domestic taxpayers, so that a withholding tax, or a final tax, is employed in lieu of the generally applicable tax. In the case of Type 2 indirect transfers, the domestic person whose equity is transferred (the last entity in any chain of domestic entities) will be the withholding agent for the tax and will be required to comply with all reporting requirements.

   c. Examples
   - Entity G is an entity organized under the laws of Country X and holds a mining licence. Entity G transfers 30% of the mining licence to Entity H, another entity organized under the laws of Country X. Such a transfer is a direct transfer for the purposes of this tax and Entity G will be subject to capital gains tax.
   - Entity G is an entity organized under the laws of Country X and holds a mining licence. Entity G is owned by Entity I, another entity organized under the laws of Country X. Entity I transfers 51% of its interest in Entity G to another person. This is a Type 1 indirect transfer, and Entity I will be subject to capital gains tax.
   - Entity G is an entity organized under the laws of Country X and holds a mining licence. Entity G is owned by Entities L and M, both organized under the laws of Country X. Entity L is owned by Entity N, which is organized under the laws of the United States. Entity N transfers 100% of its interest in Entity L to any other person. This is a Type 2 indirect transfer. A withholding tax will be imposed on the value of the transfer and Entity L is liable for withholding the tax.

A6.1.2 Rules

A6.1.2.1 Taxable Event

   i. Any direct transfer of a licence related to minerals in Country X, either in whole or in part;[3] and
   ii. Any indirect transfer of a licence related to minerals in Country X, either in whole or in part, except that the taxable event will be limited to two tiers of

---

[2] The transfer of equity interests in any domestic entity by a person liable for income tax in Country X should be subject to a standard capital gains tax. The Type 1 indirect transfer where the seller is a taxable person should naturally fall within the scope of the general capital gains provisions. It is important that a capital gains tax be imposed on indirect transfers made by domestic persons. Foreign companies may be able to escape the tax if they create domestic companies for the purposes of title transfers absent a domestic capital gains tax. At the minimum, more anti-abuse rules would have to be developed.
[3] There may have to be special rules for cases of liquidations, bankruptcy, and corporate organizations.

nonresident ownership structures. Two tiers mean that the scope of the withholding tax will be limited to one nonresident entity or entities owning all or part of the domestic entity holding the licence.

iii. Exceptions:
- The domestic capital gains tax on any indirect transfer will not apply if the shares of the domestic entity are traded on an internationally recognized stock exchange. (The transferor should be subject to capital gains tax.)
- The withholding tax will not apply on any Type 2 indirect transfer if the shares of the entity or entities directly or indirectly owning the domestic entity are traded on an internationally recognized stock exchange.
- Type 2 indirect transfers will be limited to two tiers of the nonresident corporate structures.

iv. Examples
- Corporation G is a domestic person holding a mining licence in Country X. Corporation G is a wholly owned subsidiary of Corporation H, a corporation chartered in the Cayman Islands. Corporation H is a wholly owned subsidiary of Corporation I, a corporation organized under the laws of the Netherlands. Corporation H is a first-tier corporation while Corporation I is a second-tier corporation. Furthermore, the gain from transfers of shares of Corporation H by Corporation I will be subject to withholding by Corporation G as long as Corporation H's shares are not publicly traded.
- Same facts as the last example, except that Corporation I is a wholly owned subsidiary of Corporation L, a corporation organized under the laws of France. Corporation L is a corporation with a tier higher than two. With the exception of the anti-abuse rule (see below), any transfer of ownership from Corporation I to any other person will not come within the scope of this law. If Corporation I transfers all or part of Corporation H to any other person, then the provisions of this law will apply.
    a. Anti-Abuse Rule: The second-tier limitation will be suspended if it can be demonstrated that the higher-tier entities were organized for the purpose of avoiding the withholding tax. In this case, the transfers by higher-tier entities will be deemed to have been made by the second-tier entity.[4]
    b. Source Rule: Any transfer, either direct or indirect, of a licence related to minerals in Country X is deemed to be from sources in Country X.
    c. Taxpayer
       i. In the case of any direct transfer, the taxpayer is the domestic person holding the licence at the time of the transfer.
       ii. In the case of any indirect transfer, the taxpayer is the person transferring the shares or other ownership interest of the first-tier nonresident person or persons. When the person transferring the shares or other ownership interest is not a domestic person, the

---

[4] As stated, it might be sufficient not to limit the number of tiers and simply have a direct or indirect ownership test.

domestic person whose equity is held in all or in part by the person transferring the shares or other interests will withhold a tax on behalf of the nonresident. Such a charge will be treated as a final tax for domestic purposes.

e. Only domestic persons may hold any licence related to minerals and mining within the territory of Country X.

f. Accrual: The tax accrues at the time of ownership transfer (as that time is defined), regardless of whether cash or other compensation is made at the time of ownership transfer.

g. Base of Charge:

   i. In the case of a direct transfer: the difference between the value of the accrued transfer on the date of the transaction and the adjusted basis of the licence on the audited books of account of the seller.

   ii. In the case of an indirect transfer: the difference between the adjusted basis of the value of the domestic person at the time of the transfer and the pro rata share of the adjusted basis of the seller's total assets based on the audited books of account of the tier-one entity at the time of the sale. 'Pro rata share' for the purposes of this law means: the proportion of the adjusted basis of the licence to the adjusted basis of total assets of the tier-one entity multiplied by the proportional net gain resulting from the share transfer.

   - Example: Corporation M is a domestic person holding an exploration licence and is a wholly owned subsidiary of Corporation N. Corporation N is a corporation chartered under the laws of the British Virgin Islands. Corporation N is a wholly owned subsidiary of Corporation O, a corporation organized under the laws of Germany. The adjusted basis of Corporation N's interest in Corporation M at the time of the transaction is 100, while the total assets of Corporation M are valued at 500. Corporation O transfers full ownership of Corporation M to any other person for consideration of 1,200. The basis for the withholding tax in Country X will be 140 [or (1,200–500)/(100/500)].

   iii. In the case of a direct or indirect transfer where the seller retains an economic interest in the property in exchange for an overriding royalty or other periodic compensation, the base of the charge is equal to the compensation for the transfer at the time of the transfer and any subsequent overriding royalty or other periodic compensation.

h. Rate: The generally applicable corporate tax rate on the value of the transfer at the time of the transfer and the same rate on the gross value of any overriding royalty or other periodic compensation.

i. If the capital gain is zero or below, then no tax is charged. The loss may be used to offset capital gains to the extent that the gain is domestic source in the year the capital loss accrues or in any subsequent tax year. In the case of an overriding royalty, any capital loss carryforward may be used as a deduction from overriding royalty payments until the carryforward is exhausted.

j. Adjusted Basis: Adjusted basis is defined as the value of transferred assets measured on the transferor's audited books of account on the date of the transfer. The adjusted basis will include the initial value of the licence in question plus any additions (including capitalized expenses related to the licence) less any accumulated amortization, depreciation, or depletion allowed for tax purposes. In the case of a direct transfer, the adjusted basis is the basis of the licence itself. In the case of an indirect transfer, the adjusted basis is the value of total assets on the transferor's books of account at the time of the transfer multiplied by the proportion of the ownership interest transferred.

  i. If the books of account used to measure the adjusted basis are not audited, are not maintained according to international accounting standards, or are otherwise unavailable to the domestic authorities, then the adjusted basis for computing the net gain will be deemed to be zero.

  ii. If the transfer is between related parties (however defined), then the Minister of Finance has the power to adjust the value of the transfer to reasonably approximate an arm's-length value.

k. Currency: The value of the transfer will first be measured in the currency used to measure the adjusted basis of assets where the exchange rate used for the compensation is measured at the time of the transfer. The tax will then be computed in the currency used to measure the adjusted basis and the tax will be payable in domestic currency, or US dollars converted using the exchange rate at the time of the transfer.

l. Notification: Any person holding a licence related to minerals or mining in Country X is required to notify the Ministry of Finance of any change in the ownership of either the domestic entity, or of any entity holding an equity position in the first-tier nonresident company, either before or at the time of the change in ownership structure. Failure to notify will result in the immediate revocation of the licence by the State of Country X without compensation. The relevant person will be exempted from this rule to the extent that the shares of the equity of the transferor are publicly traded on an internationally recognized stock exchange. This is a harsh rule and may create incentives for bribery and avoidance. The tradeoff is lack of compliance given the probability of getting caught.

m. Only a domestic person may hold any mining or exploration licence. Any attempt to transfer a licence to a nonresident person will result in the immediate revocation of the licence without compensation.

A6.1.3 Examples

- Corporation A is organized under the laws of Country X and is a domestic person. Therefore, Corporation A may apply for any licence related to mining in Country X.
- Corporation B is organized under the laws of Country X and is a wholly owned subsidiary of Corporation C, a company incorporated under the laws of the United States. Corporation B may apply for and hold any licence related to mining in Country X. Corporation C may not own any licence related to mining in Country X.
- Corporation D is organized under the laws of Country X and forms a joint venture with Corporation E, organized under the laws of France. Corporation D currently holds a mining licence related to mining in Country X. Corporation D would like to contribute 30% of the mining licence to the joint venture and in effect make Corporation E a partial owner of the 30% licence. Such a proposal is a prohibited transaction.
- Corporation H is organized under the laws of Country X and currently holds an exploration licence. Corporation H would like to transfer the exploration licence to Person M, a resident of the United Kingdom. Such a proposal is a prohibited transaction.
- Corporation X currently holds a mining licence with an adjusted basis equal to 10. Corporation X transfers the licence to Corporation Z, a domestic entity. Such a transfer is a direct transfer.
- Corporation X currently holds a mining licence with an adjusted basis equal to 10. Corporation X transfers 25% of the value of the licence to Corporation Y, a domestic entity, as Corporation X's contribution to a joint venture between Corporation Y and Corporation X. Such a transfer is a direct transfer.
- Corporation R is a domestic entity holding a mining licence in Country X. Corporation R is a wholly owned subsidiary of Corporation S, a corporation organized under the laws of China. Corporation S's only asset is the equity shares of Corporation R. Corporation S is a subsidiary of both Corporations Z and A. Corporation Z is organized under the laws of the United States while Corporation A is organized under the laws of Spain. Both Corporations Z and A own 50% of the equity in Corporation S. On 1 March Corporation Z transfers 30% of its ownership (15% of total shares) of Corporation S to any other person. Corporation Z's adjusted basis in Corporation S is 100. The share transfer made by Corporation Z is an indirect transfer. Corporation R is required to notify the Government of Country X and to withhold tax on the net gain.

7
Summary

7.1 Introduction

A collection-driven perspective of each tax in the standard approach (except property tax) was presented in Chapters 3 through 6. This chapter contains a summary of the approach and some concluding comments. Recall that the long-term objective[1] is to impose one tax on income for revenue purposes and to use selected excise taxes to correct for negative externalities.[2] In addition, taxpayers will know, and perhaps participate in, the computation of net income. There is no one-size-fits-all from our perspective, and the starting point will be unique in each country. That said, sufficient common elements exist to warrant discussion of how the tax instruments in the standard model can be coordinated—at least initially.

7.2 Summary of the Approach

Emphasis has been placed on the economic proposition that only individuals will bear the burden of any tax. This emphasis is combined with the administrative power of the state to require tax prepayments. The VAT shares with excise taxes and tariffs the administrative advantage that taxes are paid prior to, or consequent to with, the transfer of title to the taxpayer. We seek to replicate this advantage by attempting near universal withholding on income accruing to the taxpayer, thus further reducing the reliance on voluntary compliance.[3] Our hope is that through time taxpayers and tax administrators will summarize the transition path as:

---

[1] We want to be clear that we have little expectation that this objective will be achieved—certainly not in our lifetimes. There needs to be an objective, however, to help frame the analysis and to determine the path for reform.

[2] Of course, the revenue can be used to offset other distortions in a second-best environment. Our objective is to impose one income tax. A country might choose another objective, such as imposing one tax on personal consumption. The path to that objective might be similar except that income taxation would yield to consumption taxation. For example, if the consumption tax is flat rate, then only a VAT might be used. Alternatively, if progressive elements are sought, then the ultimate structure would be income taxation with an adjustment for flows into qualified savings vehicles. APAs would not charge advanced payment flows into legally defined savings vehicles but would impose advanced payments on disbursements. The VAT would be eliminated.

[3] There is evidence to support the claim that advanced payments increase compliance even more than information reporting. See Gale and Krupkin (2019).

Evolutionary Tax Reform in Emerging Economies. Robert F. Conrad and Michael Alexeev, Oxford University Press.
© Open Society Institute (2024). DOI: 10.1093/oso/9780192847089.003.0012

- Every supply of a good or service to a taxpayer is valued at a tax-inclusive price, and
- Every payment for a return to capital is valued on a tax-exclusive basis.

What happens after the advanced tax is collected depends on administrative capacity and taxpayer knowledge. As soon as administratively practical, advanced income tax payments will be used as a credit against a measure of comprehensive income. An initial measure of comprehensive income can be computed by the tax authority with the taxpayer making necessary corrections and adjustments.[4] Such an approach reduces reliance on voluntary compliance by the taxpayer and, hopefully, frees administrative resources for increasing compliance by difficult-to-tax groups.

Those involved in the production, supply, or importation of goods and services are explicitly exempt from tax. The definition of an Advanced Payment Agent (APA) is used to delineate the roles of producers, suppliers, and importers from taxpayers. Also, the distinction makes it possible to clearly delineate the APA's role as the government's agent for the imposition and collection of advanced taxes.

The approach builds on the standard approach by using the existing administrative and tax structures. The VAT's structure and the corporate profits tax structure remain, and existing wage or other withholding taxes on domestic residents remain. In fact, the initial shift to a collection-driven system could be achieved simply by changing taxpayer and APA definitions and expanding withholding on income payments.

Given this result, it might be claimed that nothing is gained by adopting a collection-driven approach. We believe, however, that the change in language and definition can change the perceptions of taxpayers, administrators, and APAs. Thus, at a minimum, form is consistent with economic intent. The perceptual change, if encouraged by public education and administrative improvements, can change the dynamic of tax reform. The change can occur by establishing a set of clear objectives for the system's evolution. Changes can be made consistent with the objectives tempered by current institutional and economic constraints.

While a country may choose to adopt the collection-driven language within the existing structure, there are many structural and substantive changes embodied in our approach. These changes were developed in the previous chapters, and a few are highlighted in Table 7.1.

The ability to implement any provision or set of provisions will depend on the economic and administrative conditions as well as the structure of existing taxes. Some provisions will be delayed until income levels, administrative capacity, and public awareness conditions warrant. For example, at an initial stage, advanced payments can be final taxes for all taxpayers except a specified group of high-income individuals either who accrue income not subject to advanced tax or have business interests beyond those covered by small business taxes.

---

[4] Electronic filing is available in Sweden where taxpayers are provided with an initial assessment which can be modified or approved with a final assessment later in the year. Swedish Tax Agency website: www. skatteverket.se.

Table 7.1 Summary of important elements of proposal

Tax	Proposal
Income tax	i. Income is defined by the nature of the return to capital (human or nonhuman), eliminating the need for definitions by type of payment. ii. Border withholding taxes are eliminated and replaced by nondiscriminatory advanced payments on all gross-of-tax income payments. iii. The double taxation of corporate income is eliminated with the structure converted to an advanced payment system. iv. Advanced tax is imposed on all returns to capital, including but not limited to wages, other income to labour, and returns to debt and equity including capital gains. v. The longer-term objective is to treat capital gains as ordinary income on an accrual basis using mark-to-market rules. Gains are deferred because market valuations are not possible but absent trade will be adjusted for interest cost to all taxpayers. During early reform stages, advanced tax is imposed at rates lower than but a function of the maximum individual rate and will be a final tax until comprehensive reporting is feasible. Comprehensive reporting will include a method to reduce deferral and locked-in effects by imposing an interest charge on gains and losses made on a realization basis. vi. Advanced tax is imposed and collected by APAs to the extent that APAs pay returns to human and nonhuman capital. Advanced tax will be paid by the taxpayer in cases where advanced tax has not been withheld via payments directly to the government. vii. Gross income paid for the supply of goods and services by APAs and accruing to persons not registered as APAs will be subject to advanced tax. In effect, gross income accruing to such persons is deemed to be income for advanced tax purposes and can be credited against the taxpayer's final tax. viii. Transfer pricing is reduced to determining an independent, publicly available, market price for output. Tax administration is simplified for related party transactions for inputs by imposing advanced tax.
Tariffs	1. A uniform tariff is proposed. 2. Tariff is for revenue purposes only.

Excises	1. Excises are composed of two components:
	    1. A per unit charge to correct for negative externalities to the extent present.
	    2. An ad valorem charge for revenue purposes.

2. Excises are restricted to:
   a. Alcoholic beverages
   b. Tobacco products
   c. Petroleum products
   d. Automobiles
   e. Cell phone service
3. Ad valorem rate is computed by reference to market data converted to a per unit value and imposed at either the factory gate or at the time of importation.

VAT

1. The taxpayer is the resident individual and VAT is defined as either an advanced tax (at upstream stages in the chain of value added) or the final tax on the domestic resident taxpayer.
2. One rate is imposed, except that exports are zero-rated.
3. There are limited exemptions:
   a. Personal savings instruments traded on markets and the market cost of savings.[a]
   b. Personal savings via investments in the form of human capital, including:
      • Medical care
      • Education
4. VAT imposed on mixed-use goods (goods that are investments and have consumption characteristics):
   a. First sale VAT during the initial reforms
   b. Treatment of APA (VAT imposed at the time of supply with credit) as VAT matures (real property in particular).
5. VAT on financial services is imposed using cash flow methods as reform proceeds.

Small business tax (preferred option)

1. The SBT will substitute for the personal income tax, at least initially. This is because the SBT is restricted to taxpayers supplying goods and services.
2. Very small business:
   a. A sole proprietorship with turnover below twice the exemption level for the income tax
   b. Exempt

Table 7.1 *Continued*

Tax	Proposal

	3. Micro business:
	  a. A sole proprietorship with turnover between twice the personal exemption level and a stated fraction of the VAT turnover level
	  b. Charged a fixed fee
	4. Small business:[b]
	  a. A sole proprietorship with turnover above the maximum level for a small business and below the VAT turnover level
	  b. Charged on net cash flow at the standard income tax rate
	5. Any small business supplying goods and services to an APA will be subject to advanced tax that will serve as a credit against the small business tax.
	6. Through time it is hoped that the SBT will be phased out.

Natural resources	1. Separate payments for returns to resource ownership and taxes. 2. Impose the generally applicable tax system without modification to all contractors. 3. Discretionary use of rent capture schemes.

---

[a] Personal savings and investments are exempt because the taxpayer is an individual and the investments of entities are owned by the residual claimants.
[b] VAT thresholds should be reviewed in order to be consistent with the small business requirements. Our view is that cash flow taxpayers should be VAT taxpayers. The turnover level for VAT should not be determined by a simple comparison of revenue to VAT administration costs for reasons noted below.

7.3 Common Elements

One advantage of the collection-driven approach is that it is possible to exploit common elements between all taxes.[5] The most obvious common feature is the advanced payment feature of VAT, excises, tariffs, and withholding under the existing income tax. A country considering the collection-driven approach will need to examine specific interrelationships. Some of these common features are noted here.

7.3.1 Amend Tax Regulations

Countries undertaking tax reform should change the wording of the tax laws and regulations to clarify who is the taxpayer. In most cases, this will require a change in definition for all taxes except the personal income tax.

- The VAT, excise, and tariff definitions of taxpayer should be clearly stated as the domestic resident individual.
- The income tax on entities should define the taxpayer as any individual.

These changes are more than form for three reasons. First, form follows economic substance. Second, the changes will help establish the basis for a dialogue between the government and the public about the intent of each tax and how the system might evolve. Third, combined with the definition of APA below, it should be clear that persons imposing advanced payments are performing a tax administration function.

7.3.2 Introduce the APA Concept with Implementing Regulations

An APA is defined as any person:

- making a payment that is gross income for either the supply of labour (the return to human capital) or the supply of any capital (the return to any nonhuman capital),
- supplying any good or service, or
- importing any good or service.

---

[5] Drafting traditions differ by country and legal system including common law, civil law, religious based, or traditional. We believe that economic terms and concepts can accommodate any legal system. There are certain advantages to having a tax code, however, including having one set of common definitions, administrative procedures, and the ability to coordinate policies across taxes. One example of code that might be applied, with some adjustments, is based on the reform in the Dominican Republic (see Hussey and Lubick, 1996).

A registered APA is an APA that satisfies the minimum conditions for making advanced payments for excises, VAT, and income tax. Satisfying the minimum conditions for excise tax or VAT will be sufficient for the APA to serve as an agent for the advanced tax on income.[6]

All legal entities should be registered APAs regardless of thresholds, and all entities that are related parties should be required to register. Our view is that owners who are capable of meeting the legal requirements of an entity, including the ability to periodically report, should be registered APAs.

Registration requirements should be the same for individuals and entities. New and/or extended APA registration will depend on the state of existing registration. For example, some countries began revising registration procedures by registering those who had been either VAT taxpayers or large taxpayers. Registration should proceed as practical until all APAs are registered. Of course, registration will be relatively straightforward for modern sector enterprises, large NGOs, and government entities. That said, effort should be made to extend registration beyond these known groups. Such expansion should be as comprehensive as possible in order to increase both revenue and compliance.

It should be clear that an APA is compensated for acting as the government's agent. In general, compensation includes the interest income on the float from holding advanced payments between the time of collection (or accrual if interest is charged) and the date that funds plus other payments prescribed in either law or regulation are transferred to the government. Other payments might include reimbursements for forms and other direct costs associated with the performance of the tax administration functions. Reimbursable costs should be subject to audit. Because advanced payments are incremental to established internal procedures, only the direct cost of the incremental expenses should be reimbursed.[7]

The distinction between tax collector and taxpayer is essential because a tax collector should be indifferent to the nature of the tax as long as compensation for the service provision is sufficient. In addition, management of entities can be held individually and severally accountable for failure to comply. The APA has no property right to the advanced tax. Advanced taxes are assets to the taxpayer because they are prepaid taxes, and they are a liability to the government because taxpayers can use the credits to offset tax obligations at the time of accrual or reporting.[8]

---

[6] There will be minimum requirements for being the government's agent for income tax in cases where the APA is not an agent for VAT. APAs can make supplies that are exempt from VAT and make income payments. Such APAs include: educational and religious institutions, most government agencies, and individuals who retain labour services unrelated directly to the supply of market goods and services (household servants, for instance).

[7] In most cases, income from the float will be more than sufficient to compensate for all costs. It is important, however, for costs to be estimated, particularly during the transition.

[8] In the case of the indirect taxes such as VAT, excises, and tariffs on supplies, the advanced tax and the time of accrual coincide with the transfer to the taxpayer. So, the taxpayer has no prepaid tax. Government should use accrual concepts for revenue, as opposed to cash receipts, so the indirect tax does not become government revenue until the taxpayer is charged. Thus, the full tax becomes the property of government with credits for prior payments.

The fact that taxpayers are individuals is important for the public dialogue because there could be no change, at least initially, in the form of payment. That is, the legislation about the computation of the VAT, the corporate tax, excises, and tariffs might not change. Such computations are, however, advanced taxes that are intended to be borne by the taxpayer. Perceptions should begin to change, however, because of an increase in public education and explanation.

APAs should be subject to comprehensive audits. We noted that, other things equal, APAs should be indifferent about the tax system because they are not taxpayers. There are conflicting incentives for APAs, however. The APA is acting as the government's agent, but management has its own interests that might conflict with the government's objective of withholding advanced taxes in correct amounts. In addition, APA management may be individual owners who are taxpayers or are agents for individual taxpayers who are owners. Thus, maximizing the net-of-tax return to the investor in the APA may conflict with the objectives of government and management. Investors are aware of incentive compatibility problems and provide compensation schemes to better align management's incentives with owner objectives.[9] In addition, investors and government may require independent audits as an additional check on management. The general taxpaying population via the government should demand no less than the investors with respect to accountability and transparency.

7.3.3 Coordinate Thresholds for Required APA Registration

Coordination of required registration criteria can be one benefit from a collection-driven reform approach. A strategy for determining the initial group of registered APAs and for expanding the registration through time should be developed. Existing registered producers of excisable goods, current VAT taxpayers, and those who are required to withhold on wages should be automatically included in the required registration group.

Going forward, with the evolution of the tax administration and increased public awareness, there should be an attempt to coordinate registration criteria between taxes. Through time, criteria, other than exemption, for registration by tax will begin to become less relevant. For example, if a small business tax base is turnover, then the maximum turnover level to qualify as a small business could be equal to the threshold for the VAT.[10]

The extent that other businesses are registered depends on administrative capacity, the organization of the tax administration, and the extent of public awareness. We

---

[9] Stock options and performance bonuses are two examples.
[10] We note, however, the irony of having a turnover criterion for a SBT that must be monitored and audited while being exempt from VAT. If the tax administration can audit turnover, then there is good reason to believe that the business can be required to keep receipts for inputs and become a collector of the advanced VAT. The need for maintaining such a position, however, could be the result of constraints on the tax administration.

believe administrative capacity and public awareness should expand simultaneously so that through time the criteria for required registration changes in a manner to systematically increase the number of APAs.[11]

Finally, we note that many potentially exempt APAs will be small retailers, traders, service providers, and agricultural producers, many of whom—we hope—fall below the threshold for paying positive income tax. Recall we have recommended that supplies made to a registered APA by a supplier who is neither an employee nor a registered APA will be subject to advanced tax on gross revenue from the registered APA and credited by the suppler. This group includes small retailers, however defined, service providers, and agricultural producers selling directly to individuals. The revenue loss from such transactions to the extent the individuals would pay tax had they filed returns should be within acceptable bounds.

7.3.4 Revise the Definition of Taxpayer and Registered Taxpayer

A taxpayer will always be an individual—whether resident or nonresident—for all taxes. There will be neither registration requirements nor residence requirements for excises and tariffs. Registration may be needed for income tax and a residence requirement is needed for income tax and perhaps VAT. A resident requirement may be needed, at a minimum, for a VAT if nonresidents are eligible for VAT refunds at the border when they leave the taxing jurisdiction.

Registration requirements will depend on the state of registration at the time of the change in definitions. At a minimum, registration should include independent professionals, certain small business owners, partners and significant shareholders in APAs, senior government officials, and employees of large enterprises and NGOs who hold management positions and/or are highly compensated. Initially, registered taxpayers should be required to report consolidated income and be able to take credits for all advanced taxes.[12]

7.4 Concluding Observations

Tax reform is an essential part of the overall reform process for many reasons, particularly because economic reforms and government activities in general are costly and need to be financed. In addition, the tax system, in coordination with expenditure and related policies, can help lay the foundation for future growth accompanied by reasonable income distribution. That said, tax reform cannot succeed without reforms in expenditure policy and overall government operations.

---

[11] We also note the need to coordinate criteria for small business APAs and the personal exemption, or credit, for income taxes.

[12] Voluntary registration should always be an option.

Compliance with a well-designed system with reasonable administration will not increase if the population lacks confidence in government and does not observe tangible results in a wide range of areas, including property rights protections; public safety; increases in the efficiency of government programmes, including health, education, social services, and national defence; and economic growth more generally.

Tax reform can help set the standard for anti-corruption activities, but, again, it has been our experience that the tax administration in any particular country may be no more corrupt than other governmental institutions. It could be the case that the demand for good government as defined by advanced economies is a normal good. That is, the demand for clean government increases with income and with a gradual change in expectations about how interactions with the public sector are conducted. Addressing corruption is a government-wide, indeed, society-wide, activity and needs a coordinated approach to be successful. Applications to particular departments will be specialized, but the commitment needs to be across the government in response to demands from the population.

Increased transparency and open interaction between government and the population is an important element of reform both broadly and with regard to the tax system in particular.[13] Advanced announcements of budget priorities and tax changes in the spirit of prebudget statements recommended by the International Budget Partnership,[14] combined with periods of public comment and discussion, will increase the quality of both tax and other budget proposals, as well as public acceptance. Publication of proposed regulations, proposed forms, and procedures combined with structured comment periods will increase both quality and acceptance as well.

Finally, our intent has been to present one vision to strive for as a tax system evolves. A vision is needed in order to understand how piecemeal actions fit into the tax system's evolution. That said, we hope that particular parts of each element will be useful to those thinking about reform. The approach, we believe, has enabled us to provide what we hope has been useful advice in a number of countries even though we have never explicitly advocated the complete approach. We also hope that the ideas expressed here will be input into a productive dialogue about both the useful and erroneous elements of this approach.

---

[13] We have suggested that the Ministry of Finance create a special office, or designate some senior officials, to develop public awareness and educational materials and organize structured interactions between tax officials and the public, including comment on proposed registration and regulations. The group could also draft explanations of tax concepts and rules that can be published by local news media on a regular basis.

[14] https://internationalbudget.org/.

References

Hussey, W.M. & Lubick, D.C. (1996). *Basic World Tax Code and Commentary: A Project Sponsored by the Harvard University International Tax Program.* 2nd ed. Virginia: Tax Analysts.

Gale, W. and Krupkin, A. How Big is the Problem of Tax Evasion? https://www. brookings.edu/blog/up-front/2019/04/09/how-big-is-the-problem-of-tax-evasion/ #:~:text=Compliance%20is%20highest%20when%20third,but%20doesn't%20withhold %20taxes.

Swedish Tax Agency: Website www.skatteverket.se

Name Index

Subject Index

For the benefit of digital users, indexed terms that span two pages (e.g., 52–53) may, on occasion, appear on only one of those pages.